Vegetable Gardening

for Organic and Biodynamic Growers

Vegetable Gardening

for Organic and Biodynamic Growers

Biographies of over 70 vegetables, with detailed accounts of how to grow them, their climate of origin, their transformation over time, and their nutritional and therapeutic potential

Joel Morrow

Lindisfarne Books | 2014

2014

LINDISFARNE BOOKS

An imprint of SteinerBooks / Anthroposophic Press, Inc.

834 Main Street, PO Box 358, Spencertown, NY 12165

This edition copyright © 2014 by Joel Morrow. All rights reserved. No part of this publication may be reproduced, stored in a retrieval system, or transmitted in any form or by any means, electronic, mechanical, photocopying, recording, or otherwise without the prior written permission of the publisher.

ISBN: 978-1-58420-167-0 (print)
ISBN: 978-1-58420-168-7 (eBook)

LIBRARY OF CONGRESS CATALOGING-IN-PUBLICATION DATA IS AVAILABLE

Contents

Foreword	1
Introduction	7
Asian Brassicas	15
Agretti	20
Artichoke and Cardoon	22
Arugula	28
Asparagus	30
Beans: Bush & Pole	39
Beet	48
Broad Bean (Fava)	55
Broccoli	60
Broccoli Raab	69
Brussels Sprouts	71
Burdock	76
Cabbage	78
Carrot	86
Cauliflower	99
Celeriac	102
Celery	106
Chard	111
Chicory and Radicchio	116
Chinese Cabbage	123
Corn	128
Cucumber	138
Eggplant	145

Escarole and Endive	153
Fennel	158
Garden Huckleberry and Wonderberry	161
Garlic	163
Ground Cherry	171
Horseradish	173
Jerusalem Artichokes	177
Kale and Collards	181
Kohlrabi	187
Leeks, Welsh Onions, and Wild Onions	192
Lettuce	198
Lima Beans	207
Mache (Corn Salad)	213
Melon	216
Mustard Greens	225
Okra	230
Onion	236
Parsnip	248
Peas	253
Peppers	262
Potato	270
Pumpkin	281
Radish: Black Spanish and Daikon	286
Rutabaga	291
Salsify	296
Scorzonera	298
Spinach	300
Stinging Nettle	307
Summer Squash	309
Sweet Potato	315
Tomatillo	321

Tomato	323
Turnip	337
Watermelon	341
Wild Salads	348
Amaranth	349
Dandelion	350
Lamb's Quarters	351
Orach	351
Plantain	352
Purslane	352
Miner's Lettuce	354
Sorrel	354
Upland or Early Winter Cress	355
Watercress	356
Winter Squash	359

Appendix

Cover Crops	369

Index   373

AUTHOR'S NOTE

These vegetable biographies began when my first garden teacher, Margareta Leuder, described how as a child she had raised watermelon in the Sonoran Desert in 1905. Where I come from on the Chesapeake Bay, watermelon is just another form of Kool-Aid, but Margareta had more faith in watermelon than the faithful have in stained glass. She regarded the red whirling swirls religiously, like a shaman, and I took everything she said very seriously.

My own version of vegetable biographies began as notes scribbled on the margins of a planting calendar, which swelled for years with old Bailey quotes (Liberty Hyde Bailey, *Cyclopedia of American Horticulture*), notes from ag books, and whatever hearsay factoids were known about organics and biodynamics in 1974, which was not much. Year after year, I struggled to dissect the descriptions in grower-oriented seed catalogs, such as Stokes, Harris, Southern Exposure, and (by far the best) Johnny's. More recently, I have poured over extension websites; quite good if the vegetable is important to a state's economy, otherwise surprisingly lean.

I realized that every vegetable is a significant historical and biochemical personality. When I became editor of the journal *Biodynamics* in the 80s, I began a series of vegetable interviews that have gone on now for over thirty years. Though these biographies are arranged alphabetically for convenience, each chapter reflects my own changing point of view, depending on the date of interview. Some begin historically, some morphologically, and some so imaginatively they seem to reawaken Margareta's childhood shamanism, which became beautifully elaborated through Rudolf Steiner's spiritual view of nature, the foundation of biodynamics.

FOREWORD

I began to garden full time in the early 1970s. Back then, when I kept my notes and observations in a schoolbook and on a planting calendar, there was always more to observe than I had time to write down. It wasn't merely that I was harried and scrambling—although I was. I wanted to keep records, but I also wanted to be ten places at once, so as not to miss something. The biodynamic garden was, for me, an invitation to be present at the creation; and I wanted to be out there every moment of the day and night. Every crop was like the arrival of a new child, or like a slowly conceived work of art that took months to complete. I especially liked this "garden art" because I wasn't doing it alone. I was working with a thousand shaping cosmic fingers, fingers of the light and the seasons, as if each plant were reflecting the highly articulated mobile of the solar system. I wanted to grasp this motion, which is our earth, in its totality, as if the garden were a wild creature I was trying to track down. I had to be everywhere, just to get a sense for this comprehensive creature. I discovered that becoming physically and perceptually immersed in every phase of growth was in itself a key. It was a feast that replenished itself in the eating. It absorbed me as I had never been absorbed before. I became like a child who will probably hear the last trumpet before he hears his mother calling. The truth is that I was making up for lost time. I had slept through so much; so much "world" had evaporated right under my nose, so much life had slipped through my fingers, that when I discovered a new way of looking at nature I had to scramble to catch up.

The first thing I had to do was trade in my old body for a new one. Before I heard of biodynamics I didn't even have a reason to move. But suddenly, every plant, the changing tonalities of every season, and every particle of earth under my feet cried out for attention. Because of biodynamics, I could hear it! The whole garden was telling me to "get up and do something." Every phase of growth, the dawn of every day, every leaf and fruit, became an instruction. I loved those instructions, even when I couldn't "make heads or tails" of them. Finally, there was something out there I really wanted, even more than an abundance of healthy vegetables. They were the goal, but they were also like good grades for passing the course. What I mean to say is that finally I was in a school I really liked. I liked the subjects, I liked the teacher, and I even liked the strain and the exhaustion. And so far, after forty years of physical work and observation, I haven't stopped liking them.

The problem was getting some of it down on paper. I couldn't possibly note down everything I wanted to; it passed by too fast. Even if I had thought to use a tape recorder (which never occurred to me), the best insights always seemed to come at the most awkward times—in white heat, in full harness, under the deafening abusive noise of a tiller or chainsaw. The insights didn't seem to have any sense for appropriate times. Still, I have never been so courteous to human garden visitors as I have been to these unbidden guests. If only I could have gotten all their instructions down! It's not that I didn't see clearly enough, but often they appeared like a long, serialized nature documentary played in seasonal installments, sometimes over a few years. Each insight was bigger than a single showing. Even the smallest garden insight is season-sized. And the reason why they seem to come when you are too busy is because you are in a position to see them only when your will is fully harnessed to phenomena. I discovered this only after I began to cultivate the fluid biodynamic way of picturing the plant. Before that time my conventional intellect would banish what I saw before it could speak to me.

Over the years these visitors began to join hands, as if each visit, season by season, were building into a complex biography. You can't know another being's world unless you enter it, and that was why I had to undergo a physical and perceptual transformation to undertake the journey. It was not unlike many other human commitments—subtle, involved, inspiring, messy. What made these biographies different, however, was that every family connection was woven right into the cosmos. You could see the weaving in the course of growth, as if each metamorphosis were woven out of depths of landscape invisible to human eyes. I realized that if these vegetable biographies were to be biodynamic, I would have to place the reader in a position to observe these phenomena in their flight. This became still more concrete when I tried to share these observations in a course on biodynamic gardening and nature observation. Later, when I became editor of the Bio-Dynamic Association's quarterly journal, I had the motive to write some of my observations down in a first draft, issue by issue. Finally, after decades of observing and reading, I revised them again for this book, adding more chapters.

In this volume, two books run side by side: an observation book and a fact book. Each is hungry for the other. Without new perspectives, phenomena pass by unnoticed. Without facts, new perspectives remain unsubstantiated and not fleshed out. One reason the fortress of chemical agriculture has taken so long to crack is that a change of perspective was not widely practiced. There was only one way of looking at phenomena. It isn't just pollution and reduced nutrition that has weakened the chemical fortress. A new generation began seeing with different eyes. Why stop now? If you are old enough, you remember the blanched and wilted vegetables that expired on produce counters in the 1950s and 60s. You remember how few varieties there were and how low they rated on the nutritional scale. Anyone who claimed that vegetables had therapeutic value was called a fanatic.

This has begun to change. Vegetables have new "rights." They are the backbone of nutrition and preventive medicine. To me, each vegetable is a work of art, a journey, a rite of passage into the natural world. Do you really imagine the cautious new recommendations of the present USDA are the end of this tale? What we know about vegetables today is just the tip of a wonderful cipher, an almost magical script, as if the tactile and the suprasensory were growing on a single stem. "Suprasensory," because the biography of every garden plant constantly grows beyond itself into every strata of existence. You can both eat the plants, and use them as a map. Take your pick. The two routes are connected.

Going on the journey (on those connected routes) requires tools; and the tools that biodynamics has developed have grown out of a different reading of the vegetable cipher. You will see the garden differently if you string the garden along a cosmic chain of events. The perspectives of chemical agriculture have become a prison camp for people and plants. Those perspectives never hinted that plants require the wider environment as much as hawks or kestrels do.

The plant is really a wide-open creature, as wide as the landscape it grows in. It's a creature of nodes and growth rings and cycles. What you see are not really leaves and flowers and fruits, but cycles that have gelled. The plant is merely a slight thickening of the cycles of rising and falling light, a gelled rhythm of cosmic activity. When you get to know a plant species, you see it is merely a shadow or a ripple of a larger picture, which takes years to see as a whole. You get glimpses of the whole—and its therapeutic power—when you see, for example, how cabbage, kale, and broccoli are part of a larger transformation, which is never seen entirely visible in one snapshot. These transformations have always surrounded us, waiting for millennia to be noticed and employed.

When biodynamic gardeners use a spray of ground silica (horn manure 501), they mediate between the larger cycles of light and an aspect of these governing cycles present in each plant species. The biodynamic gardener cultivates light assimilation as well as dark soil; plows furrows of light as these enter the plant leaves, as well as plowing the dark mold below. The spray is applied at nodal points in plant development, sometimes in relation to the cosmic cycles outlined in the *Stella Natura Biodynamic Planting Calendar*.* Even conventional growers seem aware of those nodal points; they are evident, for example, in the sensitivity of cabbage crops to sudden shots of fertilizer during the fifth to eighth true leaf stage. Conventional growers withhold fertilizer at this time, but biodynamic growers apply the silica spray. They know that the rhythms of the plant's coming into being have condensed within the form of the spiral of leaves, in the rosette stage. They hardly claim to possess a complete picture of the plant in its wider environment, but they make it a practice to locate, explore, and refine their knowledge of these cycles.

The soil has unnoticed cycles as well; unnoticed, mainly because the soil has become like an apartment that has been broken into so many times, there's nothing much left to steal. Biodynamic gardeners use a soil spray (horn manure 500) to help repair the damage, re-activating processes that have become anesthetized through chemical abuse, inappropriate tillage, and wrong combinations of plants. Again, the times of spraying are important. For example, the sap descends into the root during the evening, during the time of the waning moon, and during autumn—these are three different cycles of descending sap. A conventional grower I know noticed this cycle, although he exploited it to apply pesticides. He told me that uptake of fertilizer and pesticide is quicker during the waning moon; but he doesn't follow these ripples downward into the soil, where he would find a being as alive as a cow, but with organs as diffuse and changeable as the waves of the sea.

Part of the plan of biodynamic practice is not only to "restock the larder" of the soil (with compost, and so forth), but also to rebuild the house. All our practices relate to the joints, joists, and foundations of such a building. The small amounts of herbal preparations we use in making compost may seem like nothing more than tiny nails, but each one ties down a cosmic cycle that conventional, chemical agriculture has either washed right out of the soil or condensed into bricks. We aim to put these cycles back. The creator of the

---

* Some biodynamic practitioners do not believe these correlations are accurate.

biodynamic method, Rudolf Steiner, pictured the ecosystem to be somewhat like a series of organs, one inside another, too big to see, really, but as alive as any animal. Our goal is to reflect, even reproduce, these organs in our farms and gardens, setting a small process going in a small area to influence a larger area, like throwing pebbles into a pool.

These practices take time. They remind me of a conversation overheard by a biodynamic gardener as he was fishing through a bin of pins and clips in a hardware store in Scotland. The gardener couldn't help but hear, since the voice of the Texas oilman was rising rapidly. The oilman didn't want the ordered part in two weeks. He wanted it now! And in his opinion this kind of service was why Scotland was such a backwater. The clerk, a very old Scot, raised his eyes slowly from the parts list and replied without emotion, "in a hundred years nobody will know the difference."

The question haunts me; in a hundred years what will make a difference? How can one establish a sustainable agriculture, which requires a sense of time longer than anyone seems able or willing to practice? The economic structure doesn't permit it and the social structure doesn't support it, and the long cycles that extend that far are not known. As a result, it's no surprise that a method such as biodynamics, which tries to build on these cycles, barely has a toehold in the present agricultural scene.

In the past few years I've been observing the growth of trees to get a sense for these longer cycles, which are not unlike growth rings spread above and below the forest and fields. What we call seasons are merely the most generalized reflections of the rhythmically changing cycle of our solar system. Each plant family and species is a different mirror of these cycles; each a materialization of growth cycles. Each vegetable species is like detailed highly sculpted vortices, an illumination of cycles invisible to us. Each is a train of formative movements, spiraling downward into the soil. Each carries an imprint of its formative cycle into the humus. Each chapter in this book is, in effect, a biography of one of these vortices: its culture, history, and, in most chapters, what these cycles become when they enter the human body. When you practice biodynamic gardening, it seems as if your life extends beyond the limits of your body, down paths and between beds, until it flows like sap through the stems of the vegetable plants themselves.

INTRODUCTION

When I first met Margareta Leuder, my first garden teacher, she had pitched her tent by the garden on the top of the hill, close to where the deer grazed. I do not know why her grandson did not help her build a fence. I do know she liked to spend her nights up there. She would read by candlelight, and every half hour her head would fall to her chest. This was the cue for the deer that gathered quietly at the edge of the garden as silent, poised shadows. It still amazes me how quietly deer can move through a garden at night. The carrot tops disappear as silently as they grow. The collards and squash leaves evaporate, one by one, right down to the stems.

As she grew older, Margareta's nightly conversations with the deer grew longer and more involved. To anyone who might have been eavesdropping at 4 a.m., it must have seemed like a complicated legal proceeding in a remote country where logic had not yet penetrated. In her old age, Margareta made her arguments in an irritated tittering, somewhere between wren and crow, which usually trailed off toward some distant errand. However, even allowing for age, Margareta unquestionably spoke a language of gardening born from more exposure to the elements than I was willing to risk, like the time she insisted I join her in harvesting strawberries during a violent lightening storm. I suppose she picked up the dialect somewhere between sleep and the Sonoran Desert. Weeding her garden was complicated, too, since she ate most of the weeds, and even froze them for winter. Purslane, dandelions, rocket, amaranth, lamb's quarters, and nettle—these were daily bread whenever they were in season and took precedence over seemingly choice garden vegetables. From salads to stews to garden rows, nothing was entirely free of weeds. She insisted that cultivated plants had lost their force. As far as she was concerned, the nutritional quality of these weeds was not a solution; it was a problem. Why were garden vegetables so anemic by comparison? Anemia is not only a disease of the blood. It occurs when human insight no longer spends time out in the weather, when the slightest chill or hint of moisture drives it into the house, and it huddles shivering around hot stoves, even on midsummer evenings. Its very survival shuns the exposure that is the inherent language of plants.

I cannot say I liked this discovery any more than, as an apprentice, I liked being dragged into a strawberry patch with doom flashing on all sides. Yet, in Margareta's view, this was the only place where we could find real solutions. She believed that modern agriculture bore about as much relation to nature as a steaming greenhouse does to the midwinter days outside its walls.

What I appreciated about Margareta Leuder—and do even more so thirty years later—was that her direct relationship to nature and her fine spirituality were like a wrecking crew. She was immune to arguments issued from within the greenhouse. She would not be denied. She demolished and reconstructed at the same time.

Margareta Leuder was born on a wagon train in 1899, somewhere west of St. Louis. She learned gardening from her East European parents, the Indians of Northern Mexico, and the severe hardships of homesteading in the Sonoran Desert. She learned her methods of reconstruction from Ehrenfried Pfeiffer, one of the founders of biodynamic agriculture, whom she nursed during his final illness.

On her wall a watercolor hung, which Pfeiffer had painted during that time, of a figure standing among crudely swirling plant forms, holding a finger over its mouth. The figure seemed to reproach you as you entered the room. Even more annoying, the figure did not leave you alone after you left, but continued to reproach you when you made conclusions before you had actually *seen through* an experience. It seemed to say that the practical, hands-on secrets of biodynamics would yield themselves only to profound and consistent inner silence; consistent inwardly silent observation. You would have to stand before nature with all the inner focus at your command, silently attentive. I have never ceased to marvel, then or now, how much unflagging resolution this requires. Nature seems to yield her secrets only to profound inner silence.

I soon realized that such inner silence calls forth a "self" different from the one that issues agricultural perspectives from within the greenhouse. This other self does not require giving up devoted attention to phenomena as practiced by modern science. Nor does it mean renouncing the clarity and selflessness that are the keynotes of objectivity. It does mean renouncing the *rigor mortis* of twentieth-century education, however, which always pictures life as if it happened in the past, eons before we were born. Usually, this second self is like a sailor flung from a ship and barely able to keep his head above water—a direct result of mass education. From what I have observed, the second self seems unable to make *original* observations unless those faculties generally reserved for artists become the exact, tactile companions of everyday perception.

Introduction

In centuries past, this enlivened seeing was called *Natura,* who was pictured as a woman weeping at humanity's treatment of the Earth. *Natura* represents the part of nature that the latest findings of modern agriculture largely ignore. As a rule, agriculture passes these "latest findings" on to the next generation as pollution and environmental illness. Biodynamics has the task (which it sometimes meets, and sometimes does not) of remaining true to the larger, undiscovered portion of nature. Biodynamics views chemicals as mere corpses of an undiscovered life below and above the soil surface; a life rarely presented in textbooks, but one that strikes like lightening from imaginative perceptions of nature. The only alternative for agriculture is a kind of senility that, if we are honest, already takes hold of us in youth with the first agricultural method we are taught. It does not matter which one. In some cases, even the biodynamic method will do.

Sometimes, as I approach a farm from a distance, it appears as if the farmer on a tractor were a giant insect crawling over the fields. This might not be as bad as it sounds. Some morning, the giant insect might wake up, six legs instead of the usual two struggling with soreness. Its back might feel stiff, not only from long days of hay baling, but also from the stiff armor of chitin covering its spine. This should prove useful, since chitin is wonderfully resistant to chemicals. I am not trying to sound unkind, but those twenty-first century eyes, which previously may have peered like rats out of a dark space, will suddenly rise like crystal domes, drawn out of the head and into the dome of the sky, like so many faceted observatories. Antennae will burst from the airless greenhouse of the skull, like schoolchildren escaping from prison at recess. Reception will be infinitely better than that of the antenna formerly attached to the cab. Just as insect antennae magically snatch single molecules of scent out of an ocean of air, so single perceptions will retain the marginal context they possessed while still embedded in the ocean of the elements. Moment by moment, this future farmer will see that the human being is cut from the same fabric as the plants and insects. The farm will appear as if the human being had been cut into pieces and scattered like thousands of seeds over the body of nature.

It has become increasingly clear that we must gather the lost seeds of our humanity from nature into their original tapestry. Real solutions to agricultural problems will arise from nature, just as imaginative solutions resolve the plot of a story or play. The seeds are all there, needing only encouragement. A simple example will serve: a local farmer has lost a calf, and it will take forty people searching the surrounding hills to find it. Suddenly, a thought occurs to the farmer: *just let the mother cow loose and follow her.* The solution is simple, and so obvious and workable that the farmer is stunned. Instead of solving a problem by marshalling (and wasting) resources at odds with phenomena, the problem might solve itself. Unfortunately, this farmer's perception has not been trained to notice how that thought arose. The farmer can only wonder how he might invoke such thoughts on a regular basis.

The method involves thorough observation of the context of every natural event. Wasps, for example, are imported to control caterpillars. Notice what happens, however, when you *recreate their world* in your garden. If you grow various kinds of *umbelliferous* flowering plants successively, beneficial wasps will descend upon the garden, as thick and as magical as angels in a medieval illumination. Allow lovage to flower; replant root-cellared carrots; maintain beds of wild fennel and bolted finocchio, dill, and caraway. Throw in archangelica for good measure. Although archangelicas are far too big to grow on the head of a pin, the minute angels they attract are not. As far as I can tell, standing in a bed of tall umbels surrounded by hundreds of these winged messengers is a blessed experience, the air filled with certainty and hope and, like being in a city of the future, with inconceivable flying machines.

Such training involves wholehearted, devoted observation, like a mother watching an infant. It requires, too, the quiet strength of will to remain solely within the context of phenomena, while retaining enough imagination to avoid the enslavement of previous conclusions. One way that I train myself (and you will have to try it for yourself to see if it is valid and works for you) is to see each plant as a visible imagination of the forces that the plant brings to the garden. In other words, each plant becomes an artistic image of the forces that brought the plant into being. Observe, for example, how the *umbelliferous* leaves seem as translucent to light as a stained-glass window. Then observe the enclosed, inward-turning pea. Pea leaves look to me like a winged airborne creature anesthetized and pinned to the top of a stem. One can almost see the frustrated wings, weakly struggling to rise in the flower. Observe how the carpel leaves fold their thick drowsy wings around the fruit. In the end, the soul of flight reclines in a casket of saturated green.

In these two plants, one has the genesis of a new language of nature. Perhaps now just two words or syllables, but a language, I am sure, that eventually will spread over the earth. In the city of the future, it will be worthwhile to listen to the pure music of the leaves and see their changes of form in the course of development, as if they were the very language of *Natura* herself, embedded in phenomena.

Introduction

How are the bees of perception trained? Unfortunately, most gardeners never enter the hive at all, since it costs something—a lot, in fact—to remain within the seething mass. Perceptions swarm with seething galactic heat, boiling like bees over one another in an open hive, molten sea roiling, a breathing melting mass. The sound rising from beneath the surface seems intensely inward, both comforting and disconcerting. It is infinitely warmer and deeper than the glassy surface of perception, which deflects the eye like a sword. The life below the surface of perception rises, falls, and heaves beneath the waxy skin of a rapidly growing leaf or a tomato deflated by decay and fermentation.

Qualities hover around each plant like an airy sea of insects, as different for each plant and plant family as the physical insects that gnaw and suck their way from leaf to flower. The point is this: each plant is a vessel, into which flows still-unfathomed qualities, nutritional, therapeutic— even aesthetic-therapeutic. Like insects, some plant qualities have wings; some are wingless; and some highly significant ones are so minute that they pass by unobserved. Some only prick our consciousness, suddenly and painfully, after the moment of attention has passed. Those who smart from their stings know how cramped, bifocal, and benumbing the old ways of observing have been. They know that what heaves beneath the appearance and dying away of plants, and is reflected in the rhythm of observation itself, is the earth herself breathing. They know that although humans may behave as though they are not obligated to anything or anyone, they can see how plants are obliged to everything around them.

I knew one old New England farmer whose worst epithet for a person was "independent," by which he meant "obliged to no one." For him, the word is a damnation for which there is no cure. He told me that the beams of the barns he built are strong, but it is the way they interlock that makes the structure stand. The trouble is, the interlocking structure of a plant in its environment is always moving. The structure is always moving, and you have to dance to keep up with it. How can you construct a building that never stands still? This question is relevant when whole farmscapes are in ruin.

In older forms of agriculture, it seemed normal that soil life would sew up in the night what humans disassembled during the day. No more! A standing army has reduced to rubble the underground fields, furrows, factories, and insect nurseries of the soil. Only perception trained to see the very shapes of plants as pictures of that hidden life can rebuild such war-torn soil—sometimes soil even under organic and biodynamic management. In the near future, such imaginative pictures of the living world will become as germinal as garden seeds.

The articles in this book took shape over decades, the length of time it took to train this perception. All the included garden facts and attempts to view garden plants in different slants of light are meant to serve this end. Even biodynamic techniques, such as compost preparations, field sprays, and planting according to the *Stella Natura* astronomical planting calendar, remain real only when they open new avenues of perception. Training these perceptions reminds me of my failed attempts to home-school my son in astronomy. Nothing stayed still, not even the boy. The earth's constantly changing position, hour by hour, night by night, kept us active. I wondered what it would be like to remain conscious of this ever-turning reality twenty-four hours a day, season after season. I imagined it would feel like being one piece of a highly articulated mobile sculpture that was discovered suddenly to be alive. My son was not impressed; he wanted to strap himself to his Estes rocket, ignite the fuse, and take off into cosmic space. I could not convince him of the obvious fact that we already stand in cosmic space; we are just unaware of it.

Over the years, I have tried to see plants as mirrors of this constantly changing cosmic organism. Like most biodynamic gardeners, I fail whenever immediate, pressing goals warp my focus. Still, when I am not gardening by habit, I use the changing slants of light in the course of the day and the season to view the turning mobile in which the garden constantly moves. I know that each plant describes a phase of movement in this mobile, and that ill-timed sowings and plant diseases occur when my perception lags behind that moving form. I may never catch this quarry, but I have learned to pursue it.

After thirty years, I can still see Margareta observing the moods of the earth, warily and steadily, hour by hour, week by week, like a hunter stalking deer. As I picture her nodding by the garden, time has turned the deer into magicians. I stand in awe of them as they make row after row of beans disappear into the predawn air. Time has worked its magic; only now do I realize how the ever-turning cosmic organism had settled into Margareta's limbs. In her, it had become "second nature." When she died, it did not die with her. Like a plant after a devastating winter, it continued to grow. In my mind's eye, Margareta Leuder continues to walk the ancient beds of the dry wash. What lived in her limbs (barely known to me at the time), now surrounds the garden like a dancing circle of insects—like the agitated dance of insects that have just received their wings for a late summer nuptial flight.

Vegetable Biographies

ASIAN BRASSICAS

Imagine a Chinese mother, perhaps 7,000 years old, selecting Asian brassicas from wild turnip (*B. rapa*), a weed common across Europe and Asia. I imagine her descendants pulling countless cultivars from the wild species, almost like pulling genies from a magic bottle. In my mind she has to be a mother, because I remember myself at age 5 staring up at leaves and yellow flowers piled on a bench in Chinatown. An incredibly wrinkled old man is smiling down at me, as he stuffs flowers and greens into a brown paper bag. In a small army town, many hours from New York, my mother steams the flowering greens with pork and oyster sauce, defying both her Jewishness and the white anemic cuisine of our neighbors. Indeed, my mother was so obsessed with green leaves that every corner of our house was overrun with hundreds of pots, even trees, which she propagated from random slips. In the end that's why I believe brassica therapy will always be administered by mothers.

My image of a Chinese mother may be pure fantasy, but the Asian setting, prehistoric era, and genies are not, since natural polyploidy, an unusual genetic potential for metamorphosis, is totally endemic to the *Brassica* genus. In Asia the eruption may even have occurred around 7,000 years ago with the speed of stopgap photography. Another eruption occurred in historic times in Europe when wild cabbage (*B. oleracea*) metamorphosed, with the aid of gardeners, into Brussels sprouts, broccoli, and cauliflower. In still more recent times, *B. oleracea* morphed with turnip to produce rutabaga, exactly how is unknown.

The point is this: at the very heart of the biological universe is the astonishing plasticity of the leaf. Vitamins, antioxidants, our very survival have their origins in the plasticity of leaves. The companies that claim to sell "balanced vitamin formulations" should in all honesty be selling leaves and flower buds. The same may be true for antioxidants. Antioxidants may be inseparable from the plasticity of the leaf itself. Eating these leaves returns this plasticity to the dark cellar of our constitution. Again: this therapy is usually administered by mothers.

As I weed my garden, I often graze on brassica flower buds, almost lost in a vast forest of formative forces each leaf presents, with their undertones of flavor, some incredibly strong, sulfurous and spicy, and others so fine they escape my tongue as if the flavor had airy wings. Aromatic undertones disappear when cooked, almost as if they never existed. Likewise in plant breeding, finer components tend to evaporate. Better to apprentice yourself to the plant plasticity, which already exists, before you accidentally wipe it away. Maybe get in touch with a mother.

Culture

Culture for Asian brassicas is similar to cabbage and other brassicas: medium clay loam, high organic matter, near neutral pH, abundant moisture, cool temperatures. Light soils exacerbate flea beetles. Asian brassicas perform better when the clay fraction of the soil combines with compost over time, which also reduces flea beetle predation. On very light soils, Asian brassicas may never outgrow the need for row cover. A few beetle shotgun holes may be tolerable for home gardeners, but not in markets. One grower nearby finds purple mustard and tatsoi less susceptible. Try removing row cover at the early rosette stage, about 4 weeks after planting. Flea beetles are worst in hot dry weather, especially warm dry autumns.

For early crops, pac choi can be sown in cells or peat pots weeks before setting in the garden. Transplants will tolerate light frost, but deep frost may trigger premature bolting. Sow directly into cells, ¼ inch deep, in a cabbage potting mix. Pac choi doesn't do well "pricked out" (transplanted to a wider space in another flat) from an initial seed flat. Keep transplant trays in bright sun. Asian brassicas grow spindly in low light. Biodynamic growers spray silica (501) when a few true leaves appear. Keep well watered until a week before setting out. Reduce watering, and expose to full outdoor sun, if possible. When setting plants in the garden, note that brassicas grow from a rosette, like lettuce, and not a central stem, like cabbage. The growing point should be planted at ground level. Set plants 8 to 12 inches apart, depending on variety, with 18 inches between plants.

Early transplants and newly emerging brassica seedlings can be wasted by flea beetles in a day. I've given up on organic pesticides and rely on metal hoops and row cover. Be sure to use iron-based slug and snail bait.

Brassicas grown for salad can be broadcast in raised beds or sown in 4-inch bands with 18 inches between bands. Other gardeners prefer tighter 8-inch rows, which allow for precise skim-weeding with a stirrup hoe. For larger pac choi, thin from 8 to 12 inches between plants, depending on variety. Cramped seedlings bolt and produce poor rosettes.

For direct seeding, test the seeder setting over newspaper a few times, since seed size ranges from 9,000 to 15,000 seeds per ounce. Seed should drop 9 to 12 seeds per foot.

Since brassicas don't hold long at maturity, sow successive crops. Home gardeners, of course, can still happily harvest the side leaves and flower buds of bolted plants. Summer-sown plants keep well into the fall. They are saleable after light frost, edible but not marketable after frost in the low twenties, and pretty much gone after a night in the teens. Home gardeners can protect against hard frost and windburn with tarps or a double layer of row cover over bails of hay on either side of the bed.

Pac choi is sometimes used as a crop in the winter greenhouse, but I don't like the result. It becomes bland and watery. I prefer the stronger *B. juncea* mustards such as Green Wave or Golden Frills. Hiroshima Green and Osaka also make good winter greenhouse salad. Overwintered in the cold frame, these mustards give a few good cuttings in the spring, but bolt quickly as days lengthen.

Brassica rotation is even trickier in the cold frame or greenhouse than in the field. Ideally, soil should have a three-year gap between brassicas. Replace soil in the greenhouse entirely, if rotation is impractical.

Varieties

Most Asian brassicas are from one species, *B. rapa*, followed by the subheading *chinensis* for pac choi, tatsoi, and mizuna; and *pekinenis* for pe-tsai or Chinese cabbage. Asian mustards, however, were bred from *B. juncea*, the wild mustard, the same species used for mustard greens in the American South, and in the mustard spread. For seed savers, this is important to note for purposes of isolation.

Flowering pac choi, called Chinese tsai shim or choy sum, has been bred to bolt quickly and yet remain tender. Sometimes wrongly called rape, which is *B. rapus*, most varieties are either *B. rapa*, which are similar to pungent Italian raab, or *B. oleracea*, which is similar to milder Italian sprouting broccoli. Both are also called guy lohn or kai lan, which probably means flowering mustard. Hon tsai tai (*B. rapa*) produces tender thin purple flower stems and green mustard leaves for salads and stir-fries. When stems are no longer tender, they become harder to snap by hand. The "other guy lohn," the one called guy lohn in catalogs, is really a sprouting broccoli (*B. oleracea*). The leaves and large sweet buds look and taste like broccoli. Several hybrids of *B. oleracea* guy lohn promise increased vigor and adaptability. When tender stems are harvested regularly, both types of guy lohn produce over a long period. Both grow best in midsummer for harvest in autumn, early winter, and in mild climates right through the winter. Plants grown in hot, dry conditions with low organic matter get too bitter. Growth should be rapid and unchecked, forty to fifty days to harvest. Irrigate if necessary.

The same is true for Asian leaf mustards (*B. juncea*), which range from tender and delicious to bitter and tough, depending on weather and water. Asian mustards can also be harvested above the growing point for re-growth and second harvest. Vitamin Green and Komatsuna are both very mild pot herbs, also good in salad when young. Tatsoi is the standard mild salad ingredient, forming beautiful deep green rosettes at maturity. Red Giant is probably the most widely beloved mustard with highly attractive maroon and green leaves and pleasant mustardy flavor. The huge rosette requires 15 inches between plants. Very slow bolting.

Still more pungent is Ruby Streaks, with deeply serrated leaves, similar to mizuna. Golden Frills' leaves are bright green, spicy and sweet. Both are fantastic salad ingredients. Still more spicy and flavorful are Ho Mi Z and Red Mustard, for light stir-fries and steaming. Both are very slow to bolt, giving a long harvest period.

I should note that the *B. juncea* mustards are the most nutritious, with the highest levels of therapeutic sulfur compounds. Carotene in *B. juncea* ranges from 7,000 to 10,000 units per 100 grams; vitamin C from 100 to 130 milligrams (mg) and calcium from 180 to 270 mg, values twice as high as pac choi and Chinese cabbage.

Some excellent mesclun mixes are pure Asian brassica. Others include the Ethiopian texsel, *Brassica carinata*, a mild spinach-like traditional green from North Africa. Still others include Cavolo Nero, *B. oleracea*, the Italian lacinato black kale, which is also very mild.

Mizunas or kyona, however, are still the favorite addition to mesclun mixes. The slightly mustardy flavor and frilly texture add character to any mix. Purple mizuna adds maroon color and bolts very slowly. Mizunas can be harvested for several weeks if cut above the growing point.

SEED: Asian greens vary widely in seed size (9,000 to 15,000 seeds per ounce) and plant size (6 to 16 inches in diameter). An ounce of large pac choi will sow about 1,000 feet. An ounce of mizuna will sow about 1,250 feet. An ounce of mesclun seed will sow about 200 feet.

GERMINATION: 5 days at about 45°F.

VIABILITY: 4 to 5 years.

ROTATION: 3 years minimum; 4 to 5 years on diseased soil.

MOON CALENDAR AND BIODYNAMIC SPRAYS: All leaf practices, even for flowering pac choi and guy lohn. Follow the schedule for broccoli or cabbage.

AGRETTI

Agretti (*Salsola soda*, 55 days) is an unusual gourmet Italian salad and potherb. Agretti mops up so much salt from soil that previously barren crop land has been returned to production of peppers and tomatoes (*New Zealand Journal of Crop Science*). Agretti got me thinking more broadly about bioremediation. Not just what plants remove, but what they return to the soil. The daily unseen tide of natural bioremediation that follows in the wake of the disturbance we call gardening.

The salt tolerance of agretti—Italians even water the crop with seawater—is possible because agretti is a beet family herb that evolved in salt marshes. Its slender stemlike growth even looks like seaweed, as if the tide had unexpectedly retreated, leaving the slender succulent stems stranded in the air. Not a stretch really, since the Japanese version (*Salsola komgrovi*) is called okahijiki, "land seaweed." Okahijiki is used in sushi. The shape and biochemistry of plants are memories of millennia of environmental conditions that, unlike our own human personal memories, are concrete, reliable records. Every plant species retains the biochemical environment of its creation, not only these curious saltmarsh chenopods. Every plant retains an ancient heritage in reserve almost like a secret offshore bank account. This is what agretti inspired: the idea that every plant possesses an aspect of bioremediation, a piece of lost environment, even a Lost World, pieces that every year erode and wash away like chunks of Antarctica. If a true companion planting were ever created, not just the present hearsay kind, communities of plants might help replenish accounts long plundered on the mainland. Obviously, saltmarsh laden agretti should be imported only moderately into the garden and the diet. Though ironically, agretti is used to reduce hypertension in Italian herbal medicine and substantiated by research (Loizzo et al., V. Calabria, Italy 2003), this effect is apparently due to the presence of anthraquinones in *Salsola* species, which includes the ubiquitous tumbleweed (whose young growth is also edible).

To be honest, when I claim to imagine agretti's native habitat, I am actually remembering another saltwort, *Salicornea europaea*. I know the saltwort's habitat well from salt marshes along the Massachusetts coast. Salicornia looks even more like seaweed than agretti, with glassy succulent emerald green stems—not even a gesture of landlocked leaf or stem. Salicornia looks like seaweed growing in the air. It is quite edible, excellent in salads and pickled, but as far as I know, never cultivated. Agretti gives more nod to the flavor of spinach, though its flavor and texture—slightly bitter and slightly crunchy—give a truly unique gourmet touch to salads (raw). Likewise, lightly braised with garlic and olive oil, served over pasta or fish. In Italy, agretti, which translates as "little sour one," is also called both barbe di frate (friar's beard) for its tangled appearance, though I think Neptune's beard would be more appropriate, as well as roscano. In Spain, agretti is known as barilla.

Both salicornia and agretti are also called glasswort, which harkens back to agretti's sixteenth-century use in glassmaking. The great Italian glassmakers burned agretti to unite its high sodium content with carbon to form an ash containing bicarbonate of soda, the "secret ingredient" of Venetian glass.

Culture

Like spinach, agretti is a cool season crop. The chive-like tufts grow best in spring, fall, and through the winter in frost free climates. Seed germination is very poor, as low as 35%, possibly, like celery, related to salt marsh origins with its intermittent tidal irrigation (see celery), but I don't know for sure. Seeds prefer alkaline soil, so as with other chenopods, consider dusting the seed with agricultural lime. Sow seeds ¼ to ½ inch deep, 12 seeds to the foot. Chive-like shoots emerge in 7 to 14 days. Thin to 6 inches.

The chive-like tufts are best harvested when young (about 55 days) and eaten raw in salads or braised briefly to retain crunch when eaten as greens. Successive haircuts are possible until stems become tough in warm weather.

Harvest cork-like seeds as you would chard: when nearly mature let dry in a brown paper bag. Re-sow in September for autumn use or mid-autumn for winter crops in mild climates. An ounce packet of seeds, 30 grams, contains about 650 seeds, which produces possibly 150 plants. Seed has limited viability. Use late sowings for next year's crop.

ARTICHOKE AND CARDOON

The distance between a wild Mexican tomato and the latest hybrid seems small compared to the gulf between a spiny Mediterranean thistle and globe artichoke. The thistle (*Cynara cardunculus* var. *sylvestris*) is a seriously spiny wild cardoon, a sort of juiced version of bull thistle, still found wild along the Mediterranean coast. The cultivated cardoon (*C. cardunculus* var. *altilis*) is twice the size of the wild one, with larger buds and beautiful silvery leaves. But the buds and floral bracts of globe artichoke (*C. cardunculus* var. *scolymus*) are so large and fleshy they look like the scales of an extinct reptile. Even heirloom Italian globe artichokes look like hybrids, yet all three types are merely variants of the same species. All three interbreed freely and erratically.

Botanists attribute this stunning metamorphosis to unusually high levels of plasticity and polymorphism in the species (Sonnante 2007), somewhat akin to the plasticity of *Brassica oleracea*, the wild cabbage, which produced broccoli, cauliflower, and collards. A range of variants can easily be called forth from wild cardoon, without resort to hybridization (ibid). But so far, the therapeutic value of this plasticity is not available in the *Cynara* we eat—nothing at all like the brassicas. Both nutritional and therapeutic compounds are blocked by blanching and a natural alkaloid.

Gardeners have been tinkering with *Cynara* since ancient Roman times, when cardoon was extremely popular, not at all the minor crop cardoon and artichoke are today. According to Pliny, a Roman writer on natural history, cardoon was in fact the most popular and highly-valued vegetable in the first century CE. Romans ate the young shoots as salad or potherb and cooked the elongated blanched stems, which are still favored in parts of Italy, France, and Spain. Cardoon buds, much smaller than globe artichoke, were also consumed in ancient Rome, but less frequently. The modern globe artichoke was not fully selected for more than a thousand years (again, by Italians) in the fourteenth century.

Researchers have proven that high levels of cynari and luteolin in cardoon leaves significantly lower cholesterol and triglycerides (University of Reading, UK 2008). The leaves are also overflowing with polyphenols, a proven anti-carcinogen. And yet we throw the leaves away. The Ancients, dead though they are, must be looking down on us in horror. We grow this gigantic hybrid-like plant full of marvelous compounds, then throw most of it away (nearly all of it, actually), ending up with a relatively worthless plate of hors d'oeuvres.

The problem is alkaloids. The green parts of the *Cynara,* the most nutritious and curative parts, are burdened by the bitter alkaloid cynardoside, which grows more plentiful and bitter the longer the leaves are exposed to sunlight. That is why cardoon leaf shoots and stems are blanched or boiled in two waters, which discards high levels of vitamins, minerals, and antioxidants. This raises the question of why the cardoon's inherent polymorphism cannot be harnessed to breed out the offending alkaloid. Isn't it possible that the cardoon's metamorphosis into a food plant is not yet complete?

Traditionally artichoke leaf extract has been used to improve digestion by increasing bile flow, and to ease the symptoms of irritable bowel syndrome. Cardoon is also a traditional source of vegetarian rennet, which imparts a distinct flavor to cheese. Like other composites, cardoon and artichoke are very high in inulin, which lowers blood sugar in diabetics. Anyone allergic to composites may react adversely to the inulin in artichoke.

Culture

Before you plant artichoke or cardoon, determine how much space you can spare for this low-yield crop. A few plants might serve double duty as a minor crop and ornamental. Many favor the red-tinged varieties as ornament, but all *Cynara* thistles are works of art. The silvery green leaves are as finely drawn as a Renaissance illustration. The flower petals glow with a purple truly as iridescent as a rainbow.

Globe artichoke grows best in coastal California, where the cool sea fog moderates the long California summer. Ideal temperatures are 75°F by day and 55°F by night. Artichokes are commercially marginal in other parts of the country, but new annual varieties have greatly expanded the range for potential growers. Plants require good drainage and a pH from 6.5 to 7.5.

Traditionally, artichokes were not grown from seeds, which produce only 60 to 70% marketable buds in older varieties (Bailey 1947). Instead, growers divided crowns every 2 or 3 years; this is easy to do in Zones 8 and 9, and possible in Zone 7 along the East Coast with winter protection. Below 15°F crowns start to die. In optimal climates along the Gulf Coast or California, stands may last up to 10 years.

Even in mild climates, artichokes require some vernalization to set buds, a 10- to 14-day chilling period around 50°F. According to the Virginia Extension, even the newer more tolerant varieties will set 25% fewer buds without vernalization. Indoor sowing should be timed so that cold frame hardening or transplant date coincides with 8 to 14 days just below 50°F. New varieties require as little as 8 days, and set buds in the first year as annuals. Heirloom artichokes only establish themselves in the first year, and set buds the following year.

Seeds of artichoke and cardoon are sown 8 to 10 weeks before the last frost: late February or early March in the coastal Northwest and parts of the South; March 15 in the eastern central states and April 15 farther north. Globe artichokes don't grow well and become bitter in areas with hot dry summers. Hot arid climates induce premature budding.

Some growers soak seeds in 130°F water for 10 minutes to improve germination, but plan that 15 to 25% of germinated seed will produce budless plants. Sow 3 seeds to each 3-inch peat or manure pot, filled with compost or potting soil. Thin to one strongest after first true leaf appears. Johnny's Selected Seeds catalog instructs to keep the greenhouse cool, 60 to 70°F by day, dropping to 50 to 60°F at night. Keep well watered, but not sodden, to avoid root rot. Fertilize with composted tea, fish emulsion, or liquid seaweed. Biodynamic growers spray silica after the third true leaf.

Artichokes are high nitrogen feeders (conventional growers use 20-20-20); but heavily composted beds with technically low nitrogen will produce good crops. In bed culture, dig 4 to 6 inches of compost deeply into the bed. If your compost has a high carbon to nitrogen ratio (due to sawdust in horse manure, and so forth) add a high nitrogen organic fertilizer. Compost tea may not make up the difference. Artichokes can also be side-dressed with liquid organic fertilizer when the rosette has established 10 true leaves.

Set artichoke and cardoon transplants with the leaf receptacle slightly above soil level, the same way you plant lettuce. Never bury the receptacle, which is the point from which the leaves grow. Plants are notoriously slow starters. They may take 2 weeks to adjust to field conditions; keep well watered. Commercial growers use ghibberellic acid, a plant hormone, to induce early production and better bud quality. Organic growers can spray fermented alfalfa tea, which contains natural growth factors, at 8 to 10 leaves and when flower stalks begin to rise.

For weed control, the effectiveness of black plastic is unclear: raising soil temperature in some climates may de-vernalize plants; i.e., prevent flowering (New Jersey extension). In cooler climates it may produce earlier harvests (Utah Extension); Virginia Extension suggests trying the cooler white plastic.

Harvest ranges from late spring for overwintered crowns to late July or August for annual plants. Harvest continues until frost. Artichokes should be harvested when buds have reached full size, but before the budscales (bracts) have begun to spread. As the bracts open, the buds tend to become bitter, although bitterness and toughness may also occur with earlier high summer temperatures. Cut off unopened buds with 2 to 3 inches of stem. Open-pollinated artichokes produce several stalks with 3 to 5 buds per stalk, 6 to 10 buds per plant. Hybrid artichokes may produce 10 to 15 buds per plant. Unharvested buds open to become attractive purple thistles, which can be cut and dried for flower arrangements. Cultivated cardoon is often grown entirely for this purpose, although the shoots and leaf petioles of cardoon can also be harvested for food earlier in the season. Cardoon rosettes can also be tied and blanched for a few weeks to reduce bitterness. Although flavor is far better straight from the garden, artichoke buds keep 3 to 5 days under refrigeration.

Three parts of steamed buds are edible: first strip off the outer bud leaves (bracts), dip the fleshy end in sauce, and strain the dipped end with your teeth to extract the flesh. Discard the middle leaves, which lack meat; and remove the tender artichoke heart (the part often marinated and sold in jars). Discard the fuzzy center. Parts of the floral stem can also be dipped and eaten.

Traditionally artichokes have been served with butter sauce, but the buds taste more piquant with vinaigrette dressings. Try blending vinaigrette with avocado or make a homemade green goddess dressing. Instead of mayonnaise, use chopped raw onion as an emulsifier. Add a few handfuls of fresh lovage leaves (a wonderful, undervalued herb), olive oil, balsamic vinegar, marjoram, and chives. Blend until the dressing thickens.

Winter Protection

Heavily mulched crowns will often survive winters in Zones 5 and 6. After several fall frosts, cut back the leaves to the ground and bury the crowns with 4 to 6 inches of soil. Cover the bed with 8 inches of damp leaves or straw. One variety, Northern Star, is alleged to survive 0°F without protection. I'm sceptical, but if you can find seed, it's worth a trial.

In regions where winter lows drop below 15°F, lift highly productive crowns and store in moist sand, peat, or leaves in the root cellar. In late April the whole root ball can either be replanted outside (allowing 10 days below 50°F for vernalization) or split into root divisions. The advantage to this method is that you can put red tape on your most productive plants during harvest. Then new divisions will be equally productive (not the case with seeds).

Diseases and Insects

Root rot may occur due to poor drainage, over-watering, packing plants too closely in the rows, dense stands of weeds, or (counter-intuitively) drought (New Jersey Extension). When root rot is present, the growing tips become yellow and die; buds become small and tough.

Crown rot, bud rot, and curly dwarf virus may be transmitted by crown division. If disease is present, purchase clean seeds or plants to break the cycle on new ground.

Black tip is a calcium disorder associated with insufficient water. Provide at least 1 inch of water per week, especially when plants have 8 to 10 leaves (New Jersey Extension).

Artichokes have no special resistance to verticillium wilt and other plant pathogens. Compost well, and water when dry to keep plants vigorous. Control aphids, which may transmit viruses.

Artichokes are sometimes damaged by cutworms, which can be prevented with paper collars. Control aphids and red spider mites with insecticidal oil. The use of ghibberellic acid, the commercial hormone used for earlier production and increased bud quality, may also induce black tip and infestations of spider mites. Use fermented alfalfa tea.

The European corn borer, a tan or whitish larva with brown spots, common on sweet corn, can be controlled with Bt (Dipel) or Spinosad.

Varieties

Imperial Star (85 days) was created for annual production, but overwinters in Zone 7. Imperial Star yields well without vernalization, but 24% better when young plants are chilled for 8 to 10 days around 50°F (New Jersey Extension). Medium-sized plants have dark green buds and some disease resistance.

Green Globe Improved (100 days) produces much better yields if vernalized 2 weeks at around 50°F (New Jersey Extension). Harvest is reliable,

Artichoke and Cardoon

hearts are large, plants overwinter for years in Zones 7 and 8 and often survive with mulch in Zone 6. Beautiful silvery leaves, a fine edible ornamental.

Purple Italian Globe (120 days) produces highly decorative edible reddish purple buds. This long season variety should be sown in late winter in milder areas for late summer or fall harvest. Buds are large and tender, with good tolerance to summer heat.

Tempo (100 days) is a highly productive hybrid of Purple Italian, with 3 to 4 large primary buds and 10 to 15 smaller secondary buds. This is a fine ornamental plant.

Seed

Because of high rates of polymorphism, heirloom artichoke seed is extremely variable and may not breed true. A percentage of plants may not bud at all. For older varieties purchase crowns. Up to 40% of heirloom seed produces barren plants; 15 to 25% of more recent varieties produce barren plants.

SEED: About 700 seeds per ounce. Packets range from 20 to 50 seeds. For annual artichokes set plants every 3 feet in rows 4 feet apart. For perennial artichokes set transplants or crown division every 4 feet in rows 6 feet apart.

GERMINATION: 7 to 12 days at 70 to 80°F. Soak seed in 130°F water for 10 minutes to improve germination.

VIABILITY: 6 years.

DAYS TO HARVEST: From seed, 85 to 120 days. From crown division, 1 year of vegetative growth with first harvest in the second year.

ROTATION: 3 years with other members of the composite family (lettuce, chicory, escarole).

BIODYNAMIC SPRAYS AND MOON CALENDAR: Biodynamic preparation 500 during bed preparation and before crown planting. Silica spray on leaf days after second true leaf and after eighth true leaf; again on flower days when the flower stalks begin to rise.

ARUGULA

I have wondered if the unusual flavor of arugula (*Eruca sativa*) is due to erucin, one of the most potent forms of the antioxidant isothiocyanate. Erucin is found in other crucifers but in much higher concentration in arugula, which is probably why this antioxidant was named after the Latin name for arugula: *Eruca*. Erucin inhibits excess levels of estrogen and inhibits the growth of cancer cells, with the highest antioxidant content found in arugula sprouts (Barillari et al. 2005).

Arugula, sometimes called wall rocket in English, and rugola, rucola, and rugetta in Italian, has been collected from the wild since ancient Roman times, where it was served in salad with romaine, chicory, mallow, lavender, and goat cheese. Arugula is still a half-wild plant with a unique pungent, nutty, slightly smoky flavor. Arugula is included in many traditional Mediterranean cuisines, not only in Europe but North Africa and the Middle East. Its range extends to India where arugula is called *gargeer*. In the United States arugula has become commercially significant only in the past twenty years. Arugula now has acquired a following passionate enough to make plausible the ancient Romans' belief in its power as an aphrodisiac. I, for one, believe arugula's unique flavor betokens significant nutritional therapeutic value. If you grow enough of it, arugula is also delicious as a green, braised with garlic and olive oil and served over pasta. Its use as a creative salad ingredient with fruits, nuts, sun-dried tomatoes, and other greens is almost unlimited.

Arugula grows best in cool moist weather, from spring sowings that grow into early summer, sowings in late summer for early fall harvest, and early fall sowings for overwintering for harvest the next spring. Arugula is very winter-hardy, even in the north. For extended harvest of larger plants, direct-seed arugula at 3-week intervals, 15 seeds to the foot, ¼ inch deep in well-composted soil. Seed can be broadcast in beds for baby salad, or sown 3 rows in a 4-foot wide bed, again 15 seeds to the foot. Skim-weed frequently. Be prepared to protect this crop from flea beetles with floating row covers. Flea beetles love arugula. Young leaves and florets can be cut and grown again for extended harvest, or whole plants can be cut for bunching. Older leaves become hot and bitter, but are still good mixed with milder greens. Bolted flowers add piquancy to salads.

Arugula

An ounce of arugula seed (about 15,000) sows 800 to 1,000 feet of row. Sow, spray biodynamic 501, and harvest on leaf days.

Sylvetta (perennial wall rocket, *Diplotaxis tenuifolia*) is marketed as wild arugula, although the plants are not closely related, not even the same genus. Called "rucola selvatica" in Italy, sylvetta adds an even more pungent flavor to salads and mesclun mixes than arugula. Wall rocket is naturally very high in nitrile (nitrate) and like agretti probably should be used in moderation. A potential natural nitrile-based fungicide has been isolated from wall rocket. Sylvetta is sown and grown similarly to arugula.

ASPARAGUS

Detailed dioramas excavated from Egyptian tombs show dozens of tiny Egyptian figures busily packing bushels of provisions for the afterlife. I can easily imagine myself among them, the bakers and butchers and gardeners, working together like a hive of bees. But I can't decide if the image of a servant girl bearing a plate of steamed asparagus into Eternity makes me grateful for the cornucopia of our existence, or just sad. So I pause for a moment to consider my final meal—asparagus, baked ibis, and barley beer.

Wild asparagus was foraged from the Mediterranean region as long as people have walked its shores. Its antiquity is reflected in its name–*asparag*—meaning shoot or sprout in ancient Persian. The name somehow has remained completely unchanged in most languages for 5,000 years. The Romans were so passionate about asparagus that they dried the delicate spring shoots for consumption out of season. Most likely, the Romans were the agents for the naturalization of asparagus as far as the British Isles. My asparagus have spread over my property so widely that I cannot imagine gathering them all up again for the afterlife, much as I might wish to do so.

The British, however, failed to follow Roman advice on cooking. Augustus had an expression for jobs he wanted done immediately: "Do it faster than you cook asparagus." Unfortunately that old-nouvelle technique, along with asparagus cultivation itself, seemed to go dormant for a thousand years. But asparagus did not die. It reappeared, as it does every spring, suddenly, out of nowhere, in the elegantly drawn herbals of the sixteenth century. I can't believe that peasant gardeners ever abandoned this reliable spring green for a full millennium.

In the seventeenth century, people began to rethink gardens rationally, just as the Romans had done in ancient times. "Sparrow grass" regained popularity in Britain and its colonies, and in Europe. Unfortunately this was quickly followed by the great blanching "epidemic" of the 1800s, sentencing thousands of tons of precious antioxidants to oblivion for two centuries. Blanched asparagus, called spargel or white gold (because of its high market price) still has a massive hold on the European market. And today, although so many studies have extolled the value of green in vegetables, and praised the unique biochemistry and antioxidant profile of asparagus, its nutrient values have once again been diminished by chemical over-fertilization.

Ancient foragers collected asparagus for the same reason we do; they were glad to have a completely reliable, green sprout after late winter rains. But they could hardly ignore the strange smell asparagus produced in their urine, a scent compared to perfume by some (the French novelist Marcel Proust) and regarded with alarm and aversion by others. The scent is caused by a mixture of sulphur-containing chemicals (aspargic acid), steroidal saponins, and a host of other compounds shared by many members of the Asparagus genus. In India *Asparagus racemosus*, an even more potent cousin of our *Asparagus officinalis*, is called the Queen of Herbs. Extracts are prescribed for gastric ulcer, depression, sexual dysfunction, increased insulin secretion, lowering cholesterol, reduction of certain tumors, and improved feminine vitality. Indian researchers back these claims with a surprising amount of data (Goyal et al., *Indian Journal of Medical Sciences*, vol. 57 2003).

Western web sites don't dispute the unique biochemistry of *Asparagus officinalis*, but substantiating research has not been carried out. Spears are high in the antioxidants quercitin, kaempferol, and rutin. Rutin (which is also high in buckwheat) has been shown to strengthen capillaries and to generally reduce inflammation. Asparagus has been shown to increase insulin secretion, of benefit to diabetics (*Journal of Endocrinology* 2007). Korean researchers have shown that asparagus extracts protect the liver from the toxifying effects of alcohol (Kim et al., *Journal of Food Sciences* 2009).

Unfortunately, chemical fertilization has drastically reduced the vitamins and antioxidants in asparagus over the past fifty years. USDA tests show a decline of vitamin C from 33 milligrams (mg) in 1963 to a mere 6 mg per 100 grams of asparagus in 2005. Vitamin A declined by half, according to USDA tests. I assume that other unique biochemicals have diminished as well; this phenomenon is a witness to what I would call "an invisible extinction" in the world of food plants. Those plants not lost to Amazon cattle farms are lost on our doorstep, leaving only a shadow of themselves in the produce aisle.

Culture

Like celery, asparagus is believed to have evolved on barren coastal ground exposed to salt spray. Asparagus developed such high tolerance for salt and beach soil profiles that in decades past, heavy applications of salt were used as an herbicide to clear weeds from difficult-to-weed perennial asparagus beds. This proved to be a terrible practice, ruining the land and polluting the water table. But unlike celery, which accumulates so much sodium even on normal soil that people with kidney problems avoid it, asparagus is a low-sodium vegetable! Asparagus is the opposite of its Mediterranean salt marsh neighbor agretti (*Salsola soda*), which is a vegetable saltshaker.

Although asparagus will grow and naturalize on a wide range of soil profiles and climates, commercial production focuses on high drainage sandy soils, such as those found in Michigan and New Jersey. Commercial growers always keep the pH high, above 7, to suppress fusarium rot, which can destroy even long-established plantings. Organic stands on well-drained ground have been known to produce for fifty years, but conventionally grown commercial stands tend to decline in twelve to fifteen years. Well-composted organic and biodynamic stands should produce for more than twenty years.

Best results come from a thorough, initial removal of perennial weeds, either by hand in home gardens during an initial deep digging of the bed, or by covering the bed with black plastic for a full year prior to planting. Small holes can be punched for tomatoes, squash, or melons in the "smother" year. Commercial organic growers can also smother the field for a year with field crops planted in black plastic; or smother the field with dense green manures such as alfalfa, vetch, or buckwheat. Some growers practice year-long, continuous tillage to remove perennial weeds, but this exposes the soil to continual oxidation, loss of organic matter, and produces no crops.

Initial composting predetermines the productivity and longevity of the planting. Washington State Extension reports that nutrient requirements and total NPK (nitrogen, phosphorous, and potassium) stored in roots and crowns are highest during initial crown establishment, but much lower after two to three seasons. For asparagus fields, they recommend high nitrogen legume smother crops (alfalfa, vetch, and so forth) plowed down with 10 tons of manure per acre. Cow manure produces the strongest, longest lasting stands and provides all the nutrients asparagus requires during early development. Biodynamic growers spray Preparation 500 on the bare soil at this time.

Even if your home gardening style is casual, remember that asparagus growers must emulate the Egyptians and prepare for the ages. Choose only well-drained sites, never a place where water stands after a rain. A 20- by 5-foot patch will amply supply most families. Consider double digging the patch to loosen soil deeply and to remove noxious weed roots from the subsoil. Pay attention to innocent looking white roots such as bindweed (*Convolvulus*), the deep growing pieces of thistle roots, and the white wires of invasive grasses. I use a spading fork to lift and sift the soil in a windrow to one side of the trench, carefully removing weeds and roots as I go. I then re-dig the second layer so that my trench (at least 3 feet wide) is down 10 to 15 inches deep.

Next backfill a low 3-inch ridge along the bottom of the trench, mixing the backfill with half compost. Many organic growers also add a sprinkling of rock phosphate, which has been shown to strengthen root structure and future production. Other options include fortifying non-manure compost with a general organic garden fertilizer, most of which have about 50% more NPK than cow manure, but may lack the valuable biological activity of the cows. Consider fortifying bag-fertilized asparagus crowns with dilute liquid seaweed or manure/nettle teas at planting time, or side-dress during early crown growth. Always provide some sort of decayed organic matter. Rotted leaves are excellent.

Purchase only one year-old crowns. Two year-old crowns suffer more transplant shock. Crowns look somewhat like a sea plant washed up on a beach. Place the growth point facing up and the fleshy roots draped on both sides of the ridge. Crowns spaced as close as 8 inches in the row produce very slender gourmet spears. Those spaced from 14 to 24 inches between plants produce larger juicier spears. I should note that the older, really long-lasting stands were traditionally planted with wider spacing. Liberty Hyde Bailey's *Cyclopedia of American Horticulture* (1900-1902) recommends 24 inches; that is not often practiced anymore. He also recommends back-filling entirely with 100% composted manure or leaf mold, rather than the half-and-half I suggested. If you've got the compost, do it! Also note that with most varieties the growing point can sit 6 to 8 inches deep, but Purple Passion should sit 5 inches deep.

Back-fill in stages, covering the roots with 1 to 2 inches of compost or compost/soil mix. As the shoots emerge and grow, add an inch or so every few weeks, similar to hilling potatoes. Some biodynamic growers soak the shoots with a slurry of compost, clay, and 501 prep. Sprouts also benefit from sprayings of dilute liquid seaweed, or blended and strained alfalfa greens and water. In soils with imperfect drainage, mound the row to keep water from collecting over the crowns. Hoe weeds, and remove perennial weeds that appear during growth. Mulch the bed with up to 6 inches of leaves, semi-rotted leaves, or straw. Hay is not good because it contains weed seed. Crowns under heavy mulch are healthier, larger, more prolific, and fairly weed-free. Irrigate young plants in dry weather and in arid climates.

Asparagus planted in field rows can also be heavily mulched, but often growers take advantage of deep-set crowns and shallowly cultivate the entire field after dormancy. Field planting is also different. Furrows 6 to 8 inches deep and 4 to 5 feet apart are plowed across the field. Crowns are simply laid in the trench, covered with an inch or two of soil and backfilled a few inches at a time over the following month. Any hoed crops such as bush beans, cole crops (brassicas), or lettuce can be planted between asparagus rows after backfill is complete. This not only uses the land productively, but also motivates the grower to keep weeds down.

Field growers with greenhouses or cold frames may wish to start asparagus from seed. Purchased crowns produce more quickly, but are expensive. Seeds require a long period of care—three months in flats—but are much cheaper for large plantations, and allow the grower a wide choice of varieties.

Seeds can be started in a greenhouse or in outdoor beds. Greenhouse starts are sown in late winter in the north; about the time onions are sown, from mid-February to early March. Sow one seed per 2-inch pots or cells. Plant in pure compost, if possible. Germination temperatures are about 75°F by day with 65°F nights. Prick out weak or spindly plants. Feed with biodynamic compost/nettle tea if plants show lack of vigor and pale green color. Some commercial organic fertilizers may burn the ferns. Apply these sparingly, and wash residual fertilizer off leaves.

Seeds can also be started outdoors in spring. Sow 3 to 5 seeds per inch, 1½ inches deep in rows 18 to 24 inches apart. Use radish seeds to mark the rows. Keep them well weeded, but thinning is not necessary. Transplant roots to trenches the following spring before crowns re-sprout.

Follow the biodynamic spray schedule for onions. Both plants are in the lily family, and both have modified stems rather than true leaves. In asparagus, the modified stems are called cladodes or cladophylls. True leaves are vestigial. The beautiful ferns are actually very fine stems. They may have evolved to reduce transpiration in dry Mediterranean climates. It may seem an insult to call these delicate ferns a skeleton, but the stem tree is undoubtedly a skeleton of silica, which seems to diffuse into the atmosphere.

The traditional schedule for crown development delays harvest until the third year after planting: during the planting year no spear harvest is allowed. Ferns are cut back only after hard frost. In the next year as well, no harvest of spears is allowed. In the third year, however, every spear is harvested for about two weeks when the spears are 8 inches tall. In the fourth year, the clear-cut harvest is extended to four weeks. In the fifth year, harvest is 6 or 7 weeks, until the beginning of green pea harvest. Thereafter the ferns are left to grow unimpeded. Even Michigan Extension, which advises major production areas, still advises refraining from harvest until the third year.

Ohio Extension, however, claims research has shown that a light harvest during the year after planting stimulates new bud formation, and ultimately produces more spears. I don't know whether or not this translates into reduced longevity of the stand. Bailey's *Horticulture* and others think it does; so whatever you decide, keep the second year cutting light. And if at any time, in any year, spear production drops off suddenly, end the harvest immediately to protect the plants.

Special curved asparagus knives are available to avoid damaging other emerging spears. Cut at the lowest tender point or just find the tender point naturally by snapping the spear off by had. Snapping also reduces the spread of fusarium via harvest knives. Be sure to harvest all spears during the harvest window. Mixing ferns with spears only gives asparagus beetles an early start.

Control leaf pests during fern growth. Weeds decrease the next year's crop. Keep plants well mulched for strong fern growth, which builds the next year's crop. After hard frost the entire field can be brush cut and either skim-cultivated or shallowly tilled (3 to 4 inches). Tractor tires should straddle the rows to prevent crushing the crowns, but home gardeners can do well just cutting back ferns; hand weeding; and adding more compost, mulch, or wet autumn leaves for next year's mulch.

Pests and Disease

If cutworms attack emerging spears, control with Dipel (a natural bacillus). Asparagus beetles show a black-and-white checkerboard pattern on a maroon field. Egg cases cover the spears. Larvae feed on the fern, causing complete browning and severe reduction in the next year's yield. Control with pyrethrin spray late in the day when bees are not active.

Deer and rodents can make unfenced crops disappear overnight. I am amazed, however, that a small abandoned patch behind my barn—un-weeded, unfertilized, and unfenced—still bears heavily after 22 years of predation. It is doubtless a testimony to the longevity of a strong start.

Fencing helps. In gardens no more than 35 feet across, a 5-foot fence will keep out deer. For woodchuck, mouse, and vole protection add 3-foot hardwire cloth to the outside bottom of the fence. Remove blocks of sod 4 inches deep by 15 inches wide, along the base of the fence. Allow 20 inches of hardware cloth to rise vertically; bend the bottom 16 inches outward away from the garden. Replace the sod over the hardware cloth. Some West Coast gardeners have been forced to line planting trenches with hardware cloth to deal with gophers.

Asparagus rust and phyllium purple stem spot are exacerbated by humidity, excess water, and poor air circulation. In the latter, purple spots appear on spears at harvest, which infect the leaves, causing them to yellow and drop. Rusts first appear as creamy orange on stubble late in harvest followed by a darkened rusty color in midsummer on the stalks and branches, causing them to turn brown. In fall, the lesions are black. Each phase weakens the plants. Control with organic fungicide.

The most severe disease is fusarium root rot, the major cause of asparagus failure. The only preventive is extreme plant vigor, which is why I urge thorough initial bed preparation, composting, and heavy layers of mulch. I find that a mulch of maple leaves reduces insect and disease problems. Purple varieties are reported to be more susceptible to fusarium root rot than green varieties. Plant asparagus in new ground, if possible, where no fusarium susceptible crops have been planted before.

Varieties

Open-pollinated varieties have equal numbers of male and female flowers. Female plants produce fewer spears, reserving their vitality for the fruit (small red berries). The oldest heirloom still available is Precoce de Argenteuil, a seventeenth century French heirloom reselected about 1860, and still used for blanching. The rose-purple spears are thick and tender, and produce early. Colossus (Conover's Colossal) is another old European variety reselected in 1868 for its large size and unusual productivity (as much as 40 spears per crown); it is still grown in England. Both old varieties have no special disease resistance and must be planted on new ground to avoid fusarium.

Mary Washington (variety) has excellent asparagus flavor, rust resistance, and produces well on new ground. UC72 is a Mary Washington with added fusarium resistance. Likewise Viking KB3 is a Martha Washington variety with improved disease resistance.

Hybrid asparagus are all male, and therefore up to 50% more productive than open-pollinated strains. Most have very good resistance to fusarium. These include Jersey Giant and Jersey Knight. Jersey hybrids should be planted with the crown 5 inches below the surface. New strains from Canada such as all-male Millennium Hybrid show extra hardiness, excellent productivity, and (according to the *Stokes* seed catalog) very high rutin content. For warmer states (Zones 7 and 8 including the South, Southwest, and California) choose special cultivars (cultivated varieties) that do not require chilling, such as UV 157. Northern varieties planted in the South tend to sprout in midwinter and become damaged by frost.

Purple Passion hybrid produces beautiful purple spears on both male and female plants. They are lower yielding than all-male hybrids, but have exceptional roadside appeal. Spears turn green when cooked. Again, remember that extension studies have shown that one-year-old transplants are less subject to transplant setback than two-year-olds.

Growers can also divide their own plants in late winter, tagging the female plants of Mary Washington in fall before the red berries disappear. When dividing crowns make sure each division contains both root and growing point, similar to dividing dahlias and other perennial flowers. Replant immediately for best results.

SEED: Seed size varies from 13,000 to 19,200 seeds per pound. About 70% of seed planted produces usable crowns. A packet (1 gram) of 35 seeds produces a 16-foot row with 8 inches between crowns (if slender spears are desired) or a 30-foot row at 15 inches between crowns (for thicker spears). Greater spacing, up to 24 inches between crowns, is believed to extend the life of the planting. An ounce (28 grams) of 1,000 seeds produces about 700 usable crowns.

A pound (453 grams) of 16,000 seeds produces about 11,000 usable crowns, which plants an acre at 14 inches apart, and 4 feet between rows. 13,000 crowns plant an acre at 8 inches apart, 4 feet between rows. 5,500 crowns plant an acre at 2 feet apart, 4 feet between rows.

GERMINATION: about 70% usable crowns at 75° to 85°F.

MOON CALENDAR: All practices in leaf, ascending moon, if possible.

ROTATION: 15 to 30 year perennial stand, depending on drainage, soil profile, initial trench preparation, and spacing.

BIODYNAMIC SPRAYS: Preparation 500 on soil the fall before planting, during trench preparation, annual fall cultivation, and annual composting. Preparation 501 on transplants following the same schedule as onions, at least once during fern development.

COMPANIONS: Traditionally asparagus are alleged to be mutually beneficial with tomatoes. Other beneficials include parsley, basil, dill, and coriander. Marigolds are alleged to deter asparagus beetles. Alternate rows during first two years with spinach, peas, salad crops, and bush beans.

BEANS: BUSH AND POLE

Bush Beans

One December I planted bush beans in clear plastic pots, just to watch the roots grow. Conditions could hardly have been worse. Light levels were low; the wood stove pushed the temperature above 80° in the day, which then dropped to 45° at night. Germination was spotty. Many plants stunted, damped off, and died. The survivors strained to reach the faint midwinter sun. Why did I bother? Because plants and seasons are not only my outer life, but my inner life as well. I can't entirely explain that here; but observing the margin of the seasons is normal for any gardener. Gardeners always push those margins to the limit.

One thing surprised me. The snap beans that did survive produced fruits in extremely low light. The plants were dwarfed, stems leggy, leaves scanty, the 6-inch pots obviously inadequate; but the plants flowered anyway, and produced a few normal-sized snap beans. Those not eaten by my small son even produced seeds.

The variety was Provider, a reliable producer in cooler, cloudier seasons. I decided to try it in a patch partly shaded by a neighbor's spruce. It worked well enough. I realized that legumes don't fruit entirely out of the light. They seem to fruit out of themselves, darkly, almost like animal embryos, since they bear within themselves a metabolism separate from the light in their root nodule. This makes them natural companions to plants dependant on high light levels.

Bush beans don't have time to develop as many root nodules as legume fodder crops, partly because the bush beans are harvested and removed before they continue to the shell bean stage. If high production is not a goal, try an older multi-purpose variety such as White Half Runner, available from seed saver's exchanges. White Half Runner doubles as snap bean and shell bean. Modern snap beans will also produce edible shell beans. Fast-growing modern varieties make great filler as a catch crop, a midseason crop, and green manure.

Early cabbage or broccoli can be inter-sown with bush beans three weeks before those crops mature. In the warmer states, bush beans can shelter the soil between spring and autumn crops, keeping the ground shaded and alive. Beans can follow early lettuce and precede kale. Farther north, midseason beans can be harvested early enough to get in a strong stand of rye by late autumn. Where Mexican bean beetles are a problem, a quick picking can be taken, and the plants either tilled under or included as a nitrogen-rich addition to the summer weed compost.

Bean beetles serve as barometers for what the English call "heart"; that is, the soil's ability to produce healthy plants. Bush beans grown in composted well-drained medium loam (pH range from 6 to 7) are far less appetizing to bean beetles. Leached sandy soils seem to invite predation. The bean beetle also indicates something about the total plant environment. In Pennsylvania, I watched how differently my two adjoining gardens produced bush beans in midsummer. Both had identical soil profiles. One was composed of long, 250-foot field rows, while the other was an acre of raised beds. The beds area was laced with elderberry hedge, currants, Rosa rugosa, fruit trees, flower borders, lavender, rosemary, fennel, and other herb beds. Two pickings were possible in the raised beds even during the worst beetle season; in the field only one. In the field, beetles even seemed unaffected by dustings of organic pesticide; the leaves were so skeletonized, they were nearly useless as a cover crop. As a result, I don't entirely curse the bean beetle, since it convinced me of the value of soil "heart" and a mixed garden culture.

Bush beans are sub-tropical plants. When "jumping" the season I use a cool soil-tolerant variety such as Provider and heavy polyester row fabric. Even in the North, as a home gardener I have successfully sown bush beans on April 1, and harvested by the end of May. I pre-warm the soil for a few weeks with black plastic, careful to sprinkle the area with iron-based slug bait. Planting times vary; sometimes March is warm, other times April is very frosty. The soil should be at least 60°F for untreated seed. If the weather is cool, I leave the black plastic on and slit a 3-inch wide planting row, sowing 6 seeds to the foot, and covering with metal hoops and heavy row cover. For home use, I always get a crop, and in some years I am harvesting, before other gardeners sow.

Market growers have to be more careful, since extension studies have shown that chilled seedlings never fully recover. Dark-colored beans are more rot-resistant than light-colored seed. Soil temperature should really be 65°F, air temperature at least 60°F. In open ground, seed sown on May 1 will usually be harvested on the same date as beans sown on May 10. The later sowing is often more productive. However, I usually make one sowing under row cover a week earlier than the recommended date. Home gardeners can also sow bush beans and sweet corn in the same furrow. The heavy row cover will push both crops, and the corn can succeed the beans, which offer the corn a modest amount of nitrogen.

Optimum soil temperature for beans is 70 to 90°F. At these temperatures, beans return to their Central American roots. The only other trick I've used to hasten warm soil crops is to pre-germinate seed in a bucket before sowing. I have read that this can damage the seed, but I find the opposite. I once even forgot a pail until it fermented and the beans still grew well. Just remember to drain the seeds after the initial soaking overnight, and keep the pail in a warm place until the radical (rootlet) emerges. Soaked seeds must be hand-sown.

Bean furrows should be 1/4 inch deep, about 5 seeds to the foot. Beans produce best when not over-sown. In soils that crust, compost covers will improve germination. Two rows can be sown in beds 4 feet wide. In the field, single rows can be sown 2 to 3 feet apart. Early gambles should be sown a week apart. In warm weather sow later sowings, every 2 to 3 weeks. The Planet Jr. seeder I've used cracks a lot of seeds, so I sow smaller areas by hand. Cup-type seeders are better. One germinated seed every 3 inches makes a good stand; thinning is practical only on a small scale. Cultivation should be shallow and frequent until the plants spread.

In home gardens, early bean beetles can be picked off by hand. The first generation affects the entire season. At the same time, flatten the yellow egg cases under the leaves. A non-stinging tropical wasp (*Pediobius*) works if a large area is used for release (in Florida a bean-producing county was cleared of beetles with these wasps). Numbers of gardeners have reported success as well. Proper timing of release is essential. A predatory mite may also be available. Since beans are self-pollinating, row cover can also be used to keep the beetles off. Remove when beans begin to set pods.

Biodynamic growers can use silica spray (501) twice on bush beans: once when they show a crop of leaves, and again when they flower. In areas where fungus disease is a problem, equisetum tea (508) can be sprayed twice weekly. Avoid picking beans when plants are wet, and avoid overhead watering in the evening when plants will not dry by nightfall. In some areas bean mosaic, pod mottle virus, and powdery mildew are problems, especially in extended wet weather, where crops are not rotated, and in monoculture. Choose resistant varieties from catalogs that list disease resistance, and practice a three-year rotation. Alternate with rye, which suppresses disease. Good air circulation also helps. Home gardeners can thin plants to six inches apart in the row. Perpetual damp weather allows fungus that normally stays below the soil level to rise as high as flowers and fruit. Twice weekly sprayings of equisetum and silica counteract these conditions somewhat and hasten ripening.

Snap beans should be picked from 5 to 7 inches long, depending on the variety. Some home gardeners enjoy the meatiness of slightly mature snap beans, but most people favor young beans. Remember that young beans and bean varieties with very low fiber wilt more quickly. Beans that trail on the ground also tend to mold, especially in fall. Choose upright varieties and pick on the young side.

Were it not for the bean beetle, saving bush bean seeds would be easy; but to form viable seeds, strong bean plants must retain sound leaves. Home gardeners can pick bean beetles by hand, and squash the bright yellow eggs on the undersides of leaves. Plants for seeds can also be grown under floating row cover. If more than one bean variety is grown, cover the rows or isolate them by at least 100 feet. Bush, pole, and shell beans are all *Phaseolus vulgaris*. Seeds can be stored like any other shell bean and cooked in winter like kidney beans.

Late summer sowings can extend into fall using heavy row cover. Once the early frosts of September and early October are bridged, harvest can sometimes go on for 3 weeks or more.

Bush Bean Varieties

Green beans for home gardeners are bred differently from those sold in supermarkets. The main difference is high fiber in market types, making the beans firmer, less tender, and less likely to go limp during transport. Low fiber makes beans more fragile, less shippable but much better eating, with more flavor. Generally, home gardeners have no reason to plant commercial-type beans (available from seed companies that cater to growers and processors). Neither do market gardeners that specialize in fresh market sales, where taste and tenderness are the reason shoppers show up in the first place. Of course some varieties straddle the fence between home and market.

Traits to look for in choosing varieties for the home garden and fresh market include tenderness, flavor, meaty texture, wide adaptability, good yields, tolerance of adverse weather, and sustained yield over an extended period. Priorities for market gardeners may include higher fiber, concentrated pods set for rapid harvest, high yield, strong upright plants (for ease of harvest, to hold pods off the fungus on the ground, and to prevent lodging when plants fall down under the weight of pods), longer holding in the field (slow seed development), disease resistance, cold soil tolerance, and the ability to set pods in hot weather.

Some of the earlier modern varieties such as Contender and Provider are good fence straddlers for home and local markets. Contender (42 days, 1965) is valued for earliness, very good quality, and dependable yields. Contender is heat tolerant, produces under adverse conditions, and is resistant to common bean mosaic (race 1) and powdery mildew. Provider (50 days, 1965) is probably the most widely appreciated fence straddler. Few varieties beat its reliability: excellent cool soil germinator, with good seedpod development under adverse conditions, good plant vigor, disease resistance (to common and NY 15 mosaic and powdery mildew), and high yields. Taste is very good, but not gourmet.

Home gardeners have different criteria. They have loved Burpee's Tender Pod (50 days) for decades because of its meaty, extra-tender fiber-free pods; its delicious taste; productivity over a long period; and fair adaptability. But, it has a germination rate that is lower than average. There are more recent introductions, such as Jade, which is extremely tender and high-yielding, with gourmet quality (which tends to mean long and thin like French filet beans) on upright, adaptable plants for hand picking. It is resistant to bean mosaic virus.

Fresh Pick (53 days) is one of the tastiest green beans, very tender, but not slender; similar to Blue Lake pole beans in quality and flavor. Fresh Pick is heat tolerant, with stiff upright plants that hold pods well off the ground. It is resistant to bean mosaic virus. Plants bear longer than other bush beans. Pods must be hand-picked.

Bush Blue Lake (55 days) continues a long breeding tradition from heirloom Blue Lake pole beans, which set the standard for flavor for more than a century. Blue Lake flavor is unique with low fiber, slow seed development, and very productive upright plants.

French Filet (*haricot verts*) is the classic gourmet green bean. Pods must be picked young and slender (1/4 inch maximum). They must be picked frequently to maintain quality; at least 3 times a week in warm weather. For home or fresh market, try a few to see if you can keep up. Burpee's Beananza (55 days) has the sweet nutty French filet flavor with slender 7-inch pods. If picked regularly, Beananza produces twice as long as many other cultivars.

Triumphe de Farcy (48 days) is the heirloom standard with a crunchy texture, rather than the usual fleshy texture. The 5 to 6 inch pods are too short for some gourmet markets, which require at least 7 inches. Burpee's French Filet and Maxibel (50 days) can be harvested at 7 inches.

Flat Italian bush beans are dwarf versions of pole Romano. All are white-seeded. Early Bush Italian (50 days) has classic Italian flat bean flavor; they produce only compact 18-inch plants. Jumbo (60 days) is a cross between two famous beans, Romano and Kentucky Wonder. Jumbo has exceptional flavor, in huge 6 to 7 inch pods, stringless even at 10 inches. Jumbo is not upright, and beans may trail over the ground, causing mold in wet weather. In very fertile soil the plants may run, increasing the problem. Jumbo bears over a long period.

Yellow wax snap beans are a colorful novelty that supply about half the vitamin A of green beans (230 international units per 100 grams for yellow) and about the same amount of vitamin C (13 mg). Gold Mine (47 days) has one of the highest disease tolerances of any wax bean, including common bean mosaic, brown spot, rust, and halo blight. It has very low fiber, with good sweet taste. Roc d'Or (57 days) is a classy extra long Sungold from France. It must be harvested young for premier quality, and is tolerant to common mosaic and anthracnose. Heat- and cold-tolerant Romano Gold (56 days) produces pale yellow flat pods with mild sweet Romano flavor and tender texture—a double novelty.

Pole Beans

Pole beans save space in home gardens, allow for some succession of crops (spinach, lettuce, and so forth), and bear up to 7 weeks, which is much longer than bush beans. The downsides include setting up and taking down poles or fencing and the shading of surrounding crops. Native Americans solved these problems by combining beans, corn, and squash, which works well with dry dent corn and shell beans. It is harder to manage with sweet corn and green beans. Southern Exposure Seed Savers recommends combining Hickory King corn (used for grits and corn flour) with Genuine Cornfield pole beans, which are shade tolerant and produce snap or green shell. Despite its odd name, Genuine Cornfield is an old Iroquois variety, possibly of pre-Columbian origin. If you have plenty of space, you can add winter squash and plant well-composted mounds on 8-foot squares. Let the squash run till harvest and don't move vines around when harvesting the green beans. I find that the traditional Native American fish fertilizer causes raccoons to dig up the mounds.

Use 4 poles, 7 to 8 feet tall, tied at the top, teepee style, with 6 to 8 seeds sown 1 inch deep at the base of each pole. Or construct a string fence attaching #9 wire to 7 to 8 foot posts on 8 foot centers. (Use 3 strands of wire, and the fence can be rotated with tomatoes.) Tie a zigzag web of heavy jute twine for the vines to climb. In autumn both vines and twine can be composted. Sow pole bean seeds thinly (3 inches between seeds) in furrows 1 inch deep. With older varieties, harvest the green beans young. Some varieties introduced recently retain quality when more mature.

Pole Bean Varieties

Kentucky Wonder (65 days) has remained a favorite snap and shell bean since before the Civil War. Blue Lake (60 days) has set a standard for flavor for generations: stringless, meaty and tender when small, resistant to rust, and good as a shell bean. Blue Lake can be used with shorter 6-foot fencing or poles. Rattlesnake (73 days) keeps producing delicious snap beans right through summer heat waves. Fortex (60 days) a more modern introduction, is a dual-purpose bean, both for slender 7-inch filet beans, and is just as delicious when mature, even with enlarged seeds.

The unique taste and buttery texture of flat-podded Italian pole beans have had an ecstatic following for centuries. Romano (70 days) is still one of the most popular and adaptable, with heirloom varieties passed down for generations by families in Italy and the United States. Other highly praised flat-pods include Northeaster (56 days), a stringless, extremely early pole bean with "deliciously rich sweet flavor"; and Garden of Eden, a family heirloom sweet and tender from youth to maturity. "We have not seen another bean like this…" (from Johnny's Selected Seeds catalog). And finally Aunt Ada's Italian, which emigrated from Italy to Colorado around 1900; "We can hardly let a meal go by without including this delectable green bean." (Turtle Tree Biodynamic Seed Initiative).

Another much-beloved pole bean is the Scarlet Runner (*Phaseolus coccineus*), a popular bean in England. It is popular not only because of its brilliant red flower, which is edible and attracts hummingbirds, but also because Scarlet Runner tolerates the cool, moist summers. It is not, however, a European native, but like *Phaseolus vulgaris* hails from Central or South America and was cultivated by the Hopi Indians before Columbus. Scarlet Runner makes an outstanding plant for an arbor or ornamental trellis. It produces large fine-flavored green beans when picked young (6 inches); and later, it gives a crop of mottled purple and black shell beans. Scarlet Emperor (75 days) is an improved European variety.

Finally, my father's favorite pole bean, the Asian yard-long or asparagus bean (*Vigna unguiculata*) is not really a yard long. The pods grow up to 20 inches, which I remember dominating the front brick wall of my parent's house. Dad tied string to nails all along the low roof and string was lined down to the ground. The ten-foot vines covered the wall up to the roof for ten hot, humid Maryland summers. These relatives of southern cowpeas appreciate heat, especially the warm nights; they yield less in the North. Their flavor is sweet and complex with a crisp texture, always an essential ingredient to my mother's lifelong addiction to Asian cuisine. Harvest young and again when the beans begin to bulge in the pod; asparagus beans yield for a long time. The green version is often offered generically, although the variety Green Gita (78 days) is more widely adapted. Red Noodle (75 to 85 days) produces decorative wine-colored pods.

Shell Beans

Any bush or pole bean can produce shell beans, but a legion of varieties of *Phaseolus vulgaris* have been especially selected and saved for dry beans. The origin of cultivars such as Anasazi Bush (93 days) disappears into pre-history, just as did the Anasazi people who may have grown them. Anasazi Bush produces sweet, meaty, and beautiful maroon and white seeds, still popular in the Southwest, but easily grown anywhere bush beans grow. Other dry beans may bear the name of the ancestor who maintained the lineage, such as Grandmother Stallard, a productive red and white speckled pole bean for soup and stew, suitable for climbing cornstalks.

French Horticultural (65 to 90 days), also called Borlotto, Cranberry Bean, and October Bean (in New England), comes in both semi-runner and bush form. These beans are eaten as "shelly beans" in summer, just when the seeds have fully formed and the pod has begun to yellow. Undried seeds are sautéed like limas, with garlic and herbs. The balance of the pods will turn speckled cranberry red with buff-colored beans. Tongues of Fire (70 days) from Tierra de Fuego with purple-streaked pods can be eaten as young snap beans, shelly, or dried.

Black Turtle (85 to 105 days) is used for soup, baked beans, and bean spread. Nodak Pinto (85 days) is used in soups and refried beans. Jacob's Cattle (80 to 100 days) is a famously beautiful bean: white seeds speckled with maroon, for soup and baking. Yin Yang (100 days) is an American heirloom renamed because the beans are half white with a black dot and half black with a white dot. French Flageolet beans can be used dry, but in France, gourmet chefs serve them green, sautéed in butter and herbs. Flagrano (65 days) has mint green seeds, which are easy to shell and have resistance to anthracnose, bean mosaic virus, and halo blight.

Shell beans are dry when they can be barely dented when bitten. Shell the pods by hand, or beat a sack of pods with a stick or flailing paddle, or flail a pile of pods on a tarp. Blow the chaff off with a large fan. Deep freeze beans for a few days to kill weevils, then store in a dry place.

- SEED: Seed per pound is variable: Green bush 1,400 to 1,800 seeds; Yellow bush around 1,750; Pole beans around 750; French filet 1,900 to 3,400; Yard long 3,200 to 3,800; Shell American around 850; Shell French around 1,800. For bush and shell, set seeder at 6 seeds to the foot. For pole and yard-long, 3 seeds to the foot.
- MOON CALENDAR: All "cultural" practices, including biodynamic sprays, in fruit. For seed saving, all in Leo. Alternate: flower. As a cover crop, sow in root or leaf, cultivate in root.
- ROTATION: 3 years between crops.
- BIODYNAMIC SPRAYS: Horn manure (500) before sowing. Seeds can be soaked in compost tea and a pinch of 500, drained and dusted with rhizobial bacteria. Spray silica (501) after third true leaf, and again at or just before flowering. Equisetum and valerian in damp muggy weather, and where virus and fungus are common.
- COMPANION PLANTS: Beets, celeriac, celery, cabbage, potatoes, leeks, summer savory, summer radishes, and strong-scented herbs against bean beetle.

BEET

When we want to approach a garden plant in a biodynamic way, we need to experience not only the part we eat, but also the parts we don't eat. Unfortunately, only the seed saver sees the flowers and fruits of beetroots. "Fruit" seems hardly the right word for the wizened desiccated forms that appear when a beetroot is replanted the second year. As for the flower, the landscapers just pass it by. It looks similar to the greenish flowers of the wild lamb's quarters, which is a close relative. There is very little *substance* in these flowers and fruit. They lack the etheric oils present in the *Umbelliferae* (the dill and coriander family). The flowers are leafy, and the fruits are stemmy. Even when young and juicy, the fruits look desiccated; later they look burned up, incinerated! Fruitlike color and sweetness are concentrated only in the root.

Beet color is rich and deep, almost like blood. In the nineteenth century beets were called blood-turnips; if you dilute its juice, you see it is a remarkably beautiful magenta. This magenta makes a wonderful food coloring. A German garden apprentice of mine once mixed beet juice and fruit juice to make bright, tasty popsicles! The blood-turnip is built up in rings, which are the counter image of the rosette of leaves rising above it. The dark red rings alternate with lighter red or sometimes white rings, as if there were a living pulse in the root corresponding to the process of growth in the leaves (and there is!). When my children were young, I liked to slice a very large Lutz beet into a wafer-thin slice to make small stained glass windows. I ushered my children into this small church, where I still pray everyday. When you hold these rose windows up to the light, the deep color does something to your heart, like an inner bath. Maybe we shouldn't take for granted that such an intense *flowering* takes place within the earth.

In the soil, the beetroots don't scatter chaotically like the crazy hairs of celeriac. They hold together in a globe, more tapered in the Cylindra variety, more misshapen in Lutz; but still a self-contained globe. The leaf rosette forms first, producing a funnel of dark green leaves with blood-red petioles, which pour down into a very short stem at the top of the root. This is not the picture of a grasping root but of a gathering root, pouring invisibly like a funnel into the earth. Botanists who practice Goethe's habit of observation* tell us that

---

* A method developed by Johann Wolfgang von Goethe (1749-1832) that regards the sequential stages of growth in each plant (metamorphosis) as a picture of the forces that form the plant.

when any plant flowers, it displays the summation of the plant's growth in a condensed form. This is also why the final botanical identification rests with the flower. The seed tree of the beet shows the image of the forces that formed the red globe. They look like a house that has been through a fire. Taken as a whole, the seed tree looks like a sphere in which only the veins remain; veins where the blood has dried up and shriveled into the wizened seeds.

The beet has an unusual combination of qualities. It is sweeter than most fruits, but is not really fruit-like. Mineral content is high, also fiber; vitamins C and A are lower than in the carrot. Beets grown quickly have a clean sweetness; storage beets are more earthy. Carrot seeds are finely aromatic, gracefully shaped, the leaves and flowers airy, like lace. The carrot draws down this lightness and aroma into its root; the upper aromatic qualities descend into the soil. Beet leaves are round, never indented, with juicy petioles, very nutritious, with strong earth acids.

If you observe exactly where the beet is most substantial, you find it is just above and just below the surface of the ground. The root partly sits on the surface, with the leaves spread closely from a condensed stem at the top. It appears from the area that biodynamics calls the "breathing diaphragm" of the soil. The funnel of leaves pours forces into a globular beaker, perhaps making visible in its rose redness that precious funnel of life that is just above and just below the soil's surface. So fragile, it is—you have no idea how fragile! Although many of my German gardener friends dismiss beet greens as fit only for livestock, beet thinnings in late spring, and fresh greens from early beets are among my family's favorite vegetables.

Culture

The most tender, sweetest beets are grown without hindrances from lack of moisture or poor fertility. Beets mature more quickly than carrots and are far easier to grow. Normal garden soil "in good heart,"* as the British say, will grow fine beets. They tolerate most types of soil, but are highly sensitive to a lack or excess of lime. In the East they nearly always need some lime to do well, unless your soil already tests above 6.5 pH. But why bother testing? Beets will do it for you. If they grow well, you have already made a soil test. If

---

* A soil with enough clay to hold nutrients, enough sand to be friable, and enough humus to hold water.

not, then add lime to your beet beds or to your compost heap. Another trick is to dust the crinkled, multiple beet seeds with powdered lime prior to sowing, whether by hand or mechanical seeder. This invariably gives the seed a better chance to germinate in acid eastern soils. In the West, of course, the opposite may be the case. Excessively alkaline soil may cause black heart, a boron deficiency. Then a special leaf compost may help, composed of oak leaves and some cottonseed meal.

In America, beets are rarely transplanted, although the practice is easy and efficient. In Europe, acres of beets are transplanted into clean weed-free fields. Beets can be sown in flats indoors or in a cold frame. Use a planting mix of half topsoil and half sifted compost, with a dusting of lime. Because of the taproot, it is best to use deep cells, a deep flat, or a ground cold frame. Try reinforcing the bottom of a grape-shipping crate. The sowing date can be a month before the outside sowing date for your area. That means about two months before the last expected spring frost. In about four weeks, these seedlings can be transplanted outside.

A similar procedure can be used for outside seedbeds. Sow beet seed about a month before the last expected frost. These can then be transplanted to a new clean bed. You will be surprised to find that if transplanted beets are watered well for a few days to get rooted, they will be more uniform, with a more globular shape, and will mature earlier than beets direct-seeded on the same date. A dip of compost slurry* and horn manure (500) helps transplants recover quickly. Dip the roots in this slurry and plant them wet. Transplanted beets are less work in the long run, since the new bed can be weed-free and evenly spaced. Three to four inches between transplants is sufficient, except in the case of the huge Lutz storage beet, which needs 5 inches. Direct-seeded beets can be thinned by harvesting young beets as needed. Beet seed naturally forms clumps of plants. Mono germ (single plant) seed is available, but home gardeners look forward to thinnings as one of the first great harvests of the season.

Earlier I mentioned that normal garden soil will grow good beets, but good composting practices grow beets still more tender and sweet. With plenty of humus you need never fear that your largest beets will be tough or tasteless. Beets favor the phosphorus and potassium that is plentiful in compost, but

---

* A half-and-half mix of composted manure and water, which clings to the roots, prevents desiccation and provides immediate nutrients for new root formation.

are not improved by the addition of the free nitrogen often found in poultry manure. Horn manure (500) is a basic biodynamic preparation for the beds. A compost cover is also good for the seeds after they are sown, but remember to tamp more firmly than with other seeds. The air pockets of the fruit cluster need to contact the soil. Beet seeds are much larger than carrot seeds (approximately 2,000 beet seeds to the ounce, as contrasted to approximately 20,000 for carrots), so they are easier to drop singly along the furrow. However, germination is sometimes erratic, due to environmental or soil conditions. Mechanical seeders will have to be adjusted according to experience, crusting, weather, and so forth. I have found that dusting the seeds with powdered lime in the hopper improves germination dramatically.

White rings ("zoning") in beets is caused by wide swings in weather (heat to frost, frost to heat, wet to dry, dry to wet) and checks in growth due to poor fertility or transplant shock. The variety called Chioggia zones naturally. A rainy period followed by hot dry weather will cause poor color and may cause bolting. Well-composted soil usually buffers against growth disorders caused by unsettled weather. A compost-slurry dip for the roots during transplanting, and regular watering of seedlings, prevent transplant shock. Mild frost, however, does not affect seeds or young plants.

The spraying of silica can begin any time after the plant shows a rosette of leaves. At this time also begin to check for leaf miners. These are fly maggots that make crazy grey tunnels throughout the leaves, giving the impression of disease. Pull the affected leaves off early and bag them, unless you have livestock that will eat them up without a trace. Leaf miners never seem to reduce the yield of beetroot, but they make the leaves inedible (and they ruin Swiss chard or spinach; chard is actually another form of beet). I have never seen aphids on beets in the East, but have read that they can be a problem in western states. Insecticidal oil or soap controls aphids, although generally aphids are a sign of stressed, ill-nourished, or aging plants. Consider why the aphids are present before spraying.

Beets are fairly easy to cultivate and keep weed-free; beets don't mind if small amounts of soil are used for covering beet shoulders during weed control. Transplanted crops require less weeding. Mulch reduces weeds and improves quality. Unless you grow successive crops for bunching, two sowings of beets are sufficient, one in early spring and one in July. Beets remain edible in the field longer than practically any other vegetable. In fact, I can't remember growing an inedible beet in any state I've lived in, East or West.

The earliest sowings will keep you in beets until September, by which time the July sowing should be ready for harvest. If kept humid, beets keep well in the root cellar. I've even cellared spring-sown Crosby Egyptian and found them quite tasty through the winter. However, beets for pickling should be on the young side. New beet flavor is much cleaner and fresher. Cellared beets acquire a slightly earthy flavor. If kept cold, beets never sprout, and can be eaten the next summer if need arise. After handling tons of cellared beets, I can't remember one rotting.

The pests that cause the most problems are field mice and voles. When I had five cats, the beets were perfect and the songbirds scarce. After bobcats and coyotes reduced my cat population to one, the songbirds returned, and the beets were partly gnawed. I don't mulch beets; mulch increases rodent predation.

Since this chapter began with beet flowers, don't forget to save your best-shaped beets for new seed. Beet seed-saving is easy and reliable. If you've had reason to complain about beet seed germination, then grow your own seeds! Dig up several large, undamaged beetroots with a bit of soil and keep them in crates over the winter in a cool root cellar. Replant them in middle spring. Watch the seed tree rise and make your own observations. Collect the seed when it is dry, but before it scatters. If you miss, however, just leave the area undisturbed and transplant the volunteer beet seedlings next spring. Be careful not to let beet and chard flower at the same time, since they cross. Both are *Beta vulgaris*.

Varieties

One of my gardening friends once said, "I never met a beet I didn't like!" If grown reasonably well, all beet varieties are delicious. Some are sweeter, more tender for bunching; others have been bred for the main season or storage. Most are multi-purpose.

Early bunching beets: Early Wonder (55 days), a variety introduced in 1911, is a semi-globe beet, dark red with lighter zones. It is fast-growing and used for bunching, canning, and pickling. Crosby's Egyptian (60 days), developed in 1880 from an 1865 German introduction, produces flattened beets of fine quality, with some zoning, used for bunching.

Main crop beets: Detroit Dark Red Medium Top (60 days) is a consistently reliable all-purpose beet. It gives excellent yields of uniform large beets for fresh use, canning, or winter storage. According to Southern Exposure Seed Exchange, Detroit beets were selected in 1892 from a popular nineteenth century beet called Early Blood Turnip. Medium tops help prevent sunscald and corky shoulders in midsummer.

Hybrid beets show exceptional vigor, rapid sizing, and extra sweetness. Only after I learned that beets were once called "blood-turnips" did I get the gallows humor of Pacemaker hybrid, which, like many hybrid varieties, has since died. Red Ace (53 days) however, is still alive, highly praised for a decade or more for its quality and vigor under a wide range of conditions. It is an extra sweet, smooth, and tender beet for fresh use canning and pickling, Red Ace is a hybrid of Detroit Short Top, so it maintains good quality even when large. Strong greens are free of red pigments, and roots resist zoning in warm weather.

Carrot-shaped beets look like fat Nantes carrots. Cylindra (57 days) was formerly called "Cook's Delight" because of the ease of handling. Roots are 7 inches by 2 inches and produce uniform round slices.

Chioggia (52 days), called Dolce di Chioggia (Sweetness of Chioggia), has sugar-beet parentage and striking rings. The flesh is salmon red with white and pink rings. Chioggia has a sweet mellow flavor and retains its color quality when not overcooked. Golden Beet (55 days) with its yellow petioles, orange skin, golden flesh, and sweet flavor has maintained its popularity since 1940, marred only by poor seed germination. Touchstone Gold has better germination, better uniformity, smoother shoulders, and similar sweet flavor.

Beets produce multiple fruits, clusters of seeds that look like little meteorites. Each cluster sprouts four or five beets in one spot; that is one reason why so many beets are transplanted in Europe. Commercial growers can order one of the "mono" (single) germ strains, usually with mono as part of the name, such as Moneta (48 days). The single germ allows for precision seeding, no thinning required.

For winter storage, the finest beet is certainly Lutz Green Leaf, also called Winter Keeper, Long Season, and German Lutz (80 days). Lutz requires almost a month longer to mature than other roots, but many gardeners consider Lutz quality unmatched. Roots are large and oddly shaped, and produce fine-tasting mild greens that can be enjoyed over a long period. Bull's Blood is a very old heirloom beet from France, re-introduced for its very dark red leaves, useful for adding color to spring and fall salad mixes. Irregular roots are sweet and tasty with candy-cane zoning.

Beet leaves have far more nutritional value than the root. The leaves are similar in value to chard, with 6,100 international units of vitamin A, 30 mg of C, and 3.3 mg of iron per 100 grams. Roots have only 20 international units of A, 10 mg of C, and .7 mg of iron.

Store Beets in a root cellar as close to freezing as possible, in perforated bags to prevent shriveling.

SEED: Seeds per ounce average about 2,000. A packet of 350 seeds will direct-seed a 30-foot row or produce about 150 transplants for about a 50-foot row. An ounce direct-seeds 150 to 200 feet, or produces about 900 transplants for 300 feet of row. About 7 pounds of seed sow an acre; 14 pounds for an acre of baby beets.

GERMINATION: 65%, 4 to 10 days at 45° to 70°F.

VIABILITY: 4 years.

DAYS TO HARVEST: 50 days for early beets; 60 days for main crop; 75 days for storage.

MOON CALENDAR: All cultural practices in root. Alternate: leaf. For seed, replant stored root in Leo, and cultivate and harvest in the same sign.

ROTATION: 3 years between beet, chard, spinach, orach, and magenta spreen.

BIODYNAMIC SPRAYS: Horn manure (500) before sowing. Dip transplants in compost-clay slurry with a pinch of 500. Silica (501) after the rosette forms, and at least once just as root forms; once again on beets to be put in a root cellar. Nettle and seaweed spray for vigor, beginning at early rosette stage, which may help with leaf miner.

COMPANION PLANTS: Beans, leeks, kohlrabi, garlic, and onions.

BROAD BEAN (FAVA)

The broad bean (*Vicia faba*) has countless common names because so many peoples have grown it for thousands of years: fava, faba, Windsor, horse, English tick, bell, pigeon, ful, and haba, to name a few. Broad beans look and taste a bit like limas, but grow like peas and also taste somewhat pea-like. The flavor is nutty and complex, the texture meaty and rich. Favas (as I first learned to call them) can't stand the long warm summers that limas love. They would prefer a pea season that stretched on forever, which is why in milder climates favas are grown through the winter. They can take a 10°F frost that peas can't, but can be stunted by a sudden late spring or early summer heat wave and drought.

None of this would lead you to suspect that favas originated somewhere between North Africa and the Indian sub-continent. Favas are still the bean of choice for falafel in the Middle East; not, as you might have thought, the chickpea. For thousands of years the word "bean" itself meant only favas. Bailey's *Horticulture* calls favas "the bean of history" since it was cultivated during the Neolithic era (foraged to extinction in the wild), and became the dominant bean prior to the introduction of beans from the New World.

Broad beans were cultivated in Egypt long before the pyramids were built. To this day they are still the national dish of Egypt. *Ful medames* is a savory mash of broad beans seasoned with garlic, lemon juice, olive oil, cumin, and salt; and served at breakfast with pita bread. In Italy and Greece, fresh green favas are sautéed with olive oil and garlic. In India, boiled favas are mixed with curry and served on rice. Dried favas are roasted and eaten like peanuts in India, China, and South America. In Sichuan China, favas and soybeans are seasoned with chili to make a spicy fermented bean paste. In Mexico, cooked mashed favas are used as a spicy filling in corn flour pasties. In North Africa, favas remain a staple protein.

By chance, broad beans were also my first garden plant. The first year I gardened full time in California, I worked with a follower of the English garden guru, Alan Chadwick. The land was low humus silt along the American River near Sacramento. Broad beans were the main cover crop to build the soil and provide protein for the vegetarian gardeners. I was astonished by the size and vigor of the plants. Not limp and trailing like peas and bush beans, but stout, square-stemmed, almost shrub-like, with lush leaves. High in nitrogen, they are a composter's dream. We ate the young beans green out of the hand, and cooked them like limas, although at the time we didn't know to blanch off the waxy skin. We loved the soil-building powers of this nitrogen rich legume (actually a kind of giant vetch); and had we not been vegetarians we could have fed some of the greens and beans to livestock, as did some of our homesteading friends.

Large bean favas are sometimes called horse beans, and have been used as fodder and mixed with corn as silage; but in the Middle East the stronger flavor of larger beans is often preferred for human consumption. In the West, the fresh smaller seed green favas are blanched and mixed with raw vegetables in salad. Young fava leaves can be eaten raw or steamed like spinach.

Culture

Although peas and favas like the same cool conditions, favas need such conditions much longer; so unless you live in a perpetually cool moist climate, spring sowing is a "one-shot deal," as early as possible, even late winter in milder years. Favas are more tolerant of frost and grow for so much longer than peas that they sometimes run smack into early summer heat waves. Pods set from 40° to 70°F. In the warm regions where favas originate, seeds are sown in fall and grown through the winter. This works well in California, the Northwest, the southern United States, and in the coastal zones up to Cape Cod. Overwintering in other regions with winter temperatures above 10°F is worth a try.

Like peas, broad beans also produce larger leaves and greater yields with well-drained soil, ample compost, and a pH from 6 to 6.6; but favas also produce plenty of beans on poorer soils with a wider range of pH. This flexibility is, after all, a reason to grow them. Favas supply humus and large amounts of nitrogen to humus-leached soils. Adding a nitrogen-fixing inoculant suitable for vetch can improve the crop. A Canadian Extension website also notes that pre-treatment of seeds with .01% B vitamins increases broad bean yields 36%. Biodynamic growers sow seeds following their earliest application of preparation 500 and follow the spray schedule for peas.

Fava seeds are so large that even small children can handle them easily. Make a furrow 1 to 1½ inches deep with 4 to 8 inches between seeds. For children, use a stick for the desired spacing. Plants are always substantial but vary in size from 2 to 5 feet in height depending on variety, climate, and fertility. Space rows as close as 1 foot for cover crops and 3 feet for large varieties.

Broad bean plants can be slightly hilled, with some soil thrown against the stems as they grow, to control weeds. Home gardeners sometimes pinch back the growing tips after the first pod set to concentrate fruit set and force earlier maturity. Organic nitrogen fertilizers and side-dressings will only stretch out the harvest date further into the hot summer. Most gardeners treat favas like bush beans, and don't stake them. Field, fodder, and cover crops are never staked. But larger varieties in heavily composted beds may become so weighed down by fruit as to need guy lines on either side of the row. Though favas are a vetch, they have only vestigial tendrils, so don't expect them to cling to a pea fence.

Harvest and Health

Favas can be eaten at any stage. Young leaves can be cooked like spinach. Whole pods can be eaten like snap peas while pods are still pointing upward. When the weight of the seed begins to pull the pod downward, at about 2 inches long, green shell beans can be eaten raw. Later, when pods begin to swell at about 3 inches, green shell beans can be blanched and eaten like edamame. Mature shell beans should be blanched and then plunged into cold water to remove the waxy skins. Unfortunately I did not know this during my first acquaintance with broad beans, causing considerable gastric distress. Mature favas can be fully dried and stored like any other bean. Try using cooked mashed favas in authentic Middle Eastern falafel or hummus. Soak dry favas overnight then simmer for 75 minutes.

The young green seeds contain good amounts of vitamins A and C, potassium, fiber, and are 8% protein. In dry broad beans, protein rises to 25%, and is a major source of protein in the Middle East, North Africa, and India. Broad beans also contain high levels of L-dopa, the drug used to treat Parkinson's disease, which also appears to reduce hypertension.

In prehistoric times an anemic reaction to favas suppressed a deadly malaria protozoa endemic in countries of origin. Though the threat from malaria has diminished, some descendants may still become severely anemic from eating broad beans (favism). The reaction is strongest in children where favas are a staple (Mediterranean to India). In one limited study, however, the 42% of Saudi men who carried the deficiency gene showed no symptoms of favism. Favism may occur in 10% of people of Black ethnicity, also connected to their special genetic adaptation to malaria. Favism does not produce the sudden anaphylactic shock sometimes caused by peanuts. Iranians love cooked favas mixed with rice, and enjoy them green as well; but they prevent small children from eating the beans raw due to the offending biochemical vicine. Cooking largely neutralizes vicine (though apparently not enough for those highly susceptible to favism).

Those who plan to feed favas to livestock can include them as part of a mixed diet, or mixed with corn as silage. Too much fava causes digestive upset in poultry and occasionally causes favism in pigs (Canadian Extension).

Insects and Disease

Spring sown favas may be attacked in hot dry weather by black bean aphids (called Black Fly by English gardeners, although definitely not a fly). Black clusters of aphids cling along the stem, often attended by tell-tale trails of ants who farm the aphids for honeydew. Aphids reduce vigor by sucking plant juices, and spread a virus that blackens leaves and reduces harvest. Well-composted and well-watered plants are less attractive to aphids and suffer less injury. Home gardeners sometimes pinch off the upper branch, which holds most of the aphids (this is done anyway to force early fruiting), and spray the rest with insecticidal soap. Soaps and insecticidal oil kill all aphids. Lace wings and lady beetles provide some control. September-sown favas usually mature before the aphid season begins, another reason to give overwintering a try.

In some areas overwintered crops are plagued by chocolate spot (*botrytis fabae*), which appears in cool wet weather. Plant yield is considerably reduced. This fungus is best prevented by increased potassium (from compost) for sturdier plants. Added nitrogen produces lush growth susceptible to botrytis. Use wider spacing between plants and rows. Practice scrupulous garden hygiene. Remove and compost all fava plant debris immediately after harvest. Researchers in India (where broad beans are a significant protein source) have shown that oils of cumin, garlic, and rocket suppress *botrytis fabae* spore development, but only biofungicides offered complete control (*Plant Pathology Journal*-India-2010).

Varieties

Only a few varieties are readily available in North America. Most require no staking, unless grown in extremely fertile gardens. Southern Exposure Seed

Exchange offers the traditional Broad Windsor Long pod (85 days), with 6- to 8-inch pods and 5 to 6 large beans on plants that range from 24 to 30 inches. Johnny's offers Windsor (75 days), slightly smaller with 5- to 6-inch pods and 3 to 5 large beans. Thompson and Morgan offer a useful one-foot dwarf Sutton (95 days), with full-size pods. I don't know why this dwarf should take longer to mature.

Bountiful Gardens in California offers two heirloom favas listed by the great nineteenth century French seed house Vilmorin in 1885. It is a tasty three-footer called "D'Aquadulce a Tres Longue Cosse," and the huge "Long Pod," 4 to 5 feet tall, with 7- to 8-inch pods and 5 to 6 large beans. I can't imagine growing Long Pod without support. Seed savers should know that broad beans cross readily. Home gardeners should probably grow only one variety per year if they intend to save seed.

SEED: A packet—2 ounces, about 50 seeds—sows 10 to 14 feet depending upon variety and spacing. ¼ pound (about 225 seeds) sows 45 to 60 feet. A pound—about 450 seeds—sows 90 to 120 feet.

GERMINATION: 2 weeks.

VIABILITY: 3 years.

DAYS TO HARVEST: 75 to 85 spring sowing; up to 160 days overwintering.

MOON CALENDAR: For cover crops sown in leaf, cultivate in root. For beans sown in leaf, cultivate in fruit.

ROTATION: 3 years between peas and beans.

BIODYNAMIC SPRAYS: Silica preparation at least once during leaf growth, at flowering, and pod formation.

COMPANION PLANTING: Favas grow too densely for interplanting, but alternate rows of traditional companions celery, savory, and strawberries might work. Or try less traditional alternate rows of dill, coriander, cilantro, carrots, parsnips, or flowers.

BROCCOLI

Broccoli and cauliflower are botanically so similar that they share the same name: *Brassica oleracea*, var. *botrytis*. It is only at the level of sub-variation that they differ. Botanically, they are identical. How can this be, since the plants look so different? The cauliflower plant is squat to the ground like a cabbage and shoots out its leaves from a fairly low axis, producing a very white curd from within the center of its rosette. The leaves also have a whitish or grayish cast to them. The flower curd has an anemic, stunted appearance, which gardeners further by wrapping it with leaves to deny light. Broccoli, on the other hand, is fountain-like and expansive. The leaves are wavy-edged and glow strongly with a deep blue-green. Broccoli buds are the same color as the leaves and display the same fountain form as the whole plant. The buds do not hold long, but continue their rise into the flowering zone, rarely maintaining their head form at peak maturity longer than a week.

The nutritional profile paints the same picture, poverty and riches, as though these twins were separated at birth—one given all the advantages, the other none. Broccoli has 2,000 international units of A per 100 grams; cauliflower has 60. Broccoli has 113 mg of vitamin C, cauliflower 78. Broccoli has 103 mg of calcium, cauliflower twenty-five. Likewise, the therapeutic compounds so important to contemporary nutrition are present only in deep-green brassicas. In broccoli the vital sulfur compounds and enzymes that destroy carcinogens are inseparably bound to the greenness and its high vitamin content. Of course broccoli and cauliflower were not separated at birth, one raised in rich soil, the other poor. Their nutritional profile doesn't change even when both are grown side by side in equally rich compost. How did cauliflower become so stunted?

One key is the physiology of buttoning, which occurs when broccoli or cauliflower seizes up and stops growing because of checks in growth, cold stress or other shocks. Vital leafy growth abruptly ceases, and the plant makes a tiny white curd or small stunted broccoli head. In other words, the natural "canceling of green," which occurs normally in any plant in the transition from leaf to flower, in cauliflower seems to occur prematurely, as if its plant metamorphosis got stuck. Even when cauliflower produces large curds and environmental stress has not triggered a disorder, buttoning physiology seems to rule as part of normal growth. With cauliflower, the gardener is already faced with a potential emergency even before the emergency has occurred, and which requires far less external stimulus than broccoli. Cauliflower is born with it. That's why cauliflower culture is broccoli culture without the luxury of missing a step. Everything has to be done perfectly.

In broccoli the opposite occurs. The force of leaves pushes beyond the threshold of the receptacle (where non-green petals begin) and turns the sepals intensely green. In cauliflower the receptacle sinks downward to the level of the leaf rosette. This means that maintaining steady growth from seedling stage to rosette stage is much more critical in cauliflower than broccoli. Large basal leaves either provide sufficient strength for curd formation during this early period or the fall curd cannot form. Setbacks occur when seedlings are left too long in the flat (5 weeks maximum); the temperature drops suddenly in the field; or when seedlings are exposed to freak freezes, extended rainy periods, or prolonged dry weather. Much more so than broccoli, which is also affected, cauliflower is extremely sensitive to any environmental stress at the stage when the sixth and seventh leaves are being formed. At that stage the plants must not freeze (not be set out too soon, or exposed to frost without row cover or plastic tunnels); moisture must be evenly supplied (be prepared to irrigate); and no high nitrogen fertilizer applied.

In hybrids, too much fertilizer or extended hot wet weather can make both plants, but cauliflower especially, grow too fast. Cauliflower head formation will be delayed and disease resistance will be lowered dramatically. When broccoli is over-fertilized during head formation the florets become susceptible to head rot, stem rot, and fungal infection. Fermented manure or compost slurries can be applied during the first flush of large basal leaves.

Culture

Early broccoli requires careful timing and heavy row cover. Growers generally stagger plantings during the "gambler's period" when sharp frost alternates with warm days. Young plants gradually acclimatized (hardened) to take regular light frosts can be set out, but stem rupture occurs in the low 20's F. Plants never fully recover. Stagger sowings over a four-week period (the harvest window sometimes will condense to two weeks). With heavy row covers, I have had good luck setting out transplants at the end of March in New England.

Unprotected plants can be set out in late April or early May, depending on latitude.

Plants that are four to six weeks old work well for me, four to five weeks for brocciflower. (See CAULIFLOWER for culture.) Sometimes the thicker stems of the six-week plants hold up better if the spring is dry, although many growers aim for four weeks. Older plants, especially from nurseries, are often a waste of time. Since seedlings can be transplanted up to a month before the last expected frost, site and composting should be prepared the fall before. Choose ground where no crucifers have grown for at least three years. This includes Chinese as well as European cabbages. Where club root is known to be a problem, this rotation may have to be longer. The best soil type is clay loam with clay subsoil. The worst is sand. The pH should be close to neutral and the plants well supplied with calcium, either through compost or applied to the soil the autumn before. Insect problems are often in direct proportion to soil type. A well-composted medium clay loam produces the healthiest plants. Some growers save the bulk of their compost for the crucifer rotation. In productive garden soil, you can omit compost for carrots, lettuce, legumes, beets, and chard. Sweet potatoes are great because they want nothing and are related to no other garden plant.

Stokes's catalog notes that 90% of all commercial crucifer growers have gone back to transplants rather than direct-seed because of uneven germination, ragged maturity, and reduced uniformity. But home gardeners can have very good results sowing six seeds to the foot, covered by ¼ inch of fine compost, and protected by heavy row cover over wire hoops or bent rebar. Thin 12 to 15 inches in the row. Transplant trowel-thinned plants to another location.

Spray the field to be used for broccoli with biodynamic horn manure (500) in both the fall and spring. Also be sure to reserve sufficient supplies of frost free soil and compost, so that it is accessible in late February when you are preparing seed flats. The mix I prefer is half fertile clay loam and half well-rotted cow manure compost. I get steady healthy growth from this mix, with no damping off. I have found that additives such as peat and sand produce weaker, more disease-prone seedlings. If your soil is heavy clay, then mix sand, peat, soil, and compost the autumn before, using the biodynamic compost preparations. By next spring the ingredients will become thoroughly permeated by new soil life. The route of the living always pays off.

In the central states, sow the earliest broccoli at the end of February, using bottom heat to speed germination (75°F). I've used oil heat, sun heat, germination mats, and cold frames, with fresh hot horse manure layered a foot below the soil surface. Hot horse manure is a lot of work, but produces very strong plants. Leave some broccoli 12 inches apart in the frames for an extra-early crop.

For transplants, seeds can be germinated on heat pads in shallow furrows in flats or cells and covered with compost and a light sprinkling of lime. As soon as the seedlings germinate, move them to a cool greenhouse, or a protected cold frame. When the first true leaf appears, plants can be pricked out into new flats (about 30 plants to the flat), or deep cell or peat pots. Plants can be set slightly deeper than they grew at all stages. If damping off has been a problem, try naturalizing your potting soil as described above, using a cow manure compost, and spray regularly with equisetum tea, perhaps alternating with a weak solution of baking soda. I have found that damping off is not "caused" by a soil fungus. The fungus is always there. The cause is a poorly growing plant. High air temperatures invite the fungus to multiply. So keep your greenhouse or growing area cool at night, as low as 45°F.

Broccoli seedlings need lots of light. They get weak in the reduced light of some solar greenhouses. Preparation 501 is really important for plants under glass. Use it twice. Temperatures can range from the 40's at night to the 70's by day. Hot nights cause problems in greenhouses that include tropicals. In that case, start the broccoli inside and transfer to a cold frame. Second-early broccoli can be sown in the cold frame around March 15 (central states) and set in the field at the end of April. A week before field transplanting, plants should be hardened by reducing water and exposing to full sun during the day. The last few days should be full exposure day and night. If it's too cold for exposure, you have jumped the season (I do it regularly). Keep them under cover for another week. Seven weeks is the outer limit. Heavy row cover will blunt frosts and prevent wind desiccation down to 25°F.

Home gardeners unsure of soil fertility can mix a trowel full of compost in each planting hole. In some soils this will spell the difference between large heads with side shoots and stunted plants. The biodynamic ideal, however, is to work with the fertility of the garden as a whole, not to grow plants in fertile pockets. Set plants from 14 to 18 inches apart in the row, but leave at least 30 inches between rows. Some varieties give high yields packed as close as 12 inches apart in the row, but I have never succeeded packing plants in 15-inch squares. Use wider spacing in the rows for older open-pollinated varieties that produce abundant side shoots. Transplants dipped in barrel-fermented compost nettle slurry are less prone to setback.

In areas where cabbage maggot is a problem, a few handfuls of ground lime or wood ashes can be put around the base of each transplant. This seems to keep the fly from laying her eggs. I have also noticed that in one field where the soil type varied from clay loam to sandy loam, the plants in the sandy loam were always attacked, while the ones in clay loam never were attacked, even when unprotected. It has to do with "soil-heart." Maggots are present if transplants wilt in the mornings.

Organic fertilizers can be applied two weeks after the plants have been set out, but don't apply high nitrogen organic fertilizer between the emergence of the sixth and ninth leaves because it may cause shock in crucifers. Some gardeners apply organic fertilizer during the rosette period to increase the leaf scaffold, but high nitrogen organic fertilizer applied before head formation may leave nitrogen residues. In most ways, compost applied before planting is better, since it feeds plants slowly and steadily like trickle irrigation. Commercial growers give two liquid feedings, one early to form the leaf scaffold and another just as the heads begin to form. Nettle and compost tea can be used for a late liquid feeding. Some organic growers spray liquid seaweed (a teaspoon per gallon of water) on the foliage several times after the rosette forms. Biodynamic growers spray silica (501) at rosette stage and during bud formation.

Incompletely composted manure makes broccoli watery, with a downright unpleasant flavor. Broccoli, more than any other vegetable, seems to pick up off-flavors from fertilizer. Furthermore, one rotten tomato or melon won't ruin all the other fruits on the vine, but a rotten broccoli floret ruins the whole plant.

Cabbage worms usually don't appear on spring-grown broccoli until bud-formation. Sometimes first harvest passes without a worm. Once I was sitting on my bicycle gazing over a small field of broccoli, trying to decide whether to spray Bt (a natural *bacillus thuringensis* control of caterpillars.) At that moment a wasp landed on my handlebars clasping a cabbage worm and proceeded to eat the creature before my eyes. Thereafter I refrained from removing wasp nests on house eaves, and began to grow flowering *umbelliferous* plants that wasps love, such as fennel. In late summer, when the weather gets really warm, it is usually necessary to use Bt, especially on the undersides and developing stems of broccoli heads.

Broccoli prefers skim cultivation, never deep. Some gardeners hill the plants as they grow; just enough to cover emerging weeds. I've used the push plow on a high-wheel cultivator for this, as well as the hiller on a rototiller.

The push plow was even better because it throws dirt between the plants in the rows. A hoe can be used across the row and pulled toward you to create the same effect.

Harvest heads before they begin to form individual florets, called "ricing" in the trade. For home use, cut high, taking only the center of the head. The outer buds of the head will fill in and give you more broccoli. Cut at a slant to avoid rotting. For sales, the full heads must be cut; often they are the size of dinner plates. Although market gardeners discard plants after one cutting, many varieties produce side shoots for home gardeners until Thanksgiving, even through the winter in some regions.

Time autumn plantings to do most of their growing during September and October in the central states, and November further south. Seeds can be sown in outdoor seedbeds in shallow furrows and covered with ¼ to ½ inch of sifted compost or rich friable topsoil. In the central states, sow seed around June 10, expecting first harvest two or three months later. Outdoor seedbeds must be watered twice a day because of heat. Flea beetles often attack emerging seedlings, depending on soil and stress (hot, dry weather). Plants in clay loam with high humus are less troubled. Those in light sandy loam are a losing battle. Cover seedbeds and transplants with floating row cover.

Finally, remember that broccoli doesn't hold long in the field, nor does it store long, even when chilled immediately. Know what you are going to do with a crop before you plant it.

Varieties

Ask yourself the following questions when selecting a broccoli variety: in what season will the broccoli be sown and harvested? Does the plant have stress tolerance? Are the heads tight beaded and domed to vent moisture that might cause head rot? Or is the head flat and better suited to drier climates? Does it have heat resistance? Does it tolerate autumn cold and light frost? Can it resist downy mildew under cool conditions? Does the plant need wide spacing or can it be packed closely in the row? Does it produce only a large central head and no side shoots or a small central head and a long harvest of side shoots? Does it hold well in the field or bolt to flower quickly?

Then there is the question of flavor. This is tricky to pin on a particular variety; flavor seems to reflect the qualities of the fertilizer used, how well the manure was composted, and how much nitrogen it contained. I have often seen the same variety taste quite different according to where, how, and when it was grown. Consider other factors: was there too much rain? Was it the wrong variety for the time of year? Did a short crucifer-family rotation build up low levels of fungal organisms? What about basic soil type or the way compost was made? Did I neglect an essential biodynamic practice? Did I fail to make a critical observation about the weather? Did I fail to change my practices on the basis of what I observed? Or was it the variety itself? To answer these questions, it helps to learn to taste a broccoli with your eyes.

Open-pollinated strains are still useful for home gardeners, and may well stage a comeback in the future as more is learned about sustainable fertility and the reduction of nutritional value through hybridization. Early Purple Sprouting is a very old form of Italian broccoli exclusively adapted to long cool seasons, or for overwintering in low frost climates (above 15°F) or cool moist frost-free coastal climates. These large bushes produce florets rather than heads. With regular harvest, pruning, and moderate winters, this broccoli bush will last a year or more. Italian Green Sprouting, Calabrese or Calabria (60 to 80 days) produces moderately large central heads and a long season of side shoots from a spring sowing. It is vigorous, early, and has a delicious taste. If the plant is kept watered and shoots are pruned during summer, Calabrese produces many side shoots until frost. De Cicco (49 days) is newer (c. 1890) and produces a 3- to 6-inch central head, followed by a long season of side shoots in spring or fall. To produce more side shoots remove the central head at 3 inches.

Green Goliath (55 days) bears in a manner similar to De Cicco, with several larger blue-green central heads and tight buds. It has a long season of lateral harvest for home gardens, and is one of the few relatively new open-pollinated strains, introduced by Burpee. The flavor is very good. Umpquah (51 days) from Oregon produces dark green 6-inch heads with good production of side shoots. Waltham 29 (74 days) was developed in the Northeast for fall production only, but works farther south for fall harvest as well. Variable size heads 4 to 8 inches hold well with a long harvest of side shoots, sometimes until Thanksgiving. These plants tolerate dry weather during late summer.

By far the most beautiful vegetable in the garden is Romanesco, which is really a colored cauliflower. You have to examine Romanesco carefully to appreciate it. It's composed of endless spirals, spirals within spirals, spiral towers composed of smaller towers, a fantasy of fractals. No one ever told you this in school, I am sure, but the world was created out of fractals and chaos. When I see Romanesco, I imagine I'm seeing what otherwise is invisible space filled to the brim with vortices, something like Van Gogh's vision of a starry night. Heirloom Romanesco (100 days) can be planted for fall harvests. It is a very large plant with chartreuse florets and fine cauliflower flavor. Romanesco Minaret (75 days) is a more uniform selection for spring or fall. Both require cool conditions, ample water, and extra fertility to produce 5-inch heads. Romanesco is a superb gourmet crop for market growers who have the space, climate, and fertility.

Breeders of hybrid broccoli have focused on solving horticultural problems: domed heads less inclined to rot, increased plant vigor for better yields, uniform heads, and wide adaptability to various climates. As breeders develop new traits useful to growers, broccoli hybrids change every few years, although some hybrids such as Premium Crop have lasted for decades. Other desirable traits include: 1) small tight beads (florets) that shed rain and rot less easily; 2) tolerance to early summer heat and autumn cold; 3) tolerance to specific broccoli diseases such as downy mildew, head rot, brown bead, and hollow stem; 4) good holding ability in the field or garden before harvest; and 5) good holding ability after harvest. Remember that the push for increased size through hybridization and over-fertilization significantly lowers nutritional value.

Decades after its introduction, Packman Hybrid (57 days) is still widely used by growers throughout the season. With adequate water, Packman's domed large uniform heads tolerate summer temperatures, with ample production of side shoots. However, very early Packman transplants may "button up" (form tiny heads and stop growing) in cold spring weather. A newer early hybrid, Blue Wind (49 days), will not button up, and is more uniform with a more attractive smaller-beaded head. Windsor (56 days) adds very good disease tolerance to downy mildew, brown bead, and black head rot.

Premium Crop (65 days) is probably the longest-running hybrid. With large tight-beaded domed heads, good holding ability in the field, tolerance to downy mildew, and wide adaptability, Premium Crop set the standard for reliability in both commercial and home gardens. Still, others may surpass it. Gypsy (58 days) has similar stats with added heat tolerance for summer and warmer fall harvest; Gypsy also has an unusually extensive root system, able to extract nutrients in lower nitrogen organic soils. Belstar (66 days) is an organically grown hybrid with 6- to 8-inch domed heads, wide adaptability, and good side-shoot production. To be safe, always mix newer selections with varieties tested over time under diverse conditions.

Home gardeners might consider the "new" heirloom like Piricicaba (peer-a-see-caba) from Brazil (56 days). This sprouting broccoli produces loose heads with large beads and edible leaves during the hottest summers, and produces still more through the fall. It is sometimes described as raab-like, but actually it is broccoli-sweet. Purple Peacock is another unusual broccoli, one fairly hardy in mild winters. A central purple head is followed by purple side shoots and edible leaves similar in appearance and taste to Russian Red Kale, each scalloped with pink venation.

SEED: Seed per ounce 6,000 to 9,000. A packet of standard broccoli that contains 200 seeds produces 175 plants. A packet of hybrid with 100 seeds produces about 80 plants. An ounce produces 3,000 to 5,000 plants.

GERMINATION: 75% (better with hybrids). 10 days at 70°F; min. temp. 60°F. (Plants can grow much cooler.)

VIABILITY: 4 years.

DAYS TO HARVEST: 60 to 80, depending on variety.

MOON CALENDAR: Sow in leaf. Cultivate alternately in leaf and flower. Harvest in flower. For seed cultivate in Leo. Spray silica (501) on flower days.

ROTATION: 3 years if normal crucifer rotation, 6 years if disease builds up in a garden or field.

BIODYNAMIC SPRAYS: Horn manure (500) before sowing and on potting soil. Silica (501) after transplanted seedlings are established. Compost-clay slurry with pinch of 500 as root dip for transplants. Silica just as buds appear. Equisetum (508) for damping off and in disease prone areas.

COMPANION PLANTS: Aromatic herbs (catnip, dill, mint, thyme, wormwood, tansy) deter pests. Onion, garlic, dill, chamomile, mint, caraway for plant health and flavor. Flowering *umbelliferous* plants (fennel, dill, caraway, coriander, and so forth, especially fennel) for attracting beneficial insects.

BROCCOLI RAAB

Broccoli raab, also called rabe, rapini, and rapine, is nutritional and therapeutically so important I can't believe how long it took me to discover it. I'm embarrassed to report my four-year-old introduced me to it in a tiny Italian dive on the New Jersey coast. Sasha noticed some raab piled on a plate of pasta at an adjoining table. Bitter though it was, he scarfed up the raab like cake, which at the time he had never tasted—probably part of the reason he liked the raab.

Though raab florets look similar to broccoli side shoots, raab is actually a Mediterranean cousin of the turnip and the *Brassica rapa* greens of Asia. To me, raab tastes less domesticated than its Asian relatives, with higher antioxidant levels, which, I believe, rise as bitterness increases at maturity. Flavor and tenderness, however, are most acceptable when plants are grown and harvested quickly in well-composted, well-watered soil from weekly or biweekly sowings. I wish I could find the time for more than two sowings, but I never do. Crops always fail from inattentiveness. Forget to water, or forget to harvest soon enough, and the crop will become spindly and too bitter for most people, though apparently not for some four-year-olds who have not been spoiled by sweets.

In very early spring, sow 10 seeds to the foot in a ¼-inch furrow. If your planting is small, cover the furrow with ¼ inch of finished compost. "Small" is good for this crop, since three small sowings are more usable than one. Raab doesn't hold very long in the field or fridge. Johnny's Selected Seeds catalog mentions sowing in 1 ½-inch plug trays; that's a lot of work for a small plant, but possible if you have extra space and water conscientiously. Transplants could be sown 5 to 6 weeks before setting out (when spring is still mildly frosty). Transplants would certainly get established well before the height of the flea beetle season, which begins in June in New England and becomes ferocious in hot dry weather. Spray transplants with pyrethrin/rotenone before setting out; spray seedlings when they germinate in the field, and a week to 10 days later; or use floating row covers for both. Either harvest whole plants when florets form, or cut out florets with their surrounding leaves for an extended harvest.

"Spring" (42 days) is the traditional heirloom variety, still widely grown. Spring is fast growing, slow bolting, and given optimal conditions can be sown throughout the season in climates with cool summers. Sessantina Grossa (35 days) has earlier larger buds, with more broccoli color and bloom. Early Fall Rapini (45 days) is more robust with larger leaves and buds, best for milder climates with a long autumn season.

Another sprouting broccoli, Spigaviello Leaf Broccoli (45 days) also called Minestra Nero is sometimes listed under raab, but really belongs to the much milder true broccoli species, *Brassica oleracea*. It yields delicious sweet greens over a long season. Sown in July for fall harvest (even into the next spring in mild climates), similar to Asian Guy Lon and Happy Rich Hybrid. Culture is similar to raab.

Raab averages 13,000 seeds per ounce and sows 1,200 feet. A packet sows about 160 feet.

BRUSSELS SPROUTS

Brussels sprouts are not widely planted in the United States; when they are, they enter late in the season as a side dish of minor importance. Few gardeners use them for what they are—a valuable, space-saving succession crop in the garden. What makes the plants so valuable is that they can succeed by themselves. Not just briefly either, in the sense that beets and lettuce provide thinnings; but nonstop, substantially. This is not surprising, since Brussels sprouts belong to that therapeutic fountain, *Brassica oleracea*, a single species that behaves like five. Since the species produces so many vital variants, why should not a single variant—*gemmifera*—do the same?

The discovery of this fact was inadvertent. In an unusually rushed spring, I grabbed several six-packs of Brussels sprouts and collards at a local nursery, instead of sowing them myself. All summer, I harvested leaves from the plants labeled collards, and because of the labels I cancelled the perception that small buds were growing in axils of the leaves. As summer progressed, however, it was clear that none of the plants were collards and all were Brussels sprouts.

I complained to the nursery, but in retrospect I should have thanked them. The plants, even those whose leaves had been moderately harvested all summer, produced an abundant crop of spouts. The taste of the leaves was indistinguishable from collards, and their quality after frost was so fine and tender that I found myself choosing them over kale until late fall. This was a good discovery, since previously I had considered Brussels sprouts to be a minor vegetable that occupied too much space, for too long in the season, and produced a small crop my family appreciated even less than I did. It was even more important than the other Brussels sprouts "trick" I had discovered the year before—that sprouts should never be "saved" for fall harvest. Eat them as they mature, about the size of a large cherry tomato, just as they start to swell and become glossy. Peak size will vary according to fertility and available water. Sprouts do not improve by leaving them past the full emerald green stage. They only deteriorate when the small wrapper leaves show a trace of brown, finally cracking and bursting open.

Together, three harvest tips have transformed the Brussels sprouts from an occasional side dish into a staple green. These tips are: using some young leaves as greens, harvesting the sprouts anytime as they mature, and eating the leaves into late fall. Kale and Brussels sprouts are the last things I harvest from the garden, often in January. Yet so far the Brussels sprout barely owns a place in American cuisine. I hope two small revolutions in the American diet will change that.

The first is "nouvelle cuisine." Unlike many diet crazes, this is not a fad, but a significant transformation in the way we value food. Regardless of the national or regional style of cooking, vegetables and fruits are treated with new respect and startling creativity. The rule of combination is now "no rules," just fresh vegetables of every kind, of striking color, and unexpected pairings. Nouvelle chefs have given new life to all the ethnic cuisines of the world.

The second change comes from an increasing conviction that brassicas grow at the center of the therapeutic universe. It doesn't bother me that I haven't found specific research on Brussels sprouts. The biochemical well of the *Brassica* genus is so bottomless that very likely cooks will do more for medicine than medicine has ever done for cooks. Some cooks sauté greens and sprout halves in garlic and oil or minimum water. Others boil a pot of water first, dropping the greens or sprouts in just long enough to become tender. The boiling method definitely preserves the deep green color. Often I cook a mixed vegetable and sprout soup, to which I add *al dente* wheat or rice fettuccini, tofu and miso—a family favorite.

Brussels sprouts are similar to collard greens because sprouts probably arose from an older, coarse form of collards called tree cabbage or tree kale. The roots of tree cabbage go back to Roman times, and were eaten by the Celts even before the Romans arrived. Although references to cabbage abound in ancient languages, few old names and few old varieties of sprouts exist. Brussels sprouts seem to have appeared in Belgium in the seventeenth and eighteenth centuries, and spread to France and England in the nineteenth. Sprouts are a major crop throughout Northern Europe; and a fetish in England, where half the world's crop is produced and consumed. The cool, damp English autumns and winters, so little appreciated by human beings, are perfect for growing Brussels sprouts.

Culture

The flavor and size of Brussels sprouts and leaves will never be satisfactory without ample compost, and an even supply of water. One variety can seem like two if fertility varies greatly in different parts of a garden. The sprouts interplanted in my new heavily mulched raspberry bed were twice the size and a deeper green than the same variety growing unmulched nearby. Also, aphids attacked the unmulched (but well composted) plants late in a dry season. Aphids are always a pest when sprouts are stressed.

The problem with sprouts is the sheer length of time they stand in the garden. Broccoli produces its main head not long after the full structure of the plant is developed. Small florets appear in the wake and flush of optimum growth. Brussels sprouts can sit in the garden for up to six months of variable weather. This probably reflects their Northern European origin, with its long cool growing season. Aphids appear in hot dry weather and indicate that the plant has been pulled too far from its native climate. In cool moist years I don't even see the aphids.

Cultural conditions for Brussels sprouts are otherwise the same as cabbage: pH should be 6.5 to 7, the soil well supplied with calcium and organic matter. A medium loam over clay is ideal.

Where the growing season is long, cool, and moist, flats sown indoors in very early spring will produce over a long period. In short season areas, sprouts are sown four months before the first fall frost, usually at the end of May, in outdoor flats or in outdoor seedbeds.

Seedbeds should not be lean, up to 30% compost, since stockier seedlings take transplant shock better than scrawny ones. I've tried many teas, compost and nettle or seaweed, both in the seedbed and in the field to good effect. In climates where sprouts can be overwintered, sow in late summer and protect the seedbeds with polyester row cover against flea beetles. Sprouts overwinter well in the South and on the Pacific west coast, especially in damp coastal areas.

With Brussels sprouts, side-dressings of fertilizer are no substitute for long-term composting. With cow manure, Brussels sprouts are larger, longer lasting, and more resistant to aphids. Compost made from hardwood leaves and lawn clippings, including clover, comes a close second. I've found horse manure, even with little bedding, doesn't work as well. Transplants dipped in compost-clay slurry grow more strongly without transplant shock.

Best not to let transplants sit in flats or seedbeds much longer than five weeks. Space plants generously 24 inches in a row, with 36 inches between rows. Sprouts repay wide spacing. In dry weather, irrigate and use row covers if flea beetles get out of hand. Row covers also prevent cabbage flies from laying their maggots at the base of the plants. Cabbage maggots eat the roots, causing young plants to wilt and transmit bacterial diseases. A heavy ¼-inch-deep dusting of wood ash or lime six inches around the plants prevents the fly from laying her eggs.

Often gardeners remove lower leaves and petioles of Brussels sprouts in order to encourage sprout formation. Topping the plant when sprouts are larger than ½ inch in diameter (mid-September in the North) is widely practiced by market growers to hasten maturity and uniformity of the upper sprouts. If you do top plants, use the tops for greens. They are similar to Savoy cabbage. But there is no reason for home gardeners to do this, since the tops are superb eating in November or December, even in January if protected from windburn. Untopped plants still produce plenty of sprouts.

Sprouts can be harvested from the bottom up as soon as they swell and shine, starting at 1½ inches in diameter. Early unharvested sprouts will burst open and be wasted. Sometimes lower sprouts branch out, producing new greens that are very good to eat and higher in vitamins than the closed sprouts.

Sprouts and leaves improve with frost. Plants can be protected from winter winds by placing hay bales on either side of the row and covering with heavy row cover. Freezing wind does more damage than frost. Before a hard freeze, whole plants can be lifted and held for two to three weeks in the root cellar. Many people blanch sprouts in boiling water for the freezer, but the quality does not compare to protected plants left in the garden.

Varieties

English, Dutch, and German seed catalogs list dozens of up-to-date varieties, some of which have successfully crossed the Atlantic. Most have not, since our hot continental climate interrupts the cool, moist growing season favored by sprouts.

Nearly-heirloom Long Island Improved (100 days) produces large, rough sprouts packed tightly along the stem. Long Island is widely adapted, except for rainy climates where varieties with more open spacing, such as Seven Hills, may be less inclined to rot. Generally taller varieties have wider sprout spacing. The purple leaves and sprouts of Rubine (90 days) add color to market displays and have excellent flavor. The color and flavor of Rubine and other purple Brussels sprouts intensifies after light frost and stays purple when cooked. Since ambitious home gardeners usually produce far more sprouts than they can consume, open-pollinated strains may be quite satisfactory. The uniformity of hybrids is more important for market growers.

In general, hybrid sprouts are more vigorous, earlier maturing, and with heavier crops. Traits to consider are wider spacing of sprouts on the stem for better formation and aeration (Diablo, 110 days and Jade Cross E, 97 days). "Wider" usually means "tall"; and the tall ones sometimes do fall, so be prepared to stake taller varieties. More compact varieties include Jade Cross (95 days), also quite early. Oliver (90 days) earlier still, can be sown in early summer and still mature a crop, producing well in diverse climates. Diablo also holds longer in the field without bursting, which allows all sprouts to mature evenly for market displays of the entire stalk.

SEED: Seed per oz. 6,500. One packet of non-hybrid grows about 50 plants. One packet of 80 hybrid seeds grows 50 to 75 transplants. One ounce produces 3,000 to 5,000 transplants.

GERMINATION: 70% (better with hybrids). 10 days at 70°F; min. temp. 60°F (plants can grow cooler).

VIABILITY: 4 to 5 years.

DAYS TO HARVEST: generally 90 to 140.

MOON CALENDAR: All culture practiced in leaf. Harvest late morning or early afternoon in leaf or flower signs.

ROTATION: 3 to 6 years crucifer rotation depending on build-up of soil-borne disease.

BIODYNAMIC SPRAYS: Horn manure (500) before sowing and on soil for flats. Silica (501) for transplants and early rosette and as sprouts appear. Compost-clay (500) slurry for transplants. Equisetum (508) for damping off and disease prone areas.

COMPANION PLANTS: For health and flavor: onions, garlic, dill, chamomile, mint, and caraway. Aromatic herbs (catnip, dill, mints, thyme, sage, rosemary, marjoram, oregano) deter pests.

BURDOCK

Burdock root, *Arctium lappa*, a native from Eastern Europe and across Asia, was once cultivated in Europe, and was spread by colonists in North America to the gardens of Native Americans. Shoots were harvested as greens in spring. Roots were eaten like parsnips. In modern times, burdock consumption has been largely restricted to Asia, where the root is almost revered nutritionally and medicinally. The Japanese call burdock root *gobo*, the Koreans *tong u-eong*, and the Chinese *ngau pong*. Macrobiotics enthusiasts, who cook in the Japanese style, consider burdock root indispensable.

Burdock roots are crisp, sweet, and pungent, with earthy undertones. Earthiness can be reduced by peeling and cutting julienne strips; and soaking the strips in water and a few tablespoons of vinegar for ten minutes. Burdock strips can be stir-fried with julienned carrots, onions, garlic, mirin (a Japanese rice vinegar), soy sauce, and sesame oil. The Chinese add strips of roast pork.

In spring, burdock leaves can be cooked like spinach. Later on, young crisp roots can be peeled and eaten raw like radishes; immature flower stalks can be battered and fried.

Like other composite food plants, burdock is high in inulin, which lowers blood sugar. Limited research from the Far East confirms burdock root as a blood cleanser and liver detoxifier. Traditional Eastern medicine extends these claims to the kidney and colon.

There are no confirmed negatives to burdock root as a food, although its high levels of tannins may bind to iron, making the iron less available.

Culture

Burdock root may be the longest root you'll ever grow. In extremely deep, friable soils, roots may reach 4 feet, with tops 8 feet high. In normally friable soils, roots range from 18 to 36 inches, 1 to 1 ½ inches in diameter. Best to double-dig your burdock bed to loosen subsoil down 16 inches. Compacted soils will not produce usable roots.

Root diameter will also be determined by spacing. At 2 to 3 inches apart, roots will be narrow (about an inch); at 4 to 5 inches, roots will be much wider. Normal composting is sufficient. Whatever works for carrots and parsnips, works for burdock.

Sow burdock in spring whenever carrots are sown in your area. Sow 5 to 8 seeds per foot, in rows 18 to 24 inches apart. Thin plants 2 to 5 inches apart, depending on desired root size. Roots reach full size in about four months. Harvest roots as needed in the fall. Store unwashed roots in perforated bin liners in the cold cellar. Washed roots wilt quickly. Leave some roots in the ground for late winter or early spring harvest. In cold areas, mulch heavily after first hard frost for easier access.

Varieties

Varieties include Takinogawa Long (2 feet) and Chiko (1 to 2 feet). Both four months to harvest.

> SEED: An ounce of seed (average 2,000) sows 235 to 350 feet at 2- to 5-inch spacing, in rows 18 to 24 inches apart. A 2-gram packet (110 seeds) sows 15 to 22 feet.
>
> VIABILITY: 1 to 2 years.
>
> MOON CALENDAR: All practices in root.
>
> BIODYNAMIC SPRAYS: Follow the schedule for carrot.

CABBAGE

When a cabbage is cut in half, the leaf arms unfolding look remarkably like a highly magnified picture of the meristem. The meristem is the mobile, magical point, microscopic in size, where plant cells are most intensely alive and most malleable. The meristem never stays the same, but is always becoming the next stage of the plant, from cotyledon to broad leaves to seed, always leaving the past behind in the form of maturing and aging leaves.

To my thinking, it is no coincidence that a cut cabbage looks like a meristem; one that is macroscopic, not microscopic. In cabbage a normally invisible sequence rises into visibility, from an egg-shaped ellipse, opening to a growing parabola, and then folding out farther into an aging hyperbola. From above, the rosette looks like a giant flower bud about to open, but the bud only gets tighter and more intense. The leaves crumple and fold on themselves. They become water-forms flowing internally between the midribs; flowing densely into vortex, like a river blocked by a dam, with only an indented watery ripple lapping at the leaf margins. The flesh becomes denser, sweeter, and more nut-like, surprisingly similar in texture to the juvenile cotyledon stage.

I don't believe this comparison to the meristem is a metaphor. I believe the meristem has found a literal image of itself in the cabbage species *Brassica oleracea*. This single species has embodied the meristem and become the single greatest fountain of food plants. Collards (variation *acephela*), kale (var. *tronchuda*), Brussels sprouts (var. *gemmifera*), cabbage (var. *capitata*) and broccoli/cauliflower (both sub-variations of *Brassica oleracea* var. *botrytis*) form a single plant. Even rutabaga is thought to be a natural hybrid arising out of *Brassica oleracea*. No other species shows this power of metamorphosis. In the cabbage species, the Greek god Proteus has risen once again from his ancient seabed and shows that even today he can change shape at will. Like a magician, he retains the juvenile mobile qualities of metamorphosis hidden within the leaf and holds them at a youthful stage within the vegetative zone—in thick broad leaves and leaf buds, in the succulent green sepals of broccoli, and even the strangely stunted and thickened curds of cauliflower. I believe this is why the species has such astonishing therapeutic power.

The cabbage species not only retains the potential of unhardened childhood, but also some of its vulnerability. All crucifers are prone to insect, disease, and rotting. Off flavors may be taken up from poorly composted manure, poorly fermented liquid manure, pig manure, or anaerobic compost. Like a small child, the leaves immediately take up the impressions of their surroundings. Very high nitrogen organic fertilizers speed up growth, increase susceptibility to fungal disease and rotting, and pass nitrogen residues on to consumers. Excess nitrogen makes the leaves watery, destroys nut-like flavor, and reduces storage life. Fertilizer for cabbage and kin should correspond to baby food: abundant, predigested, and entirely bound to the organic. None should be applied during head or bud formation.

Cow manure compost—well worked by manure worms—is ideal for cabbage, producing vigorous but balanced growth. Whenever liquid compost and nettle slurry is used as a "kick" in early to mid-growth, the brew should be well aged for three months with the biodynamic compost preparations. In a regularly composted biodynamic garden, side-dressings are unnecessary. Studies have shown that young cabbage plants can be stunted by sudden shots of nitrogen given between the time of the fifth and eighth true leaf. Keep liquid feedings dilute; otherwise yield, size, and quality will suffer. There is no sense in violating the natural breathing cycle of the plant by forced feeding. Better to transform the soil life over many seasons.

Because cabbages are shallow-rooted and susceptible to grabbing available nutrients, it is important to lure roots into a wider circumference. Horn manure (500) helps to integrate root, compost, and soil life (over many seasons) with the mineral portion of the soil, especially the clay fraction. A compost/horn manure (500) dip gives transplants a good start. Silica (501) is indispensable in a crop such as cabbage that is tending to close off from the sun's light. Use silica especially during a waxing moon, when nutrient uptake will be greatest. The clay fraction of the soil—especially a permeable clay loam with clay subsoil—improves the interior quality, flavor, and yield of cabbage crops, an important indication for market gardeners.

The right soil type with a near-neutral pH and the use of finished compost will go a long way toward plant health and insect resistance. I have made experiments growing cabbage and their kin on both sandy and clay loam in the same year. The difference was striking. More than 30 percent of the cole (brassicas) crops on sandy loam wilted from cabbage root maggot. Those on clay were hardly touched. Yield, of course, was much lower on sandy loam. The next year

I tried again, this time piling several cups of limestone around the base of the stems of those on sandy loam. This fortress prevented the egg-laying of the cabbage root maggot; nevertheless, yields were still twenty-five percent lower than on clay. Sandy loam can be improved over the years through biodynamic composting. Hardwood leaf compost with its durable organic matter and high trace mineral content can significantly counterbalance the problems of sandy soil.

Culture

Early cabbage can be started in flats, cells, or cold frames. If you have access to cow manure compost, use it. It has been my experience that cow manure produces less damping off and stronger growth. Make your own potting mix, if possible from materials on your own property. Peat and vermiculite mixes are not ecological, and they are distinctly dead. Dead materials result in weaker plants susceptible to fungi. After countless flats per year, an equal mix of rich clay loam (neither sterilized nor pasteurized, but from a garden sprayed with horn manure in the fall) and (preferably) cow manure compost never produced a single damped-off seedling. I also have good results with compost made from mixed materials. Steady, unbroken growth is the key. Keep the greenhouse fairly cool, and don't accelerate growth with heat, especially at night. Never re-use potting soils or soils used in cold frames. Re-cycle them into the garden rotation.

The cabbage family likes a sweet soil, between pH 6 and 7. If your soil is under 6, you may have to add ground limestone directly as a stopgap; but for the long term, add lime while building the compost heap. Apply to the crucifer rotation. The same goes for potting mix. If the pH is below 6, a light dusting of lime helps germination. Sow seeds four rows to a flat and cover with ¼ inch of fine compost, gently tamped. Or sow directly in cell-type containers, which transplant even better, 2 seeds per cell. Use bottom heat (75 to 80°F) from a greenhouse heating pad for the brief period of germination (4 to 5 days), but once seedlings appear, remove flats to a place where the temperature is cool, 55 to 65°F. I've found, however, that cabbage seedlings in the greenhouse tolerate swings of 80°F in the day to 45°F at night. This applies to other *Brassica oleracea* seedlings, as well. When seedlings show their first true leaves, they should be pricked out promptly from flats and spaced 5 x 6 inches in flats, peat pots, or cow manure pots. Air circulation is important. Spray with silica (501) when the cabbages show a few true leaves, which means that they are established enough to make use of it.

Unless you are gambling to beat the season (which I always do, by using heavy row cover), avoid sowing cabbage seeds too early and never plant more than six weeks before your last expected hard frost. Steady unchecked growth will always out-distance plants struggling an extra two weeks in the flat. A vigorous five-week flat will outgrow flats or cells that sit seven weeks. Try gambling a few flats two weeks earlier, but aim for outdoor transplanting two weeks before last spring frost. Plants should look vigorous and stocky five weeks after sowing. If they don't, then find out why; check temperature, potting mix, water, and so forth. Make notes.

Hardening-off means exposing the flats to cooler temperatures and direct sun for a week. Setting out transplants directly without hardening works only during extended cloudy periods without sharp frost. Hard frost can rupture the cells of transplants; they never recover. You can hedge your bets by staggering sowing dates. Sow three times, at one- to two-week intervals. The resulting harvest may be closer than that depending on weather, but this will cover unseasonable setbacks. Another method is to sow all seeds at a safe date, but sow varieties with maturing dates from 60 days to 100 days. A spread of varieties spreads risk. Varieties known to withstand midsummer heat hold longer in the field without splitting.

Red cabbage is harder to grow than green, probably just because it isn't green. Green cabbages often grow through less than optimum fertility and checks in growth from weather, especially dry spells. Reds often don't. They stunt like cauliflower, so I guess it's best to regard them as cauliflower and cater to their every wish, especially constant water.

Mid-season crops mature rapidly in July heat, so avoid planting a lot of summer cabbage without an assured market, even if that market is your kitchen.

Cabbage seedlings can be planted more deeply in the field than they sat in the flat. Home gardeners uneasy about soil fertility can put a trowel-full (or two) of cow-compost in each transplant hole. In compost, transplants don't miss a beat, and in my East Coast garden they required only one initial shot of water. If the springtime is very dry, keep seedlings watered until they perk. Use biodynamic silica in the field three weeks after transplanting, when plants are established.

In areas with long hot summers, a break should be made before sowing the fall or overwintering cabbage crop, according to the length of summer in your area. Fall sowings range from early May to late June, depending on latitude.

Commercial growers have found that every day you shift later sowings for autumn harvest (May or early June, depending on latitude) causes a three-day shift in harvest date. That is, a sowing ten days earlier in May can result in a harvest thirty days earlier in fall; in other words, too early for unrefrigerated storage. Late sowings require extra care, since transplants are usually set out under hot midsummer conditions. Cabbage maggots are usually past breeding, but heat and drought drive flea beetles into a feeding frenzy. Under the worst conditions (very sandy or silty soil) nothing seems to stop them. Some gardeners say that frequent shallow cultivations disturb the breeding cycle. I use row covers until the plants have established a rosette. In small to medium-sized gardens, mulch and mixed culture *definitely* help. Mixing herbs in the cabbage rows, even on a field scale, has been practiced successfully by European biodynamic growers. See the herb suggestions at the end of this article. Once plants are established, flea beetles are usually not a problem.

In mixed garden culture, wasps often take care of cabbage moth caterpillars. Monitor cabbage worms carefully (the green ones are hard to see) and spray Bt (Dipel) if the problem increases. It is usually worse in later sowings. Flowering dill, fennel, caraway, and other *umbelliferous* plants attract beneficial wasps.

Spacing of plants depends on variety. If you want to grow baby cabbages, early varieties can be crowded one plant per 8 to 12 inches, with 18 inches between rows, . Storage cabbages need 2 feet between plants and 36 inches between rows. Cabbage tolerates closer spacing in the row, but roots dislike touching between rows. Skim off weeds with a scuffle hoe or the stirrup hoe on a wheel cultivator; deep cultivation disturbs cabbage roots. Burying weeds through hilling also works, so long as the implement does not cut too close. Maggot-damaged plants often re-root from the lowest leaf node when hilled. Mulch is better yet. Control slugs with an iron-based bait. If mature heads begin to split, cultivate deeply to break roots and slow growth. Home gardeners can slow splitting of mature heads by forcibly giving the heads a half-turn in the ground.

To control cabbage diseases, practice a three-year cabbage family rotation. If disease occurred on any crucifer, clean up scrupulously and compost diseased refuse for use only on tree fruit and ornamentals. Rotate five years and choose resistant varieties. In "black leg," a seed-borne fungal dry rot begins as leaf spots and then becomes larger dark areas, with leaf edges turning bluish or red. In "black rot," bacteria causes veins to darken, wilt, and become foul-smelling, with either poor head formation or rotting of mature heads. West coast-grown seed is free of black rot. Club root fungus cannot be eradicated once soil is infected, but vigorous cabbages grown in 4- or 5-inch peat pots for an extra six weeks will produce heads when planted in infected soil. It's not a real solution, but is the only possibility in some areas. "Watery soft rot," a cool wet weather fungus, causes whole heads to collapse. Alternaria, a seed-borne fungus, begins as small water-soaked leaf spots that grow larger brown or purple. However, if you build up your soil over the years biodynamically, these diseases should be a rare sight, if they occur at all. Instead of feeding liquid nitrogen between the fifth and eighth leaf stage, spray silica, equisetum, nettle, and dilute seaweed.

Cabbages may be harvested whenever the head feels firm. A mature to over-mature cabbage looses its sheen and often has a beige papery leaf at the top. Fall cabbage improves in flavor with light frost, but cannot endure hard frost. On the other hand, the storage crop should not be cut prematurely, lest the root cellar be too warm. In the past I've used an exhaust fan to draw the icy night air into the root cellar in the fall. The autumn earth is so warm! Storage cabbage should be cut only when the cellar temperature can be brought below 45°F. Cabbages lose quality and spoil easily when put in a warm place just after harvest. Stored cabbage can last until March if temperature is held close to 32°F. Some people pull whole plants including roots and hang them upside down in the root cellar, but this takes up a lot of space. If frost is moderate in your area, earthen clamps piled with straw sometimes work if the earth has cooled sufficiently before hilling. The cabbages rot if the fall stays warm. In Zones 7 and 8 cabbages can be left in the ground all winter (with wind protection in some areas). If cabbages freeze before the storage date, let them thaw before harvesting. Frozen cabbages rot in storage.

Varieties

Tolerance of the disease fusarium "yellows" increases in importance the longer the cabbage sits in the ground. Fusarium tolerance is present in Early Jersey Wakefield (64 days), a fine-tasting old favorite with a pointed head. Likewise Caroflex (68 days), a conical hybrid with excellent flavor. The tolerance is absent, however in Golden Acre (65 days), a good early cabbage often used for bedding plant sales, but not by growers themselves. Most early hybrids also lack yellows resistance, except for Charmant (65 days), a high-yielding hybrid similar to

Stonehead (67 days), which forms its head slowly without bursting for extended harvest. Useful for both fresh market and home gardeners. Farao F1 Hybrid (64 days) also holds well without splitting, with crisp leaves, sweet and spicy.

Cabbages for sauerkraut generally have lower water content, with greater density and dry matter. These may include vigorous open-pollinated (O.P.) European varieties such as the tasty Holsteiner Platter (90 days) or the high yielding hybrid Kaitlin (94 days). Both can be stored for the short term.

Main season varieties should have greater vigor and adaptation to hot weather, with tolerance to yellows, black rot, and splitting. These might include hybrids such as Blue Vantage (76 days) and Blue Thunder (85 days). O.P. Early Flat Dutch (85 days) has good heat resistance but unknown disease resistance. Early Flat Dutch is also suitable for kraut and winter storage.

For long-term storage try one of the O.P. European varieties bred for that purpose. Dottenfelder Storage (90 days), a sweet, slow-growing cabbage originating at the Dottenfelder Hof biodynamic center in Germany, is grown in the United States by Turtle Tree Seeds. Novatov (110 days), one of the most popular hybrid European storage cabbages is tolerant of yellows, internal blackening, and tip burn. The American Hybrid Storage No. 4 tolerates adverse weather and less than optimum fertility, and can be used fresh at 75 days and stored at 95 days until spring. It is yellows-resistant.

Savoy cabbages are considered the sweetest and best-tasting cabbages because they mature during light frost, the same frost that turns tough summer kale into the sweetest and tenderest of delicacies. And they are beautiful plants, slightly more nutritious than regular cabbage, and easier to grow than red. Savoy can be overwintered in the ground in Zone 7 with protection from the wind, but it is not tolerant of wet winters. O.P. Vertus Savoy produces large green heads with fully blistered leaves. January King (100 to 160 days [1885]) can also be left in the ground throughout the winter in Zone 7 (again with protection). Its heads are purple-tinted with semi-savoy leaves; the hearts are tender and mild. Deadon (105 days) is pretty much the same plant hybridized and yellows-resistant. Its purple color deepens and the heads sweeten with frost.

Red cabbage, like cauliflower, is more subject to checks in growth due to weather and disease. Red Drumhead (85 to 100 days, heirloom [1860]), a dense deep purple, tolerates both heat and wet weather. O.P. Red Acre (76 days), a smaller red cabbage that stores well has yellows resistance but is not tolerant of heat. It is best for early spring sowing and fall sowing. These open-pollinated varieties grow best given "cauliflower care"; but for red cabbage, hybrid vigor also helps. Only one, Cardinal Hybrid (80 days) is described as "reliable," along with resistance to yellows and splits. Other hybrids carry plaudits for exceptional taste (Super Red, 80 to 73 days) or excellent uniformity and resistance to yellows, black rot, and tip burn (Red Dynasty, 76 days), but no mention of reliability.

SEED: Seed per oz. average 7,000. A packet of standard seed will grow 25 transplants. A packet of hybrid seed will produce 75 transplants. An ounce will grow 4,000 to 5,000 transplants.

GERMINATION: 75% (better in hybrids). 7 to 10 days at 70°F min. Seedlings grow best from 55 to 65°F, but tolerate a wider range of temperatures, down to 45°F at night.

VIABILITY: 4 years.

MOON CALENDAR: All cultural practices in leaf.

ROTATION: 3 years between crucifers is essential to prevent build-up of disease; 6 years for club root.

BIODYNAMIC SPRAYS: Horn manure (500) before sowing and on soil for flats. Silica (501) for transplants, early rosette, as leaves curl to begin forming heads, when heads begin to show size, and as heads mature for storage. Compost-clay 500 slurry for transplant root dip. Equisetum (508) can be used prophylactically in extended periods of warm wet weather prior to the appearance of fungus.

COMPANION PLANTS: Aromatic herbs balance the heavy vegetative tendency in cabbage—fine-leaved herbs, such as dill or chamomile, or very strongly scented ones, such as mint or wormwood attract beneficial insects. Gardeners who grow mixed cultures know the benefits of these herbs. For health and flavor use onions, garlic, dill, chamomile, mint, caraway, sage, and rosemary. Against pests use catnip, dill, caraway, thyme, sage, mint, rosemary, marjoram, tansy, wormwood, and southernwood. For intercropping in wide plantings try bush beans (not too crowded), beets, celery, chard, lettuce, onions.

CARROT

Over the years I've become more and more partial to gray November days; they are insect-free and just the right temperature for work. The monochromes of brown and gray are quieting and peaceful. I accept that the summer sun has traveled elsewhere and has taken its life with it. The sun now shines only faintly, like a message from another hemisphere. I'm thankful the sun has left a legacy of its descending course, as day by day it sent spears of light into the ground. Somehow (and it's a miracle, if you think about it), the spears still stand there, like a bulwark from ancient Greece, against the winter snow. We call these spears of light "carrots."

The carrot carries the force of sunlight through the winter. Its lacy foliage is especially suited to prepare for this. Even during early growth, the fern-like leaves show a refined, sparse quality usually reserved for leaves closer to the flower. Their flavor is both pungent and aromatic, as if to say, "Yes, I touch the earth very firmly, but I am not overcome. I bring a flowery scent from the airy regions into the root, and yet never lose my form." In a carrot the balance of earth and light can hardly be surpassed. The effects of light are visible even in the slender seed leaves, which are nearly identical in form to the forked bracts under the flower. This shows a markedly different relation to the earth than does a succulent cotyledon like cabbage.

The root itself is rounded and shoots down smoothly and deeply, as far as five feet in some soils. Even in the wild carrot (Queen Anne's Lace) this tendency of form is maintained. It lacks the endless branching of root hairs found in plants less bound to the light. If stones or hard clay block its path, it may become forked or short-stumped, but internal qualities remain constant so long as the soil drains well. Poor drainage makes for poor color.

The soil must be prepared to receive this spear of light, so that it can develop qualities of summer sun within winter conditions. This depends on the way sand, clay, and humus are wedded in a particular piece of ground. Over the years it has become clear to me that carrot quality is a kind of barometer for the garden as a whole.

Ordinary carrots are fairly easy to grow; but large, sweet, and tender ones require a mature garden bed. They relish the humus most when it has become fully bound to the soil life. Nature has already provided good quality humus in some areas. Especially in parts of New England, there is abundance of old humus in the soil. Old humus is different from organic matter, or even fresh compost. It requires the inter-working of earthworms and other small soil creatures over long periods of time. But as I said, the quality of carrots can be used as a barometer for soil culture. The garden as a whole can be improved by improving the carrot beds.

Short, stumpy varieties of carrot, such as Planet or Kinko, will not solve the problem of a shallow compacted soil, or soil low in humus. For home gardens with compacted soil, consider raised beds and double digging. The combination of well-matured compost and deep cultivation will always produce the best carrots. If this work is daunting to your back, just do a bed or two a year.

Double digging a bed is really not much more difficult than ordinary digging. The effect will last for the life of the garden. It means a concentration of work in late autumn—the perfect activity for gray November days. Poorly drained soils, or soils with compacted clay, are the first candidates. Double digging simply involves throwing a spit of dirt forward across the width of the bed so that the subsoil is exposed. Apply several shovelfuls of mature compost to the opened spit, dig it into the subsoil, take a step backward and repeat the process. When I was young and foolish, an apprentice and I double-dug an acre of raised beds in late fall and early spring. To save time, we used picks to break up the subsoil. I enjoyed the work. Thirty years later, I still do — but not as much.

Most market gardeners cannot afford this labor-intensive system, made famous by the English garden sage Alan Chadwick. Many use a chisel plow and sub-soiler on heavy soils, and legume plants to penetrate the depths. Danvers and Chantenay carrots grow well on loosened heavier soils. Stony soils, however, produce too many forked roots for market use.

If a choice of soil types is an option on your land, choose a sandy to medium clay loam. A percentage of sand (silica) adds warmth and light to the soil, producing roots that are smooth, clear, and fiberless. A percentage of clay mediates between plant and humus, improving color and keeping qualities. If heavy clay soils are worked over a few years, they can also yield good roots, but midsummer crusting of seedbeds is a problem until humus levels are built up.

In choosing land for carrots, take note of pernicious perennial weeds such as wild morning glory, *convolvulus*. These can make a hopeless job, even for the home gardener. Cleansing can be achieved by continuous tillage, rye in autumn and buckwheat as a smoother crop. In small beds, fork-sifting is possible, but time consuming. New sod ground is also difficult because of wireworms and un-decayed organic matter.

Horn manure (500) is used by biodynamic gardeners to build a carrot soil, helping humus, earthworm, sand, and clay to interact and form a working whole. This cannot be achieved overnight, but is indispensable to the gradual development of land to be used for biodynamic carrots. Applied during the autumn, horn manure will hasten the decay of organic residues lying dormant in the soil. In the spring, the manure preparation will activate the soil prior to seeding. Horn manure is most effective when sprayed during the descending moon on root days in the afternoon.

When I first showed my children the roots of Queen Anne's Lace, they wouldn't believe it was carrot. Still, they had to admit the bruised root smelled like carrot; and with some encouragement they tasted it, and it tasted like carrot. I explained to them that carrot was selected from the wild in ancient times, but that the very orange sweet crop we now harvest was developed in France fairly recently. Then we dug around until we found a wild carrot faintly tinted with orange. "That's it," I cried, "that's the beginning of the carrot we grow!" Lest they poison themselves and their friends, I also initiated them into the dangerous members of the family: poison hemlock, whose purple streaked stems and fetid smell are unmistakable, and fool's parsley, more similar to wild carrot but also evil-smelling. The leaves of wild carrot are sharp, herbal, "resiny," and bitter; the fibrous wild root is similar, but not as strong. Bitter terpenes and a soapy flavor abound, both still constituents of modern carrots, but sugars seem absent. The fine flowery fragrance of the root, however, is unmistakable!

Apparently prehistoric Afghan farmers recognized the potential in this scent, since selections of Queen Anne's lace spread East and West throughout the ancient world. For millennia, though, the "carrot" was white or pinkish and low in vitamin A. Such carrots were found in China and Japan (more than three feet long), in Greek medical texts, in the gardens of monks, and in the storage houses of the Iroquois in 1779 by General Sullivan (who promptly destroyed them). By the sixteenth century, red, orange and purple varieties were found everywhere in Europe, but only in the nineteenth century did the French select the very sweet, tender, orange carrot we enjoy today.

If you take a fancy to the "wild" taste (which may yet prove to provide therapeutic properties), you can try a seed-savers' variety that preserves the original Middle Eastern strain in a cultivated form. In the past, Southern Exposure Seed Exchange carried Afghan Purple (65 days), which is similar and harkens back to the original purplish red roots still found in Asia Minor. Dragon looks similar, with deep purple flesh wrapped around an orange-yellow core, spicy and not as sweet as modern orange carrots—a colorful addition to stir-fries and salads.

Who knows? If "supersweet" gene manipulation goes too far and breeders accidentally drop some essential nutritional or therapeutic ingredient of carrot, they may have to do what a French plant breeder did in the nineteenth century. He created the modern sweet, low terpene, low-fiber carrot from selections of orange-rooted Queen Anne's Lace. One of the first very high-vitamin hybrid carrots, Juwarot, seemed to suffer from mis-breeding. It tasted soapy to me. To discover the original terrain, close examination of the wild plant and ancient breeds would be a good practice for seed savers.

Culture

Carrot seeds are very small (and delicately aromatic, so be sure to savor their aroma as the first carrot meal of the season!). There are about 20,000 carrot seeds to the ounce, 320,000 seeds to the pound. I emphasize this fact because carrots must be sown very thinly and require some care to produce good results. In Europe only the oldest peasants were allowed to sow carrot seeds. Younger people must make a special effort to duplicate their restraint. Sowing by hand should imitate a very fine spring rain. Pretend you suffer from arthritis, if you don't have it already, and move slowly. Another trick is to "cut" carrot seed in half and mix with baked millet seed, sand, or baked old carrot seed. The latter is especially good for mechanical seeders. On the other hand, extremely thin carrot stands are not as vigorous as those with some company. For some reason germination and early growth are more vigorous in groups. A balance has to be struck between a paltry stand and the need for excessive thinning, which can deal a heavy blow to any carrot grower. Pelleted seeds can solve a lot of these problems.

Settings on mechanical carrot seeders seem so variable that I cannot give any indications. I have used #8 and #6 in Planet Jr. with fair success in a spring sowing. Most growers start lower than the company's plate-hole or cup-size suggestion. Test the seed fall on newspaper first. Try several settings the first year under the same soil conditions. Much depends on soil type and available moisture. Cup type seeders (Nibex, and so forth) are much more accurate. Aim for about 20 to 30 seeds per foot. Spacing of plants determines size, shape, and even root color. For mature roots plan for 2 inches between plants; for baby carrots, ¾ inch.

In my early gardening years I frequently broadcast carrot seed. This takes skill and patience, the second of which I completely lack. I do better with closer-set rows. A bed 3½ to 4 feet wide can support three rows of mature carrots or four rows of baby carrots. With this spacing, the yield of early carrots will be enormous, and the weeds under better control. On a field scale, you can increase carrot yield by using tight double rows (5 inches apart) with an 18- to 24-inch tilling path between double rows. Mechanically raised beds also increase yields and decrease compaction.

Soil type dramatically determines the success of carrot crops. Sandy loams produce the sweetest and best-shaped carrots, no matter what the type or variety. Some catalogs (such as *Stokes*) note the soil type recommended for particular varieties: sandy, mineral, high organic, muck, or clay.

On a small scale, circumvent the crusting of heavy clay soil by covering the seeds in a shallow furrow (¼ inch deep) with sifted compost. The compost should be about the thickness of black velvet. To make the process easier, I have collected horse manure in sawdust to make special compost that requires no sifting. Be sure to tamp or roll the seedbed after covering. Besides rapid emergence in heavy soil, the great benefit of compost covering is that the black band allows for immediate cultivation, since it demarks the slowly germinating rows. For spring sowing, or on lighter land, this method is unnecessary. In dry weather, emerging seedlings require irrigation.

Carrots can be sown from three to five weeks before the last expected frost in spring. The day-night temperature should average around 50°F, but such rules cannot replace a little instinct and second-guessing about how the season will be. In warm years I've sown carrots in March in Pennsylvania, watched 6 inches of snow cover the seedbed, and found the seedlings just emerging as the snow melted. Learn to sense the moment when winter is over and spring is just beginning; that's the right moment for carrots. For the autumn crop, count back three and a half to four months from the first hard autumn frost, which in Pennsylvania ranged from June 15 to July 7, depending on irrigation. Carrots keep best in the root cellar when they attain full size, so give them enough time to size up. Small carrots tend to dehydrate more easily in storage. Carrots color and sweeten best at temperatures between 59° and 68°F. Autumn harvests should be timed to mature during the cool period called Indian summer in the East.

In large plantings of late carrots, I have preceded the crop with dwarf English peas. Peas prolong the soil life of early spring and keep the ground moist. Rows of early carrots can also alternate with dwarf peas. The composite family is also a good companion to carrots. In Europe the black salsify or scorzonera, a tasty root grated in salads, is used widely as a companion. Scorzonera helps to repel the carrot fly. The onion family—chives, garlic chives, and garlic in particular—improve growth and repel carrot fly. In areas where carrot fly is a serious pest, try planting double rows, 5 inches apart, one of which is onion, one carrot. Aromatic herbs such as catnip, horehound, rosemary, sage, hyssop, and lemon balm also repel the fly. The carrot variety Resistafly is unattractive to carrot flies. In later plantings, rows of carrots can alternate with beans. Beans can also follow the spring carrot crop without any addition of compost. Chicory, escarole, and lettuce are also good companions to carrots, perhaps because they attract earthworms.

Biodynamic growers spray silica (501) up to five times on the storage crop. Each spraying will increase the light assimilation so important to the development of "light storage" in the root. The carrot is especially receptive to silica when the leaves are just beginning to feather out. Sprays are most effective on root days, descending moon, if possible. Leaf days can be used as alternatives. The beginning of root formation is the next crucial stage for the use of silica. Spray when roots are about the same color and size as your pinkie. Though silica is usually sprayed with the rising light of the morning, switch to afternoon sprayings at this point, when saps are descending into the root.

Alternaria leaf blight begins on older leaves, *cercospora* leaf blight on younger leaves. The latter shows dark spots with yellow, the former larger brown-black lesions with yellow margins. Equisetum (508) can be used as a preventive; but it will not cure an existing attack. Use copper sulfate sprays. Danvers and some hybrids are tolerant of leaf blight, but always practice three-year rotation for carrots and other *umbelliferous* plants (dill, fennel, caraway, and so forth). Rotate six years for blight-infested soils. Nutritional sprays help and give additional vigor to the tops, even if blight is not present.

Nettle tea and dilute seaweed tea are excellent foliar stimulants during leaf growth. Valerian spray (507) is used to sweeten roots during later development, especially in periods of extended cloudy weather. Late silica sprayings help prevent deterioration of vitamins and quality during storage. September and October are the best times for such sprays, depending on latitude.

Many growers skim-cultivate carrots prior to seed emergence. With compost covering this is very easy. Another method is to demark the row with a 10% mixture of radish seed. A lot of unnecessary hand weeding can be avoided by keeping all but a 1-inch band skimmed clean, before, during, and after emergence. Since emergence can vary from 10 to 20 days, this is very important. Summer weeds appear overnight. For home and small market gardens the stirrup or wheel hoe works perfectly. Push or drag it behind you in a straight line, razor-close to the compost cover, radish seedlings, or barely emerging carrots.

Early on, I took an old high wheel cultivator and adapted the head of a stirrup hoe to fit the mounting bracket, replacing the iron wheel with an English bicycle tire. For market growers, the low European style wheel hoes are worth the money. They focus the pushing force directly at the line of cultivation, increasing efficiency and accuracy. Seed rows should be sown absolutely straight to dramatically reduce weeding time with a European style wheel hoe. Whatever method you use, use it often and shallowly. Practice shaving very close to carrot seedlings; there are usually enough excess seedlings to risk slicing off a few.

Careful thinning is essential to a strong stand of carrots. Unless you use pelleted seeds or a precision seeder, carrots usually have to be thinned to 2-inch spacings. Don't try this immediately after emergence, unless the seedlings come up as thick as grass. First slice off those that deviate from the furrow line. Then give the stand a chance to establish itself. Cotyledons like company for a while. Begin when the first true feathery leaf emerges from between the seed wings. Baby carrots can be thinned to 1 inch, and other carrots to 2 inches. Home gardeners can vary spacing, but carrots for market or storage should be thinned rigorously.

Besides interplanted onions, a thick dusting of wood ashes is often used to provide an inhospitable nest for the carrot fly, whose maggots tunnel through the roots. Wood ashes also add potassium and phosphorus, which helps to sweeten the carrots. The carrot worm is a beautiful green, black, and yellow caterpillar, which appears when the foliage is fully developed. The caterpillar is the larval stage of the swallowtail butterfly. Use Bt (Dipel) only if the damage looks serious. The excessive presence of any insect indicates an unbalanced cultural environment. Give more attention to soil, compost, and mixed planting.

Harvest and Storage

Many people harvest carrots at finger size, but most varieties develop flavor, color, and sweetness only at maturity. New hybrid Nantes are better for early baby carrots. Most carrots mature 55 to 70 days after sowing. Storage carrots should be in the ground 75 to 85 days. They need some size and more dry matter in order not to shrivel in storage. Summer carrots crack or get woody quickly; fall ones hold longer. Some hybrid carrots mature very rapidly as they approach maximum harvest date, and may split. The strong foliage of Danvers (and Danvers crosses) makes harvest much easier. Danvers and specific hybrids have been bred for strong tops. Others require lifting with spading fork or chisel plow. If you intend to store carrots for the winter, time maturity as close to hard frost as you dare; in Pennsylvania that meant mid-November; in New England, late October. Sow storage carrots three months before hard frost.

No matter what method is used for harvest, mechanical injury should be avoided. Cull fork-speared and broken roots, and either use them within a month or feed them to livestock. Carrot roots don't rot easily, but it is better to store only perfectly sound ones. I have never had problems with pulling the foliage clean away from the carrot, instead of leaving the suggested few inches of stem. Because of the retention of field heat, never put sun-heated carrots directly into a big pile. Let the roots get cold (40°F) before you put them into storage. Field dirt can stain roots in storage. Roots can be washed (not scrubbed) in water.

There are many different ways to store carrots. Some people layer them in boxes with slightly damp sand. Kept very cold (33° to 35°F) this works fairly well, but I have tasted off-flavors from sand. Hardwood leaves, especially maple with their natural growth inhibitor, maintain better flavor; but if the pile generates heat, like a compost heap, the pile can be ruined with carrot root hairs. Leaf moisture must be just right, only very slightly damp, and the temperature as close to freezing as possible.

By chance I found a carefree way to store carrots. I was overwhelmed by several tons of carrots, and had little help. I left most of them in the same woven plastic feedbags used to haul the carrots off the field. They kept better than any other method I had tried. Later I read a USDA report claiming that roots store best in perforated plastic box liners. Plastic may not be biodynamic, but the bags are easy to move around; burlap dries carrots out, rots, and rips. The one factor that cannot be changed is temperature. In autumn it is more difficult to get a root cellar below 40°F than to keep frost out. I use a fan blowing *in*.

In Zones 6 and 7 some home gardeners mulch carrots through the winter. They mulch lightly when frost is regular, but not deep. When ground frost begins, they mulch more heavily with leaves or straw. For example, if the ground normally freezes down to 10 inches in their area, they put on 15 inches of mulch. Caution: if you mulch heavily before hard frost, rodents move in. Second caution: roots may not be accessible in midwinter due to frost and snow.

Seed-saving of open-pollinated carrot is usually not successful in the East because carrot and Queen Anne's Lace cross easily and produce a wild pale-orange offspring. Commercial seed is usually grown in the West, where wild carrot does not grow. If you live in an area with no wild carrot, choose the best-looking roots from your fall crop. The shape should be evenly tapered, the color deep orange; the flesh will be smooth, clear, and free from bumps and side roots. Practice by looking and testing, noting the visual appearance of carrots with excellent taste. After some practice you should be able to determine taste visually. Selected carrots can be stored vertically in boxes filled with soil. The foliage can be pulled off, but don't cut into the growing point. In early spring, replant these roots in the garden, giving each root 2 feet all around. These will produce umbels of seeds that can be harvested when dry. Carrot seed is viable for at least three years, and often much longer.

Varieties

From the nineteenth century to the most recent hybrids, Nantes has produced premium, bitter-free carrots. Roots have a beautiful cylindrical form, 7 by 1½ inches thick, with a characteristic blunt tip. Flesh is clear, brittle, and deep orange. At peak maturity all Nantes types have superb quality, sweetness, and excellent flavor. They are suitable for juicing, and many store well. Nantes Half Long, Scarlet Nantes, and Coreless (75 days) are the same carrot. Scarlet Nantes Touchon (60 days) was selected for smoothness, earliness, greater uniformity, and extremely good color. Touchon Deluxe (58 days) was selected from Touchon for brilliant orange color, greater length, uniformity, and internal quality. Touchon is still one of the best carrots for fresh eating.

Nantes Hybrids have raised a high bar even higher, with exceptional sweetness, smoothness, brittleness, and internal quality. Some carry a sugar gene and are pure candy, with as much sugar as muskmelon (8%). Such sweetness has now been matched in Imperator and Kuroda hybrids as well. Nelson hybrid (56 days) can be forced very early under row cover (which also excludes the carrot fly), and sweetens even in hot weather when others fail. Nelson has typical hybrid Nantes smoothness and brittleness with excellent color. Bolero (75 days) is a Nantes hybrid bred for fall harvest and storage. Bolero holds well in the field without cracking; although not as tasty in the fall as other Nantes, it beats all the others in maintaining flavor during storage. Bolero resists alternaria leaf blight, cercospora blight, and powdery mildew. Sweet Baby Jane (57 days) does not store quite as well, but has unusually fine flavor, sweetness, and internal quality from baby carrot size right to maturity. It has nearly perfect Nantes quality for home or fresh market.

Another breeding direction of interest to carrot growers is insect resistance. One Nantes hybrid has the unappetizing name Resistafly (70 days). According to *Nichols* catalog, Resistafly has "low levels of chlorogenic acid [which interferes] with the pests' life cycle, making it unattractive to them." Sounds good to me, but I always wonder if these deletions have nutritional consequences.

When I lived in New Hampshire and had perfect well-drained carrot soil and cool summers, the open-pollinated Imperator (74 days) was my favorite carrot. It was sweet even at 12 inches, and tasted nothing like the plastic packet Imperators from California. Imperator is still sold as Tendersweet, and under the right conditions it can be absolutely delicious. Growers should know that sweetness and color are highly influenced by soil temperature (optimum is 59 to 68°F) and good drainage.

Imperator hybrids are sweeter, though their length (10 inches) requires very permeable soils. Some, like Maverick hybrid (63 days), require sandy soils. Many Imperator hybrids are now crossed with Nantes to create truly memorable carrots. Sugar Snax (68 days) has unusually high brix (sugar content) as well as very high carotene. The tenderness, smoothness, and internal quality are pure Nantes; the shape and length (up to 10 inches) are Imperator. It resists alternaria, cercospora, and pythium.

For years I resisted growing hybrid carrots. But the hybrid Nantes, Imperator, and Japanese carrots are so good, it is impossible to stop eating them. Their big drawback is also their strength. Hybrid vigor makes them grow rapidly past their harvest window (3 weeks maximum). Thereafter, they tend to split. Bolero holds longer than others. Check for new hybrids with tolerance to cracking.

Were its flavor not so variable, with occasional wild carrot flavor (*terpenes*), Danvers would be the ideal carrot. Seeds germinate strongly; plants are vigorous with full, strong tops. Roots are large, high yielding, high in carotene, and produce well in heavier soils. Strong tops make harvest easier than any other carrot, and the roots store well through the winter; much better than Nantes or Chantenay. The problem with Danvers is uneven flavor. Flavor is sometimes sweet and carroty, sometimes laced with a bitter herbal flavor reminiscent of the tops. Danvers is perfect for stews and stir-fries and salads with tangy dressings, variable as carrot sticks, and not really suitable for carrot juice unless you like the herbal tang. Danvers Half Long (75 to 100 days) has been a preferred storage carrot since 1871, 7 to 9 inches long, 2½ to 3¼ inches across, tapering with blunt ends. Danvers 126 is a more uniform selection of Danvers Half Long, selected for processing but similar in quality to its parent.

Chantenay carrots are also reliable growers on most soils, fairly sweet and fine-flavored with no bitterness. Color is variable, not as deep as Danvers, and tops are weak and susceptible to leaf blight. They are a lot more trouble to harvest. The shape is strange, with very broad shoulders and a steep taper, 5 to 6 inches long. Good fresh or for winter storage. The Chantenays are still grown for processing but not as widely as in the past. Quality is good, but not exceptional. Useful when heavy soil is a problem.

Biodynamic growers often worry about what will be lost with the complete hybridization of plants. Studies generally indicate a loss of nutritional value through hybridization, although many hybrid carrots are higher in A than older varieties. Breeders are still playing with ancient traits. Cosmic Purple (70 days, Nantes & Imperator) with its deep purple skin, orange or yellow interior, and sweet spicy flavor, harkens back to Afghan Purple carrots, first recorded in the tenth century in Asia minor. Atomic Red (70 days, Imperator)—whose name makes me wonder if its traits were perhaps developed using radiation—has dark red-orange skin and a strong wild flavor. Purple Rain Hybrid (73 days, Imperator type) has almost black-purple skin flesh and cores, surrounded by white, yellow, or orange rings. Purple haze (73 days, Imperator type) has a vivid, thin purple skin with orange interior and sweet flavor.

Japanese carrots are widely respected for taste and sweetness. Shin Kuroda (68 days) is very early with exceptional sweetness, shaped like Chantenay with broad shoulders tapered to 6 inches. Sweet Treat (70 days) is a similarly shaped Kuroda hybrid which according to Burpee is "one of the tastiest carrots we've every offered." Kuroda carrots are prized for juicing. Burpee also reserves its highest accolades (higher than Sugarsnax hybrid, which it also carries) for the Asian import Big Top. Burpee calls Big Top, apparently a non-hybrid with extremely sweet crisp red-orange flesh, "our finest quality carrot." These Asian carrots are worth trying when disease resistance is not an issue.

Since vitamin A is one reason we eat carrots, I haven't mentioned white carrots. Perhaps it's prejudice, since I like white potatoes and love Japanese white sweet potatoes. White carrots can be found in Rainbow (70 days), a single hybrid variety that must be reverting to the fountain of carrot types. Carrot colors range from white through all shades of yellow, apricot, and orange, each with a slightly different flavor. Kaleidoscope Mix (75 days) is a more colorful choice, a mix of four varieties, deep orange, yellow, red, and purple. Striking for the fresh market or the home garden.

For long-term storage I've already mentioned Nantes, Danvers, and the hybrid Bolero. Saint Valery (80 days) also stores well. A very large carrot, 10 to 12 inches with 3-inch shoulders and smooth bright orange flesh, it can overwinter in the ground in Zone 7, or root-cellared farther north. Open-pollinated Autumn King has similar stats and can be stored in the same way. Be careful, however, of very large hybrids such as Envy (66 days) that are sweet, smooth, and widely adaptable, even in clay loam, but do not store well. For a large hybrid with excellent taste that does store, try Olympus hybrid (67 days)—or its successors, since hybrids change from year to year.

The baby carrots sold in supermarkets are often cut and shaved pieces of larger carrots. True baby carrots are smaller Nantes types such as Minicor (54 days) and Sweet Baby Jane Hybrid (49 days), which have higher brix (sugar) ratings than the "cut and peel" versions.

> SEED: Seed per ounce about 18,000; but varies hugely with variety. A packet, 750 seeds, sows 25 feet at 30 seeds to the foot. An ounce of seed sows 600 feet at 30 seeds to the foot and 1,000 feet at 20 seeds to the foot. 2 to 3 pounds of seed per acre for Nantes and Imperator. 1 to 2 pounds of seed per acre for Danvers and Chantenay. 10 pounds of seed per acre for baby carrots.
>
> GERMINATION: 55%; 21 days at 50°F; 6 to 14 days at 60°F; 6 days at 70°F, if kept moist.
>
> VIABILITY: At least 3 years, often much longer.

MOON CALENDAR: All cultural practices including biodynamic sprays in root, descending moon if possible. For seed, replant roots in Leo.

ROTATION: 3 years between crops; 6 years if leaf blight is prevalent.

BIODYNAMIC SPRAYS: Horn manure (500) before sowing. Horn silica (501) up to 5 times from appearance of true leaves to harvest. Equisetum (508) for blight, but well before its appearance. Valerian (507) late in root development. Later sprayings of silica can be applied in the evening for this root crop.

COMPANION PLANTS: Peas, beans, chicory, endive, escarole, lettuce, chives, onions, leeks. Aromatic herbs such as rosemary, horehound, sage, catnip, lemon balm, and scorzonera help repel carrot fly.

CAULIFLOWER

It seems perverse to characterize cauliflower by its faults, but I would even go further: I think its signature as a plant is inseparable from the problems cauliflower gives to growers. A cauliflower crop can be ruined by any check in growth at any time: 1) uneven watering or poor nurture of seedlings in flats or peat pots; 2) use of transplants more than five weeks old; 3) steady drop to below freezing in outside temperatures after transplants are set out; 4) using transplants not slowly hardened to prevailing outside temperature; 5) planting in insufficiently composted ground; and 6) not providing an even supply of water at all stages. Stressed plants "button up," that is, they prematurely form tiny curds before the leaves are large enough to support full-sized heads. In other words, in cauliflower the trigger for stunting is lurking at every stage of growth, because the plant is intrinsically held back and stunted within the stem.

All plants button up when they are ready to flower. The green vegetative stage is suppressed and condensed; and the signature of the plant, its "soul," so to speak, appears in the flower. In cauliflower, however, this always occurs much sooner, at the height of the vegetative state. If you look carefully you can see the spirals of buds hidden within the curd, barely visible. In Romanesco cauliflower, described below, these flower spirals become more prominent and striking, but in white cauliflower the impression is different. It looks like white foam bubbling up from within the stem, flooding and drowning the flowers. The bubbling stem is quite tasty. It is similar to the pith of broccoli stems, but not as nutritious. It is somehow a "no man's land"—neither leaf, nor flower, nor fruit. Even the more nutritious curds of the colored varieties are entirely buttoned up.

Culture

Cauliflower culture, for white or colored, is the same as for cabbage or broccoli, but more exacting. If you learn the steps for growing good cauliflower, your cabbage, broccoli, and Brussels sprouts will improve as well. Cauliflower needs a well-composted soil with a pH between 6.4 to 7.4, which can be prepared the autumn before or early in spring. Cauliflower is sensitive to boron deficiency, so if you grow for market, have your soil tested. Generally if your beets have no hollow heart, boron is sufficient. For early summer harvest, sow seed in deep cell packs (70°F during germination), four to five weeks before April 15 in the north; earlier in the central and southern states. Follow biodynamic soil treatment and sprays for cabbage or broccoli.

Market growers make weekly sowings, starting February 1, to offset any unfavorable weather that can cause buttoning up. Keep seedlings at around 60°F. Crops for autumn harvest are sown outside from late June well into July, depending on latitude. Liquid feedings of seedlings in the third week with fermented nettle tea and liquid seaweed ensure vigorous transplants with strong roots. Harden plants a week before setting in the field by lowering the temperature gradually to the outside median. Plants can be set outside several weeks before the last expected frost, around April 15 in the north. That our climate is probably moderating is also a good reason to make two or more successive sowings. Dip transplants in a slurry of compost mixed with some clay or compost tea. Discard transplants that are older than five weeks. Set plants 18 inches between plants, in rows 30 inches apart.

Home gardeners unsure of garden fertility can mix in half a shovelful of compost per planting hole. If purchased organic fertilizers are used, then select one with nitrogen (the first number) from 4 to 8. Excess nitrogen can cause leafy curds, sometimes caused by high nitrogen poultry manure used in compost or bagged fertilizer. Side-dressings can also be applied during the rosette stage, (6 or 7 leaves longer than 1 ½ inches). Keep plants moist during dry weather.

Varieties

Because hybrid cauliflower is much easier to grow, the selection of open-pollinated varieties has dwindled. For home gardeners who do not require hybrid vigor, uniformity, or high production, try Early Snowball (50 days) for spring or fall, with good leaf coverage and dense heads. Plant Snowball Self-blanching (68 days) for fall only (day-length sensitive). Amazing (68 days) has some tolerance to heat and cold stress. O.P. varieties require optimum organic fertilization and ample water.

When choosing hybrids look for vigor, uniformity, density, well-domed heads, self-blanching, wide adaptability (heat, cold, day length) and tolerance to various diseases. Some seed companies, such as Stokes, have specialized in cauliflower for generations and note particular disease resistance, susceptibility, heat tolerance, and so forth, for market growers. Good choices include

Snow Crown for its vigor both early spring and late fall (down to 25°F), Fremont (62 days, self-blanching) is presently a growers' favorite for its uniformity and dependability. Burpee's First White is a very cold-tolerant hybrid, with very large uniform heads.

I feel better recommending the colored cauliflowers and brocciflower because they are so much higher in vitamins and antioxidants. The oldest known cultivar of cauliflower is called Romanesco, an Italian heirloom from the 1500s or earlier. I find that Romanesco is one of the most fascinating garden vegetables—almost mesmerizing. If you study it carefully, you get lost in its spirals; endless layers of chartreuse spirals, spiral towers composed of smaller towers, a fantasy of fractals. Some mathematicians think the world was created out of fractals and chaos. In Romanesco you can see what is not so apparent in all the other garden plants: that nature is filled to the brim with vortices, in endless combination, denser and more fantastic than Van Gogh's "Starry Night."

You may have to search seed-savers' exchanges to find heirloom Romanesco (100 days), a very large plant for fall harvest with bright chartreuse heads and fine nutty flavor, with no blanching required. Many catalogs offer Veronica (78 days), one of several hybrid Romanescos available. Both heirloom and the hybrids are planted in summer for a fall harvest. Culture is the same as for white, except that obviously no blanching is required.

Hybrid green cauliflowers have the same chartreuse color as Romanesco types, but look and taste like white cauliflower. Some have "yellows" resistance. Culture is the same as regular cauliflower.

Purple brocciflower, such as Violet Queen Hybrid, stands in between. The plant looks and grows like cauliflower, while the texture of the heads is similar to broccoli. For climates with winters not too deep, Purple Cape (200 days) from South Africa can withstand temperatures in Zone 6 down to 10°F. According to Bountiful Harvest seed catalogue, Purple Cape can be planted in a cold frame in fall and harvested in late winter on the northwest coast of the U.S. It's worth a try.

Graffiti Hybrid is an intensely purple cauliflower, which grows best in fall but will also produce in spring. The color of Cheddar Hybrid grows even brighter when cooked, combining cauliflower taste with more vitamins, but no disease tolerance.

FOR SEED, MOON CALENDAR, AND BIODYNAMIC SPRAYS, see
    the section for broccoli.

CELERIAC

Whenever I try to characterize the *Umbelliferae* in classes on plant metamorphosis, I find myself describing the top growth in great detail and with great enthusiasm. Everyone is struck by these round flower "tables," set for thousands of insect guests, and by the panoply of scents and tastes as exciting as the insects that visit them. Each year their reappearance seems as fresh and surprising as a walk into Eden. Yet all these experiences refer only to the sunlit life above the soil, as if only the tops of plants contribute to the magic of a mixed garden culture. Does this family go in only one direction? What about the roots? Do the roots of the *umbelliferous* plants have a beneficial effect on the garden?

One of the striking features of the taste of a carrot is how "un-rootlike" it is. It stands out among the roots for failing to betray even a faint hint of that musty quality we associate with earth. Beetroots, for example, may develop this musty quality in late winter storage. In the carrot, the topmost life of this plant family streams down into the earth, creating a sweet, clean, fruit-like root. When dug up from the soil, the domestic carrot even separates cleanly from the soil. Even its wild progenitor, Queen Anne's Lace, (although it grasps the earth tightly) is as wonderfully scented as a flower!

Celeriac is different. It is as finely intertwined with the soil as the top is subdivided in the upper air. I know hardly a garden plant with more tenacious roots! They cling so tightly to the soil that unless you cut the roots, it is very difficult to dig them out. The roots themselves look like gnomes with gnarled features and filthy, matted hair. You're not quite sure of their intentions. In fact, I used to make gnome dolls for my children by using barely pruned celeriac roots for the heads, and several dramatically forked and twisted carrots for arms and legs. The children found them too frightening to play with.

Celeriac spreads quite far into the soil, making a wide sphere of roots and root hairs. What surprised me, however, was the quality of the soil around the roots. I always found it noticeably better than the soil around other plants. Earthworms were more abundant, and the soil itself often looked like pure worm castings—much darker than the surrounding earth. Then it occurred to me that the soil creatures and the shape of the root sphere might be the counter-image of insect and flower umbel above. The finely incised form of the upper plant seems to be present in the total circumference of the root zone. I don't know why earthworms are attracted to celeriac (and celery), or if celeriac by itself alters the soil, but the total effect is significant. It reminds us that what is below the root zone is as astonishingly vivid as the region above. We just can't see it. The same contrast separates the frightening celeriac skin from its smooth white pith inside. Its grubby face is so hard to clean! But hidden underneath is the aroma of summer air! In celeriac, the sweet herbal quality has been pushed down into the earth. These qualities, in my opinion, make celeriac a good companion in the garden rotation.

In the early stages, celeriac is very similar to celery. In the first true leaves, the only visible difference is a slightly sharper leaf margin in celeriac. I learned this distinction when dozens of unlabeled flats of celery and celeriac got mixed up in the greenhouse. I was relieved that identification was possible, since the plants tolerate different garden conditions. Celeriac is not nearly as demanding as its sibling.

In celery the petioles or leaf stalks swell and fill with a fragrant, slightly sweet sap. In celeriac the stalks are much drier and more fibrous; the leaves are more pungent and the green is a shade darker than celery. In celeriac the sweetness accumulates at the base of the petioles. The white pithy base found in celery enlarges into a rough, sweet sphere, with a stronger and more concentrated flavor. Most important of all, this flavor can be stored all winter in the root cellar. Although difficult to clean and pare, celeriac adds an excellent celery flavor to soups, stews, and sauces. Incomparably good in soup with fresh lovage leaves (another close relative of celery), celeriac can also be grated raw as a salad ingredient. Gardeners who like the taste of celery, but lack the conditions to grow it well, might try celeriac.

Celeriac varieties all originate in Europe, where the roots continue to be popular, especially in Central Europe. Europeans eat grated celeriac and carrot salad in the winter; include cubed celeriac in soups and stews; make cream of celeriac soup; or serve steamed celeriac with cheese sauce. For American cooks, the problem with celeriac is preparation. Celeriac is a pain to clean and pare; this is easier if it is cut into quarters first. I think preparation has been the main reason for its low popularity in the United States. This is a pity, not only because celeriac adds a fine lovage-like flavor to cooking, but also because European seed firms are improving external smoothness and internal quality year by year.

Culture

Celeriac should be sown 10 weeks before the last expected spring frost. Culture is similar to celery. In both plants the hardest part is the minuteness of the seed. With more than 60,000 seeds to the ounce, you don't need much, even at 50% germination.

To increase germination rate, some growers lightly abrade the seed coat between sheets of extra fine sandpaper. Sow thinly with great restraint in dead level flats at about 6 seeds per inch, in rows a bit less than 1/8 inch deep and 3 inches apart. Germination takes 10 to 15 days at 70°F, improved by alternating temperatures. Water with a mister or very gentle fan sprayer. Celeriac and celery seeds are sunlight-responsive germinators; so don't use a dark room for germination. Air circulation and lots of sunlight are a must at all stages of growth to prevent damping off and other fungal problems. Lower the temperature to 60°F after plants show seed leaves. Early fungus problems are fewer in celeriac than celery.

Delicately prick out flats when the second true leaf appears. Lift, holding the true leaf not the stem. Transplant to flats in a 2- to 3-inch grid or cell-type containers. Soil mix can vary from 25 to 50% compost for less damping off and more vigor. Temperature should not drop below 55°F, which may cause bolting. Harden plants by reducing water for a week before setting in the field, at least a week after last frost. Plant 7 inches by 15 inches in the beds, or 8 inches by 2 feet in rows. Celeriac requires only normally fertile garden soil, pH around 6.5, neither as fertile nor as wet as celery, although fast-draining soils need bolstering with extra compost. Black heart will appear if soil calcium is low. Celeriac does not tolerate drought and extreme heat. Be prepared to irrigate.

Biodynamic gardeners spray plants with silica (501) at least once in the flat, again a few weeks after transplanting, when a good rosette is formed, later as the root begins to form, and finally a few weeks before harvest. Celeriac is not as susceptible to leaf blight as celery, nor to aphid-borne viral diseases (which stunt or mottle plants). To control leaf blight, practice a three-year rotation for the carrot family. Control aphids with insecticidal soap or neem. Aphids always signal low humus, or stress from drought or heat. Mulch is good. The earthworms love it. Quality is improved with an even supply of water.

Harvest in late fall before hard frost, using a strong, sharp harvest knife to cut the roots as the plants are lifted with a fork. Store in a very humid (more than 95%) and cold (32 to 38°F) root cellar. Celeriac will keep until spring.

Celeriac

Varieties

Previously only Large Smooth Prague (Giant Rooted Prague) was available in seed catalogs in the U.S. I used it for years both for cooking and for making troll figures. It is variable in size and internal quality. Breeders have reduced hollow heart, pithiness, and discoloration in newer varieties. Recent varieties such as Brilliant (100 days) are smoother, less knobby, and easier to prepare. They have better internal quality with little pithiness or hollow heart. Mars (95 days) is similar to Brilliant, but appears earlier and holds longer without pithiness.

SEED: Seed per ounce, averages 60,000. A packet will produce 400 transplants. An ounce produces 10,000 to 25,000 plants.

GERMINATION: 50%; 15 to 20 days at 70°F; grow at 65°F.

VIABILITY: 4-6 years.

DAYS TO HARVEST: 120 days.

MOON CALENDAR: All culture in root, if possible, or in leaf. Biodynamic sprays in root.

ROTATION: 3 years for this and other carrot family members. Leaf blight is a pain!

BIODYNAMIC SPRAYS: Horn manure (500) on field and in flats. Silica (501) at least once on greenhouse transplants. Compost-clay-500 root dip for transplants. Silica twice during leaf development and at least once during root development. Equisetum (508) and valerian (507) during fungous weather. Silica can be sprayed in the evening for root crops.

COMPANION PLANTS: Alternate with lettuce, shallots, leeks, garlic, chives, onions, and tomato beds. Beneficial to cabbage, bush beans, scarlet runner beans. Promotes earthworms and soil life.

CELERY

I've heard it takes more calories to chew and digest celery than it returns, but if that's true how do gorillas build muscle on a diet of wild celery leaves? Is it because gorillas eat the dark green leaves, which we discard in favor of juicy stalks? Humans have never eaten celery for nutrition, but for its sweet herbal flavor and for its saltiness—three times that of collards. For us, celery is not really a vegetable at all. It's a big salty herb, akin to its finer-flavored cousin, *Levisticum* (lovage). In that sense celery is like every other plant in the family *Umbelliferae*. Even the vegetable members such as carrot or parsnips are herb-like. I find the sweet, piercing scent of *umbelliferous* leaves and the intense etheric oils in many of their seeds inseparable from the play of sunlight itself, dramatically condensed. A whole atmosphere is condensed into the space of a seed. Salt, too, is endemic to the origins of celery.

Celery evolved in wet saline meadows on the Mediterranean Coast and saline marshes inland. Celery is still found wild throughout Europe and eastward through Asia Minor to the feet of the Himalayas. Like many *umbelliferous* marsh meadow plants, it has a fairly narrow range of conditions in which it thrives, which is why celery is so particular about growing conditions. It is an ancient medicinal herb, even mentioned in Homer's *Odyssey,* circa 850 BCE. Only recently has it been bred for smooth, watery cell structure. Yet even as a medicinal herb, I find celery hard to understand. For example, it contains biochemical components that actively lower blood pressure—along with three to five times more sodium than any other vegetable! Do they just balance each other out? As it is, celery became a vegetable only in the 1600s, and then became popular only by denying its relation to light through blanching in the nineteenth century.

Since celery originates in marshland, commercial growers often choose muck soils with the water table within 2 feet of the surface for best culture. Areas of frequent fog, such as parts of the coast of California, are famous for growing celery. Gardeners who violate the conditions of the marsh origins of celery cannot expect success. For dry climates, replace the flavor with celeriac or lovage.

There are three aspects to the conditions of celery's marsh origin. These include the need for slightly acid humus, constant availability of moisture, and a very peculiar pattern of seed germination. Celery seed germinates slowly and unevenly. There are many seeds to the ounce, many more than the 10,000 plants an ounce will produce, but germination is a problem. One must imagine the conditions for marshland germination of seeds. Water flows in and water flows out, the seeds sometimes being submerged under water and then drying out again. Those by the shore become wet and dry many times before they germinate; and believe it or not, the celery seed has not forgotten! Alternate wetting and drying have been shown to considerably promote more rapid seed germination. Still, the shortest time you can expect is about 10 days; the longest, 3 weeks. Since the seeds are so small, you always need fewer than you think. Even a tiny packet will produce 400 plants, although through lack of care, you may not get a single usable stalk.

Most families eat celery, but few grow it. Some seed catalogs don't list a single variety. Others list only one. Why? Celery is a nuisance in many ways. It must be sown very early in a warm space, which many gardeners don't have; needs lots of light when there isn't any; needs warm temperatures and breezy air circulation. It damps off easily when there isn't enough air. In other words, it's a typical *umbelliferous* plant, which also means it does not like the greenhouse very much. It wants light and flowing air. It wants muck and moisture on a blithe summer day. It hates dry heat. It wants what only a specialist can supply perfectly. Its culture difficulties are typical of a plant that's been *carried too far from its point of origin.*

Culture

Celery is grown for market in cool coastal areas, or in regions where summers are cool and soils are muck or high in organic matter. Hot dry summers are a losing battle; although, at home, deeply composted beds, mulch, and steady irrigation will grow good celery far from its comfort zone.

Celery is usually started in flats 10 to 12 weeks before the last expected spring frost. Commercial growers sometimes use seed more than 3 years old, since aging weakens the blight fungus. If you depend on the harvest for market, consider soaking seeds for 30 minutes in water that is 118°F (use a yogurt maker) to kill the fungus that causes late blight, a nemesis of the celery grower. Afterward, dry the seeds before sowing. (Obviously this treatment is not suitable for pelletized seed.) To aid germination, some growers *lightly* abrade dry celery seed between two sheets of very fine sandpaper. This will break the seed coat. Again, not for pelleted seed, which has a higher germination rate than non-pelleted.

Prepare the seed flats with well-rotted compost and soil, half and half; I have never had any damping off (fungal-rot on seedling stems) from this mix. The addition of sand and peat somehow lowers resistance to fungi. Seed flats should be firm, dead level and free from pits and gullies, where seeds could sink too deep. Even with pelleted seed, maintain control in sowing. In seed flats sow 3 or 4 rows with 6 seeds to the inch in each row, 3 or 4 rows to the flat. Over-sown seed flats are a nightmare. I like to cover seeds with 1/8 inch pure sifted compost and then tamp gently with a small board. Water very gently, using an upward turned English rose sprayer or a spray mister. Direct watering may wash the seeds to one side of the flat. Keep the flat moist, but not flooded, at around 70°F. Temperature fluctuations are good, since they hasten germination. Celery seed is sunlight-responsive, so don't leave germinating flats in a dark room.

During germination stage and thereafter, water gently with equisetum tea against fungus. After germination, continue to use a spray of strong equisetum tea. If flats germinate too thickly and grass-like, thin even during the cotyledon stage using tweezers. Leave room for air circulation, lest plants elongate before they leaf out. When the second true leaf appears (the one with serrations, instead of two tiny wings), then the plants may be loosened and pricked out with a penknife. Gently lift each plant by a true leaf, not the stem. Soon you'll get the knack and learn to do it quickly. Replant 5 by 6 inches in flats or in cell packs with the same 50-50 compost-soil mix. I drilled holes in a board with dowel stubs for accurate spacing of planting holes. Drop the taproot into the holes and lightly firm. Set the celery seedlings at the same level they grew in the seed flat. For even growth, drop the temperature to about 65°F but above 55°F to discourage bolting. Occasional drops don't seem to trigger bolting. Biodynamic growers spray equisetum even more frequently than silica after the plants are established, to discourage fungus. Give full sunlight. Avoid overheating. Aim for 65°F.

Use your richest soil for celery. Market crops require optimum fertility and perfect summer moisture. If you can't control moisture, don't plant celery. Some home gardeners solve this problem by planting celery as if they were setting out a 30-year asparagus bed, with a deep trench, and compost and mulch on top. At the very least, apply as much compost as you would use for a cauliflower crop. In the old days, that meant up to 50 tons to the acre, which is unrealistic by today's standards. Row composting is more economical. Biodynamic growers apply horn manure (500) after the compost is tilled in or after the furrow or trench is made. The normal, slightly acid range of pH is satisfactory for the crop. Boron deficiency, which is a consideration for commercial growers, is not usually a problem for compost users.

Plant hardening involves reducing water for about a week to 10 days prior to setting plants in the field, usually 2 weeks after last frost, when the weather is stable and warm. Lowering temperature may trigger the flowering process. Expose the plants to the open air for a few days prior to setting out on a cloudy day, if you can. Transplant 8 inches apart in rows 30 inches apart; or as close as 6 inches by 20 inches in fertile beds. Always set the growing point level to the earth. Setting it deeper invites rotting; but mulch against the outer petioles helps and does no harm. In open soil, skim-cultivate to avoid root damage.

Commercial growers fertilize celery every 2 to 3 weeks. Well-composted and mulched celery can produce a reasonable imitation of commercial crops, if steady moisture is maintained. A drip system is ideal. For small gardens without an irrigation system, use plastic gallon jugs filled with water with a pinhole on each side between two celery plants. Fill as needed. Home gardeners can water with compost tea.

Insect and disease are worse in packed field plantings stressed by drought and in soils low in organic matter. Celery worms and leaf tier can be controlled with Bt (Dipel); mixed culture and interplanting significantly encourages beneficial insects. In home gardens celery is easy to interplant with the onion family.

Blanching spoils the hard work you've done throughout the season. Boards and bales for blanching are what negate celery's nutritional value, and should be a thing of the past. Market celery must be dipped in cold water after harvest to remove field heat and refrigerated immediately at 35°F to preserve quality. Celery does not take much frost; but it lasts a month or longer in Zone 7 in an improvised clamp (boards and bales) and overwinters in Zone 8. In Zones 6 and 5, home gardeners can lift whole plants, root and all. Wash them off and stack in crates in a root cellar. At 32 to 40°F, celery will keep for a few months.

Varieties

Some seed companies offer pelleted seed, which is a real plus in a plant that produces over 65,000 seeds to the ounce. The standard open-pollinated early variety is Utah 52-70R. After decades it is still one of the most dependable. The "R" indicates disease resistance, because celery is susceptible to fusarium yellows, which is also a problem in cabbage and other plants. Fusarium shortens the celery petioles (stalks). One amusing solution for fusarium-infected land is Picador, which has been bred too tall to grow on uninfected land. Look for fusarium resistance. Descendants of Utah (Ventura and EA Special Strain, both about 90 days) offer slower bolting to flower and greater adaptability. Conquistador is widely adapted even to normal garden soil. Hybrids such as Tango (80 days) and Monterey (85 days), named after an optimal seacoast-growing environment, offer greater vigor, tenderness, and fewer strings.

For a still sharper celery flavor, try a cutting celery such as Safir (78 days), whose stalks impart a strong flavor to soups and stews and double as fresh scented greens in flower arrangements. Cutting celeries are easy to grow and last a long time if the flower stalks are removed.

SEED: Seed per oz. average 60,000 (pelleted seed about 9,000). A packet will produce about 400 transplants, an oz. about 10,000 plants.

GERMINATION: 50% for naked seed; up to 90% for pelleted seed; 10 to 20 days at 70°F. Grow at 65°F.

VIABILITY: 5 years.

DAYS TO HARVEST: 85 to 120.

MOON CALENDAR: All practices, including biodynamic sprays, on leaf days, ascending moon, if possible.

ROTATION: 3 years for all plants in the carrot family, more in blight infected soil.

BIODYNAMIC AND ORGANIC SPRAYS: Horn manure (500) in field and in flats. Silica (501) several times on greenhouse plants. Compost-clay 500 root dip for transplants. Silica twice during leaf development and once more for storage celery. Equisetum (508) and valerian (507) in the greenhouse and during fungus-promoting weather. Nettle tea and organic foliar spray during first two months. Liquid seaweed spray at one-tablespoon concentrate per gallon.

COMPANION PLANTS: Alternate with bush beans, leeks, shallots, garlic, chives, onions, and tomatoes, beneficial to cabbage.

CHARD

Green leaves play such an irreplaceable role in human nutrition, especially in child development, that I was surprised when biodynamic farm families I met in Germany wouldn't eat beet greens. I had not tried to convince them to eat weeds, which had also occurred to me, but I knew that beet thinnings were delicious, one of the high points of the early summer garden. No matter. A German farmer just stared at me, as if my radical suggestion undermined the social order. Without smiling, he delivered the final word on German behavior: "It is not done." However, if he had thought a minute he might have modified his reply to: "We do eat beet greens, but in a form where the oxalic acid content is less dominant. Perhaps you are not aware that Swiss chard is not merely related to beet; it *is* beet. Both are *Beta vulgaris*."

When I rechecked my favorite sixth-grade garden book, *The World in Your Garden*, I was reminded not only that this was so, but also that the beetroot as we know it is a comparatively recent innovation. European people ate the greens of *Beta vulgaris* for thousands of years before the beetroot was selected. Red Chard, for example, now advertised as a novelty in seed catalogs, was described by Aristotle in ancient Greece. Theophrastus distinguished the same light green and dark green types still popular in various countries. In ancient Greece the red root was collected only from the wild sea beet (*Beta vulgaris maritime*), the ancestor of chard and beetroot, and was used only for medicinal purposes. In late Roman times, the third or fourth century CE, some enterprising Italian gardener began to select beetroots for size and tenderness. Roundness, however, did not enter the picture until the Renaissance. Great sweetness did not appear until the nineteenth century.

It may surprise many readers that the word *beta*, the "beet," does not refer to the root at all, but means "greens" in Latin! The word "chard," on the other hand, is also a misnomer. "Chard" originally referred to the leafy buds of cardoon, the wild artichoke, which has also been enjoyed by Mediterranean people since antiquity. Only later was it applied to the greens of *Beta vulgaris*. And so, Europeans are quite correct when they say "beetroot" and never just "beet."

For the next millennia only the Italians seemed to eat the root, which was called "Roman beet" to distinguish it from the greens. The beetroot crops up occasionally in medieval sources, but only during the sixteenth century did the sweet root begin to become popular in Europe. In the eighteenth century it grew rounder and sweeter; and then sweeter still, reaching a high point of sweetness in 1800, when the German scientist Franz Karl Achard found that beets could be used to produce white sugar. Thus began the modern pattern of separating the plants' parts from their nutritional whole, an increasingly deviant practice in regard to human health.

Beet greens and Swiss chard differ only slightly in their nutritional profile. Beet greens have about twenty-five percent more calcium (which may be made less available because the calcium binds with oxalates present in the plant); and more minerals in general. Chard has about the same amount of vitamin A (6,500 units versus 6,100) and C (32 mg). High vitamin, calcium, and oxalic acid content are, in fact, a characteristic of the family. In kindred species (wild lamb's quarters and spinach), both vitamin content and oxalic acid content are even higher. In fact, were it not for the oxalic acid, lamb's quarters would surpass kale and nettles in nutritional value. Maybe I should have tried to get my German friends to eat lamb's quarters. I knew plenty of Europeans who used lamb's quarters in soup during World War II. My old gardening teacher certainly did.

What makes chard more useful than all the others, however, is its length of harvest. Chard is always available, and if harvested regularly, is always of high quality. Young chard thinnings are phenomenally tasty and can be pulled when the leaves are the size of spinach. I find mature chard leaves and stems delicious too; mature plants can be revitalized by pulling off all the leaves except the smallest at the center. Few garden plants are so prolific and so long lasting. What other garden subject can maintain quality in such a range of temperatures, from midsummer heat to moderate frost? Finally, chickens and pigs relish chard, even when the leaves have been damaged by leaf miner, a significant problem in some areas.

Culture

Chard seeds look like tiny asteroids. They appear pockmarked and desiccated, and if you look closely, you can see that each seed is composed of several aggregate parts similar to beetroot. Each withered facet can become a plant; and since, to my knowledge, mono seed is not available for chard, thinning is necessary. Not a problem, since gardeners welcome chard thinnings as the best eating of the season. Most limit their seed rate to 10 seeds per foot, or half that many, to avoid thinning entirely. For large leaves, thin mature plants to 6 inches in the row. In dry sandy soils the pocky seed may germinate and die for lack of moisture. Ample organic matter, compost, seed cover, and irrigation help, as does firm tamping of the seed row, which packs soil particles into the empty seed pockets. In soils with a pH below 6, dusting the seed with ground limestone prior to sowing substantially increases seed germination and does not interfere with mechanical seeding.

Chard is not fussy about soil or fertility, once established. Sandy and medium clay loams are best. Since compost is needed elsewhere for more demanding crops, chard need not be fertilized at all, but high organic matter improves quality. Because the plant lasts so long, it has time to establish a good root system, which spinach lacks. Biodynamic growers apply horn manure (500) prior to sowing, which helps plant roots expand into the soil horizon.

Sow chard 5 to 10 seeds per foot, ½ inch deep, in rows 18 to 24 inches apart, as soon as soil can be worked. Except for red-stemmed chard whose seedlings may bolt from frost, late snow and frost don't seem to affect germination or seedlings. Chard can be thinned late, when plants are 6 inches tall; and if rows have gaps, it can be transplanted easily. Just make sure the hole is deep enough to accommodate the long taproot. Set the plant at the same depth it originally grew.

Home gardeners who cover the seed furrow with compost will make pre-germination weeding easier, since a thin black line is visible. Later when the growing point has risen above the ground level, soil can be thrown against the plant during cultivation. Biodynamic gardeners apply silica (501) at rosette stage.

Harvest is usually done by stripping the outermost leaves by hand. If the leaves are pulled out and down, they come off by themselves. In large plantings you can also cut off the entire plant with a knife, leaving a few inches of leaf above the growing point. This method produces younger, more tender leaves, and lower total yield; but most gardeners plant more chard than they can use anyway. If the leaves develop numerous beige translucent blotches and tunnels (caused by the leaf miner) this method helps reduce infestation. Burn infested leaves, or feed to livestock and remember to do the same for spinach, orach, and beet leaves, which are also susceptible.

Mixed culture and closeness to aromatic herbs reduce many insect problems. In worst-case scenarios, home gardeners can construct a fly-screen cage for susceptible plants and remove it only for harvesting leaves. Market gardeners can use floating row covers throughout the season.

Chard survives light freezing in autumn and often holds well into winter in milder areas. Leaves are not marketable after heavy frost, but home gardeners should not prematurely remove plants. Hay bales to either side and a plastic roof will protect them for a long time. In places with mild winters, cover the top with a board and another bale or two. The plants will probably produce greens early in the spring. In southern areas, chard overwinters easily with some wind protection. Some varieties, such as Swiss Chard of Geneva, are said to be more hardy in cold temperatures. Overwintered plants will bolt the next summer and produce seeds, since the plant is biennial. If beet is not flowering at the same time, seeds may be saved. In very cold areas the whole plant may have to be lifted with the root ball, stored in a cold cellar, and replanted in spring. Lifted plants may also be replanted in a cool greenhouse for winter greens. Fresh chard seed germinates beautifully. Just remember beet and chard are the same plant, so alternate years for seed saving, or share the task with a gardening friend some distance away.

Varieties

Although the Romans probably ate chard greens with olive oil and garlic, the later breeding of chard seemed to favor the snow white stems, the petioles. The greens were fed to livestock. The stems of Lucullus, Glatter Silber, and Fordhook Giant (all 55 days) still produce large delicious white petioles to serve with cream sauce, but the green leaves are just as delicious. Spinach beet, also called Perpetual, may be closer to the original Roman green; it produces an endless supply of tender leaves that taste exactly like spinach, and it tolerates summer heat. Bountiful Gardens catalog claims Perpetual is perennial in Zone 7; however, as far as what I have come to know, the species is biennial, producing flower and seed in the second year, and then dying. Perhaps frequent cutting extends its tenure.

Rhubarb Chard and Ruby Red (both 60 days) are prized for their beautiful red stems, perfect for mixing with ornamentals in a flower border. For some reason red chard seedlings are prone to bolting in frosty weather, so must be planted a bit later. Though Rhubarb Chard has been around since the beginning, I never would have suspected that so many colors could be extracted from beneath the red. Pink, magenta, and purplish red I would expect, but bright yellow, golden, and orange are a surprise. Bright Lights, Neon Lights, and Rainbow (all 60 days) all live up to their name, beautiful in the garden and striking at the green market; but sadly, all lose their color when cooked, and like red chard, their seedlings bolt from untimely frost.

All chard can be harvested small (always cut above the growing point!) for baby greens or salad, but Italian baby leaf chard such as Erbette (30 days) has been bred for the purpose.

SEED: An ounce of seed (1,900) will sow 200 to 300 feet. A packet (¼ oz.) sows 50 feet to 75 feet.

GERMINATION: 65%; early to late spring, 5 to 10 days at 50° to 70°F.

VIABILITY: 4 years.

DAYS TO HARVEST: 50 to 60 days.

MOON CALENDAR: All practices in leaf days, including biodynamic sprays, ascending moon, if possible.

ROTATION: 3 years between chard, spinach, beets, lamb's quarters, and orach.

BIODYNAMIC SPRAYS: Horn manure (500) on land prior to sowing. Silica (501) twice during development, during the morning, ascending moon, if possible.

COMPANION PLANTS: Bush beans, onion family, cabbage family. Interplanting with strong-scented herbs helps repel leaf miner.

CHICORY AND RADICCHIO

You may have noticed that your whole organism reacts more intensely to bitterness than to salty, sweet, or sour. Bitterness shoots suddenly through your body. Plants that are extremely piercing, such as tansy, may even produce violent ripples of revulsion from head to toe. We are over a million times more responsive to bitter than to sweet, which is probably why we eat so much sugar! In regard to sugar, we stumble along like drunks. It takes a dope slap to wake up: at least one part sugar to 200 parts dilutant. We are twice as sensitive to salt, which can be detected in a dilution of 1 to 400, and still more so to sourness at 1 to 430,000. But we are unbelievably sensitive to bitterness, which can be detected at one part to 2 million, a dilution that is downright homeopathic!

A chapter on the physiology of taste published online notes that bitterness may alert the grazer to toxic alkaloids. You could also add that it alerts the grazer to a valuable nutritional package. Animals sense this. Those huge vegan gorillas favor bitter greens. It may be hard, even impossible, to separate the bitterness from **its** package. Agronomists in New Zealand use chicory forage to reduce intestinal parasites, nematodes, and lungworms in young lambs, which increases growth, vigor, and weight. Chicory also increases bone mineral density and decreases glucose uptake. Getting humans to eat it is another question, though I know from experience that the culprit is sugar.

As a forager, bitter greens have always intrigued me, drawn me by the nose into the wild, right into the details of plant composition. Taste and smell want to eliminate for a time the distraction of sight, as if a blind person were led by the nose and tongue into a magical realm, a biochemical fairy tale. Over the years many gardeners acquire a bit of the stereonasic forked tongue of the snake, which enables the snake to navigate entirely by tasting floating molecules of scent. They become able to navigate by taste and smell alone, perhaps more conscious of what a grazing animal knows instinctively. They notice how just as certain volatile aromas lead us out into wider nature, the exploration of bitter greens leads us into the formation of our own bodies.

You probably have observed how small children taste food with their entire bodies, given over helplessly to taste and smell, especially pronounced when nursing. The way they move makes them look like they taste with their toes. Tasting with one's entire body is a profound gift; either aided or thwarted by how one was fed as a child after being weaned. I know from experience how sugar (even sugar from pureed fruit) lures small children away from exploring nature through food. I was surprised that my third and fourth children, both of whom were somewhat deprived of sweet food, always ate their greens, while the older two took longer to come around. The fourth consumed platefuls of bitter greens by the age of three and continues to do so through his teenage years.

Many biodynamic practitioners believe that cultivating their "serpent's tongue" allows them to sense the play of formative forces that brought each plant into being. Over the years, I've set my sights lower, but such attentiveness has given me tremendous observational mileage. Even though our sensibilities will always be rudimentary compared to other animals, each plant has acquired an extraordinary tactile biography composed solely of taste and smell.

Most bitter greens are members of the daisy family, the *Compositae,* and retain more wild biochemistry than other garden subjects. Endive, escarole and the misnamed Italian dandelion are chicories. French dandelion is a selected cultivar of the common lawn weed. Traditionally these greens were considered spring tonics, especially for the overburdened liver, for so-called blood cleansing, expelling waste products from the blood. The overburdening of the circulatory system with such waste products has been then and is now a primary cause of disease. I am also certain that breeding or blanching out bitterness completely reduces the storehouse of nutrition and therapeutic agents. Bitterness and its attendant antioxidants are a single package. Best to find a breeding compromise and a newly acquired taste.

Italian Dandelion

Italian dandelion, also called Sicilian chicory and radichetta, is actually a blue-flowered chicory, *Chicorium intybus*. Italian dandelion is probably as close to wild as any garden plant gets. Though not a dandelion, Italian dandelion has a similar appearance to the lawn weed, but with larger, deeply cut dark green leaves. The true dandelion, *Taraxacum officinale* is available as French Dandelion. Both are nutritionally extremely strong. For example, 100 grams of dark green cos lettuce has 2000 units of A, 70 mg of calcium, and 18 mg of C; Italian dandelion has 4000 units of A, 86 mg of calcium, and 22 units of C. But French dandelion has 14,000 units of A, 187 mg of calcium, and 35 mg of C, far more than carrots in every category! Chicory and dandelions are among the great untapped nutritional resources available to the gardener, each containing an extraordinary reservoir of antioxidants and anti-inflammatory agents.

Baby forms of bitter greens have become well established in the salad trade. Stronger greens can be mixed with lettuce. Creamy hearts and some cultivars are less bitter. As a potherb, endives, dandelion and Italian dandelion can be added to stir-fries and cooked in traditional French and Italian styles.

Endives and escaroles (*Cichorium endivia*) are also chicories, closely related to *Cichorium intybus*, though the true endives are much older garden plants, extending through Rome and Greece to ancient India. These include the reliable Batavian escarole, a broad leaf green with creamy mild hearts, which I discuss in another chapter; the French frisee types such as Salad King, the well-known frilled curly endive widely adapted to three season culture; the similar Giant Fringe Oyster grown for late fall with large blanched centers; and tall endives such as Travista with large self-blanching heads, useful for specialty salads. (See ESCAROLE AND ENDIVE.)

Italian dandelions are best used young, after 30 days, for salads; mature leaves (50 days) can be steamed as greens with basil and olive oil. The old cultivar Magdeburgh or Sicilian chicory, with dandelion-like foliage, makes a fine salad. *Cicoria catalogna* or radichetta is more deeply indented, with whitish green petioles and bittersweet flavor. Magdeburgh roots can also be lightly roasted and ground and used as a coffee substitute. The old-fashioned French chicory (Pan de Sucre or Sugar Loaf), forms large romaine-like self-blanching heads with a creamy, mildly bitter heart. Dried ground up mature roots (100 days) can be used as a coffee substitute or mixed half and half with coffee.

Witloof Chicory

Witloof Chicory is grown like a root crop in summer, root cellared and then forced in tubs of sand to produce blanched Belgian endive. The resulting "chicons" are crispy and mildly bitter, but lack the vitamins of green salad. An indispensable ingredient in continental salad, they are sometimes steamed in gourmet dishes. The standard cultivar is Witloof Improved. New hybrid cultivars produce more uniform heads. Some can be forced without sand.

Witloof is grown and stored like carrots. After frost kills the leaves, roots are root cellared until needed for forcing. Chicons are usually forced by burying in damp sand in a dark warm cellar. Apple crates, wooden tubs or bushel baskets can be used. The root grows a torpedo-shaped shoot, 4 or 5 inches long depending on the size of the root, in about three weeks. Handle gently when removing from sand, especially for market. In Germany I observed the almost fanatic care workers took in harvesting these little blanched heads. When bruised, they turn a lovely, but unmarketable pink.

Radicchio

Radicchio is the chicory most altered from the wild, forming colorful maroon heads, a chicory version of red cabbage. Uniformity is highly variable. Up to 40% of plants revert to open or partially closed rosettes. Commercial growers consider 50% marketable heads acceptable. Round types (chioggia) vary enormously in size in the same sowing from baseball to bowling ball. Some older cultivars require cutting back prior to head formation. Most are bred for specific times of year. Some cultivars, such as Red Verona, produce romaine-shaped heads (trevisio), some of which are green. Older cultivars were sown at the same time as fall romaine. Rosettes were then cut back in early September for re-growth as heads. Cool temperatures increase color and sweetness.

For early crops choose varieties with high bolt resistance such as Chioggia Red Preco No 1. New hybrids of chioggio or trevisio types have a higher ratio of marketable heads and greater head uniformity, but taming wild variability has so far eluded breeders. Plant a variety of cultivars to determine what works for your climate. Some cultivars are better suited for spring or fall, but even three season cultivars will have to be tested.

Radicchio Culture

Older Italian cultivars were adapted to Mediterranean winters and produced heads by over wintering or by cutting back just above the growing point in late summer to force re-growth. Plants cut back in late summer will produce heads 4 to 6 weeks later. California Extension notes that growing radicchio on plastic significantly increases percentage of heads. Heading is generally better in cool autumn weather. Sow radicchio about 85 days before first frost. Spring sown seedlings may bolt if chilled below 50°F, and should not be set out until nights rise above 50°. Ideal nighttime temperature is 60° F. In fall after the plants are beginning to head or are already headed, moderate frost does not damage plants. Home gardeners can retrieve frozen heads, after the heads thaw late in the day.

Radicchio grows best under weather and growing conditions that favor the largest heads of lettuce: cool 50 to 60°F nights, with fertile loam; pH 6.5, with moderate compost. If kept watered, radicchio handles heat better than lettuce, but like lettuce, radicchio may bolt and leaves may burn and become more pungent under drought and heat stress. Under normal conditions, radicchio seems to tolerate less rainfall than lettuce. Like lettuce, radicchio germinates best at 75°F, but unlike lettuce, low night temperatures during the germination and seedling stage may also trigger bolting. Keep night temperatures above 50°F under glass and delay spring transplanting until weather settles.

First time growers may wish to start with a fall cultivar, when successful heading will be more likely. Otherwise, they can try several different cultivars in both spring and fall, observing soil type, fertilizing method, rainfall, irrigation needs and biodynamic amendments. Compare percentage of usable or marketable heads for each cultivar and conditions. Be sure not to confuse generic lack of uniformity with poor soil culture. Radicchio appreciates compost. Try new cultivars annually as these appear. New cultivars are bred for specific seasons, and as far as I know these seasons are in Europe, not North America.

Seed companies that conduct trials and/or report growers experience differ in their opinion whether radicchio heads more successfully direct seeded or transplanted. Johnny's Selected Seeds insists that transplants are reliable. Stokes catalog reports that direct seeded produces 20 percent more marketable heads. In my own limited experience both methods have produced uneven results.

For transplanting, sow radicchio directly in cells at two-week intervals (to offset changing environmental conditions). Bottom heat will improve germination, but day and night temperatures above 50°F are required. As with most members of the composite family, radicchio requires light to germinate. Cover lightly with 1/8-inch loam of sifted compost. Two weeks after germination fertilize with compost tea or liquid seaweed. Set in well-composted soil with good drainage after three or four weeks. Space as you would buttercrunch lettuce, 8 inches by 12 inches in beds or 8 by 18 inches in rows.

For direct-seeded crops sow in well-composted soil at the same time you direct seed fall lettuce—the end of June through July, depending on latitude. Sow 6 to 12 seeds per foot. Thin to 8 inches in the row. Apply biodynamic practices on a lettuce schedule.

Diseases and Pests

Technically chicory could be susceptible to diseases and insects of lettuce, which argues for at least a 3-year rotation, but chicories and dandelion are fairly problem free. In extended wet weather, bottom rot may be a problem. Choose resistant cultivars. Some cultivars are also subject to leaf tip burn. Slugs and snails need to be controlled with baited iron, especially when plants are gown tightly to force blanching. Radicchio is the most susceptible. Bottom rot begins as sunken lesions on the leaf stems and slimy rot closest to the ground, especially in wet weather. Rotate all lettuce family crops with other families such as onion, garlic, and corn. Tip burn is a disorder that becomes a disease. When hot dry weather follows wet weather or irrigation, too much water transpires from the leaves. Leaf edges become translucent and die and may become infected with soft rot bacteria. Choose resistant varieties. Maintain an even supply of water when conditions change abruptly.

Harvest heads when firm like head lettuce, usually beginning six weeks after transplanting. Heads mature unevenly over several weeks. Heads hold best in cool weather and can take light frost. Refrigerated heads keep up to a month in perforated plastic bags.

The seed and cultural indications below focus on radicchio. Seed for Italian dandelion is the same size as radicchio. Seed for Witloof is 33% larger. Adjust seeding accordingly.

> SEED: Radicchio Seed per ounce averages 20,000, slightly less seed per ounce than most lettuce seed. A packet of 100 seeds sows about 8 feet; 500 seeds sows 40 feet, 1,000 seeds sow 80 feet. An ounce sows 1,500 feet to 1,800 feet at 12 to fifteen seeds per foot. For transplants, calculate about 50% of seed sown. An ounce produces about 12,000 transplants.
>
> GERMINATION: 4 days at 75°F. Nights above 50°F.

VIABILITY: 4 to 8 years.

DAYS TO HARVEST: Approximately 70 to 85 days from seed.

MOON CALENDAR: All biodynamic sprays, and culture in leaf, especially ascending moon. For seed sowing, sow in leaf, cultivate and harvest in Leo.

ROTATION: 3 years between all composites.

BIODYNAMIC SPRAYS: Horn manure (500) on flat soil, seedbed and garden, also again in prolonged dry weather. Silica (501) when several true leaves appear, when plants have formed rosettes, and when plants begin to form heads. Equisetum (508) against damping off and bottom rot.

COMPANION PLANTS: Onion and carrot family. All chicories are an excellent subject for mixed plantings. Root environment stimulates earthworms and soil life.

CHINESE CABBAGE

In late November an Amish man backed his tractor-trailer up to my garden shed. I should say "former Amish man," since the Amish shun both trucks and the rototiller that he was delivering. I had no loading platform, so we first lowered the tiller by hand onto a pickup bed and then by ramp to the ground. All the while George Klinger, a handicapped man who worked with me, chattered non-stop to the driver in Dutch. George wasn't Amish, but throughout his youth, his relatives regularly hired him out to Amish farmers, and among the many things George learned from them was how to eat beet sandwiches. "A thick slice of boiled Lutz beet on fresh bread with butter—ooh that was good!" Neither of the men bothered to translate, but I did notice that the Amish man couldn't take his eyes off the vegetable garden. Against the general grays and browns of November, the Chinese cabbage stood out like a field of emeralds, a green seeming to glow almost supernaturally in the half-light of evening. Finally the driver turned to me and spoke in Amish-accented English: "That's an organic garden, isn't it?"

"Biodynamic," I replied, and described a bit what biodynamics is about. He nodded, and I could see him measuring with regret the life he had left behind. "The chemical gardens are dead at this time of year," he said. And then added, "They don't last." Then he fell silent for a very long time, just staring at the bright green as if hypnotized. His silence seemed to be re-considering our whole civilization.

Since that day I celebrate the bright green of Chinese cabbage as a festival for a saint no longer in fashion; a festival for cool autumn days with low light levels. Chinese cabbage may not be as hardy or store as well as its European cousin, but it has the advantage of coming up quickly just after the dead heat of midsummer, which is so hard on the Europeans. Chinese cabbage can be sown as much as 2 months later (July 15 in Zone 6), and still out-produce the Europeans two to one.

Chinese cabbage is also a better succession crop, simply because it does not tie up the ground for such a long period of time. It does what it does without hesitation. Contrary to some seed catalog info, it can be transplanted quite easily; therefore, a seedbed sowing on July 15 does not need to occupy garden ground until August 15. In fact it grows so quickly that transplants are often ready in 3½ weeks. Longer than 4 weeks triggers bolting.

In taste, Chinese cabbage is lighter, sweeter, and more delicately flavored than its European cousins. Although it lacks the intense concentration of nutrients found in its open-leaved *Brassica rapa* brethren, its freshness and crispness have become indispensable in salads and nearly instant stir-fries.

Culture

Although Chinese cabbage is vigorous, it prefers rich soil, preferably clay loam, composted as heavily as any other brassica. Chinese cabbage grown with biodynamic compost sometimes elicits no interest from insects, even the flea beetle. Sandy soils, however, are a losing battle, especially in mid-August. Even with row cover to protect from flea beetle, the plants head poorly. As a stop-gap, home gardeners with inadequate supplies of compost, or with lean sandy soil, can compost transplants individually with a grapefruit-sized lump at planting time, although long-term plants grow better with well incorporated compost. Chinese cabbage requires a soil pH between 6 and 7, with ample soil calcium. Remember that most diseases left over from previous brassica crops can infect Chinese cabbage. Rotate on a three-year schedule. Biodynamic growers spray soil with horn manure (500) the autumn before, and again in the spring. Chinese cabbage is not tolerant of dry spells; plan for irrigation.

Spring sowings of Chinese cabbage must be handled more carefully than any other crop. Choose bolt-resistant varieties especially bred for spring. Seedlings of any variety may bolt if sown too thickly, left un-watered in the flat, exposed to frost in a cold frame, chilled below 50°F for a week or more, or transplanted bare root. Spring seedlings should be sown directly in peat pots, cells, or plug cells, 4 weeks before the last spring frost; earlier only if transplants will be protected by heavy row cover. Seedlings can be watered with alfalfa tea, compost/nettle tea, or liquid seaweed once or twice in the greenhouse. Plants require bright light. Transplant after last frost date, without disturbing roots, 12 inches apart with 18 to 24 inches between rows. Keep them well watered. Protect against flea beetle with floating row covers. Row covers also deter root maggots. Alternately, a layer of wood ash or ground lime 6 inches around the base of plants also prevents flies from laying root maggot eggs. Biodynamic growers spray with horn silica (501) when transplants become established, and several times during the rosette stage.

Chinese Cabbage

In fall, with declining day length and cooler temperatures, Chinese cabbage heads more surely. For an autumn harvest, sow in flats, cells, pots, or directly in the garden from early June to late July, depending on latitude. Plants are stressed least and head most quickly when sown directly into large cells or peat pots, 2 to 3 seeds per pot, thinned to the one most vigorous.

For many years I sowed my fall crop in July in an outdoor seedbed (20 seeds to the foot, ¼ inch deep, 6 inches between rows). After 4 weeks I transplanted them semi-bare root into the garden and watered them twice a day until they perked up. None ever bolted; all headed well. Flea beetles were at a low point at that time of year. I know this is "Old School," but certainly for home and small market gardeners this is still the cheapest and least resource-intensive method. I also prefer transplanting of some sort to direct seeding because direct seeding is vulnerable to crusting, uneven stands, flea beetles, poor spacing, and weeds. In cool moist areas not prone to crusting, direct seeding might work well if precision-seeded 3 to 5 seeds per foot, and skim-weeded promptly and tight to the row following emergence.

Transplant from seedbeds or cells after 4 weeks (not much longer), preferably on a cloudy day, a rainy day, or late afternoon, especially if the weather is hot and dry. Cells and pots suffer far less transplant shock, but be prepared with irrigation and row covers for drought and flea beetles. Once plants are established and heat subsides, flea beetle damage diminishes. Set plants 12 inches to 18 inches apart: 12 inches for Michihli and smaller hybrids; 18 inches for the broader Wong bok and Napa types; 18 to 24 inches between rows. Unlike European brassicas, set plants no deeper than they grew in the seedbed, cell, or pot. The growing point is close to the ground, so do not throw soil against the plants, as you might with cabbage or broccoli. Cultivate by skimming very shallowly. Irrigate if August and September are dry. Chinese cabbage likes water.

Biodynamic growers spray silica (501) when rosette spreads, and just as rosette condenses into head. Mulch is excellent for this crop, especially if planted in beds rather than field rows. Cabbage worms usually do not care for Chinese cabbage, but use Bt if they appear. Grasshoppers have been a problem for me on hybrids only. Michihli was never touched.

Harvest can take place whenever the heads are firm. You can judge density by gently squeezing at the top of the head. Sowings timed to head in mid-autumn will not bolt, and so can be left until just before damaging frost. Light frost does not hurt the heads. If they freeze slightly, do not cut while frozen.

Left alone, they will often be in good shape for an afternoon harvest. Chinese cabbage stores fairly well, though not as well as European cabbage. In a cold to near-freezing root cellar, it will keep well through December. I've even eaten Michihili in February. Stack the heads three deep or stand them vertically in boxes with no roots attached. Heads keep even longer under refrigeration, some quite usable at the beginning of March. My parents kept some Michihili I gave them in an old basement refrigerator all winter, and said they were quite fresh tasting even in April.

Varieties

Because of day length and the possibility of bolting, varieties of Chinese cabbage are carefully selected for season of harvest. Only bolt-resistant strains can be spring sown for summer harvest. Strains that lack bolt-resistance are sown in July after the sun begins to descend. A few varieties are tolerant of both seasons.

Unless you live in a region with cool moist summers, open-pollinated Napa cabbages are difficult to grow from an early spring sowing. O.P. Honshu forms a compact 9-inch barrel with the exceptionally tender cream-colored interior typical of Napa types.

Wong Bok (80 days) tends toward more open growth. 10- by 6-inch heads are variable and require a long season. With tangy flavor for salads and stir-fry, Wong Bok is usually sown in July for autumn harvest.

Many Napa hybrids have exceptional disease resistance, and are for sowing early spring through July. Jazz (65 days) is tolerant to virus, bacterial soft rot, alternaria leaf spot, and even some races of club root. Jazz has excellent quality, is very slow bolting, and is tolerant to midsummer heat. Stores up to 2 months if kept cold. The smaller Minuet (48 days), also highly disease-resistant, can be packed 12 inches in the row. Very slow bolting, with exceptional flavor. The large Bilko is not as tasty but is widely adaptable, with resistance to club root, fusarium yellows, and black speck.

Open-pollinated Michihili (78 days) produces very tall slender heads, 18 inches by 4 inches, with good uniformity and sure heading. Leaves are dark green, crisp, tender, and tightly folded, with excellent sweet flavor. Sow in mid-July for fall harvest with storage into late December, if kept close to freezing, 33°F. Granat (60 days), a slender variety of Chinese cabbage bred in Europe with very fine flavor, is another open-pollinated variety suitable for limited winter storage.

Hybrid Michihili is uniform, sure heading, and high yielding. Jade Pagoda (72 days) produces high yields of tall, elegant, medium green heads, 16 by 6 inches, and is tolerant to black speck, bacterial soft rot, and virus; vigorous and slow bolting. Greenwich, a beautiful dark green 14-inch hybrid Michihili, is also slow bolting, with resistance to bottom rot and black speck, and strong tolerance to tip burn.

SEED: Seeds per ounce about 9,000. A packet of 100 seeds produces about 35 transplants or 35 feet of row. An ounce of seed produces 6,500 transplants or will direct seed about 3,000 feet at 3 seeds per foot.

GERMINATION: 75%; 10 days at 70°F.

VIABILITY: At least 3 years.

DAYS TO HARVEST: 75 days.

MOON CALENDAR: All cultural practices in leaf, including biodynamic sprays. For seed, sow in spring in leaf; cultivate in fruit, especially in Leo; and harvest seed in Leo.

ROTATION: 3 to 6 years between brassicas, depending on disease build-up and crucifer rotation.

BIODYNAMIC SPRAYS: Horn manure (500) in seedbed and field. Silica (501) after transplants are established, at rosette stage and at beginning of head formation. Silica on heads at maturity for storage crops.

COMPANION PLANTS: Precede with early peas, early bush beans, broad beans, and early beets. Interplant with *umbelliferous* plants such as dill, caraway, coriander, carrots, chervil, or among celery or celeriac; also the onion family. For insect pests, interplant with pungent herbs such as wormwood, sage, tansy, catnip, rosemary, and southernwood.

CORN

Corn is everywhere. It is so commonplace that its true identity is invisible. No one notices that corn, as a phenomenon, is so uncanny it must be a folktale. Think about it. Corn originally meant "grain." Grains are tiny; they are seeds. Seeds are condensations of a "type" shrunk into a dot of matter. I once tore open the wall of a house built before 1750 and found corncobs not much bigger than Bic lighters! Those cobs were so tiny, they almost looked like giant ears of wheat.

Leo Tolstoy tells a folktale about grains the size of a hen's egg. The Czar rubs his beard and thinks how well such grains would feed his troops. He calls before him a decrepit old peasant—blind, toothless, and lame. Yes, the peasant had heard of such grains, but only in his grandfather's day! The corns were as big as hen's eggs. So the Czar, who can order the earth to stand still, commands a still older peasant to appear, who walks in without a limp and still has all his teeth. Yes, he too has heard of such corn, but only when he was a small boy. So the Czar sends emissaries far and wide, until they find the oldest peasant in Russia. This peasant not only has teeth, but also fire in his eye. He strides through the palace, as straight and tall as a cavalry officer. "Corn like this used to grow everywhere!" he says. "We lived on corn like this and had enough to give it to others. We knew nothing of money. No one thought of buying and selling. My field was God's earth. With every generation the corn has shrunk, because men have ceased to live by their own labor and now depend on the labor of others."

When I read this folktale, I thought of maize.* Were maize as rare as Tolstoi's corn, folktales would be written about it, and nobody would believe a word of it. An ear of field corn is more than thirty times larger than an ear of wheat. If you had described such ears to a Russian peasant, described a field of grain with stalks as thick as water pipes and leaves broader than swords, he would have called you a dreamer and gone back to his plowing.

---

* Maize was the original word for our American corn. In Europe "corn" means the seed of any grain plant, but in the United States maize corn became the household bread of poor farmers, right into the twentieth century. For them it was the only corn.

He would not have believed you, because the genetic history of maize reads like fantasy. Otherwise how can a grass, belonging to a thin vertical tribe whose fruits as a rule are very small, produce a fruit so lush it is eaten like a vegetable? No other plant in the grass family produces a fruit anything like it. Nor is anything like maize found in the wild today. The problem is simple enough for botanists. They explain the leap from a small wild grass to an ear as big as a club by saying "the mutations did it." But why is maize the only grain naturally subject to these mutations? Why did it leap so willingly from form to form, growing larger and starchier over the millennia? Why not rice or rye? Why is it still so changeable today, so eager and malleable in the hands of geneticists that it jumps like a genie into soda bottles and bio-diesel fuel? Whatever else it is, maize is certainly the greatest example of metamorphosis in the history of agriculture. In the end, the Czar got just what he wanted!

Representations of an extinct small pod corn can be found on ancient Peruvian pottery, showing each kernel still enclosed in a separate husk. But the progenitor of maize became extinct so long ago that even the Indians have lost the name for it. After this *ur*-maize abandoned its husk "by mutation," it crossed with a distant relative of maize, *Tripsacum*, producing *Teosinte*, which does not look like corn either. *Teosinte* re-crossed with *ur*-maize, mutating, and eventually producing flint and dent corn, the maize that sustained Native Americans for millennia. However, these leaps are so fantastical that one might just as well believe the Native American version that corn was wrestled from the body of a spirit being. Many Native Americans must have been midwives to the birth of corn, observing, collecting, evaluating, selecting and perpetuating.* Who knows? Maybe behind the mystery stands a prehistoric breeder who would make Luther Burbank look like an amateur.

Maize must be inherently suited to mutation. As a grain it must exist in an entirely different category from wheat or rice, but its inherent plasticity had

---

* The original forms of corn seem to have a high protein content and a hard starch. The hardest is popcorn (*Zea Mays Everta*). The second hardest is flint corn (*Zea Mays Indurata*), which is all hard except for the center. It is relatively high in protein and is used for cornmeal and tortillas. Original types include the enormously variable Indian corn, whose various forms and colors (red, tawny, calico, blue, and black) still possess the genetic abundance that modern strains have lost. In dent corn (*Zea Mays Indentata*), the entire crown is composed of soft starch. This is the largest type and the most widely grown. It is used almost exclusively for fodder and silage. There is still another type called soft corn (*Zea Mays Amylacea*) used for corn flour. Sweet corn (*Zea Mays Saccharata*) includes several types that do not develop starch so quickly or so abundantly. Sweet corns are selected for high sugar content and more recently for special sugar genes.

never struck me so forcefully as it did one day when I was examining corn smut, a grotesque fungal disease of corn. This disfiguring fungus shines a strange light on corn plasticity. It seems uncanny the way the kernel seems to flow out of itself in huge grey swirls. The kernel loses control of itself, loses all form and spills out like molten batter, glistening silver and strangely metallic as moonlight. At that moment I was reminded of Johann von Goethe's remark that plant aberrations often reveal the archetype. Time and again Goethe observed how a plant's response to abnormal conditions often expresses the most significant formative gesture of the plant. Suddenly I realized that in corn smut I was not seeing the *usual* magic of plant growth. I was not seeing the elements rush together from the four points of the compass to form the kernel. In corn smut that magical process was flowing in reverse, unraveling the golden wires of sunlight into a river of silver metal, spilling, exhausted, into a black earthen pool.

I realize that other grains are also subject to disfiguring fungi, such as the ergot of rye, but maize as a genus seems to flirt with the boundaries of form. Corn seems ever ready to take up too much from its environment, swelling to its limit and beyond, until its cells glisten, like an overfed child. Corn swells to the point of bursting, whether by mutation, the manipulations of a geneticist, the intrusion of a fungus, or the addition of too much fertilizer. I wonder where the center of this grain lies, so inclined to one-sided traits of size and sweetness; a grain that apart from its blessings lies at the root of overproduction and agricultural pollution in the West.

In a grain such as rice, the grain of the East, air travels down hollow stems into the water. Rice seeds are open and airy, dancing above the water on rivulets of air, even appearing to dance rhythmically in the structure of the panicle. In maize, the grain of the West, vast amounts of water flow up the stem, like a water pipe. Corn kernels themselves are closed off from the air and swollen with liquid almost to bursting, touching the air only umbilically through the silk.

One consequence of exchanging an individual bran surrounding each grain for naked swollen kernels surrounded by an umbilical husk is the loss of the B vitamins found in the bran. People dependent on maize, especially in Africa, where maize has been introduced relatively recently, suffer from the severe B vitamin deficiency called pellagra. In Central America, natives learned to combine corn with beans to compensate for this deficiency. Steamed sweet corn provides some vitamins A, E, and C, although I think no one chews the kernels enough to get full benefit from them. As a garden crop, I recommend corn as a delicious candy.

Maize takes on more weight, water, and carbohydrates than any other grain. Maize has become the darling of industrial exploitation of the earth. As much fertilizer as water now courses through the veins of maize. In European farmlands where fertilizers have saturated the water table, maize is used as a sponge to mop up the mess. In other places, maize is part of the problem.

Corn continues to be the impressionable child in the history of agriculture, putty in the hands of those who may or may not have the best interests of the earth at heart. In a future court of law, one with more far-sighted standards than our own, a strong case may even be made for the agricultural equivalent of child abuse. We will feel particularly guilty when we discover someday how those plastic, magical, malleable forces were really meant to be used. Of course, in such a trial, it will be hard to know whom to blame, since as the predator we suffer from our own shrinking predatory base.

Culture

Almost any good soil will grow corn, as long as compost, warmth, and water are available. A medium clay loam with high organic matter is ideal, only slightly acid, pH 6 to 6.8. Sandy loam warms up fastest for early crops. Compost by itself (depending on quality) produces good ears, but side-dressings increase yields substantially, especially for modern hybrids. Sugary, enhanced, and supersweet types may require additional fertilizer for good tip fill, requiring about twice the nitrogen as potassium and phosphorus. An organic 8-6-4 can be applied after plants are about 18 inches tall (at 12 inches, corn may suffer physiological stress). Southern Exposure Seed Exchange notes that old Southwestern Indian varieties grow in association with particular *mycorrhizae*, which makes roots 10 times more efficient in extracting soil nutrients. That may be a piece of the future coming from the past.

Corn land should be sprayed with horn manure (500) both the fall before and again in the spring. For extra-early crops, leave some ground with no fall cover crop, otherwise too much fresh organic matter will be left in the soil, causing the seeds to rot.

Deeply prepared soils allow roots to go more deeply early in the season and compensate for low supplies of water later on. Deeply prepared beds that are mulched often produce well in the driest seasons, even without irrigation, and they provide better tip fill and flavor. For an extra-early gambler's crop use only finished compost, directly on the seed. In extra-early crops, organic matter invites rot and pests on untreated seed. Choose varieties that will germinate at 55°F and consider Natural II organic seed treatment. Most varieties need a soil temperature of 65°F to get off to a good start. For untreated seed, pre-heat the soil with black plastic or wait for warmer weather.

Farmers of old never planted corn until they felt comfortable sitting on the soil with their pants down. I heard this first-hand from an old New Hampshire farmer who did it every spring. Others more modest wait until oak leaves are the size of mouse ears. However, a touch of frost on early seedlings will not kill them, as long as they have not been pushed by high nitrogen fertilizer. For gambling crops, side-dress with a lower nitrogen 4-6-4 organic fertilizer after plants are established (4 inches).

When sowing, try not to leave seed corn exposed on the soil surface. Crows are smart. They'll dig up the whole block. Home gardeners can deter birds by stretching two strings 1 inch apart, 2 inches high over the furrow, or roll chicken wire over the entire block. Seeds can also be protected with row cover, which can stay on until leaves press against the fabric.

Native Americans planted corn in hills along with pole beans and winter squash; this is easiest for dry corn, shell beans, and winter squash, which can be left fairly undisturbed until harvest. What I don't understand is how Indians dealt with raccoons if they used fish fertilizer. I stopped using it years ago. Raccoons tore up the beds looking for fish. I couldn't even harvest corn until I got a varmint dog.

Because corn is wind pollinated, plant in blocks of at least 4 rows, 30 to 36 inches apart. Sow 3 seeds to the foot, 1 inch deep, ¾ inch for supersweet. Thin to one strong plant to the foot, 6 inches in extremely fertile soil. In larger areas, sowing rates may have to be adjusted, depending upon soil type, crusting, and available moisture. For later sowings when the ground is warm (90°F) corn can be sown shallowly and the entire corn block covered with 2 inches of mulch. As the corn reaches above the mulch, more mulch can be applied up to 6 inches. Mulched blocks bear well without water in dry seasons.

Biodynamic growers apply silica spray (501) as soon as corn leaves curl downward. Silica can be sprayed at other nodal points in corn's growth: when it forms a full sheaf of leaves, at sucker and tassel formation, and when ears just begin to be visible. Other sprays that are useful for corn are fermented nettle and liquid seaweed, both of which are stimulant as well as directly nutritive. In areas where corn smut has been a problem, regular spraying of equisetum tea is helpful before smut appears. Corn smut is the grey, ugly, but quite edible fungus that makes the corn kernels look so grotesque. It should be removed early on, before its seed spores spread over the soil. The spores remain viable up to five years.

Corn pests vary from region to region; only a few will be mentioned. Home gardeners can control corn earworm by squirting a few drops of mineral oil into the silk of each developing ear. In severe outbreaks, spray Dipel, which is sprayed in the silk several times after the worm appears. Corn borers are often hard to control, but some growers spray pyrethrins (late in the day to avoid beneficials) into the crown and leaf-axils at 4-day intervals after the borers appear. Yellow stripes on corn leaves from late June into July may be caused by Stewart's wilt, transmitted by flea beetles. Choose wilt-resistant varieties in catalogs, and provide strong organic culture for the crop with ample water, side-dressings of liquid seaweed, and so forth. Rotate crops, with three years between plantings.

Raccoons are the bane of sweet corn lovers, especially near wooded areas. The only sure protection is electric fence, 3 strands at 4-inch intervals from the ground. Some gardeners have kept coons out with continuous replaying of ranting talk shows, but talk can never be relied upon. Raccoons know better than people just when to harvest sweet corn. A good dog is often the best solution. Animal repellents don't work in high-pressure areas. Birds can be kept off corn in home gardens by placing 16-inch paper bags over the ears a week before harvest.

Harvest begins at the milk stage, roughly 18 to 24 days after half the ears show silk. When the silks begin to turn brown, open a few ears and check kernel size. Press your fingernail into a kernel. If milk squirts out, the ears are ready to harvest. Varieties differ in how quickly they turn to the dough stage, when the sugar turns to starch. Supersweets and sugar-enhanced types hold longest in the field. Others have narrower harvest windows. For processing, the kernels should be large enough to cut easily off the cob in the early milk stage for O.P. and normal hybrids; more mature for sugary, enhanced, and supersweet.

Corn for seed, meal, or dry feed should be sprayed with silica (501) once when the ears are forming, and again as the ears are ripening. Sweet corn can also be ground for cornmeal, but is not as starchy as flint, which in this case is desirable. Meal and seed corn should be crackling dry before harvest and must be cured for a month in a warm, dry place before shelling. Dry corn keeps best on the cob, since shelling injuries to the kernels pave the way for aflatoxin, which is caused by a fungus. Aflatoxins on damp cracked corn are a leading cause of animal illness and early death. Aflatoxins cause damage to human organs as well.

Varieties

Indian flint and dent have survived as ornamental corn. In Rainbow Inca or modern Earth Tones Dent (90 days) and Underwoods Ornamental (100 days) you can find an entire rainbow: blue-black, purple, blue, magenta, red, green, brown, tan, yellow, and white, another testimony to corn's astonishing plasticity. Indian heirlooms are mostly single colors: dark red (Blood Butcher, 120 days), blue-black (Black Iroquois sold as Black Mexican, 76 days for sweet corn), and yellowish-greenish blue (Oaxacan Green, 95 days). Tennessee Red Cob (100 days, used to support pole beans) and many cultivars from the western reservations (see Seed Savers Exchange) produce full cobs with very little water. For polenta with a pink cast and rich complex flavor try Floriani Red Flint (100 days), an Indian corn bred for centuries in Italy. Flint and dent corns are grown to maturity and left to dry until after a few frosts. Kept dry, they can be ground coarsely for grits or fine for flour.

For most gardeners, however, the main event is sweet corn, where varieties proliferate like fruit flies and disappear just as quickly. Breeders are constantly toying with the cloud of qualities that make sweet corn, triggering one trait at the expense of another and floating their creations before the public; these sometimes catch a current, but just as often sink out of sight.

The sheer number of constantly changing varieties is both an opportunity and a problem. Unlike the case with broccoli, you can't simply try five different varieties per bed. Wind pollinated plants require a minimum of 4 to 6 rows 15 feet long, of a single variety. And the new supersweets don't tolerate companions at all, unless the second is another supersweet. When cross-pollinated in the field by an open-pollinated corn or another kind of hybrid, supersweets revert to field corn quality at harvest.

Best to pore over seed catalogs with more care than ever, noting every wanted and unwanted trait. That's a problem, since seed catalogs are not *Consumer's Report*. Seed exchange catalogs such as from Southern Exposure and Seed Savers Exchange are informative for open-pollinated strains and give a broad picture of the species. Also useful are catalogs written especially for growers, such as Stokes, Johnny's, and Harris, which detail more accurately the advantages and pitfalls of each variety.

Corn traits are divided roughly between those helpful to growers and those appreciated by consumers. Horticultural traits to consider include: 1) cold soil germination (55°F); 2) range of suitable latitude for a variety; 3) adaptation to environmental stress (in some varieties changes of weather affect quality and yield); 4) disease resistance; 5) ease of harvest; 6) how easily the corn pulls off the stalk; 7) tightness of husks (which keep out ear worms and birds); and 8) yield. Equally important are traits affecting eating quality. These include: 1) traditional corn taste; 2) brix (sweetness); 3) holding sweetness in the field and after harvest; 4) tenderness; and 5) crisp texture. These traits are rarely if ever found all at once in a single variety.

Open-pollinated seed is the only kind that can be saved by the home gardener. Standard open-pollinated (O.P.) corn is lowest in sugar of the sweet corn types; but harvested exactly at early milk stage and steamed immediately, it has good sweetness and traditional corn taste. Once mature, standard corn does not hold long in the field, but its lack of uniform ripening also means that harvest is staggered. Although standard sweet corn is less greedy for fertilizer than hybrids, it requires larger blocks of 5 to 6 rows for good pollination and appreciates plenty of compost for plump sweet kernels.

Country Gentleman (93 days), which I knew as Shoepeg as a child, covered thousands of acres and filled the Maryland canning factories, where I worked one summer. Rows of black women stripped kernels off the cobs, corn juice in turn stripping the skin off their hands, their feet surrounded by piles of fermenting cobs rank as vomit. The stench was surpassed only by the tomato cannery six miles down the road. Nevertheless, we found Shoepeg sweet and flavorful in the milk stage, which held in the field longer than other O.P. sweet corns. I was also fascinated by the irregular kernels that were not in rows like other corn. Shoepeg is adapted from the mid-Atlantic north to the Hudson Valley. Stowell's Evergreen (98 days), which can be traced back to Native American stock, also holds longer in the milk stage, adapted to the mid-Atlantic States, and south through Virginia.

Black Mexican (76 days) was apparently misnamed back in the nineteenth century; it actually it descends from a black Iroquois flint corn. Black Mexican has exceptional flavor when eaten at the milk stage, before the kernels turn blue-black. Golden Bantam (78 days) is a relatively recent Massachusetts variety. It was introduced by Burpee in 1902, and is still sold in their catalog. The small golden-yellow ears need to be harvested very early in the milk stage.

Not only has O.P. corn virtually disappeared from seed catalogs, but also the "normal" hybrid has, designated in catalogs as SU. One of the last holdouts is Silver Queen (91 days), still popular for classic corn flavor if harvested and eaten the day it is picked. Normal SU hybrids must be isolated from all other kinds of corn by 100 feet. Sugar content and holding have been far surpassed by sugar-enhanced, supersweet, and synergistic varieties.

Sugar-enhanced corn (SE and SE+) is created by including a modifying gene to increase sugar content and tenderness, and to slow the conversion of sugar into starch (holding capacity). Corn flavor is good. SE alone means that an SE gene has been crossed with a normal SU hybrid for better corn flavor; it is 20% sweeter than normal hybrids. SE+ means that both parents were SE, making a "fully sugar-enhanced" corn even more tender and twice as sweet as normal hybrids, with much better holding in the field. SE and SE+ types can be grown together, but isolate them from all other corn by 100 feet (some breeders insist 250 feet). Otherwise, time the maturity dates of different corn types to be 2 weeks apart, to thwart wind cross-pollination, which ruins quality.

Standard supersweet corn has a shrunken (SH2) gene, which dramatically increases sugar content (it is many times sweeter than other corns); and just as dramatically slows the conversion of sugar to starch. This means incredible holding capacity in the field and post-harvest. After a week in the fridge, supersweet still tastes fresh; it is still good in soups two weeks later. Kernel texture is crisp and crunchy, which many people like, but the earliest varieties were not high in classic corn taste. My family thought of them as absolutely delicious candy, and the crisp kernels are terrific frozen. "Augmented supersweets" have the sugar-enhanced (SE) gene added to the supersweet (SH2) gene, adding tenderness and more corn flavor.

Supersweets require warm soil to germinate: 65°F if treated with organic Natural II, or 75°F if untreated. Shrunken seeds are smaller, making seed count higher and planting depth shallower (3/4 to 1 inch). Optimal harvest date will be 1½ to 3 weeks after half the ears show silk. Both augmented and standard supersweets must be isolated (100 to 250 feet) from all other corn types, lest kernels be reduced to field corn quality. Otherwise, avoid cross-pollination by staggering maturity dates 2 weeks apart.

Synergistic (SY) varieties combine sugar-enhanced (SE) and shrunken (SU) genes differently than the augmented. About 75% of the kernels on a cob are SE while 25% are SH2. The result is increased tenderness, better germination, and greater vigor. Synergistic types are compatible only with sugar-enhanced

(SE) corn, but not with other supersweets (SH2), O.P. sweet corn, popcorn, field, or ornamental corn. Planting with normal SU hybrids won't ruin SY, but may affect quality. When using incompatible types, stagger maturity dates 2 weeks apart, to avoid cross-pollination. Synergistic corn develops sweetness during the mature milk stage. Immature kernels taste watery.

The sheer number and changeability of sugary, sugar-enhanced, supersweet, and synergistic corn make recommendations impossible. Make a list of the traits that you require and search for varieties that fit: cool soil germination for early crops; wide adaptability, crispness, tenderness (too tender won't ship); good husk and tip cover; ease of harvest, and so forth. All of them are sweet enough, but look for a balance of sweetness with traditional corn flavor.

SEED: Seed per ounce, 150 to 275 (Supersweet seeds are smallest); seed per lb. 2,500 up to 5,000. 2 ounces (300 seeds) sows 4 rows, 25 feet long at 3 seeds per foot; or 4 rows, 35 feet long at 2 seeds per foot. A pound (2,500 seeds) will sow 6 rows, 200 feet long at 2 seeds per foot.

GERMINATION: 75 percent ; minimum soil temperature 55°F; optimal temperature 65°F or higher for untreated seed in early spring.

VIABILITY: 3 years.

DAYS TO HARVEST: 55 to 95 days.

MOON CALENDAR: All cultural practices, including biodynamic sprays in fruit, especially in Leo.

ROTATION: 3 years between crops; 5 years on smut-infected land.

BIODYNAMIC SPRAYS: Horn manure (500) before sowing and during drought. Silica (501) when plants are established, at sucker and tassel formation; seed and storage corn can be sprayed again as ears are maturing. Valerian (507) can be sprayed in extended cloudy weather with silica (501).

COMPANION PLANTS: All legumes, both bush and pole, especially shell beans and cowpeas. All *cucurbits*, melon, pumpkin, squash. Purslane should not be weeded out; leave pigweed and amaranth in limited amount, without letting too many of these weeds go to seed.

CUCUMBER

A disciple of the great English gardener Alan Chadwick once showed me how to construct a cucumber mound. It was not quite as large as the Indian burial mound in Ohio, but it did involve digging a pit big enough to bury a half barrel. At the bottom, about three feet down, he placed a thick 10-inch layer of sticks, stones, and forest litter. This was followed by successive layers of compost, lime, leaf mold, and soil; then coarse compost, followed by finer compost mixed with soil, until the pit had risen high—15 inches higher than the surrounding garden.

Why do this? Why do I still recommend a very modified version of this for home gardeners thirty years later? Because it works! Chadwick's French Intensive Method originated in market gardens around Paris in the nineteenth century, and specialized in getting extraordinary yields in limited space. And that's what a cucumber mound should do. I've used a modified version for cucumbers and for a half-acre of squash for years, and I can tell you it really pays—in size, color, yield, and taste. It pays because, unlike other methods, it provides a deep reservoir that backs up the crop throughout the season. Roots quickly go deeper. They establish strong plants before the onslaught of insects. They remain almost drought-proof. They produce longer, and with less water than irrigated crops.

The Chadwick method addresses all the conditions required by cucumber. The high mound warms up early in spring. It is rich in organic matter and compost. It contains lime, and its pH tends toward neutral. It provides perfect drainage, even in prolonged wet weather. Once the roots have reached the depths of the easily permeated well, it provides a steady supply of nutrients and moisture, even during drought. Time lost in mound construction is gained in minimal irrigation, greater vigor (and therefore disease resistance), and higher yield—much, much, higher yield.

My modified version of Chadwick's urn burial works almost as well, and it also takes less time. I remove a disc of topsoil about 30 inches across, 9 inches deep, piling the topsoil to one side. I excavate a 2- by 2-foot hole, 1 foot deep, and pile that subsoil on the opposite side. I back-fill the subsoil mixed with a few shovelfuls of half-rotted organic matter, usually half-rotted hardwood leaves. I put back the topsoil, mixed with 2 heaping shovelfuls of compost.

I suppose cucumbers are so fragile because we grow them so far from their place of origin, the warm valleys of India between the Bay of Bengal and the foothills of the Himalayas. Cucumbers are one of the oldest garden vegetables; their history disappears into prehistory more than 3,000 years ago. They were grown for thousands of years before most of the world knew what a garden is. In fact, cucumber is so old that its wild ancestor became extinct in prehistoric times. By the dawn of written history, cucumber had reached China and Italy, where the Romans even grew forced cukes out of season. (The Emperor Tiberius had to have cucumbers for lunch every day of the year.) Columbus planted cukes in Haiti in 1494, and by 1539 Desoto reported that Florida natives were growing cucumbers better than those of Spain.[*]

Culture

With all of the cucumber, melon, and squash family (the *cucurbitae*), the size and quality of the crop depend upon the health of the leaves and vines. Hence the deep mound. Leaves must grow quickly and suffer no early checks in growth from striped or spotted cucumber beetles and the wilt they transmit. The plants never recover from early damage to leaves. The white powder of two fungus diseases, downy and powdery mildew, obstruct photosynthesis and reduce yield. Use potassium bicarbonate or biofungicide for control. The dark green outer skin of the cucumber is actually a green leaf wrapping around the fruit, a continuation of the health and functioning of the leaves themselves. To stimulate leaf growth, use half-ripe compost in the cucumber hills. Biodynamic growers cultivate and spray silica (501) and equisetum (508) on leaf days. Leaves benefit from liquid seaweed and nettle or alfalfa tea.

To prevent damage from cucumber beetles (which also transmit bacterial wilt), use row cover. Home gardeners sometimes make cages out of old fly screen. Both should be wide enough for vines to grow several feet in all directions before removal. Bury edges to keep beetles out.

For extra-early crops, cucumbers must be sown under glass 4 to 5 weeks before the last frost date in spring. Biodynamic cultural practices are similar for muskmelons, watermelons, and squash. Since cukes cannot be pricked

---

[*] *The World in Your Garden*, Camp et al., National Geographic Society.

out, use 3-inch peat pots, 3 seeds to the pot, each filled with sifted compost and sandy loam, half and half. Germinate at 75°F soil temperature and keep day temperatures above 70°F, at night above 60°F. Plants may elongate as they struggle for light, get checked in growth, and later become sunburned outside, which causes them to fail. Thin the weakest of the three seedlings. Commercial potting mixes can be improved with compost or fermented nettle or seaweed tea after the true leaf appears. Biodynamic growers spray with silica (501) and equisetum weekly. When transplanting, don't break out the bottom of the pot. Cucumbers don't tolerate root disturbance. If the season is cooler than normal, pre-warm the soil with black plastic at least a week before setting out. The shock of cold soil and bright sun can cut production in half. Cool nights cause blossom drop. Protect extra-early crops with heavy row covers or hot caps. Wire screen cages for insect control can also be covered with slatted plastic to increase temperature. Cucumber beetles are most intense in early summer, from June 15 to July 15 in New England. Unprotected transplants can be sprayed with a neem preparation before setting in the field, and then sprayed weekly until vines began to run.

On a field scale, row covers are the only pesticide-free solution, especially when direct-seeding. Some of the benefits of mound preparation can be achieved by creating well-composted raised rows. For good germination, soil temperature must be above 65°F, best between 70 and 80°F. Seed rots below 50°F. In cool spring weather, black plastic can be set out two weeks in advance of sowing to warm the soil for cucumber and melons. If possible choose a well-drained sandy loam with a southern exposure.

For unprotected direct-seeding wait until 2 weeks after the last spring frost. Note that for every region there is an optimal time for outdoor cucumber seeding, which allows unprotected seedlings a bit of a start before the cucumber beetle breeding onslaught begins. Plant seeds 2 to 3 inches apart, ½ inch deep in rows 6 feet apart. Thin to 9 to 12 inches between plants. Obviously, denser sowings require more fertilizer. Biodynamic silica sprays can continue after true leaves develop through first fruit set. When using open-pollinated or susceptible varieties, spray equisetum and potassium bicarbonate at first sight of whitish mildew. Bees improve fruit set. Commercial growers provide one beehive per acre. When affected by drought, cucumbers will be stunted and short. Remove all the short fruit and irrigate for the new fruit set.

Cucumbers can be harvested and eaten at all stages of maturity prior to yellowing, although eating quality varies from variety to variety. Burpee Pickler, for example, is surprisingly good even when far beyond pickle stage. Optimum size for thin-skinned hybrids is 4 to 5 inches, not the usual 8 to 9 inches for slicers. Asian, Armenian, and English Telegraph types grow extremely long by nature, with best quality at under 2 inches in diameter. Long cucumbers are often trellised for straighter fruit. All harvested cucumbers have a short storage life, a few weeks under refrigeration at best. For best quality pickles, cucumbers should move from field to jar as quickly as possible.

To save open-pollinated cucumber seed, choose two or three healthy looking, dark green fruits from very healthy vines during about midseason. Early fruits are weaker in seed formation. Remove all the other fruits and flowers from that plant. Let the chosen fruits vine ripen to yellow orange; it's no problem if they over-ripen and get soft. Scrape out the seeds and allow them to ferment in a crock for a few days with a small amount of water. When stirred, the viable seeds will sink. Wash the good seeds, dry thoroughly on a screen and store in a dry place.

Varieties

Cucumber varieties fall into nine or more types: picklers, table slicers, burpless, Asian, Armenian, Middle Eastern, French, dwarf, novelty, and European greenhouse. Disease resistance varies greatly, indicated by the following initials:

DM (downy mildew): this white cottony mold cuts production and may kill vines.

PM (powdery mildew): spotty powder on the leaves cuts production, causes plants to wither, fruits to sunscald and ripen prematurely.

CMV (cucumber mosaic virus): mottled curled leaves, yellowing, and loss of production. CMV overwinters in many perennial weeds: catnip, milkweed, ragweed, burdock, mints, and so forth.

AN (anthracnose): causes sunken spots on leaves and fruit.

ALS (angular leaf spot): fungal spots on leaves.

S (scab): brown scabs on leaves, oozing spots on fruit.

B (bacterial wilt): there is no resistance. Spread by cucumber beetles; causes wilted plants, sticky ooze from leaves. Use row covers to deter the vector.

Many open-pollinated picklers show good disease resistance and yield; Burpee Pickler (53 days) has stood the test of time. It is vigorous, high yielding, has good tolerance to cucumber mosaic (CMV), and is usable in salads and pickles in all stages of growth.

The key to the longevity of the open-pollinated Marketmore lineage from Cornell is disease resistance. Marketmore 76 (68 days) is still widely grown commercially many decades after its introduction. High-yielding and well adapted to both north and south, Marketmore is resistant to bitterness, CMV, PM, DM, ALS, and AN. Marketmore 80 has similar stats, with some resistance to cucumber beetles. There are many other Marketmore cultivars.

Edmonson (70 days) is an old heirloom from Kansas, adapted to the dry plains, with excellent resistance to disease (ALS, AN, CMV, S) and drought. For pickles and slicing. Wisconsin SMR 58 (65 days), a black spine pickle, has also stood the test of time; tolerant to CMV, S, and black leaf spot.

Cucumber hybrids have typically increased vigor, yields, and disease resistance. Many are now *gynoecious,* producing only female blossoms with a high concentrated fruit set and much more fruit, with a compatible male variety included for pollination. Hybrids with male and female flowers (*monoecious*) may yield as much, but spread the yield over a longer harvest. Other cucumbers don't require a pollinator. *Parthenocarpic* hybrids can grow fruits without pollination and therefore without bees, making them useful for greenhouses and tunnels. All other cucumbers produce more fruit with beehives nearby.

Hybrid traits to look for include disease resistance, high yield, good color, shape, length, general appearance of fruit, edible skin, freedom from bitterness, crispness, sweetness, flavor, and uniformity. Every hybrid has some but not all of these traits. For example, a high-yielding hybrid such as Olympian (52 days) may have very good appearance, with resistance to all the major cucumber diseases (A, ALS, CMV, DM, PM, and S) but may be just average in taste with a crisp fresh flavor. In other words, it is a good supermarket hybrid. Diva, however, with far less disease resistance (DM, PM, S) has extraordinary eating qualities, with smooth edible bitter-free skin and a sweet crisp delicious flavor. Diva (58 days) is *gynoecious* and *parthenocarpic* and its non-bitter leaves are less attractive to cucumber beetles.

Home or market growers who use their vacant greenhouses for cucumbers in summer should use only trellis-compatible varieties with mildew tolerance. Mildew can be intense in hot damp summers. Traditional English Telegraph is not resistant. European *gynoecious* hybrids, such as Carmen, are.

The same criterion holds for hybrid pickles. One of my favorite pickles is the vigorous reliable good-tasting Burpee Pickler (53 days), which is resistant only to CMV. Burpee Pickler has been around so long I didn't even remember it was hybrid. Little Leaf (57 days) is a still stronger plant, which yields well even under adverse conditions, with brighter emerald green color and good taste for fresh eating and pickles. Little Leaf has terrific disease resistance (A, ALS, DM, PM, CMV, S and B). Plants are *parthenocarpic*.

Asian cucumbers from Japan and China tend to be longer (12 to 14 inches), burpless, tender-skinned, sweet, and crunchy. All require a trellis. The O.P. Suyo Long has no disease resistance but is widely adapted and grows well in hot weather. Hybrids such as Tasty Jade are mildew tolerant, vigorous, high yielding, *gynoecious* and *parthenocarpic*.

For an exotic touch, market gardeners can add the curious Armenian "cucumber," whose pale ribbed, 24-inch fruits look like aging dolphins. The skin is tender, no peeling required. Striped Armenian, also called Painted Serpent, is best eaten from 8 to 18 inches, and resembles a cucumber crossed with green striped marrow. Both Armenians are not technically cucumbers but melons, *Cucumis melo*. Both require trellises.

If you have a yen to taste a descendant of the original cucumbers of India, try the strange-looking but crisp and tasty Poona Kheera. The skin of Poona Kheera is white when young, russet brown when fully grown, but looks like a regular sweet cucumber when sliced.

SEED: An ounce of seeds (average 1,000) sows about 130 hills at 8 seeds per hill, or about 220 feet of raised row at 5 seeds per foot. A packet of 100 open-pollinated seeds sows 12 hills, or about 20 feet of raised row at 5 seeds per foot. A packet of 30 hybrid seeds sows 4 to 6 hills.

GERMINATION: 80%; 10 days at 70°F; 7 days at 80°F. Minimum soil temp. 65°F.

VIABILITY: 5 years.

DAYS TO HARVEST: 50 to 65 days.

ROTATION: 3 years between all members of the squash family, *cucurbitae*. Some diseases are shared with nightshades.

MOON CALENDAR: Sow on fruit days. Cultivations, foliar, and biodynamic sprays in leaf. Harvest on fruit days.

BIODYNAMIC SPRAYS: Horn manure (500) on flat soil and/or field. Silica (500) at least once on greenhouse plants. Compost tea with a pinch of 500 to water peat pots at transplanting. Silica after second true leaf, when vines begin to run, or at first flowering and at fruit set. Equisetum (508) and valerian (507) in extended wet weather.

COMPANION PLANTS: Dill planted thickly in cucumber mounds; also tansy, catnip, yarrow, castor bean, wormwood, nasturtium, mints, and marigold to deter flea beetle. Zucchini and radish seedlings are preferred by beetles and can be planted in trap mounds or in sections of field row.

EGGPLANT

Most years our New England climate never quite catches up with eggplant, which is native to subtropical India. In India, eggplant becomes a seven-foot shrub with huge leaves and two-pound fruit. Fortunately this fruit doesn't need to sweeten like melons, or we would harvest even fewer of them. Eggplant originates from the same climate as melons and requires exactly the same cultural conditions: a well-drained soil, fairly high fertility, plenty of organic matter, and moderate moisture. Most important, both require two months of warm nights (70°F) for serious market crops.

In very warm climates eggplant grows easily; from Southeast Asia through the Middle East, eggplant is a staple. It is the "King of Vegetables" in India, the backbone of Indian cuisine. And considering how much eggplant I ate growing up, it may seem odd that I have planted it only haphazardly over the years. Eggplant was my mother's favorite food. She served it stuffed, fried, and sautéed, and fed us ratatouille more frequently than other kids got hamburgers. Later I stopped eating eggplant because I decided that anything not green or brightly colored, or a plant somehow deprived of sunlight (mushrooms, for example) was not healthful. I was proved wrong about mushrooms; likewise about eggplant. I didn't understand the role eggplant plays in traditional cuisine, or in my mother's cuisine for that matter.

What makes eggplant such an indispensable ingredient in so many cuisines from Thailand to Spain is not so much its own qualities of flavor. Eggplant does have a subtle complex flavor, but it doesn't stand alone like a fully ripe tomato. Eggplant is valued for its meatiness and texture, and how it absorbs and presents other flavors. It enhances meat, tomatoes, peppers, and garlic, and provides the foundation (along with lemon, tahini, and garlic) for Middle Eastern baba ghanoush. Large eggplants are delicious stuffed with rice, raisins, walnuts, and spices. My mother's problem was my father's habit of dousing her creations with ketchup. Perhaps she should have done as Indian wives do, and tempted him with a sauce made with tahini and tamarind. She also could have tried stuffed eggplant with ground coconut, peanuts, and masala, as is done in India with the green eggplant called brinjal. Had Dad poured ketchup on her ratatouille, her all-time favorite food, however, she certainly would have divorced him.

The soft seeds of eggplant contain minute amounts of a nicotine-like alkaloid. Considering how much eggplant I ate as a child, I probably suffered nicotine withdrawal when I left for college. Europeans shunned eggplant for centuries because the fruits looked like giant versions of deadly nightshade. The problem, of course, was that they received the fruit without the cuisine. The transition was easier for the Arabs who traded in India and spread the eggplant westward as far as Moorish Spain. Eggplant fit perfectly into Middle Eastern cuisine. The Chinese adopted eggplant even earlier. Eggplant was already endemic in 544 CE. All of the narrow "Japanese" varieties were developed by the Chinese, although a trip to an American Chinese restaurant would never convince you that the Chinese still grow and consume more eggplant than any other country, by far.

Eggplant has more food value than I realized in my late teens, but the best parts of it are found in the skin. The flesh alone is not high in vitamins, but contains good amounts of foliate, potassium, fiber, and beneficial phenols, which help lower blood sugar and blood pressure. These benefits, plus low soluble carbs, recommend eggplant to diabetics. USDA tests also show that the phenols caffaic and chlorogenic acid found in eggplant are antimutagenic, antimicrobial, antiviral, and anti LDL (they lower the "bad" cholesterol).

Through the skin, however, you enter another dimension. Dark-colored eggplants are high in an apparently completely unique, potent antioxidant, an anthocyanin called nasunin. The Department of Nutritional Science in Japan reports that nasunin is an angiogenesis inhibitor, which means it prevents the formation of new blood vessels that feed the spread of cancer. Although not suggested or prescribed as a treatment, nasunin may play a long-term dietary role in preventing cancer. One variety, Black Magic, which I cannot find in seed catalogs, is reported to have 3 times the amount of nasunin found in standard eggplant. Harvest time is also a factor. Antioxidants are highest and solanine (an alkaloid found also in tomatoes and peppers) lowest when the colored eggplant skin has a high sheen. The skin becomes tougher and antioxidant levels go down again when overripe fruit becomes dull.

Culture

Eggplant grows best and is most disease-free in sandy or silt loam, which allows for deep root penetration down to 3 or 4 feet. Eggplant produces most easily wherever melons are sweet and abundant, commercially throughout the

South up to New Jersey, in the Southwest, and California. Eggplant requires 80 warm days and 60 warm nights to produce really well. Plants do nothing below 62°F and deteriorate under 50°F. The pH ranges from 5.5 to 6.5. Greenhouse sowings begin 8 to 10 weeks before outdoor soil will be 70°F, which means seed is usually sown from March 1 to April 1 in the East.

Some growers tweezer-sow 72 cell trays and transplant into 18 to 36 cell trays after true leaves are established. Others sow thinly in flats 3 to 4 seeds to the inch, ¼ inch deep at 85°F using bottom heat or heat lamps, and prick out the strongest plants to 3-inch pots or 2-inch cells after true leaves are 3/8 inch in diameter. Grow seedlings and plants at about 72°F. Harden seedlings by reducing water and lowering the air temperature to 60°F after 7 weeks. Set out transplants 1 to 2 weeks later in warm 70°F soil. Many growers use black plastic and row covers to raise soil temperature to about 70°F in spring. Some claim higher yields using clear plastic. Clear plastic does not suppress weeds. Optimum temperatures for pollination and growth range from nighttime lows of 62°F to daytime highs of 95°F. Eggplants are much more sensitive to cold than tomatoes and peppers.

For a fruit, eggplant has fairly high NPK requirements. Conventional fertilizer recommendations for long seasons are 20 to 40 pounds of N and 80 to 120 pounds of P and K per acre before planting, with 5 to 10 pounds of nitrogen per week during vegetative growth. This much nitrogen, however, will create heavy vegetative growth and set fruit too late for cooler regions. Good quality compost is the key not only to good yields, but also to the vigor that rides out viral attacks and fungus infections. Compost also contains natural biofungicides. Side-dressings can include fermented nettle and compost tea, fish emulsion, liquid seaweed, or organic fertilizer while the scaffold of leaves and stems is being built. Cease when flower buds begin to form.

Most growers space plants 18 to 24 inches apart with 30 to 36 inches between rows, although some California growers allow 5 feet between rows for better color (University of California Extension). New transplants should be carefully set vertically to prevent sunscald and heat damage from leaning over hot black plastic. Transplanting holes should be filled evenly to prevent wet spots favorable to collar-rot fungi. Many growers stake plants to maintain verticality and to provide an even leaf canopy. They also remove the lowest leaves and flowers to keep fungi at bay and to hold fruit well above the ground. Others use a modified Florida weave system, tying the eggplants to guy lines as is done with greenhouse tomatoes.

Eggplant does best with moderate amounts of water. Too much at any stage, either from rain, fog, or irrigation, promotes fungi. In dry climates or dry periods, critical watering times extend from flowering to fruit set and fruit enlargement. Fruits become bitter tasting with too little water and or too little organic matter in hot dry weather. These critical watering times are also key nodal points for spraying biodynamic silica (501). Flowers are all self-fertile, so mixing of varieties for pollination is unnecessary.

Fruit is ripe when the skin becomes glossy, and over-mature when fruit loses its sheen and becomes less firm with darker seeds. Harvest at 7- to 10-day intervals, 5 to 6 times a season, depending on latitude. Market growers wash fruits if necessary, and air-cool to 50°F. Water-cooling and refrigeration damages the skin and hastens deterioration. Fruits lose quality below 50°F and suffer surface bronzing and internal darkening at 41°F, but even at 52°F eggplant won't keep longer than 2 weeks.

In July, growers in the South and California sometimes cut the plant shrub back to 6-18 inches, which forces new growth and a second harvest in the fall. Two to four weeks before expected fall frost, pinch off all remaining blossoms to hasten ripening.

Plant Diseases

Chances of fungal disease are reduced by perfect drainage (raised beds or raised ridges), plant vigor, and steady growth (excellent compost, no lapses in fertility or irrigation, and no checks due to insect predation). Best to use drip rather than overhead watering to prevent splashing of fungal spores. Practice long (4 to 5 year) vector rotation of nightshades and cucurbits. Practice mixed planting, if possible. Keep plants vertical and staked, with leaves and fruit well off the ground. Prune off lowest leaves and flower buds. These measures will improve quality and yield, and minimize use of the amazing and expensive biofungicides mentioned below. Beneficial fungi are present in well-made compost.

Damping off of seedlings due to pythium or phytophthora fungus is exacerbated by non-vital potting mixes, overcrowding, and poor drainage (heavy soil or tractor compaction). Pythium and fusarium-controlling fungi can also be purchased as Root Shield® or Soilgard®.

Early blight, caused by *Alternaria solani*, affects stressed seedlings and transplants, producing round to irregular lesions, often with concentric rings *only on the leaves*. Treat with a copper fungicide or a biofungicide (Actinorate®).

Phytophthora blight is spread by too-short rotations of plant vectors nightshades and cucurbits, especially. Rotate 4 to 5 years. Phytophthora peaks early in high humidity at 68°F and spreads from splashing rain and irrigation. Eggplants set on raised beds or ridges with lower leaves pruned are less susceptible. Phytophthora is also called collar-rot and stem canker because first symptoms show stems infected with dark streaks followed by sudden collapse of the entire plant. Fruits show water-soaked dark brown patches coated with white fungal spores. This distinguishes phytophthora from phomopsis (also called collar-rot), which produces dark brown lesions that circle the stem and pale sunken areas in the fruit but have no white mold. Phomopsis fruit decay can also appear after harvest from fruits that appeared healthy in the field. Fungal infections are hard to reverse once established. In the early stages the biofungicides Plant Guardian® (Gardens Alive) and Actinovate® provide protection. Some eggplant varieties such as Florida Market and Florida Beauty are partially resistant to phomopsis.

Verticillium wilt begins with yellowing between the veins of lower leaves and V-shaped lesions at the leaf tip followed by complete wilting of the entire plant. Losses in some eggplant growing areas range from 5 to 50%. Practice a 4- to 5-year rotation. Some eggplant varieties show resistance to verticillium on infected soils, including Classic, Epic, Irene, Nadia, and Black Pride (New Jersey and Cornell Extension).

Bacterial wilt causes plants to wilt and die more quickly. Diagnosis: cut stems will ooze when placed underwater. Use biofungicides or liquid copper fungicide.

Bacterial soft rot (Erwinia) causes fruit rot after harvest. Avoid picking when crop is wet or during the hottest part of the day. Clean up all residual debris.

Viral diseases are not treatable by sprays or soil drenches, but are reduced by the same cultural practices that reduce fungal disease: excellent plant vigor and long 4- to 5-year rotation of nightshades, cucurbits (cucumber, melon family), and beets. Some varieties show tolerance to viral disease. By far the most persistent disease is tobacco mosaic virus (TMV), which infects all nightshades, cucurbits (cucumber, melon), squash, and the beet family. Symptoms begin with mottled light and dark patterns followed by characteristic puckering and distortion of leaves and fruit. Large dead areas (mosaic burn) appear in hot and dry weather. Plants are stunted, but do not die. TMV is spread by seed, not a problem from major suppliers but of concern to seed savers. It is transmitted through poor sanitation of pruning tools, handling, insect-chewing wounds, and short rotations. Insects themselves are not primary vectors. Remove all plant debris and boil pruning-shear heads in water for 5 minutes. Plant TMV tolerant/resistant varieties such as Dusky, Nadia, Epic, and Black Bell II.

Insects

Keep plants warmer and protected with wire hoop and row cover until the flowers appear, then spray the exposed plants with neem or with kaolin clay (Surround®) every 7 to 14 days for flea beetle. Though kaolin is non-toxic, it leaves a white film on the fruit; avoid applications within 30 days of harvest. Beneficial nematodes (Gardens Alive) applied to the soil will reduce pest larva for the following year.

Overwintering larvae of Colorado potato beetles, which emerge in May or June in Zone 6, will also be reduced by beneficial nematodes. If they are unchecked, the larvae can totally destroy transplants. Obviously an overlap occurs with this insect on potato crops. Bt (*Baccilus thuriengensis tenebrionis* called Novodor®) prevents larva from feeding. Bt works only on newly hatched and small larvae. However, even 30% defoliation after the bloom stage will not significantly reduce yield (New Jersey Extension). Sprays containing Spinosad provide extremely effective but very expensive control. Alternate with Bt to reduce pest resistance.

Outbreaks of mites, tiny eight-legged, spider-related pests, are sometimes precipitated by pesticide-induced reduction of predator species (such as lace wing). This includes use of broad spectrum organic pyrethrins, and is further aggravated by monoculture. Mites are extremely destructive in hot dry weather. Like aphids, mites suck on plant saps, reducing plant vitality. Control with insecticidal soap and insecticidal oil (a cottonseed oil that suffocates mite eggs.)

Aphids pierce plant cells and suck sap, causing stunting. Sooty mold grows on the sticky ooze from the wounds. Aphids can be controlled by lady beetles, lacewings, insecticidal soap, and insecticidal oil. Again, overuse of pesticides decreases predators, which include syrphid fly (hoverfly) larva and the larva of true bugs. Pesticide overuse has been linked to large-scale aphid infestation (New Jersey Extension).

Symptoms of non-beneficial nematode damage look like disease, with anemic yellowish plant color (chlorosis) and reduced vigor. Nematodes also transmit verticilluim wilt, a rapid interveinal yellowing and wilting of the entire plant. Rye, timothy, and brassica cover crops (rapeseed, and so forth) exude butyric acid, which reduces nematode populations if planted the year before. The fungi found naturally in compost, and purchased beneficial nematodes, also provide control.

In new sod, cutworms can be devastating to transplants. To the stem of each transplant, apply a 2-inch cardboard collar, pushing it a bit into the soil.

Varieties

Black Beauty (80 days, 1910) is still the standard open-pollinated variety: large dark fruits on vigorous plants that need a long warm season and require staking. Italian heirlooms include Prosperosa (65 days), one of the most delicious eggplants, deep violet, heavy yielding, adaptable; and Rosa Bianca (84 days), a round ribbed eggplant, white with magenta purple streaks, shaped a bit like a pumpkin. Uncooked fruits make a centerpiece worthy of a still life composition. Smaller Asian types include Apple Green (62 days), which quickly produces apple-sized fruits with tender skin; no peeling required. Early production makes Apple Green good for the North. Thai Long Green (80 days), traditional pendulous 10-inch Asian eggplant on compact 2-foot plants; and Ping Tung Long (70 days), with prolific 12-inch purple fruits from Taiwan.

Nadia Hybrid (67 days) is a large Italian style fruit on a strong scaffold, adaptable with some tolerance of cooler seasons, one of the few eggplants with some resistance to verticillium wilt and tobacco mosaic virus. Other vigorous, productive, and reliable large purple-fruited hybrids include Classic (76 days), Burpee Hybrid (70 days), and Park's Whopper Hybrid (62 days). Vigorous hybrid Asian eggplants include Orient Express (58 days), with extremely early black purple fruits, adaptable to both early cool and midsummer heat, with tender skin and gourmet quality and Fairy Tale (65 days), with abundant clusters of small (2 to 4 inch), white-streaked purple fruits, bitter-free and flavorful, on very compact 20 inch plants. Hansel (55 days) bears clusters of similar deep purple fruits on slightly larger 30-inch plants. Kermit (60 days) is a prolific hybrid version of a traditional Thai eggplant—the green "ping pong balls" used in curry dishes.

SEED: An ounce (about 6,000 seeds) produces 3,500 transplants. A packet of 25 seeds sown carefully with tweezers should produce 15 strong plants.

GERMINATION: 5 to 10 days at 85°F

VIABILITY: 4 years

DAYS TO HARVEST: 60 to 80

ROTATION: 4 to 5 years between nightshade and cucurbit (cucumber/melon) family due to shared disease susceptibility.

DAYS TO HARVEST: 55 to 80 days

MOON CALENDAR: Sow on fruit days, ascending moon. During vegetative phase spray on leaf days, on fruit days after flowering.

BIODYNAMIC SPRAYS: Spray horn manure (500) on potting soil and equisetum (508) on seedlings and seedling soil. Silica (501) when seedlings produce true leaves and at least once during vegetative growth, again at flowering and fruit enlargement.

COMPANION PLANTS: Insects and disease are reduced in raised beds with mixed vegetables and herbs (monitor flea beetles). Many varieties make a pleasing addition to ornamental landscaping. Marigolds reduce nematodes. Intercrop with salad between eggplants under row covers.

ESCAROLE AND ENDIVE

Most winters I have made a pilgrimage to a botanical garden. My first impression is always the Asian splendor of the glass houses, which often look like buildings from the Middle East or India. It seems out of place that snows should bank their bases and frost climb their glass walls. Yet wide spaces of snow lie just a pane of glass from the deep greens of tropical vines and trees.

Anxious to reach my Dream of the East, I push across the snow-swept parking lot and eagerly anticipate the steaming warmth beneath the glass dome. In an instant my winter coat becomes a burden. The clean, sharp December air is quickly replaced by dense, unmoving steam. I enter a different kind of breathing, a different hemisphere of plants. I step cautiously into the jungle, remembering a panther I once heard near Palenque, Mexico (a place where a rope of vine might turn out to be a snake). As I pass waxy greenhouse *anthuriums* and orchids with dream faces, I cast a backward glance at the ice flowers on the glass and the snow piled high around the conifers.

I stand there with one foot in the northern hemisphere, another foot in the southern, and it occurs to me that compared to the average American consumer, the stone colossus that straddled the harbor in ancient Rhodes was a mere child. Today we stride multiple continents with ease. Without thought of consequence we shift the continents around, importing Brazil into Peoria, Thailand into New York. Before me stands an orange tree with hundreds of golden suns ripening in December! Their golden fruits could hardly be expected to fly like birds to ripen in their place of origin. Those fruits are offspring of a different sun!

I'm not the first person to believe the world will die of transportation. This thought sobers my sense of reality, and reminds me of the enormous amounts of oil used to feed our colossus, the greenhouse boiler. A huge price is being paid merely because plants are being grown away from their natural environment. With that thought, another falls on my head—a fruit, as it were, from the orange tree. This must be a general law: the farther plants are taken from their rightful season, the higher the price we pay—in every sense of that expression. Even in the temperate garden, harmonious balanced growth depends upon growing plants intimately timed to their season. The further plants are taken from their seasonal timing, the more cultural problems they seem to have. A whole complex of native factors has originally brought each garden crop into existence: soil, climate, season, air, and so on. Each plant is like a reading of a special climate, of a special place of origin. That really needs to be acknowledged.

One of the main goals of both home and market gardeners is to extend the season, both early and late. Gardeners want techniques that don't depend on foreign oil. They want plants that are inherently timed to the season. One such plant I found by chance, and when I discovered it, I was very impressed.

When I returned home from my tropical revelation, I decided that I was going to import less of Brazil into Pennsylvania. The greenhouse I was using at the time was an old glass house from the early 1950s. Its roof was made of lapped glass. This had the virtue of breathing, but the disadvantage of being nearly un-sealable. Since the greenhouse was divided into three sections, I decided to turn off the heat in two. In the third, I had a carpenter put an inner translucent fiberglass drop ceiling with a center vent, which reduced the heated space by 30%. It also created a warmed attic of air above the heated area. The biggest disadvantage was dust on the topside of the fiberglass ceiling. It needed frequent washings. I decided to heat this section to just above freezing, but no more. The sun would have to do the rest.

Having made these decisions, the question was what to grow. It was very simple to grow greens of all kinds in the above-freezing house. Lettuce grew all winter fairly well. But how to best use the two cold houses? We grew spinach, lettuce, various Chinese greens, and an oddly named salad called Batavian escarole. Batavian escarole is not (as some people might think) an exotic folk dance, but an endive probably first cultivated in the Mediterranean. The thing about growing under glass is that plants will taste blander under the weakened light. Delicate-flavored lettuce and bok choy become tasteless under glass, whereas bitter greens such as chicories and biting mustards become delicious during the winter months. Escarole, especially, produced large dandelion-like leaves, full of flavor and vitamins. To my taste, they are the perfect mix for use with root-cellared Chinese and European cabbage in fall and winter salads.

Around January 15, however, a very heavy frost seemed to kill everything in the cold houses. Above-ground benches froze solid and the escarole leaves went flat. If it hadn't been so cold so suddenly, we would have dug up the benches and ground-level beds and prepared them for February plantings of onion and spring salad. But the soil was like rock, so we let them be. It was lucky we did, because at the end of February the Batavian escarole began to grow again. In only a few weeks, hundreds of large creamy-centered heads appeared. These heads were even better quality than the fall harvest. But what was most gratifying was that this was the second harvest from the same plant. So long as we didn't cut into the growing point, the plant put out lush new growth. Its temperature requirements for good growth were low enough that a crop could be harvested before the bench space was needed for spring lettuce.

In the fall I decided to try escarole in cold frames. These frames were also not especially tight, but in the spring the fall crops reappeared without much attention. Imagine getting your first spring salad without having to plant in the spring! In our case this resulted in a continual staggering of crops: first the slightly heated greenhouse, next the waist high benches in the cold houses, then came the escarole planted at ground level, and finally the escarole in the cold frames.

Culture

To grow Batavian escarole outside, prepare a good deep seedbed in the middle of August. The bed should be well composted. Make very shallow (¼ inch) furrows for the seeds about 6 inches apart. Sprinkle the seeds in a light rain, a little lighter than you would for carrots. These seeds are easy to handle; they are larger than lettuce seeds and have a distinct almost tubular form, like desiccated flowers. Cover with ¼ inch fine soil or sifted compost and tamp lightly. Both the seedbed and the young plants should be kept moist. When the plants are about 5 weeks old, transplant them into cold frames.

The most economical spacing is a 10-inch checkerboard pattern. Escarole is a large plant. Cramping accomplishes nothing and invites rot. Like lettuce they cannot be transplanted at any other depth than they grew in the seedbed. Bare root plants survive quite well. Transplants with a root ball or from a cell pack hardly stop growing.

As for any cold frame crop, intensive production requires high fertility. That means very deeply dug beds, with compost being up to 30% of the top 6 inches of the beds. Biodynamic growers spray with horn manure (500) prior to transplanting. Keep the cold frames open until the weather gets really cool. On the other hand, I don't know many plants that so successfully survive overheating. Late October days can be hot and the frames steamy, but so long as the escarole is watered daily, it will continue to grow rapidly. To avoid fungus and rot, soak the frames early in the day and open them if the weather is balmy. Some of these plants may grow their creamy rosettes by late fall. Harvest the rosette without cutting into the growing point. Cutting off the top of the root prevents re-growth. Some people tie the plant together with a large rubber band for blanching, like cauliflower or blanched celery. This takes a week to ten days. Since by Christmas I crave every ounce of true green I can get, I never do this. I just mix these slightly pungent fall leaves with milder Chinese cabbage. The fall harvest can be extended quite a long time by covering the frame with an old rug at night. A tight, draft-free cold frame produces longer. Again, don't forget to water. In sheltered locations the temperature can still soar during warm spells.

Unless you have a solar cold frame, frost will probably overcome the plants sometime in December or January. Leave the rug off during the dormant period. By late February they may start to grow again, depending on your latitude. Begin to water as soon as new growth appears.

The creamy quality of spring heads is quite appealing and have proved quite marketable. They grow quite large, but never need to be tied. I've never had one bolt. With corn salad, this can be your earliest spring salad, by far.

Varieties

Escarole and endive are both offshoots of the same species of chicory, *Cichorium endivia*. The wild chicory of roadsides (*Cichorium intybus*) is the source of the misnamed "Italian dandelion," see pp. 117-118. Escaroles generally make heavier, denser heads with smoother leaves, while endives are frillier (frisee) and deeply cut. Some endives, such as the heat- and cold-tolerant Bianca Riccia are grown exclusively for baby salad mixes. Others such as Keystone and Salad King form large frilly rosettes with frilly crème hearts, similar to lettuce, but more frost-hardy. The old standard Batavian escarole, which I describe in this chapter, is still widely grown, even available in pelleted seed from Harris for accurate spacing. Newer improved escaroles such as Natacha make heavier heads with larger hearts and have a higher tolerance to bolting, tip burn, and bottom rot in hot weather. All endives and escaroles are good subjects for extending the season.

Escarole and Endive

SEED: Seed per ounce. Endive, average 19,000. Escarole, average 14,000. A packet of 100 seeds sows about 30 to 40 feet of full heads. An ounce sows up to 3,000 feet. Approximately 1 ounce to 1½ pounds of seed per acre, depending on seeding rate. Follow guidelines for lettuce seed. Less pelleted seed is required.

GERMINATION: similar to lettuce.

VIABILITY: 4 to 5 years.

DAYS TO HARVEST: 33 days for baby salad, 45 to 55 days for heads.

FOR MOON CALENDAR, ROTATION, BIODYNAMIC SPRAYS AND COMPANION PLANTS see "Lettuce."

FENNEL

Despite its alleged reputation as a bad companion plant (retarding the growth of its neighbors), I love having fennel in the garden, especially at the flowering stage. Any plant that brings such abundance of beneficial insect life to the garden has to be good. Florence fennel or finnochio (*Foeniculum vulgare dulce*) is valued for the celery-like swelling of its stalks. It has market possibilities in Italian neighborhoods and in nouvelle cuisine. Its flavor lies somewhere between anise seed and celery. The swelling of the bulb is very graceful and the stalks rise into an incredible feathery fountain of foliage, wonderfully indicative of the entire family of *umbelliferous* plants. When fennel comes into flower, the garden bed is utterly transformed into a fairytale forest of tall yellow umbels, overflowing with insect life. You would need an entomologist to identify the dozens of harmless wasps it attracts, which in turn become predators of all kinds of insect pests in the garden. If I could shrink in size I would love to spend my life in a fennel forest.

I have also grown the wild seed fennel (*Foeniculum officinalis*), which produces a still greater abundance of flower seeds and insects. The wild fennel is a perennial, hardy in zones up to Zone 6 with winter protection, but it produces no edible stalks. It creates a beautiful herbaceous border, twice as tall as Florence fennel. Some varieties have reddish-bronze feathery leaves. As to the effect of either plant as an unfriendly companion, I've never seen it, but its strong scent, both sweet and a little stupefying, certainly has an effect on me! The odor is dense and deeply intriguing. It captures the senses just as it captures the hundreds of insects that inhabit its flowers.

In herbal medicine, fennel seed tea has been used to stimulate milk flow in nursing mothers and to relieve infant colic (a very weak tea made with only a few seeds), as well as to aid digestion and relieve flatulence in children and adults.

Florence fennel is primarily grown as a fall crop because it bolts so easily in spring. However, if growing seed for flavoring of bread, cakes, or sweet tea, an early spring sowing can be left to bolt. Perennial fennel is fairly permanent in Zone 7, and requires little if any care. Florence fennel is not listed in all seed catalogs. Zefa Fino (80 days), the standard Swiss variety, is so slow-bolting it can be sown in spring. Widely adapted. The bulbs of Perfection are larger and more bolt-resistant. Hybrid Orion (80 days) is large and higher yielding. Some catalogs list fennel as an herb with either green or bronze foliage for flavoring, or to produce anise-flavored seed when wintered over in Zone 6 or 7.

Florence fennel has the same high fertilizer requirements that celery has. For spring crops, transplants can be sown in the greenhouse on a celery schedule or direct-seed on a carrot schedule, remembering that fennel is not tolerant of dry soil. Any loam will grow good fennel, but never be skimpy with compost and water, lest the bulbs fail to flesh out. When horn manure is sprayed preceding the fall carrot sowing, include fennel as well. Sow the seed in shallow drills, ¼ inch deep at a rate of 9 seeds per foot. In heavy soil use a ¼ inch compost cover instead of soil. Thin seedlings to 6 inches apart, with 18 inches between rows; or 6 by 12 inches in well-composted raised beds. Fennel seed is similar to carrot seed and the seedlings look quite similar, too, but have longer, more graceful wings. Bed culture is preferable to field. Bulb fennel always seems to do poorly when extra moisture is not available. It benefits from mulch. At the early stages, weeding is essential since the plant is quite delicate. Spray silica when plants show their true feathers and again as the bulb begins to form. Side-dressings and liquid fertilizers are not desirable; the flavor of fennel is too delicate. Fennel is not quick growing, but needs ample nitrogen to thrive, so prepare for the crop in advance.

Harvest when the bulb swells to the size of a teacup. Spring sowings may bolt quickly, making the bulb fibrous. Early thinnings are delicious in the early summer, raw for salads and steamed with fish. Allow some of your spring crop to flower. You, as well as your garden, will be enchanted by the tiny beneficial wasps attracted by the blossoms. Gather your courage and sit quietly in the middle of the bed on a sunny day. You will find yourself in the midst of another world, which is brimming with inconceivably important activity, activity that does not pay us any attention at all, as if the sun's rays had become populated with her very own creatures. It is truly a wonderful unknown world, sustaining all the pollinating activities in nature. See how many wasps you can identify. I haven't found one that bothers to sting, even when touched. They are much too intoxicated by finding a plant that gives them the fullest expression of their cosmos. They swim in it; and it makes me unbelievably happy to watch them and to be alive within their world.

One last practical note: though midsummer-sown Florence fennel can be left in the ground through the early fall until needed, it cannot bear more than a light frost. In fine markets, bulbs are usually displayed with some feathers. Bulbs keep for a month or longer refrigerated or in a cold root cellar at 35 to 40°F.

SEED: An ounce of seeds (about 7,000) sows 700 feet at 9 seeds per foot. A packet of 100 seeds sows about 11 feet.

GERMINATION: 55%, 10 to 14 days at 60°F.

VIABILITY: 3 years.

DAYS TO HARVEST: 90 days.

MOON CALENDAR: For celery-like bulbs at base of stalks, culture in leaf. For seed crop, cultivate and spray remaining plants in fruit, especially in Leo.

ROTATION: 3 years for the carrot family (fennel, dill, caraway, cumin, parsley, carrot, and so forth).

BIODYNAMIC SPRAYS: Sprays can accompany fall carrot sowing. Horn manure (500) before sowing. Silica when feathers are established and at bulb swell. Silica again when the plant bolts to seed, with Valerian (507) in cloudy weather, especially to develop oil in seed.

COMPANION PLANTS: Reputed to be a poor companion, but I have not found this to be true. Said to harm bush beans, caraway, tomatoes, and kohlrabi. Wormwood and coriander said to adversely affect fennel. Make observations over a number of years. An isolated fennel forest is just what I have in mind for my retirement years.

GARDEN HUCKLEBERRY AND WONDERBERRY

Both garden huckleberry and wonderberry were selected from the fruit of the rank hedgerow weed, black nightshade, *Solanum nigrum*. Garden huckleberry (*Solanum nigrum* var. *melanocerasum*) produces clusters of black berries that look somewhat like blueberries or huckleberries (*Vaccinium* genus). Garden huckleberries are used to make mock blueberry pies and preserves. Wonderberry (originally called Sunberry) was developed by Luther Burbank to improve the flavor of garden huckleberry. Burbank claimed to cross *S. nigrum* var. *guineense* with *S. villosum*, producing *S. x burbankii*. Botanists insist Burbank's wonderberry is a variant selected by Burbank from *S. nigrum* var. *retroflexum*. He thought a cross had occurred, but apparently it never happened. His selection, however, does have better flavor and less aftertaste, although in both berries the key is to harvest fruit "dead ripe."

At first glance unripe fruit may look fully ripe. Never harvest shiny hard black berries. Wait until the berries become a dull purple-black. When fully ripe, the interior of the berry turns from greenish to purplish. Although neither fruit is tasty out of hand (both need to be cooked with added sweetener and lemon juice to be palatable), it is important to teach children to recognize fully ripe fruit. Unripe or half-ripe fruit could make children ill from the toxin solanine, which diminishes through ripening. The flavor of both fruits is improved by light frost, a good time to schedule harvest and processing.

Garden huckleberries and wonderberries can be prepared for pies, jams, and freezing by covering berries in water with a pinch of baking soda. Simmer for 10 minutes and drain. Garden huckleberries require more sugar than blueberries—60% for jam, 40% for pie; like blueberries, they require the addition of lemon juice. Most recipes also add ¼ teaspoon of pumpkin pie spice, nutmeg, or orange juice to pick up the flavor. Add a thickener for pie filling; follow the directions for blueberry jam on packets of pectin.

In third world countries, wonderberry leaves are eaten as greens. They too, however, contain solanine, though the levels are low. A similar plant,

Chichiquelite huckleberry (*Solanum scabrum*) is actually one of the most widely consumed greens in Central Africa. Africans eat the greens up to 3 times a week, switching to other greens such as amaranth for a few days if the low levels of solanine cause stomach ache.

Culture

Garden huckleberry and wonderberry plants range from 2 to 3 feet tall, with smooth pepper-like leaves. The plants are not as particular as tomatoes or peppers about soil type or regular watering. They produce plenty of fruit in partial sun (60%), but fruit will not ripen as well and off flavors may predominate. Sow 3 seeds per 3-inch peat pot, 6 to 8 weeks before soil temperature is 65 to 70°F. Germination is longer than tomato—up to 2 weeks. Berries appear in 60 to 90 days. General culture is similar to pepper or tomato.

The Long Island Seed Project notes that flea beetles prefer wonderberry to garden huckleberry. Use floating row covers. Otherwise, plants are not as susceptible to nightshade disease and pests as tomatoes.

Garden huckleberry is marketed without any varietal name in England as *S. nigrum guineese*. Wonderberry is marketed sometimes as wonderberry, sometimes as sunberry, sometimes as *Solanum burbankii*, and sometimes merely as *S. retroflexum*.

GARLIC

Before me lies a book that for decades has helped me nose around the plant world. The subject is centuries old, yet the active principles involved have been isolated only fairly recently; they require an extensive knowledge of botany and biochemistry, which I lack. The subject is pharmacognosy, and this particular volume is pretty skeptical about the claims of herbalists, but I don't care. I crawl around the plant world on my hands and knees, for reasons I myself barely understand, knowing that what I really want from plants is nameless, almost religious in nature.

I didn't begin reading pharmocognosy for medicinal purposes. I still don't. Rather, I have the idea that the active principles, particularly the smells, are the greeting cards of the plants' essential identity. Often I am lured into better acquaintance by smell alone, since smell is the portal that offers a discreet insight into the inner biochemical principles of plants. Where my nose fails, I pay close attention to the listed biochemical ingredients (the terpenes, the geraniols, the menthols, and so on), noting how plants of diverse origin seem to share groups of active principles in common. I still believe that this list has almost unfathomable meaning. An abstract of these smells might form an alternative map of the botanical world; a map of magical forces playing and combining, appearing and disappearing, more wonderful than fantasy, unveiling kinships not evident to exterior classification; a kinship of formative forces.

Of course, I was stopped in my tracks by the sheer complexity of the task and the limits of my education. There was irony in that conclusion as well. Just think what a task it would have been to preserve a flexible and imaginative approach to the subject through six years of biochemistry! Probably impossible! My nose, however, remained undaunted, and like a dog on the scent of a paradise of game, led me from plant to plant. Not that all the scents are pleasant or delicious. On the contrary, some are quite repellent. But the nose is smarter than the mind in one important respect—it penetrates with shocking directness into reality. It leaves the mind far behind, stubbornly stumbling through the underbrush, just as a hunting dog leaves the hunter behind. Nor does this analogy stop there, for the mind shoots the game dead just as surely as the bullet from a gun, or a biochemist. The question then remains: can one know these active principles, these potent biochemicals in their living form; in a form that relates them to the map of the formative forces?

Garlic (*Allium sativum*) is a very potent example. Its scent has a long history, actually as long as history has been recorded. Garlic graced the pharaoh's table, and the patriarchs longed for it in the wilderness. So impressive is the active principle that Julius Caesar surrounded himself with soldiers, not as Shakespeare mistakenly assumed, to protect himself from Brutus and other assassins, but to shield himself from the garlic breath of common people who crowded around to kiss him. Such are the burdens of great fame. The Romans were great believers in the strengthening and curative value of garlic. They imagined it had the power to ward off just about everything.

Although the authors of *Pharmacognosy* (Tyler et al. 1981) are reluctant to ascribe curative value, they admit that as little as 50 grams of garlic per week (less than two ounces, or about one large bulb) significantly lowers blood cholesterol. Persons on a garlic-free diet "had significantly higher serum triglycerides and beta lipoproteins." Other effects, not so well-researched in the United States (though they are in Europe and Russia), include the "stimulation of bile production; lowering of blood sugar and blood lipids; reduction of hypertension; acceleration of wound healing; and curing of the common cold." Apparently Caesar was not aware that garlic's potent antibacterial principle—allicin or diallyldisulfide-S-oxide—is inextricably wedded to garlic odor.*

So far, the most powerful principle found in garlic is prostaglandin, an anti-inflammatory hormone usually found in animal organs. Garlic contains the first reported occurrence in higher plants. According to the *Encyclopedia Britannica*, prostaglandins lower blood pressure, immobilize free fatty acids, regulate excitability, inhibit aging, and act as an anti-inflammatory agent (especially against excessive histamines released during injury). It cannot be a coincidence that these are just the conditions that traditionally garlic is said to address. Although prostaglandins are found in the liver, brain, and other tissues, the high amounts found in semen indicate its deep connection to birth and the reverse of aging. It remains a mystery why such a substance should be found in garlic at all, and to a much lesser extent—about 92% less—in onions.

Key substances in animals and plants share an uncanny correspondence. The molecules of hemoglobin and chlorophyll, for example, are remarkably

---

* Supplement makers claim to remove garlic odor, making higher consumption possible, but recent research questions whether any active principle (vitamins, etc.) have full value separate from the plant.

similar. The difference is that animal organs are closed off from the environment, secretive and hidden, almost womblike. The animal is hidden within the dark cave of its organs, crouching and furtive, and longs for the cosmic environment it is shut off from. We become carnivores of scent, tracking down the lost pieces of our being spread out in the garden, in wider nature. Our relation to all plants is biochemically very, very, deep; none deeper than to garlic.

In terms of taste, garlic (and to a lesser extent onion) is a food that has some similarities to salt. Garlic has a potent smell and taste of its own, but its function (even at 50 grams per week) is as a flavor enhancer. It stands behind other foods, making them more palatable. This is quite annoying to the dairy farmer, since cows really relish wild garlic, which spoils the taste of the milk. Cows, however, sense that garlic brings the whole organism into relation to its protein and fat metabolism. This may have something to do with garlic's strong connection to sulfur. Garlic provides cosmic information right down into the soles of our feet (or the hooves). In fact, so quickly does allicin permeate the organism that the body seems almost transparent to it.

Perhaps for this reason herbalists have noted that garlic goes particularly well with meat. Garlic complements meat, prevents the development of toxic intestinal flora, and counteracts the mucous-forming effect of many other foods. English herbalist Juliette de Bairacli Levy says that the active principle in garlic for the latter is crotonaldehyde, which allegedly heals mucous linings of the nose, throat, and intestines.

Garlic in milk may bother some consumers, but studies have shown that garlic in mother's milk does not repel babies (*Pediatrics* October 1991). Garlic may yet prove to be essential to childhood development. Lifelong consumers of garlic, besides having lower levels of blood fats, have less stomach and colorectal cancer. Why fight it? Perhaps milk from cows fed on wild garlic could be made into specialty cheese. It could be called "rocambole," after the slightly wilder predecessor of domestic garlic.

Culture

Because garlic is a hardy perennial, it prefers autumn planting. Perennials need the fall to establish their root system and prepare for immediate recovery in early spring. In fact, most perennials want to "do their thing" by midsummer. In cool climates the garlic cloves can be planted in spring, but the bulbs will be smaller. Even in New England the tops wither before the bulbs develop fully. I have many garlic volunteers and have transplanted self-sown garlic plants into the garden. Results were only fair. Cloves can be planted in late September in the North, late October in the central states, and November in the South.

In the wild state, garlic grows best in damp pastures and light woodlands, in areas with high humus. Like the rest of the onion family, garlic requires large amounts of decomposed organic matter. Adequate amounts will assure garlic's moderately heavy demand for nitrogen, which would otherwise have to be supplied later. In fact, garlic really prefers its nitrogen from compost rather than side-dressings. Quality is much higher, flavor is better, and the bulbs much stronger. This is well known to commercial growers.

Some biodynamic gardeners plant garlic following a heavily composted crop harvested in late summer or early fall. They top-dress the bed with compost, till lightly, and spray horn manure 500. They plant the separated, unpeeled cloves, pointed end up, 1 ½ to 2 inches deep, 4 inches apart, and a foot to 18 inches between rows. Then they mulch 4 to 6 inches deep with straw. In areas with dry summers, drip lines go down before the mulch. Except for biodynamic leaf sprays, often nothing more is needed for this crop.

Because of its semi-perennial nature, even market gardeners find that garlic fares better under bed culture. In beds, less mulch is required for the same yield, and garlic appreciates the untrampled soil. Otherwise, choose the spongy tilth of deep lowland soil or former pasture. Garlic also likes the water- and nutrient-holding capacity of clay loam. Soils low in organic matter or suffering from compaction call for bed culture immediately. Drench plants with equisetum tea. In areas with high winter rainfall, some growers leave the beds unmulched to prevent the bulbs from rotting. Unmulched beds should be kept weeded. Fall planted garlic grows quite late, even in December in the central states.

When garlic greens up again in early spring, spray silica (501). Again, keep weeded, if necessary. Some weeds are okay but yields plummet in beds overwhelmed by weeds, and harvest becomes really difficult. Many bulbs are missed, and then re-sprout. In beds of less than optimum fertility, or for extra-large bulbs, plants respond to side-dressings in mid spring of compost/nettle tea, fish emulsion, or organic fertilizer.

Causes of crop failure in garlic may stem from seed cloves that have rotted slightly in storage or have disease hidden in the root plate. Disease in the root plate will cause the bulbs to break apart prematurely. Discard seed cloves that show signs of rot, soft spots, or black streaks. But even sound cloves may rot in poorly drained soil, and less hardy varieties may rot in cold wet winters. Hardy types like rocambole never seem to rot. Unharvested rocambole cloves always reappear in spring. In general the success of garlic will be in direct proportion to the size, vigor, and dark green color of the leaves. Garlic is a leaf through and through, and the leaves always forecast the harvest. Though garlic likes nitrogen, too much will adversely affect flavor and storage quality. Sudden changes of weather can also cause garlic to fail, especially unmulched garlic. Drought stressed garlic can shut down prematurely and become dormant (re-vernalize) as it does during winter. I have found that mulch alone has prevented this; but be prepared to irrigate in areas with a prolonged dry season.

Later in summer, garlic will reach a point of natural metabolic slowdown. When softneck tops begin to brown, dig one clove and peel back the sheaths one at a time; 3 or 4 sheaths means the bulbs are ready. In general, 2 or 3 bottom garlic leaves will have turned half yellow. Storage is not merely a question of bulbs drying out, but of the process leading to winter dormancy's being completed. Immature bulbs rot in storage. Over-mature rocambole cloves may pop right out of their skins. Lift bulbs with a digging fork. Never pull them.

Lay out bulbs in a warm, dry shed to cure for a few weeks. Be sure to select a good supply of the best bulbs for fall planting. Note fullness, symmetry of shape, good size for the type, and absence of disease and mold. The rest should be stored in near freezing, at 65 to 70% humidity.

Some home gardeners maintain a fully perennial garlic bed. I discovered this method by accident from a bed crop that I neglected to harvest. When garlic leaves reappeared in the fall, I mulched the bed with half-ripe compost. Next summer, I harvested some cloves and left the others to grow. I kept the bed weeded and harvested, and it produced a steady supply of small cloves for home use for five years. Garlic has volunteered everywhere on my property.

Elephant garlic is also planted in the fall. The giant bulbs need 7 inches between plants, 18 inches between rows, with cloves set 4 inches deep. It is a huge gobbler of water and fertility, so if you grow it, do it right, with lots of compost. Mulch plants 6 inches deep in the North, since elephant garlic is the least hardy of the garlics. Along with your order, seed companies usually send a manual on growing and selling elephant garlic.

Garlic is not very susceptible to pests; thus it is useful as a blended spray for insect pests on other plants. Thrips seem to appear only on humus-deprived and drought-stressed plants. Maintain early vigorous growth and apply insecticidal soap or oil, if necessary. Garlic blended with egg is a proven deer repellent; but to keep the deer uncomfortable, alternate from year to year with other alien scent formulations, such as vegetable grade fish oil (1 cup per 3 gallons water) rosemary oil or cinnamon oil.

Varieties

There are hundreds of varieties and strains of garlic. Try a few varieties according to your taste and region. The more pungent garlics are closer to the wild plant and are generally hardier. Some are downright hot, but heat is different from flavor, and heat diminishes with cooking. Garlics are broadly divided into the wilder hardneck (rocambole) variation, which produces hard flower scapes and tiny top sets in the first year; and the soft neck variation, which retains leafy necks right into harvest. Other types include selections of wild garlic from different species and elephant garlic, also a different species.

The great thing about hardnecks (rocambole, *Allium sativum* var. *ophioscorodon*) is their toughness and adaptability. A rocambole variety long-forgotten has naturalized itself in beds everywhere on my property for twenty years. It grows in shrub and perennial borders, in soft fruit plantations, in hedgerows and under fruit trees. The bulbs are smaller, but they're always there! Grown in the garden, the cloves are much larger, but yields are lower than softneck. Hardnecks grow better in the northern and central states. The plants are called hardnecks because in August they send up a hard flower stem out of the center of the bulb, producing flowers and tiny bulblets. Yield will be increased substantially if curled scapes are removed after the scapes have first curled 360 degrees and then begun to uncurl. Scapes can be used in cooking. When hardnecks are not harvested on time—about 4 weeks after the 360-degree turn—the cloves will split off and either re-sprout or be less storable. Hardnecks have only one layer of fairly large easy-to-peel cloves surrounding the scape, whereas softnecks have successive layers of smaller bulbs where the scape would rise.

German Extra Hardy is one of the strongest growers, with vigorous leaves and long roots, which resist heaving in the winter. Cloves are very large, 4 to 5 per bulb with good strong flavor. Stores well. German Porcelain is similar but larger still, half as large as elephant garlic in fertile soil. It grows well in the mid-Atlantic. For the South and warmer regions try a Creole-type stiffneck such as Ajo Rojo, which tolerates heat and drought. Also try other exotic varieties from central Asia and the Caucasus for their different flavors; or wild garlic relatives such as *Allium longicuspis* (Brown Tempest) with its very hot, wild garlicky flavor. Asian garlics such as Blossom are very hot eaten raw, but mellow out when stir-fried or baked. Asiatic garlic grows like a hardneck in cool climates and like a softneck in hot ones. Go online to explore other garlics from Poland, Russia, Yugoslavia, and the Middle East.

Softneck garlics (*Allium sativum*, var. *sativum*) have been bred not to bolt and form bulblets. Though slightly less cold-hardy than stiffnecks, they are easier to grow, yield more, don't break apart as easily, and store better; and the softnecks can be braided. Cloves are smaller but more numerous, with 3 to 5 layers. Artichoke softnecks are the largest with up to 5 layers of lumpy cloves, very productive and adaptable. Silverskin softnecks are best for warmer, drier areas where these beautiful bulbs are traditionally braided.

Inchelium Red, an artichoke type, is one of the most productive garlics, with prizewinning flavor. Mild French Silverskin is best for the South and West, with excellent flavor, keeping qualities, and appearance.

Elephant garlic is wonderful to grow but a disappointment to eat. Bulbs grow as large as small grapefruit, and have no more flavor than a single clove of silverskin. Too mild for garlic lovers, a disappointment really; but good sliced in stir-fries and salads or used as a creamy spread on hot bread. Elephant cloves are very expensive to start. It takes a year or more to build up enough planting stock, if you plan to market the bulbs. One bulb will produce eight times its weight, enough to supply a family for the winter (but not my family!).

A beautiful garlic to grow in containers is *Allium tuberosum*, called garlic chives. It is a must in every kitchen garden or in the perennial border. The beautiful swirl of flat leaves might have been drawn by Leonardo da Vinci. It has star-like elegant white flowers in abundance. Superb chopped in salads, salad dressings, or garnishes, better than chives. Left in the ground, it produces many small plants in the spring.

The giant flowering *Allium* (*Allium giganteum*) gives an archetypal picture of the genus. The leaves die back somewhat, and we are left with two spheres, a pungent bulb in the earth connected to a radiating sphere and starry flowers by a long, hollow tube. This is an archetypal biodynamic picture of how the earth (the bulb) is connected to the cosmos. Although the flower seems to originate from the bulb, the forces that produced the bulb itself are coming from another direction, pictured by the radiating seed-head. Garlic rarely sets fertile seeds; but it repeats the set of cloves up in air where seeds normally form, holding back what flies away in seed formation. The reproductive force, expressed as prostaglandin, is reserved, held back for the general well-being. Herbalist Juliette de Bairacli Levy says the ancient name for garlic is *moly*, the herb given to Odysseus to protect him from the wiles of Circe, freeing him to continue his life's journey. Garlic may have a similar function in relation to the entire human organism, reserving what otherwise supports the reproductive forces for the use of the organism as a whole.

- SEED: For regular garlic: 4 pounds of cloves sow about a 100-foot row or a 30-foot bed with 3 rows, depending on the size of the cloves. For elephant garlic: (8 times larger) a pound will plant 15 feet; 7 pounds will plant 100 feet, or a 30-foot bed with 3 rows.
- GERMINATION: Plant in time for a month's growth before hard frost; grows from middle fall into frost.
- VIABILITY: Cloves keep 5 to 8 months.
- DAYS TO HARVEST: 80 days from the time re-growth begins in spring.
- MOON CALENDAR: Plant in root but cultivate and apply biodynamic sprays in leaf. Spray maturing bulbs with silica (501) on root days in the afternoon.
- ROTATION: Three years between members of the onion family to avoid bulb-rotting fungi.
- BIODYNAMIC SPRAYS: Horn manure (500) on soil before planting. Dip cloves in compost-clay slurry with a pinch of 500 stirred in. Spray silica when plants show good top growth in fall and re-growth in spring. Spray maturing bulbs with silica in afternoon, when the leaves show slight yellowing.
- COMPANION PLANTS: Garlic is good for practically all garden plants, as well as around fruit trees (against peach borers, and so forth) and roses (for fragrance), and against pests. Mixed culture for garlic lessens the effect of thrips. Garlic sprays are useful as fungicide and pesticide. Celery or celeriac and garlic are good companions. Garlic repels celery pests, and both require similar fertility, water, and mulch.

GROUND CHERRY

Ground cherries (*Physalis pruinosa*) are sweeter more fruitlike members of the husk tomato, tomatillo genus, sometimes called strawberry ground cherry, sometimes Cossack Pineapple. Both names refer to flavor undertones that make ground cherries a pleasure to eat out of hand. Children love their very sweet pineapple like flavor. Different from tomatillo, ground cherries are allowed to ripen, which means allowed to fall to the ground. Fruits are delicious in salad, mixed into fruit compote, or made into pies and preserves. The very sweet berries can be dried like raisins. Because ground cherries originate in Eastern Europe, they are much quicker to fruit than tomatillos, and less dependent on a long season. Plants are also more compact, 12 inches high by 24 inches wide. They fit easily into any size garden, even containers. Fruits are very high in antioxidant vitamins C and A.

Leaves look like Jimson weed but are velvety and fuzzy. Like Jimson weed they can become invasive; extremely so in the beautiful ornamental husk cherry called Chinese or Japanese Lantern (*Physalis alkekengi*), which is extremely hardy and the devil to eradicate once established. Chinese lanterns only look like ground cherries. Their fruit may cause miscarriage in pregnant women, and severe abdominal pain, especially in children. On the positive side, research indicates that xanthophylls extracted from Chinese lantern may prevent vision loss due to age-related macular disease.

Ground cherries produce well in sun or half-sun in most soil types, but fruits not fully ripe (half-sun) have lingering musky off flavors. The flavor of fully ripe fruit varies from pineapple to strawberry to grape and tomato. Like tomatillo, the seed cavity is not juicy but firm, with high pectin, making it easy to thicken preserves or pie filling. One plant will make a pie.

Culture is the same as tomatillo or tomato and subject to some tomato disease and insects. In regions of low frost, ground cherries will overwinter.

Varieties

Cossack Pineapple (60 days) produces small sweet ½-inch berries with complex flavor. Goldie (75 days) produces larger ¾-inch berries, which are very sweet and flavorful. Aunt Molly's Ground Cherry has gotten mixed reviews because of off flavors and seediness.

Cape gooseberry (*Physalis peruviana*) is another sweet long-season ground cherry very similar to *P. pruinosa*. Fruits look a bit like true gooseberries (Ribes). For 100 years Cape gooseberry has been useful to isolated cattle stations in Australia where no other fruit was available. Cape Gooseberry is by far the most widely grown ground cherry—stretching across South America, Africa, Egypt, India, China, Southeast Asia, Australia, and New Zealand. It is used in commercial jam, pie, chutney, curry, and spicy sweet sauces. The fruit is dried as raisins, used raw in salads, and eaten out of hand. Golden fruits are sometimes squeezed as a ground cherry orange juice. It grows only in long warm-season climates. Fruit must be completely ripe, as unripe fruits have proved toxic to some people. Fruits are high in vitamins, polyphenols, and antioxidants. Plants are favored in the third world because they produce well with no fertilizer. Added potassium, however, increases fruit quality. Fruits are ripe when the husk splits. Varieties include Goldberry, whose 1- to 2-inch fruits are sweet enough for raisins or juice, and Garrison's Pineapple, similar in flavor to Cossack Pineapple or ground cherry.

HORSERADISH

I've observed a patch of horseradish (*Armoracia rusticana*) growing near the remains of a nineteenth-century foundation for more than thirty years. The house was gone long before I moved north in 1983. The locals claim that four generations of family members have harvested the roots every fall, but none had a clue when the patch was planted.

For home gardeners the advantage of a wild horseradish patch is a constant supply of roots, with no work. The disadvantage is that roots are small and rangy. None grow large or smooth enough to peel or grate easily.

Market growers treat this extremely hardy perennial (up to Zone 3) as an annual. They plant 3- to 6-inch root pieces in loose deeply cultivated soil every spring. To get a larger central root they sometimes use a hooked rod early in the season to lift the huge rosette up about 2 inches. This breaks the smaller side roots, throwing energy into the central root, which may weigh 2 pounds by fall.

Horseradish, originally called *meer rettich* (sea radish), is a native of Asia and Eastern and Southern Europe, and is still found wild in damp places and along sea coasts. Its common name is a confusion between *meer* (sea) and *mare* (horse). In late summer and early fall dry spells, when the central root is putting on weight, remember that this is a moisture-loving plant.

Since antiquity, the medicinal value of horseradish has been praised so extravagantly as to seem unreasonable. The Delphic Oracle claimed that horseradish was literally worth its weight in gold. In recent times her claim has gained credence, since grated horseradish has been shown to contain 10 times the antioxidants of broccoli, available in a long-lasting package accessible to any gardener. Roots also have 81 milligrams (mg) of vitamin C per 100 grams, enough to ward off scurvy in hard times.

Like Upland Cress (early winter Cress) horseradish has higher levels of antioxidant glucosinulates (*gluconasturtiians*) than most other cruciferous vegetables (University of Illinois). Horseradish has shown promise for inducing cancer cell arrest (apoptosis) under laboratory conditions (University of Dundee, Scotland); and it stimulates enzymes that aid in liver detoxification (Cornell University).

Therapeutic effects are increased by grating, which initiates enzymatic activity and the transformation into isothiocyanates (antioxidant). Wait 5 minutes before halting enzymatic activity with 2 to 3 tablespoons of white vinegar and ½ teaspoon salt to each cup of grated horseradish. Although lemon juice, balsamic, or wine vinegar would achieve the same result, white vinegar makes eventual darkening more apparent, which will alert to the loss of isothiocyanates, and indicate the time to grate a new batch.

Horseradish oils and the enzyme myrosinase rapidly open clogged sinuses (Virginia Extension). In India young horseradish leaves are eaten in salads and added to curries, a significant increase of vitamins and antioxidants to the diet.

Japanese horseradish (*Wasabi japonica*) is an entirely different species, grown for its green leaf petioles, which are ground into a pungent green paste. Wasabi is grown like watercress in running streams, rice paddies, and hydroponic greenhouses. Some commercial wasabi preparations are created by dying European horseradish green.

Culture

Horseradish is well suited to organic and biodynamic production. Nitrogen needs are low to moderate, phosphorus moderate, and potassium high (Virginia Extension). Compost produces good results. The pH range is fairly wide, but like other crucifers, horseradish prefers a neutral soil. Lighter soils produce the best roots and make harvesting much easier. Roots don't tolerate hardpan or shallow soils. Soils should be cultivated a foot down using a spading fork or chisel plow.

When roots are received by mail, notice that the upper part of the root is cut straight across, while the lower part is cut on a slant. This indicates original growth orientation. The same applies to harvesting your own root sets: make a straight cut above, slant below. Root sets can be harvested in fall and refrigerated or cold-cellared at 30 to 38°F, or left in the ground and harvested in spring. Horseradish does not require vernalization (winter chilling). Long side roots are used for sets; cut into 3- to 6-inch pieces and place in 6-inch furrows, when soils have warmed enough for spring planting of other crucifers. Space sets vertically, straight cut up ,about 18 inches apart in rows 3 to 4 feet apart. Virginia Extension suggests slanting sets away from the direction of cultivation to avoid lifting unrooted plants.

As mentioned above, some growers lift the rosette by 2 inches early in the season using a hooked steel rod, to break tiny lateral roots. Home gardeners can pull the rosette up a few inches by hand. Removing lateral roots makes more nutrients available to the central shoot.

Horseradish roots put on their bulk late in the season, so be prepared to irrigate during any late summer and early fall dry spells. Wait until the first frost signals the end of bulking before harvesting. Roots can be lifted with a spading fork or harvested for market using a single row potato digger; first mow any standing foliage and rake away frozen matted foliage. Roots may be washed prior to storage in perforated bin liners. Roots store 10 to 12 months at 30 to 32°F with 90 to 95 % humidity, but quality and antioxidant levels are highest in the fall. Fresh roots have higher antioxidant value than stored roots.

Commercially, roots are graded as "Fancy" when 6-inch pieces are more than 1 ½ inches in diameter; and "US #1" when 6-inch roots are 1 inch in diameter. Both grades must be internally white and free of discoloration or streaking, which adversely affects the prepared condiment.

Diseases and Insects

Like beets, horseradish is subject to black heart, which looks like a disease, but is caused by boron deficiency. This is usually resolved by compost from mixed sources, including hardwood leaves. Get a soil test, if necessary.

Foliar disease includes white rust, leaf spot (ramularia), bacterial leaf spot, and cercospora leaf spot. Control with copper fungicide.

Turnip mosaic virus presents as splotchy distorted leaves. Transmitted by aphids, which can be controlled with insecticidal oil.

Brittle root is a virus-like disease caused by the salivary juices of leafhoppers. Roots turn dark brown and become brittle. Control leafhoppers with insecticidal oil or neem (azadirachtin).

Horseradish leaves are eaten by cabbage worms, which are velvety green with faint yellow stripes. Control with Bt (Dipel). The larva of imported crucifer weevils feed on roots, making them unmarketable. Control with pyrethrins sprayed late in the day. Flea beetles should be controlled on early leaf growth with row covers, neem or spinosad.

Varieties

Crinkled-leaf types, called "common," have very high-quality large central roots, but are susceptible to turnip mosaic virus and white rust. Smooth-leaf types, called Bohemian or Maliner Kren, produce smaller central roots but are smooth and of good quality. Smooth-leaf types show resistance to white rust but not turnip mosaic.

Big Top Western from the University of Illinois shows resistance to both diseases with very good root quality. Other varieties recommended for large primary roots up to 2 pounds each include Swiss and Sass.

SEED: Horseradish is propagated vegetatively from root cuttings, not from seed. Select plants for vigor (strong top growth), size of central root, internal quality (whiteness, free of streaking and discoloration), and flavor. Save secondary roots (with top cut straight and bottom cut slanted) in perforated bin liners at 30 to 38°F until spring. Growers without cold storage can leave entire plants for propagation in ground until early spring at planting time.

VIABILITY: Roots last 10 to 12 months in cold storage 30 to 32°F, 90 to 95% humidity.

MOON CALENDAR: All practices in root, descending moon.

ROTATION: For permanent stands, plant where no gardening has occurred. In the garden practice the standard 3- to 4-year crucifer rotation.

BIODYNAMIC SPRAYS: Preparation 500 on tilled ground prior to planting, 501 on newly established rosettes, fully established rosette, and in early fall when the central root begins to flesh out.

JERUSALEM ARTICHOKE

The "Jerusalem" in Jerusalem artichoke does not really refer to the Promised Land. But the plant does possess remarkable traits that biodynamic farmers wish could be grafted onto other vegetables, the foremost being its tough perennial nature. Another name is "sunchoke," and it is indigenous to the Native American prairie, a prairie that the Land Institute and other initiatives have been trying to develop into sustainable permanent agriculture. Sunchokes can do what annual vegetables cannot; they grow more rampantly than weeds, harbor few insect pests, and every year produce (without replanting) a superabundance of potato-like tubers! This abundance will reappear even after prolonged summer drought. The flavor of the tuber is sweet, nutty, and contains inulin, a form of sugar well tolerated by diabetics. Finally, and most surprising of all, a single planting can produce reliable crops for thirty years.

Yet, like many promises of paradise, the reality of Jerusalem artichoke falls somewhat short of the Heavenly City. Sunchokes indeed grow faster than the weeds. After the first year, the tall vigorous plants shade and "choke" out the weed population. Their vigor is typified by the name of a commonly available variety, Stampede. Stampede produces very large white tubers, often more than half a pound, about a month earlier than the rest of the species; but as the name implies, the artichoke patch knows no bounds. It spreads wildly in all directions. Once established in an area, even a year of heavy black plastic covering may not keep them down. The only way to be rid of them is to leave the state, which I did.

Chokes are indeed reliable producers, almost regardless of weather. They withstand fairly wet conditions and summer drought, intense cold in winter, and intense heat in summer. The patch is as long-lived as a fruit tree and yields are never biennial. The tubers are sweet, crisp, and crunchy in salads; and sweet, soft, and nut-like when cooked. Chokes will probably always remain a minor homestead crop, because cooked chokes produce substantial gas and abdominal pain in many people. As with beans and leeks, be moderate. Some people are also allergic to inulin.

One farmer joked that "Jerusalem" was added by a seed company to conjure up visions of profit; as animal feed, the crop is so easy and prolific, there might be something to it. But Jerusalem refers to a whimsical American corruption of *girasol*, "turning with the sun," the Italian word for sunflower. Jerusalem artichoke (*Helianthus tuberosus*) shares this heliotropic tendency with its annual relative, the sunflower, (*Helianthus annus*). In the annual sunflower the resinous, intensely scented flowers produce a highly nutritious seed and high-quality oil. In the perennial sunflower (sunchoke), an overwintering storage tuber is produced by August or September.

The true globe artichoke (*Cynara scolymus*) and sunchoke (*H. tuberosa*) are both in the same family, the daisy family, *Compositae*, but *Cynara* is a thistle. "Artichoke" comes from an Italian dialect for pinecone, referring to the conelike scales of thistle buds. The flavor of sunchoke tubers faintly recalls the flavor of artichoke hearts.

Europeans gave the Jerusalem artichoke back to America. This Native American sunflower is still found wild throughout the West, Midwest, and parts of the East. Like corn and squash, the Indians grew it for centuries. Europeans discovered it during the fatal English expedition to Virginia in 1558. The French explorer Samuel de Champlain carried it back to France in the next century, where the tubers were improved by selection and finally re-introduced to non-native North American gardeners.

In her *Enchanted Broccoli Forest* cookbook, Mollie Katzen suggests not only using sunchokes raw in green garden salads and with sour cream and tofu dip, but also presents the novel idea of using sunchokes as a crunchy addition to fruit salad. Just scrub under cold water and slice. Raw sunchokes can also be pickled or marinated in wine vinegar, lemon juice, garlic dressing, or Italian salad dressing. The traditional Italian method is to sauté pared sliced sunchokes in olive oil and chopped garlic. Salt, pepper, and parsley are then added to taste.

To make a sunchoke Asian stir-fry, mix sliced carrots, broccoli, bok choy, and so forth, in equal amounts. Add lesser amounts of sliced onion, chopped garlic, and grated ginger. Stir-fry until broccoli is slightly tender but still deep green. Season with soy or teriyaki sauce. To get the effect of water chestnuts, clean and pare raw sunchokes and add to the stir-fry only when the other vegetables are nearly cooked. In another recipe sunchokes are sautéed in butter and flavored with salt and lemon juice or with Parmesan cheese or nutmeg. Still other cooks lightly steam sunchokes and serve with a creamy cheese sauce.

The scent of both the annual and perennial sunflowers have always intrigued me. In the annual sunflower, the sweet "resiny" scent is piercing, penetrating, almost intoxicating. In perennial sunflower (sunchoke) the scent is sweeter still, almost like chocolate. You can smell the group of related composites including arnica, calendula, and *inula* from a long way off. Their resins and warmth also remind me of the resins of conifers.

Sometimes I have spent a whole day in an arboretum exploring a forest of conifers with my nose. One group, say the firs of the world, might be tied together with the scent of grapefruit rind. You can walk into the forests of composites in the same way. At the right time of year the scent is almost overpowering. Where I live now, in Western Massachusetts, I grow unintentional forests of cup plant (*Silphium perfoliatum*), which overwhelm a large bed of purple lupines and invade the shrub borders and blackberry beds. The strange square stems rise up 10 feet before bowing with the weight of thousands of small sunflowers and the insects, which adore them. I often have to stop and stand still. Their sweet, intoxicating "resiny" smell is like a gate into a completely imaginary forest. Although I hate the invasiveness of these giant composites, I have to surrender at the gate of their world.

Culture

Like nettle, sunchokes don't belong inside the garden. They need a place where their rampant growth will never become a problem. On smaller properties, it might be necessary to box a bed with aluminum flashing at least a foot down. Some gardeners dig tubers in from the edges to contain the bed. Others allow a substantial mow strip around the edges of the patch.

In some situations, such as along banks, which tend to erode, the tenacious habit of sunchokes might be beneficial. Certainly they are no worse than the ubiquitous Japanese knotweed (*Polygonum cuspidatum*), a rampant bamboo-sized relative of buckwheat. Japanese knotweed was originally introduced by the USDA as a hedge for erosion control. It became virtually unremovable. The only creatures I know who seem happy about Japanese knotweed are the bees, which love the abundant buckwheat-like flowers. Bees love perennial sunflowers too.

Before biodynamic or organic farmers plant large areas to sunchokes, they should consider whether the plant will become a nuisance, if later the land is required for another crop. But, since sunchokes are well adapted to poor sandy soils, they may be an excellent choice for otherwise unproductive farmland.

Sunchokes have been used for livestock feed for generations. As with any other vegetable addition to the diet, the sunchokes must not displace the native diet of the animal. Check Extension Reports on the dietary limits for each animal. The area to be planted should be tilled and lightly composted, but if compost is in short supply just add a handful to each planting hole. Mulch can make up the difference over the years, and too much fertilizer makes watery tubers that don't keep well. Biodynamic growers should spray horn manure (500) over the area prior to planting. Tubers are similar to dahlias (a relative) and each one needs to have at least one sprouting eye at the top. Plant 3 to 4 inches deep with 15 inches between plants, and a 4-foot tiller width between rows. Keep weeded for the first year, either by cultivation or a heavy mulch of straw or leaves. In the second year the plants will take over.

Give the plants a spraying of silica (501) when the plants are well into leaf, when the first flower buds appear, and once in fall during seed formation. If large tubers are needed, compost annually and mulch well. Like any permaculture crop, the compost of the previous fall repays the following summer. For larger crops, sunchoke fields can be rotated every few years, perhaps followed with suppressive crops such as squash, pumpkins, or melons on black plastic.

Tubers can be harvested in the autumn, but unless careful storage arrangements have been made, no more should be lifted than can be used in a few weeks. Tubers keep poorly out of the ground, shriveling or rotting, depending on storage conditions. With optimum coldness (near freezing) and high humidity, they will store all winter. Some people store them like carrots in moist sand. In the central and south central states, heavy mulch keeps the ground frost-free for winter digging.

SEED: 3 pounds of tubers plant 100 feet of row.

GERMINATION: Hardy perennial, early spring.

VIABILITY: Self-propagating in the ground root cellar from 1 to 4 months. Must not dry or shrivel at near freezing temperatures.

DAYS TO HARVEST: 90 days.

MOON CALENDAR: All culture, including biodynamic sprays in root.

ROTATION: Perennial. Difficult to rotate. Tubers re-sprout vigorously.

COMPANION PLANTS: As a hedge on the north side of the garden against wind. Invasive. Shades out other plants.

KALE AND COLLARDS

Kale is the most nutritious cultivated plant. Only stinging nettle (*Urtica dioica*) and lamb's quarters (*Chenopodium album*), both wild plants, surpass kale in some ways, although nettles are burdened by a brief and painful harvesting season and lamb's quarters by high oxalic acid content. Kale is so nutritious that other vegetables pale by comparison. Kale does not just specialize in certain vitamins. It provides them all, bestowing them in a highly digestible form. An orange, for example, has only a third of the vitamin C found in kale, and oranges have 40 times less vitamin A. Lamb's quarters has more calcium, but the oxalic acid binds the calcium and adds a problem of its own for the kidneys. The same is true for the other chenopods beet greens and Swiss chard; chard is the least problematic in that regard. Kale leaves have nearly twice the protein (4.5%; collards have 4.8%). Kale is the lowest in water, highest in fiber and food energy, and contains half the sodium and twice the niacin of Swiss chard. Incredible!*

Nutrients are the tracks of the complex of forces found in each plant; and if one compares leaves and fruits and roots, one realizes the Goethe was right. The leaf is the center of the universe for the living world, a cosmic funnel for the formative forces within the plant. The leaves are the focus, the spiral, the gathering place of life, the harvester of earth and sky, and the very center of life on earth. And of all these leaves, kale is the Sun.

Kale is also one of the hardiest vegetables, solving a big problem for fall and winter gardening. Collards are more heat tolerant, but kale survives more frost. With wind protection, kale can be harvested right through the winter. Taken together, kale and collards form an unbroken chain. The stalks of wind-protected kale send out new shoots in the spring during the time that new collard plants are growing in a cold frame. By midsummer, when the spinach has gone by or bolted, collards will be thriving. Except in scorching climates, collards

---

* When I checked these figures with the 2010 USDA website, I found to my distress that all the nutrients for conventionally grown vegetables had declined drastically in the last forty years, often by half. Steiner, Howard, Albrecht, and Pfeiffer, the founders of alternative agriculture, had predicted this; but I was startled, even so. The causes—over fertilization, lowered organic matter and de-mineralization—still hold sway. I have retained the older stats, which I believe are more in line with organic and biodynamic vegetables.

produce a slow fountain of greens until hard frost, but long before that, direct seeded-kale will be flourishing. Kale can be tough in midsummer, especially when denied water, but a touch of frost makes it deliciously sweet and tender. If you've forgotten what sugar should really taste like, try biodynamically grown kale in the fall. I also like kale grown in the winter greenhouse.

Kale and collards are so similar that botanically they are hard to separate. Both are named *Brassica oleraceca*, var. *acephala*. Even the prehistoric names of kale and collards are the same. Kale and collards derive from the Scottish *caulis* or coles and the Anglo-Saxon *coleworts*. Both are considered the original form of all the cole plants that followed, including swedes, kohlrabi, Brussels sprouts, broccoli, and cauliflower. Gardeners have used both for over 2,000 years, probably going back to Asia Minor. The Greeks and Romans ate them, and so did the monks in the middle ages. It was only later that the heading, white varieties were developed, resulting in an incredible drop in nutritional value. Students of plant metamorphosis have always been fascinated by the sequence of plants that have developed out of kale and collards. As plants, they seemed ever-willing to pour forth new variations. Yet, despite the range of variations, even experienced gardeners cannot tell one cotyledon from another. Here we are dealing with a primal leaf form, a foundation from which the rest of the protean group of crucifers grows. Kale and collards remain closest to the primal form, and like all primal waters they remain the most curative.

Traditional consumers of collards are southern African-Americans. Even in the 1930s, nutritionists were puzzled by their relative good health, despite their extreme poverty and limited diet. George Washington Carver believed that the key to their health was the collard and the sweet potato. To this day, "greens" to an African-American means collards, which they spoil somewhat with pork fat. Kale was once so pervasive in the Scottish diet that the same word was used for both food and kale. Over centuries kale acquired the reputation of "vegetable doctor," now severely challenged by popular Scottish treats such as deep-fried candy bars. Though kale is a therapeutic well of great depth, treatment works best when begun in childhood, as part of a diet low in animal fat and animal protein. In the realm of "therapy," kale appears to have an edge over collards.

The palatability of kale and collards varies according to how both are grown, when harvested, and how cooked. In New England I harvested tender kale and collards in May by setting out transplants in early April under heavy row cover (with iron-based slug bait) as soon as the soil could be worked. Mid-May I removed the fabric and harvested until summer, when kale tends to get tough, and switched to collards and Swiss chard until frosty September nights transformed kale to the best of all possible vegetables. Both kale and collards are sweetened and tenderized by light frost.

Early and late harvests need only light steaming, though many cooks like the bright green retained by submersing the leaves completely in boiling water. One of our favorite family meals solves the problem: a kale and mixed vegetable soup served with fettuccini. We add the ingredients to a pot of boiling vegetable bouillon according to the cooking time of each ingredient, sometimes adding uncooked miso at the end, along with chopped scallions or garlic chives. Although traditionally kale has been seasoned with butter and salt, and collards with pork, my children have grown to love these greens dressed with fresh pressed garlic, olive oil, balsamic vinegar, and salt.

Despite botanical sameness, kale and collards are clearly different, probably even therapeutically. Collard leaves are similar to the large leaves enclosing heads of cabbage, while kale leaves retain the serrations of a wild ancestor. In kale an enormous amount of surface area is curled and condensed in a small space. The leaf rosette is compact and viewed from above is very flower-like, which is exploited in ornamental forms of both varieties. In fact everything has sunk into the leaf. Each leaf has become astonishingly *substantial*, storing a tremendous midsummer force of sun for months after the sun has abandoned the North. This process is usually reserved for storage roots, such as carrots, which gather the work done by leaves over the summer. In kale and collards, however, the entire cycle of the year is retained in the leaf zone.

Culture

Culture is similar to cabbage, but easier, especially with kale. Kale does not seem to be as bothered by disease or insects as cabbage, at least in the northern and central states. In the South, nematodes and other cabbage pests such as flea beetle and cabbage worms can be a problem. Collards are eaten by cabbage worms, less so in a medium clay loam with cow manure compost. Control cabbage worms with Bt (Dipel). In the South where nematodes are a problem, add more compost, which contains nematode-attacking fungi, or apply beneficial nematodes. In the early stages, especially for midsummer plantings, kale and collards can be protected from flea beetles with row cover.

In the North, kale and collards can either be started in cold frames or directly seeded outside three months before expected fall frost. In central states, kale and collards can be sown with midseason cole crops in mid-June. Kale can also be sown later, from July 15 (or in the central states, the same time Chinese cabbage is sown). Sow mid-August in southern states, and mid-autumn in low frost areas for overwintering.

Kale seedlings are fairly bolt-resistant. I've neglected them in seedbeds for two months and still found them productive. 6 weeks is normally the maximum for kale and collards. Kale can be transplanted in beds in a 12-inch grid, or 10 inches in a row with 20 inches between rows.

Collard plants, however, grow very large, even larger than cabbages. Give them 2 feet all around, unless you are planning to harvest immature rosettes for bunching, in which case they can be planted closer like kale. When putting in a lot of plants, biodynamic growers prepare a compost-clay slurry with preparation 500 as a root dip. Silica (501) can be sprayed when transplants have established themselves in a few weeks and when the plants form a rosette.

Kale grows more quickly than collards, and can be harvested as whole rosettes, rather than stripping the individual leaves. Some growers market young collard plants the same way, but plants in home gardens will produce far more leaves when stripped gradually over a three-month period.

Varieties

The best collard selections are found in southern catalogs, such as *Southern Exposure Seed Exchange*. Vates, and slower bolting, more winter-hardy forms of Vates, such as Champion, grow well in most regions, but some collards are adapted to local conditions. Georgia is favored in the South, where it withstands hot summers, though Georgia also improves in sweetness and tenderness with a touch of autumn frost. Georgia Green (*Southern Exposure*) is an heirloom variety adapted to southern Atlantic sandy soil. Worth a try elsewhere, especially where sandy soils produce poor growth in the cabbage family. Green Glaze (*Southern Exposure*, 1820, 79 days) offers excellent resistance to cabbage worm and cabbage looper in southern areas where worms are a problem. Other heirlooms, such as the slightly savoyed Morris Heading, are half-heading cabbage collards. Faster growing hybrid collards may be useful for bunching and for earlier harvest.

Blue Curled Scotch (55 days) is still considered the best-flavored kale. For some reason, perhaps sheer lack of imagination, Virginia Extension has called its selection of Blue Curled Scotch "Vates." Not to be confused with Vates Collard. Vates Kale (55 days) is resistant to yellowing due to heat and frost in the Mid-Atlantic states, but may yellow in deep frost. Winterbor (60 days) is a hybrid of Vates with greater frost tolerance for later harvests and overwintering, with higher yields than its predecessor. Winterbor is tall (2 to 3 feet) but re-grows vigorously when cut above the growing point. Popular with market gardeners. When overwintering under snow or between bales of straw, choose a compact variety, or time a later planting. Even hardy tall varieties are subject to windburn. For added color try red-leaved kale such as Redbor, similar in other respects to green kale. Flavor and red color are enhanced by light frost.

Tuscan kale, the Italian lacinato, (65 days) is a beautiful large plant (hence the nickname Dinosaur kale), with long dark green leaves, increasingly popular in organic markets. Not with me, though. The leaves are not as flavorful as regular kale and not as hardy. I enjoy looking at the plants much more than eating them. The leaves of Tuscan kale hold up better than other greens after harvest.

For fall harvest, Red Russian (Ragged Jack) is an attractive plant with purple stems and slightly wavy, deeply toothed, green leaves. Excellent for salads and stir-fries, the tender leaves of Red Russian need to be handled like cut flowers. They wilt easily and seem more prone to insect attacks. Nevertheless, they appear frequently in health-conscious markets.

Gourmet restaurants often use "flowering" kale and "flowering" cabbage as attractive bedding for salads and platters. Not really flowers, the leaves form a highly colored palette of purple, rose, white, and red. This is a feast for the eyes, all edible. Cool weather, short autumn days, and light frost bring out the best color. Flowering kale and cabbage make really spectacular fall and winter bedding material. When I visited Washington D.C. after Christmas, I was delighted by the ornate bright midwinter design in rose, white, and green kale, planted directly above the underground Islamic wing of the Smithsonian Museum. I've never seen such a successful winter garden or a finer use of design. It was like a reflection of the ancient Islamic carpets below.

If you wish to create your own magic carpet, Stokes has a beautiful collection of ornamental kale and cabbage, all edible. Nagoya Red Garnish (60 days) is used widely by market growers for the restaurant trade.

SEED: Kale seed averages about 7,500 seeds per ounce; collards about 5,000. A packet of 100 seeds produces about 80 transplants; about 80% of seed sown produces viable transplants.

GERMINATION: 75%; 7 to 14 days at 70°F.

VIABILITY: 4 years.

DAYS TO HARVEST: 50 to 65 days.

MOON CALENDAR: All culture, including biodynamic sprays, in leaf.

ROTATION: 3 to 6 years for cabbage family, depending on disease (6 years for club root).

BIODYNAMIC SPRAYS: Horn manure (500) on field and seedbed. Compost-clay-500 slurry as root dip for transplants. Silica (501) when rosette begins and 3 weeks later.

COMPANION PLANTS: Same as cabbage. Since plants can be transplanted late, kale is good for fill-in for summer gaps. Be aware of three-year crucifer rotation, however. For health and flavor: onions, garlic, dill, chamomile, mint, caraway, sage, and rosemary. For pests, use aromatic herbs: catnip, dill, caraway, thyme, sage, rosemary, marjoram, tansy, wormwood, and southernwood. For intercropping: bush beans, beets, celery, chard, lettuce, and onions.

KOHLRABI

In the last century an artist named Turpin tried to illustrate Goethe's observation that each successive plant organ (leaf, sepal, petal, ovary, and so forth), is a metamorphosis of the previous one. Turpin didn't seem to get it. He randomly pasted together parts of a dozen species, in effect creating the first "Frankenplant." At first I thought this was a joke or a vicious cartoon attacking Goethe's ideas, but later I read that Turpin was sincerely trying to illustrate the archetype of metamorphosis. The problem goes beyond a drawing, which not only does not illuminate, but also actually prevents the viewer from being active in the logic of transformation. Turpin created a botanist's nightmare, really an unconscious vision of the future, in which every natural relation is torn from its roots; in which the pieces of percep-

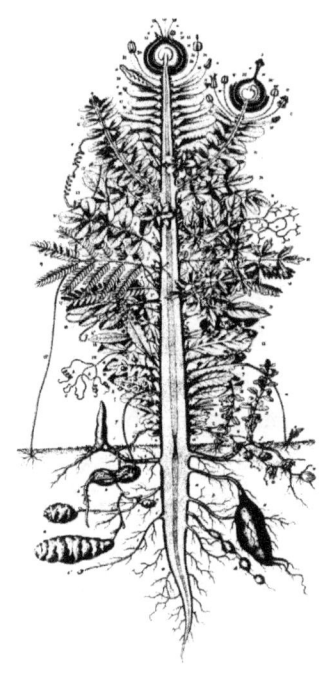

THE IDEAL PLANT
by P.J.F. Turpin

tion themselves have no connection whatsoever to the truly magical transformations in nature. Turpin's picture is a blunt instrument. In many ways it reminded me of a normal American biology class—at least the ones I knew when I was in school. Doubtless Turpin and his successors were unaware that their disjointed picture of nature laid the foundation for an agriculture that will destroy large portions of the earth.

The problem with Turpin (and most biology teachers) is that they never look at nature using her own power of imagination. Probably none of them ever took a good look at kohlrabi, either. I doubt that an artist not intimate with metamorphosis could really have invented kohlrabi. To do so, a human artist would have to experience the formative space out of which kohlrabi arises. There would be no other choice, since kohlrabi is part of a still larger imagination, larger even than the magical *Brassica* genus itself, although the plot of this play is still quite a mystery to me after fifty years of observation and thought. Johann von Goethe made many rueful remarks about our inability to follow nature's plot and method of change. He said, for example, that unless you can understand the secret of transformation, you will be a sorry guest upon this earth!

Using forked carrots and gnarled roots I've made countless fantasy creatures for my children, but the strangeness of kohlrabi is no fantasy. It is as if an unsettling childhood dream were suddenly to stand before you—a green eyeless head with leaves for hair. In the dream, part of me wants it to speak, part of me does not. I try to run but my legs are paralyzed, and the leaves become fingers that explore the contours of my face. They won't let me go until I answer a question.

The question appears to be a stem that has changed into a turnip surrounded by leaves. Has a root pushed abnormally up from the soil, just as the stem of a potato uncannily swells underground, imitating a root? It can't be that—kohlrabi isn't earthy at all. Kohlrabi tastes almost like a fruit, clean, sweet, and apple-crisp. The stem has swollen as if a fruit were forming *inside* the normal spiral progression of leaves. In kohlrabi the juvenile plastic force of the meristem has reappeared in an unexpected place, but typical of the *Brassica* genus. Kohlrabi reminds us that every spiral sequence of brassica leaves, every Fibonacci dance of repeated nodes (each like a repeated musical phrase, really) mathematically describes an egg-shaped space that prefigures the flower and becomes filled with substance in the fruit. Kohlrabi reminds us that in the brassicas, the stem cells are the rulers of the kingdom, and that their rule is long and just.

If kohlrabi is a fantasy, it is a fantasy arising from the ground plan of the genus. Kohlrabi swells in the rhythmical space described by its leafy fingers, open and airy in collards, tighter and denser in cabbage, clotted and curd-like in cauliflower, but never, ever becoming the indiscriminate jumble drawn by Turpin. The sphinx-like question, on which my miserable life depends, is to understand the exact agenda of this juvenile ever-changing creature, whose therapeutic power, despite our advanced knowledge of its chemistry, still somehow eludes us. The power of metamorphosis in kohlrabi speaks somewhat like Jehovah to his servant Job: "Were you here when I created the earth? Answer if you have understanding!"

Kohlrabi is a footprint left for the tracker, a footprint that might eventually lead us to create such spaces in nature ourselves, when little of nature is left outside us.

Culture

Novice gardeners often imagine that kohlrabi is a root. They treat kohlrabi as a root and harvest a small crop of cordwood. Even the otherwise reliable Stokes Seed Catalog refers to kohlrabi as a "European root vegetable." True roots can be ignored for months, need only moderately rich soil, and have a long harvest window. Not kohlrabi. Think of kohlrabi in the same way you think of broccoli. Kohlrabi is the expanded stem of a fancy broccoli, which must grow steadily, with no checks in growth, and must be harvested at just the right moment. In broccoli this would mean tight blue-green buds, except that in kohlrabi, optimum harvest is not so visible. Nevertheless, kohlrabi is either gourmet quality or it must be discarded. Never forget that kohlrabi is there, or when you planted it.

Culture is no different from broccoli: medium clay loam, pH 6 to 7, ample compost, and most important, consistent supplies of water, especially in areas subject to spring heat waves. Successive sowings can be made in cooler areas. Autumn sowings can accompany bok choy sometime in late summer, depending on latitude.

Sow in seed flats or cells 4 to 6 weeks prior to setting in the field (when most frosts are over, and soil can be worked in the spring). Biodynamic growers spray seedlings with horn silica (501) and equisetum (508) on the same schedule as broccoli. In gardens with poor fertility, feed weekly with compost/nettle tea or liquid seaweed. Continue feedings weekly for two weeks in the field. When transplanting, don't bury stems quite as deep as broccoli or cabbage, because the stem will swell. A mixture of compost, clay, and horn manure (500) as a root dip hastens transplant recovery in the field and speeds growth in cell-type containers. Organize transplanting dates so that many cole crops can be treated at the same time.

Transplant kohlrabi 4 inches apart, in rows 12 inches apart in raised beds, or 18 inches apart in the field. Kohlrabi can also be direct seeded in well-composted soil when frost is almost gone, 12 seeds per foot, ¼ to ½ inch deep in 12 to 18 inch rows. Thin to 4 inches between plants.

Kohlrabi is subject to many cabbage diseases and must be rotated with other cole crops, three years between members of the family. Because I plant so many cole crops, I compost all cole crop residues in a long-term compost pile, which I use only for ornamentals, trees, and soft fruit. In some areas black rot, a serious problem in poorly rotated cabbage fields, reaches plague proportions in kohlrabi. Black rot causes veins to become black and foul-smelling with yellowing leaves. Symptoms usually appear 3 to 6 weeks after transplanting. Black rot bacteria overwinter in the soil, on plant refuse and on seed. Hot water treatment is helpful but not an absolute preventive; seeds are agitated in hot water (122°F) for 20 minutes then cooled and dried. Black rot and other diseases of kohlrabi are fostered by humid conditions. Seed grown in arid regions is free of infection. Wild rabbits and flea beetles love kohlrabi. Floating row covers will deter both.

Novice gardeners leave kohlrabi in the ground too long. To be mild, tender, sweet, apple-like, and free of wood and fiber, most varieties of kohlrabi must be harvested young, at 2 inches in diameter. Storage types allow greater latitude of harvest. Note in your garden calendar the expected date of maturity—4 to 5 weeks after transplanting or 40 to 60 days from direct seeding (longer for storage types). Start checking quality when the stem swells to 1½ inches by harvesting kohlrabi for a crisp sweet addition to salads. Once a season of sweet fiber-free kohlrabi has been harvested, you will begin to *notice* the glossy, lively surface appearance and color of active growth in fiber-free plants. Very fertile soils often produce tender 4-inch bulbs even with heirloom varieties.

Bulbs harvested at 2 inches can be eaten leaf and all. Kohlrabi bulbs are very high in vitamin C, and the leaves rival collards and kale in A, C, and calcium. Leaves are delicious when young. Kohlrabi adds a sweet water chestnut crunch when added at the last minute to stir-fries. Kohlrabi is most delicious raw (crisp and satisfying), either plain or with a dip. Purple slices form a striking edible rim around a salad plate. Purple and pale green kohlrabi, carrot slices, and various greens quickly produce an astonishingly beautiful salad.

Varieties

Kohlrabi is an important crop in Europe, but minor in the United States. This is partly due to the cooler, less extreme climate of Northern Europe, which makes for quicker, more tender growth. Previously, only Early White Vienna (55 days) and Early Purple Vienna (60 days) were available. Grown quickly and harvested early (at 2 inches in diameter), both produce sweet fine-grained bulbs. Neither is uniform; both are subject to cracking and black rot, and both become fibrous if not harvested young.

Pick and choose desirable kohlrabi traits from new European hybrids. Traits include faster growth, holding longer without splitting, holding longer in warm weather, increased uniformity, tenderness, sweetness, fruit-like flavor, and longer maintenance of the fresh clean taste typical of well-grown kohlrabi.

Purple-skinned kohlrabi is also available in both open-pollinated (Early Purple Vienna) and in new hybrid varieties.

Although kohlrabi for fresh use has a narrow harvest window, both O.P. and hybrid storage kohlrabi are more flexible and store up to 4 months. Gigant (130 days) is a traditional Czech heirloom, reselected by E. M. Meader of the University of New Hampshire. Gigant is fiber-free from 2 inches to more than 10 inches in diameter; it can be used spring or fall, and matures between 10 and 20 pounds. Its leaves can be eaten like kale. Bulbs root-cellar or overwinter in the ground under mulch, if winters are mild. Gigant resists root maggots and is used to make sauerkraut in Europe. Kossack (80 days) is a hybrid winter storage kohlrabi best harvested at 8 inches. When the hard woody rind of storage kohlrabi is removed, the inner flesh is tender and sweet, months after harvest.

SEED: Seeds per ounce 5,500 to 9,000. An O.P. ounce sows about 400 feet, hybrid 550 feet, or produces at least 4,000 transplants. A packet (1/16 ounce 500 seeds) sows 30 feet.

GERMINATION: 75%; 14 to 21 days at 70°F, but can be grown in a 60°F greenhouse or cold frame.

VIABILITY: 3 years.

DAYS TO HARVEST: 40 to 60 days from direct seeding for fresh use; 80 to 120 days for storage types. About 28 days after setting out 4-week-old transplants.

MOON CALENDAR: All culture in leaf, including biodynamic sprays.

ROTATION: 3 to 6 years for cabbage family.

BIODYNAMIC SPRAYS: Horn manure (500) on field, flat soil or seedbed. Compost-clay 500 root dip for transplants. Silica in greenhouse or seedbed once, again when plants are established in the field, and again as the stem begins to swell.

COMPANION PLANTS: *Umbelliferous* plants, *alliums*, aromatic herbs repel insects. Allegedly not compatible with tomatoes.

LEEKS, WELSH ONIONS, AND WILD ONIONS

I once saw an old photo of an English gardener displaying a leek almost as long as himself. He must have triple-dug his bed, refilled the first two stories with every ounce of organic matter available on his property, and planted the leek seedling in a 10-inch trench. As the leek grew, he must have back-filled in the trench to overflowing, creating a supremely long, supremely white pillar, which, I have no doubt, was exhibited with pride at a local garden club.

One thing I know for sure—that didn't happen in the United States. Americans occasionally grow leeks, but never with such fanatical devotion as the English. And if such a huge leek were produced, it would have the best chance in an English climate: a long moist season, very cool, with no breaks in moisture for three months or more, and no frost until Christmas. In such a climate giant leeks are not only possible, but fairly easy to produce and even easier to store. In regions with moderate frost, almost any leek variety will overwinter easily and be ready for harvest on any day until spring.

The part of this picture that bothers me isn't the possibility of exaggeration, but the very whiteness of the pillar. It bothers me because I believe that the leek and its cousins, the Chinese leek and Welsh onion, have the most value through their greenness, and the least through the obsession with whiteness that has gripped the West for more than a century.

Why couldn't leeks be bred to retain greenness? Garlic chives are tender and green. Wild *alliums* are all deep green. If leeks were green, then to quote Dylan Thomas, "the force that through the green fuse drives the flower" might "drive [our] green age." A green old age. It needs greenness to do so. Green onions and the wild cousins of leek have three times the vitamin C, 100 times the vitamin A, and twice the iron of white leek. The iron reminds us just what force the green is driving in these plants, driving strongly through every millimeter of our respiratory and circulatory systems. I suspect that the more living the vehicle, the more enlivening the effect of the active principles within these *alliums* might be. *Alliums*, as a group, have similar effects to garlic in lowering blood cholesterol, strengthening the respiratory system, and stimulating the digestive system. I believe they "tell us" (via a culinary communication) how to transform ingested food.

Choice of plant foods and recipes, even presentation, are all really a dialogue between our physical constitution and outer nature. I always wished I could be like John Muir: to be so nourished by the vision of nature that I could climb for a week on a loaf of dry bread! For most of us, the dialogue between our physical constitution and outer nature involves choosing which plants to eat, and taking care with recipes and presentation. I believe this dialogue is less instinctual than we think it is, and more trained into us by childhood nutrition.

By age four, a child should be trained as a tracker of the therapy hidden in vegetables. By age six, children should be setting off into the wilderness on their own. Otherwise, most of what we eat merely accumulates as dead stuff in our system, inevitably leading to disease. Have you ever really wondered why our constitution becomes our enemy in middle age, just when we need an ally? Rudolf Steiner gave an answer that many biodynamic practitioners fail to heed: minimize protein intake and increase the use of the deep *therapy* found in green plants.

However, diets being what they are (although my kids eat a ton of vegetables, they also eat hot dogs and grilled meats), the *allium* family, especially green *alliums*, provide some antidote in transforming animal protein and its negative effects. When the *allium* family enters the digestive tract, it is antiviral, antibacterial, and anti-carcinogenic (due to organic sulfurs). In the blood, the *alliums* are cholesterol-lowering and blood cleansing (due to saponins). A number of phytochemicals in the *allium* family have been shown to block and suppress cancer agents, especially those induced by the consumption of animal products (Beling 1997). The *alliums* inhibit the formation of nitrosamines, a cancer-causing by-product found in hot dogs (cured meats) and grilled meats. Though these phytochemicals are found in white *allium* leaf shafts and bulbs (especially garlic), the green *allium* leaves contain far larger amounts.

Diversity and Origins of Alliums

Besides leek itself (*Allium porrum*), there is Chinese leek (*Allium tuberosum*), Welsh onion (*Allium fistulosum*), wild leek (*Allium ampeloprasum*), wild garlic (*Allium canadense*), autumn wild onion (*Allium stellatum*), field garlic (*Allium vineale*, a very strong wild garlic, almost a "garlic medicine"), and a wild leek called ramp (*Allium tricoccum*). In the Great Smoky Mountains annual ramp festivals are held, celebrating the wild leek in salad, soup, and stew. The first three *alliums* are available from seed catalogs; the latter six can be found wild and identified using a wildflower book. Seeds or top bulbs of wild varieties can also be collected and sown in the garden.

The Welsh onion gets its name from *walsch*, the German word for "foreign," the foreign origin being China or Siberia, not Wales. Welsh onion is called Japanese leek in Japan. It never forms a bulb and is perennial. Chinese leek, or garlic chives, forms a delicious perennial clump of flattened leaves, which can be separated, root and all, like green bunching onions for use in fine cooking or transplanting. The swirl of leaves and flowers is beautiful.

The leek was undoubtedly much greener during its early days as a garden plant in ancient Egypt or prehistoric Mediterranean pastures; there is no question it possessed more of its original force. The Romans, especially working people, valued leeks in their original form, giving the species name *porrum*, which is the common Roman word for leek. The Romans carried the leek to the British Isles before Christ, which is why the word "leek" is derived from the old Anglo-Saxon. By 1775 the leek was being grown by the American colonists and by Native Americans. The surprising abundance of old and new European varieties attests to its longevity and continued popularity throughout Europe.

Culture

Leek culture is similar to onion. Since leek seeds are viable for only one year, purchase only what you believe you can use in one growing season. (A packet, 500 seeds, produces about 250 transplants; an ounce produces about 5,000 to 6,000 transplants). Start seeds early, in February or early March, when days are lengthening. Seedbeds and flats should be quite rich—up to 50% compost. Seeds should not be sown too thickly; large transplants produce large leeks; cramped, spindly seedlings produce less productive offspring. Cramped seedlings never fully recover.

Sow in cold frames or beds in an unheated greenhouse, 3 seeds to the inch, ¼ inch deep in rows, 8 to 12 inches apart. For flats, sow 4 seeds to the inch, transplant to flats when large enough to handle, and transplant to the field when seedlings are the diameter of a pencil, about a foot tall. Cold frames have the advantage of far less initial work, but cells reduce transplant shock and transplant more rapidly. In areas with adequate spring rainfall or with irrigation, bare-root plantings of leeks from cold frames recover rapidly (unless sown too thickly to begin with).

During seedling growth, plants benefit from several applications of biodynamic silica (501) and compost/nettle tea and liquid seaweed. Bare-root transplants are more vigorous when roots are dipped in a slurry of compost, clay, and horn manure (500).

Although leeks benefit from extra fertility and a rapid start in the cold frame or greenhouse, they require exceptional fertility in the garden for very large leeks. Good resistance to disease and leaf-rasping thrips and other insects gives leeks ample time to develop. Beds or field should be deeply cultivated prior to transplanting, especially deep (18 inches) if you plan to set plants 6 inches apart, in 6-inch deep furrows in order to hill for long blanched pillars. Leeks can also be set at normal soil level, 6 inches between plants in rows 24 inches apart, and hilled during cultivation. In either case, weeding is easier for leeks than for onions since the stems can be buried as the plant grows. This lengthens the pillar, as the growing point is forced higher up the stem. Soil can be hoed against the plants using the small plow attachment of a wheel hoe. Follow the biodynamic spray schedule for onions.

Direct-seeding requires a precision seeder, arrow-straight rows, and precise, timely cultivation. Sow 6 seeds to the foot, ¼ inch deep, in rows 24 inches apart. Sowing dates range from April to June, depending on variety, desired harvest size, and harvest date.

Leeks should be harvested and used or marketed in early maturity, when quality is highest. Leeks store best if left in the ground. In areas with mild frost (20°F), hardy strains can be harvested as needed until spring. Home gardeners in colder climates can place hay bales on either side of two leek rows and cover with boards and tarps after regular 20°F frosts have begun (November or December). In areas of deep frost, leeks should be lifted before the ground freezes solid, the leaves and roots partially pruned and the stalks packed vertically in the root cellar in leaves, peat, or perforated plastic bags. Leeks store fairly well for about half the winter, best at about 30°F with high humidity, but nothing is slimier than a rotting leek. Leeks left too long in a hay bale cloche are also subject to rot. Overwintered non-hybrid leeks can be left to flower and set seed in spring. The globular seed head should be hung to dry (over newspapers or in a paper bag) when not over-mature, lest the seed scatter before harvest.

Perennial leeks are superb for kitchen gardens and propagate easily from division of bulbs. Chinese leeks or garlic chives (*A. turberosum*) can be grown from seed or divided. Chinese leeks are suitable for bunching.

Chinese leeks, perennial leeks, and other *alliums* can be used liberally in miso soup, mixed vegetable soup, and stir-fries. Add them chopped just before serving. White pillared leeks add substance, creaminess, and sweet onion flavor to soups and stews. My family is especially fond of green *allium* dressing: blend 1 cup virgin olive oil, ½ cup balsamic vinegar, 1 tablespoon tamari, and 1 cup chopped Chinese leeks or other wild *allium* greens. I think of the *alliums* as tour guides for other flavors, backing them up or bringing them together. *Alliums* seem to increase the assimilation of other foods, and perhaps also the nutrients they contain.

Varieties

In the United States the market is so limited that even large seed firms such as Burpee don't offer a single leek. Traits for market growers to consider include uniformity, length of shaft (longer for summer, shorter for fall and winter), cold-hardiness for overwintering in less severe climates, and resistance to leaf diseases.

Broad London (also called Large American Flag, 130 days) has been the standard variety for home gardens for generations, with large 1½-inch shafts, 8 to 10 inches tall. The white shafts of King Richard grow much more quickly to 12 inches—only 75 days for summer harvest. King Richard has limited autumn frost resistance. Shorter and slower growing varieties such as Bandit (120 days) or Blau Greuner Winter (110 days) have been bred for late harvest and overwintering in Zones 4 and 5.

Hybrid leeks germinate quickly and grow faster than open-pollinated, but may not be as winter-hardy. Hybrids have great uniformity (higher percentage of saleable shafts) and higher yields.

SEED: Leek seeds per ounce average 10,000. A packet of leek seeds sows 25 to 50 feet (1 gram produces 200 transplants). An ounce direct-seeds 1,650 feet, unless leeks are cramped for bunching. An ounce produces 4,000 to 6,000 transplants, depending on how carefully the seedbed is sown. Chinese Leeks (7,000 seeds to the ounce) and Welsh onion and Chinese leeks (garlic chives) are usually listed under herbs in seed catalogs. Other *allium* seeds and bulbs can be collected from the wild in moderation.

VIABILITY: 2 to 3 years.

MOON CALENDAR: All practices in leaf, including biodynamic sprays.

ROTATION: 3 years between *alliums*.

BIODYNAMIC SPRAYS: Horn manure (500) on field and seedbed. Horn silica (501) twice in greenhouse or cold frame. For bare-root transplants dip roots in compost-clay 500 slurry. Horn silica (501) at least twice: as flags develop and when pillars begin to enlarge.

COMPANION PLANTS: Alternate rows with carrot (*alliums* repel carrot fly), celery, beans, beets, and cole crops. *Alliums* are beneficial interplanted throughout the garden. In highly mixed culture, rotation can be disregarded somewhat.

LETTUCE

Every year a wild plant rises to eight feet behind my barn, branching in all directions with dozens of tiny yellow dandelions. The leaves and midrib are stiff and exude a milky, bitter sap. Even the youngest rosettes—when I search them out—are deeply incised and bitter on my tongue. Unless I were a donkey or a goat, I couldn't imagine eating this plant, *Lactuca canadensis* the wild lettuce. Still more extreme is the prickly lettuce, *Lactuca scariola*. Here the leaf margins become spiny and the midrib develops prickles. The prickly lettuce moves even farther away from succulence, becomes thistle-like, similar to sow thistle and distinctly inedible. Nevertheless, *Lactuca scariola* is believed to be the wild progenitor of cultivated lettuce, already selected for salad in Persia in 600 BCE. By Roman times, a dozen varieties were cultivated—hence "romaine."

The milky sap of wild or bolted lettuce is so unpleasant, I can barely imagine the original process of selection. In the steppes of central Asia, the craving for greens must have been intense. Gardening of some sort existed there since 8000 BCE. So at some point mere gatherings of wild lettuce must have been succeeded by careful selection of juicier, less bitter rosettes. The strange thing about selection is that even when a cultivated plant like lettuce has been bred for tenderness and bitter-free flavor over thousands of years, it still reverts to the wild as soon as it bolts. Those tender, juicy leaves become small, triangular, milky, and bitter. To reproduce, the domestic lettuce has to revert to its wild form.

You could easily say that the wild plant retains the dynamic forces that continue to bring domestic plants into being during reproduction. The wild plant is hidden within the domestic variety, invisible but completely there, completely necessary to the domestic plant's continued existence. *Lactuca scariola* is more than an evolutionary ghost. It's a blueprint of the invisible dynamic forces we neglect at our peril.

You can observe this process yourself by letting a few lettuce plants go to seed. Observe the change of leaf shape as the wild form rises on a juicy stalk from within the quiet green bowl of leaves. If you harvest the dry seed before it scatters you can save it for next year. After flowering, when about half the flower clusters have become fuzzy, harvest the entire stalk and place upside down in a large paper bag. Dry indoors. If you miss the harvest, volunteer seedlings can be transplanted to other parts of the garden as they appear, sometimes even the next spring.

The other invisible side of lettuce is the root system, which along with other members of the composite family (chicory, dandelion, endive, escarole, and scorzonera) attracts earthworms and improves humus formation in its root sphere. You can see and smell it in the surrounding soil. Best to grow lettuce with finished compost, perhaps in association with the carrot family (dill, caraway, lovage, chervil, celery, parsnip, and so forth), which have similar requirements. The carrot family is also what I would call a metamorphic companion, since its airy aromatic branching retains openly what lettuce suppresses in the cultivated varieties. Alternate rows of lettuce and carrots, celery, celeriac, and the aromatic *umbelliferous* plants, or precede the fall carrot crop with lettuce.

Culture

Dozens of varieties of lettuce and mesclun have become such important gourmet crops that whole market operations have been built on lettuce alone. Each variety becomes known intimately, exactly when top-quality will occur and when it should no longer be marketed. Market gardeners need to know exactly the earliest and latest date each variety can be harvested. Planning sequences and harvests take years of experience. In many market gardens it becomes a major question of how to rotate so much lettuce. The downside of the lettuce boom is monoculture and the buildup of disease. Home gardeners may be dumbfounded by claims of "resistance to 25 races of downy mildew"; but market gardeners that continually push the season into hot weather, and don't rotate at least three years between lettuce family crops may discover them all.

Many methods used by market gardeners can be useful to home gardeners and fit well into any biodynamic scheme. These methods use space economically and help to insert lettuce into a diverse companion planting. Season extension in spring and fall can revolutionize the way home gardeners think about gardening. By pre-warming the soil and using heavy row cover with steel hoops, what before seemed like gambling can become routine. Practice pre-cropping, intercropping, and catch-cropping. Plant lettuce in areas waiting for warm season plants like squashes, eggplant, or melon (pre-cropping). Plant between crops that need more space only later in the season, such as cole crops. Plant fall lettuce after warm season crops are harvested, or among those that are still lingering. I've never been bothered by planting more lettuce than I could use, because I always found some way to use it. Lettuce is immensely appreciated by pigs, chickens, rabbits, and local wildlife. The last stop is feeding earthworms in the compost heap. Earthworms thrive on composted lettuce. Always save enough compost and topsoil in a frost-free area to prepare flats and cells in the spring.

Biodynamic gardeners awaken the soil life in early spring by spraying horn manure (500) after winter dormancy. Horn manure draws earthworms up from the depths. For lettuce any permeable loam will do. A pH of 6.5 is ideal, which in biologically active soils comes about naturally through earthworms and compost. Some biodynamic gardeners spray lettuce soil with valerian (507) in mid-spring as an earthworm stimulant.

For lettuce I use the same potting mix as for squash and cole crops, but many growers prefer a lighter, sandier mix, which warms up quickly in a cool greenhouse. Too much sand as a dilutant may produce weaker plants. In the field, naturally occurring sandy loam warms up faster in spring for early crops. For cole crops, I mix half biodynamic compost and half medium loam; but I also get good results with compost made entirely from vegetable refuse and hardwood leaves, both in cell packs and in the garden. I find the horse manure and sawdust too light, unless it has been composted for two years; the carbon-nitrogen ratio is too high. How lettuce plants maintain stable, steady growth and deal with damping off fungus, mildew, and aphids will be determined by initial compost and soil preparation. High temperatures, however, are the biggest problem; most lettuce types require moderate days and cool nights to grow well.

There are over 20,000 lettuce seeds per ounce. To avoid overcrowding sow thinly, 4 rows per flat, 4 seeds to the inch about 4 weeks before setting transplants in the field, or sow directly into cell-type containers. Lettuce germinates best at 68°F in a sunny location with minimal seed cover. Lettuce requires light to germinate. Direct seedings germinate above 40°F and grow well at 50°F with wind protection. Optimum temperatures range between 60 and 70°F. Seed flats respond to light watering or misting. Given a moist atmosphere I have germinated flats tamped with no soil cover at all. I often sprinkle seeds carefully and thinly over a graded and lightly tamped flat and cover with a fine sprinkling of compost, like a layer of gauze. I water carefully with a very fine spray. Flooding washes seeds away. Overheating at night is the greatest cause of failure with lettuce, a problem not corrected by fungicide.

When the first true leaf appears between the round cotyledon seed leaves (about 2 weeks after sowing) prick plants out promptly and transplant to new flats with 2-inch spacing all around. Grow cool 60-65°F with daytime highs below 75°F. When lettuce transplants are established, spray with silica (501), stinging nettle tea, and liquid seaweed, especially if your flat mix contains peat or vermiculite. Plants can grow on the cool side, even 45°F at night, so long as full sun is available by day. Watch for stem elongation due to cramping in the flat or inadequate light. Sow waves of succession every 18 to 21 days. Three sowings under glass should extend the lettuce season into June. First lettuce can be transplanted under row cover as soon as the soil can be worked.

Depending on latitude, outside sowings begin as soon as the ground can be worked in spring. Though lettuce begins to germinate at 40°F, it comes quicker in the 50°s. Outdoor seedbeds have an advantage over direct seeding, where weeds and crowding prevail unless a precision seeder is used. Transplanted lettuce grows faster and larger due to better spacing. For outdoor seedbeds choose heat tolerant varieties, since outdoor sowings mature in warmer weather. Sow a very fine rain of seed in furrows 1/8 inch deep and cover with a layer of fine soil or compost 1/16 inch thick. Lettuce fails from a too-deep sowing. Tamp firmly with a tamping board. Keep well-watered with a fine gentle spray. Thin two plants per inch.

At the same time outdoor sowing begins, harden off the earliest wave of cold frame lettuce seedlings by reducing temperature to near freezing and reducing water for three days prior to setting in the field. Over-watered or over-fertilized transplants have expanded plant cells that are susceptible to frost. Plant cells with less internal water can survive frost down to 20°F, although chilled plants are susceptible to bolting when exposed to temperatures below 50°F for extended periods during the second and third leaf stage. Open the cold frames by day. Cover at night if cold weather and frost threaten. Even in Pennsylvania I never found much advantage to setting lettuce out unprotected before April 10. In New England, I often transplant in early March with no problem, using heavy row cover, followed by succession planting every few weeks. Space plants 8 inches apart in the row for medium-sized looseheads and butterheads; 12 inches for Romaine, larger looseheads, and Batavian lettuce, with 12 to 18 inches between rows. Remember that maturity dates will be later in cool weather and earlier in hot. Lettuce is 2½ times sweeter if harvested in the early morning, a time that also minimizes field heat. Field heat causes lettuce to wilt and reduces quality.

With four sowings you can cover the optimal spring season for a home or small market crop. Later sowings require irrigation. Select heat tolerant varieties, and use shade cloth in warmer climates. The new Batavian lettuces take summer heat very well. Plantings to the north side of pole beans or a sunflower hedge (not too close) will help. Mulch cools the soil. Weekend gardeners can take a midsummer break and resume sowing around July 20, weather permitting. Lettuce may fail to germinate in temperatures consistently above 80°F. Home gardeners can germinate small seed flats in the refrigerator for 4 to 6 days. Summer sowings will mature in the cooler nights of September. Follow these with sowings on August 1 and 20. These three will supply lettuce into hard frost. Be prepared to cover late-maturing lettuce with row cover.

In both spring and fall, biodynamic silica (501) can be sprayed on each succession when transplants are established and also when heads begin to form. Horn manure (500) can also be sprayed on surrounding soil in prolonged dry weather to maintain humus activity. On less fertile soils, liquid feedings of compost tea should be restricted to early stages of growth. No nutrient foliar sprays should be necessary, but stinging nettle spray can be used to offset growth imbalance, which gives rise to infestations of aphids. Liquid seaweed also has a beneficial stimulant effect. I would not use either within two weeks of harvest, lest flavor be affected. Equisetum spray (508) can be used in sustained muggy weather.

Lettuce crops do well under mulch, but be sure to apply iron-based slug bait. Lettuce doesn't like deep cultivation, which disturbs roots. Skim or scuffle early, as soon as weeds germinate. Skim direct-seeded lettuce before weeds appear, as soon as seed leaves are visible.

Except for slugs in the greenhouse and under row cover, in my experience I have never encountered pest or disease problems with lettuce. Pests and diseases can be averted by thorough rotation and ample composting. Aphids are always a sign of plant stress. Even heat-tolerant varieties can be stressed in midsummer. A few aphids can be washed off with a hose, but the cost of organic field sprays (insecticidal oil or soap) is hard to justify with lettuce. Likewise for organic mildew control. In new sod, cutworms are likely to be present; home gardeners can make paper collars to deter them. Practice frequent rotation against mosaic disease and mildew, and compost all crop residues to feed livestock. For home gardeners, creative interplanting solves most problems before they appear, since the intensified soil and beneficial insect life seem to pull plants through every time.

To prevent crossings, I often allow a single cultivar to bolt and set seed. When about half the flowers become fuzzy (called "pappus"), I cut the plant at ground level and dry it upside down in a paper bag. Bolted lettuce will also scatter volunteers in late summer, early fall, and the following spring. Volunteers can be transferred for autumn harvest or the winter cold frame.

If water is reduced, cold frame lettuce survives some freezing, but never cut heads when frozen. Some cultivars, such as North Pole, have been bred for the extended late fall and winter cold frame in Zone 4, perhaps protected by old rugs or hay bales on very cold nights. A cold-hardy looseleaf, such as Red Tinged Winter, can be harvested gradually by peeling lower leaves.

Varieties

Most of the types and textures of lettuce we consider novel were present in ancient Rome. Many were grown in China by 600 CE or earlier, including oddities such as celtuce or stem lettuce, which was enjoyed by the Chinese when tribal Europeans were still gnawing bones. The Romans carried lettuce culture to Gaul (France) and later to Britain. Looseheads and red and green Romaine were passed on by Rome to the Gauls, who, after they became French, grew them in cloches outside of Paris for centuries. At one point the signal American contribution to lettuce culture was the mass production of Iceberg, a variety that demoted salad to a worthless side dish. Fortunately the reintroduction of color, texture, and flavor has saved not only consumers' health, but also thousands of market gardeners from extinction.

Even so, it's horrible how much iceberg is still sold. Disease-resistant iceberg apparently "saved" the lettuce industry in the 1920s but helped (along with white bread, absurdly high intake of protein, and correspondingly low intake of vegetables) to make Americans the most disease-ridden First World country on earth. Loose leaf and romaine have 6 times more vitamin A than head lettuce, and 3 times more vitamin C and calcium. Iceberg varieties are hardly worth a mention, so I won't, although Green Ice (45 days) provides a similar crunch, with better quality, and greater nutritional value.

Although lettuce still largely conforms to cultivars sold in the nineteenth century, varieties are now distinguished by use (heading or baby/mesclun), shape, texture, color, flavor, heat resistance, disease resistance, slowness to bolt, and slowness to become bitter. Many gardeners plan their lettuce year based on these traits.

For home gardeners, the heirloom loose leaf lettuces, such as Black Seeded Simpson (41 days), have always been the first lettuce of the season. Simpson's light-green, tender, cut-and-come-again leaves can be grown all season long, but wilt quickly after cuttings. Waldmann's Dark Green (49 days) and its heat- and bolt- resistant successors form full frilly green heads for spring or fall. Note resistance to races of downy mildew and other diseases in recent cultivars. Red loose leaf such as New Red Fire and Red Sails (55 days) have beautiful frilly burgundy leaves, slow to bolt and slow to become bitter. Dark Lollo Rossa is similar. Market growers also should note the MTO-30 or M.I. designation, which means that seed is mosaic free (within the limits of the test).

I find oakleaf lettuces too fragile after harvest, but their tenderness and texture are appreciated in salads fresh from the garden. On the other hand, oakleaf (45 days) is fairly heat- and bolt-resistant. Red oakleaf varieties range from cherry red to burgundy. Many have good resistance to downy mildew. Cocarde (49 days), a large French trumpet-shaped oakleaf, has dark green leaves tinged with rusty red, held well off the ground. Thai Oakleaf (39 days) was selected in Thailand for excellent quality under high heat. Upright, fairly slow bolting. Deer Tongue or Matchless (54 days) is an heirloom favorite, with sweet, crisp triangular leaves and some resistance to bolting.

Boston, bibb, and butterheads have unusually tender leaves, with a soft creamy texture, really hard to stop eating when harvested at just the right time. I've always loved the slow bolting Buttercrunch (46 days) with its sweet delicious crisp hearts. Capitane (62 days) is a large Dutch butterhead, with smooth velvety leaves and award-winning quality. Tolerant to heat and cold, with resistance to lettuce mosaic virus. Butterheads grow best in cool weather, spring or fall, but some, such as Ermosa (48 days), tolerate hot weather if kept watered. The already mentioned North Pole (50 days) can be overwintered in a cold frame in Zone 4. Sow 2 to 3 weeks before first frost and harvest winter to spring. Red butterheads such as Skyphos (47 days) make a beautiful presentation, with excellent flavor, wide adaptability, and disease resistance (downy mildew, mosaic, and so forth). Marvel of Four Seasons (50 days) can overwinter without protection in mild climates. Brick-red leaf tips contrast with yellow-green hearts. A beautiful heirloom with no special disease resistance.

For many, romaine (or cos) is the king of lettuces, the backbone of a substantial salad, longer lasting on sandwiches, with sweet crunchy midribs, a salad fit for Caesar. Tall upright leaves are extremely high in vitamins. It appreciates good fertility, but is easier to grow than its reputation. Organic and biodynamic romaine makes heavy crops, easily twice the size and quality of romaine found in supermarkets, with sweeter midribs and crisper hearts. Never let seedlings become stressed or stand longer than 4 weeks in flats or seedbed. Plant in fertile soil and keep watered. You'll be astonished at the results.

Green Towers (74 days) is the most popular romaine in the eastern United States and Canada, an earlier, heavier, taller high-quality version of Parris Island Cos. Jericho (60 days) is a heat-resistant version from Israel and remains sweet even in midsummer. Very slow bolting. Older types such as heirloom Cimmaron (65 days) from the eighteenth century make huge open heads, deep green right to the center. Red romaines have deep red to cranberry red outer leaves with sweet lime green hearts. Recent red varieties also have excellent disease resistance to downy mildew. Rouge d'Hiver (62 days) is an open-headed French heirloom romaine with deep red leaf margins. Overwinters under row cover in states with moderate winters.

Romaine butterhead crosses, such as Winter Density, are actually heirloom varieties from the nineteenth century. Winter Density (54 days) is a much loved English strain, tolerant of mild frost. Grown fall, winter, and spring in the British Isles. Heads are upright, like romaine, about 8 inches tall, but very tight-leaved, like buttercrunch.

The French Batavian lettuces, marketed as Summer crisp, were created by crossing romaine and Batavian escarole. They have fantastic texture and taste. Harvestable longer than any other salad in warm weather, with remarkably fine gourmet appearance. Excellent quality both as a loose leaf and as a cos type, with sweet, crisp juicy leaves, bitter-free. I find them delicious even when over-mature. Sierra (56 days) has red-tinged, wavy, cos-like leaves around a sweet creamy heart. It is resistant to tip burn, bottom rot, and bolting. Victoria (55 days, Johnny's Seeds) shares characteristics of cos, leaf, and iceberg. Grows successfully in summer with thick hearts that maintain crispness and sweetness in hot weather. Extremely slow bolting. Anvenue (54 days) is a small Batavian imitation of iceberg, bred for hot weather in Hawaii and great for summer sowings. Magenta (48 days) is an improved Sierra, with a whorled cos-like head and crisp heart. Excellent tolerance to all lettuce diseases. Cherokee (48 days) offers a similar package with beautiful burgundy leaves.

SEED: Seeds per ounce about 25,000. A packet (600 seeds) direct-seeds a 50-foot row or produces about 350 plants. An ounce direct-seeds 1,600 feet, up to 5,000 feet with a precision seeder. A packet produces 300 transplants, approximately. An ounce produces up to 20,000 transplants.

GERMINATION: 80%; 7 days at 70°F, but can germinate at 50°F and grow at 55°F; germination drops drastically above 80°F.

VIABILITY: 6 years.

DAYS TO HARVEST: Loosehead — 50 days; Butterhead — 52 days; Romaine — 60 days; French Batavian — 55 days

ROTATION: 3 years to prevent disease build-up in market gardens.

MOON CALENDAR: All culture, including biodynamic sprays in Leaf signs, ascending moon, if possible. For seed saving, begin spraying mature plant in fruit sign, preferably Leo. Harvest seed in Leo, if possible.

BIODYNAMIC SPRAYS: Horn manure (500) on flat soil, seedbed and garden; also in prolonged dry weather. Valerian (507) to stimulate earthworm activity. Silica (501) when several true leaves appear and when plants are forming a rosette; for heading types also just as head is beginning to form. Equisetum (508) against damping off in seedlings and in prolonged muggy weather. Stinging nettle and seaweed spray before rosette forms on transplants.

COMPANION PLANTS: Shallots, onion, garlic, carrots, and other *umbelliferous* plants. Cabbage family provides shade for midsummer plantings. As an early crop preceding warm season vegetables such as squash and melons. Interplant between newly planted strawberries. Use lettuce volunteers to fill empty spots early and late in the season. Roots of lettuce are relished by earthworms.

LIMA BEANS

I was surprised to find that Delaware is the leading producer of lima beans, and not the Deep South or California. Delaware has long summers, warm autumns, and the coast is moderated by the ocean. According to Delaware Extension, high humidity, fog, and heavy dews increase pod set. In Delaware, growers plant limas as a succession crop in late June or early July, following peas or small grains. This allows limas to mature in September and October, after late summer heat waves have passed. Limas that mature during high heat (above 90°F) have reduced pod set and lower yield. Some varieties, however, such as Worcester Indian Red Pole, show good heat and drought resistance.

In other regions plantings are adjusted to grow at optimal temperatures. On the East Coast limas grow easily up to Long Island; they grow across the South, in California, and the dry Northwest east of the Cascades. Check with local growers and your state extension service to learn whether limas mature in your area. Gardeners in regions too cool for limas can try broad beans (favas), which are comparable in size and taste and really appreciate cool, wet summers.

The earliest archaeological remains of lima beans have been found—of all places—in Lima, Peru. Large seeded limas date there from 4000 BCE. But the region of greatest diversity seems to be Central America, though whether this is due to native distribution or breeding is not known. Central America is the source of small seed butterbeans, which mature earlier than the larger meatier limas. Butterbeans often succeed farther north and are less susceptible to blossom drop in cool wet weather.

Fresh cooked green limas have good amounts of vitamins A and C, and are high in potassium, fiber, folate, and magnesium. Like other beans, limas lower cholesterol and homocysteine, reducing the risk of heart attack and stroke. Green limas eaten raw would be even higher in vitamins, but they contain a toxic cyanogenic glucoside, linamarin, which is neutralized in cooking. Limas from countries of origin may have 20 to 30 times more linamarin than those bred in the United States. Linamarin from uncooked limas (or unprocessed cassava) may aggravate glucose intolerance and diabetes. So cook your lima harvest, and never let children eat them raw. Fresh green limas are delicious sautéed. Dried beans should be soaked overnight and simmered 75 minutes. In many countries limas replace meat when mixed with rice.

Culture

I have compiled a list of rules for growing limas, which will increase yield and minimize disease. Some were long known to me, some gleaned from state extension websites about limas grown commercially.

- Choose high drainage soil, if possible, or make raised beds.
- Avoid compaction. Dig garden beds deeply (double digging) to improve drainage or subsoil with a chisel plow.
- Use plenty of compost for plant vigor.
- Keep nitrogen levels moderate to avoid saturated watery vegetation susceptible to fungus.
- Keep pH between 5.8 to 6.5; lower or higher pH causes metabolic imbalance.
- Avoid overhead irrigation, or irrigate overhead only on sunny days in the morning to allow foliage to dry.
- Where bean diseases have been a problem, allow 30 inches between rows with 4 inches between plants for better air circulation.
- Clean up, remove, and compost all bean debris immediately after harvest.
- Rotate beans 3 years in a given plot.

Limas stunt so badly in cool soil (60°F) that it's never worthwhile to jump the season. For untreated seed, soil should be 75°F. (Commercial growers sow treated seed between 65 and 75°F.) Seed germinates quickly (5 days) in soil 75 to 85°F. Home gardeners in marginal areas can pre-warm the soil with black plastic for a few weeks and sow under heavy row cover. Use a rhizobial seed inoculant suitable for limas, if limas have never been sown on that ground before.

Sow seeds 1 inch deep. For small butterbean types sow seeds 3 inches apart in rows 24 inches apart. For larger lima beans sow 4 inches apart in rows 36 inches apart. Pole limas can be sown at the base of a four-pole tepee 8 feet high. Plant 3 seeds to the pole and thin out the weakest seedling.

Diseases

The list of lima bean rules listed under "Culture" solves many disease problems. Pythium fungus is present in all soils, but it can spread rapidly in sodden wet compacted soils. Pythium rot appears as water-soaked beans with fluffy white fungal growth in periods of extended cool wet weather, from excessive overhead irrigation and stress caused by poor fertility. The stress of drought followed by rain can also trigger attacks. Pythium can be controlled using biofungicides.

Sclerotinia persists on bean debris and is aggravated by poor bean rotation. White fungal growth and large black bodies (sclerotia) are found in the pith of the stem during warm humid weather.

Downy mildew appears as white cottony growth on pods. Control with copper fungicide. Eastland, a high yield bush lima, carries some resistance.

Powdery mildew appears as round whitish spots on older leaves during warm humid weather. Control promptly with biofungicide.

Anthracnose appears as reddish-brown spots on pods in cold wet weather and persists in bean debris. Compost debris promptly. Control with copper fungicide.

Fusarium and rhizoctonia root rots both show reddish discoloration of the root, changing to dark brown. Lateral roots are killed, limiting plant nutrition. Nematodes are vectors for fusarium and can be controlled by beneficial nematodes and cover crops of rye and velvet bean (Alabama Extension). Non-beneficial nematode damage itself looks like a nutritional disorder, with light-colored stunted plants. The variety Nema Green lima bean is resistant to nematodes.

Root rots are a cultural problem aggravated by low-lying land, heavy soils, and poor drainage. Consider raised bed culture, double-digging or sub-soiling with a chisel plow. Once established, the offending bacteria (*Fusarium solani phaseoli*) is persistent, requiring a strict 3-year bean rotation. Biofungicides may help to control root rot, but drainage comes first.

Halo blight appears at 65 to 75°F, bacterial blight at 85 to 90°F. Both occur during wet weather and high humidity. Both show water-soaked spots on lower leaf surfaces. In Halo blight the spots are surrounded by a greenish-yellow halo. Later leaves become completely yellow. Both blights are bacterial, transmitted on bean debris. Control with copper fungicide (which also acts as a bacteriocide.)

Insects

Both adults and larva of Mexican bean beetles (*Epilachna vaivestis*) skeletonize leaves of all bean plants. Adults look similar to lady beetles but are copper brown with 16 spots. Eggs and larva are bright yellow. In some areas of commercial bean production, larva have been fully controlled with a tiny parasitic wasp, *Pediobius faveolatus* (New Jersey and Florida Extensions). Spinosad, kaolin clay sprays, and neem also provide control.

The lima bean pod borer is the ½-inch caterpillar of the ½-inch moth, *Etiella zinckenella*. The pink, tan, or greenish larva overwinters on wild lupines in the West and on other legumes elsewhere. The larva wriggle violently when disturbed. They bore into pods, leaving little or no trace of entrance and bore out again to pupate in the soil. This insect is extremely difficult to control.

The southern green stink bug (*Nezara viridula*) is a light-green, shield-shaped bug that sucks sap and smells bad. Stink bugs inject toxins and introduce yeast infections, but the larva does most of the damage. Larvae bore into pods and are hard to kill once inside. Limit egg-laying populations by spraying pyrethrins at bloom times (very early or very late in the day to limit bee mortality), when there is about one bug noticed every 15 feet of row (Clemson Extension).

The seed corn maggot attacks the meaty lima seeds during cool weather, when low soil temperatures prevent rapid emergence. Delay planting until optimal 70°F soil temperature. Introduce beneficial nematodes.

Spider mites are present everywhere, but are more prevalent in warmer regions in dry weather above 70°F. Mites are tiny spider-like arthropods with 8 legs and no antennae, thorax, or wings. They make tiny webs and suck sap from the underside of leaves, reducing chlorophyll and causing yellow stippling. Shake an affected leaf over a white sheet of paper. Red green or black specks will cover the paper. Control with lacewings, lady beetles, insecticidal soap, or flowable sulphur. Note that mites are increased by excessive use of pesticides, including pyrethrins, which may harm beneficials. Mixed plant culture increases beneficials. Horticultural oils will smother mite eggs during the dormant period without harming beneficials. Slugs and snails, which proliferate in wet warm weather, are easily controlled with baited iron phosphate.

Leafhoppers also feed on the underside of leaves, weakening the plant and reducing pod set. Leafhoppers are small, 1/8-inch, pale green spotted insects. They look like tiny cicadas. Leafhoppers hop suddenly, move sideways, or fly away quickly when disturbed. Salivary juices of leafhoppers are toxic to plants and obstruct the flow of nutrients in the plant, as well as transmitting plant viruses. Control with pyrethrins sprayed very early or very late in the day to avoid honey bees. Be sure to spray the undersides of leaves and wait at least 10 days between applications. Leafhoppers often move in again from surrounding vegetation.

Lygus or the tarnished plant bug (*Lygus lineolaris*) also injects salivary toxins during feeding, causing deformation on roots and fruits and blackening leaf shots. Lygus bugs are brown or greenish-brown with black or yellow markings, and a small yellow triangle at the end of each wing. They hibernate on vetch, lupine, or other legumes. Spray pyrethrin early in the season. Clean up and compost all legume debris.

Varieties

Eastland (68 days) is one of the highest yielding bush limas with good resistance to downy mildew. Fordhook 242 (75 days) is equally productive, with large seeds. It is fairly adaptable for a lima, tolerant of heat and drought, and a good choice for marginal central and northern states. Classic nutty lima flavor.

Henderson Bush (72 days) has been a small-seeded southern favorite since 1885. Henderson bears early on 2-foot bushes in humid or dry conditions in the central and southern states. Baby Fordhook (70 days) produces very early small tender limas, more delicate and less meaty than the larger types. Also a good choice for marginal lima regions in warmer climates.

Pole limas are a better investment in time and space, with larger pods and longer harvest. Big Mama (80 days) produces huge 8-inch pods on 8- to 10-foot vines. Very large tender and meaty beans with classic flavor. An improved heirloom variety.

Burpee's Best (70 days) is a pole version of Fordhook 242, with larger pods and higher yields. Same classic flavor and meaty texture. Bears early and long.

Christmas (84 days), also called Large Speckled Calico, keeps yielding in hot humid southern summers. A beautiful huge bean, cream-colored with red stripes and full classic lima flavor. A traditional favorite. King of the Garden (88 days), another beloved nineteenth-century heirloom, bears heavy crops of highly flavored sweet limas over a long season. Worcester Indian Red Pole (85 days) is a tough productive lima, probably descended from a Native American variety. Adaptable to heat and drought.

SEED: A pound of large seeded limas (400 seeds) sows about 130 feet of row with 4 inches between seeds. A pound of small-seeded butter bush (about 1,300 seeds) sows about 325 feet of row, 3 inches between plants. One-quarter pound of small seed sows about 80 feet. 2 ounces sows 40 feet.

GERMINATION: 5 days at 70°F.

VIABILITY: 3 years.

DAYS TO HARVEST: About 75 days for bush; about 85 days for pole.

ROTATION: 3 years between bean family.

MOON CALENDAR, BIODYNAMIC SPRAYS AND COMPANION PLANTING: Follow the suggestions for bush and pole beans.

MACHE (CORN SALAD)

Mache, also called corn salad, (*Valerianella locusta*, 50 days), lamb's lettuce in England, is really the only member of the *Valerian* family eaten as a vegetable. It is enormously popular in Europe, especially in France, where millions of pounds are consumed annually. Although not well established in the United States, maches can extend the salad season further into winter than any other green.

It is a native European weed often found on bare and cultivated ground, and so often foraged in grain fields (all grains are called corn in Europe) that it became "the salad found in corn." For centuries, peasants collected the wild rosettes, which remain remarkably fresh and green right through the winter in Zone 7. Frost even improves their flavor. Today it is not so easy to understand how much peasants depended on these wild winter greens. In our time the equivalent urgency has been transferred to the long-term anti-carcinogenic benefits of greens. For the seventeenth-century peasant, however, the high vitamin content of mache (corn salad) (three times the C of lettuce, with very high A and omega-3s) prevented scurvy and vitamin A deficiencies, and often spelled the difference between live and still birth.

This fact is presented rather extremely in the fairy tale "Rapunzel," a tale I read countless times to my daughter. *Rapunzel* is the name for corn salad in Germany.* To this day the image of the impoverished, pregnant peasant woman continues to haunts me. Imagine the conditions masked by this fairy nightmare: the bitter cold German winter gnawing into her bones, the barely heated cottage, and the lack of greens. I see her gaze held prisoner by the neighbor's garden with its rows of corn salad and hear her begging her husband to scale the wall. But try as I might I can't understand the final forced trade. Who could possibly trade a newborn child for a handful of greens? The answer is, tragically, thousands of Third World families, every single day. Fairy tales, as they say, are timeless.

---

* The English edition translates *rapunzel* as rampion, a bellflower also sometimes foraged in winter, but in Germany *rapunzel* is corn salad.

Culture

Corn salad significantly extends the garden year by filling otherwise unoccupied niches of the cold season garden, cold frame, or cold greenhouse. Even in Zone 4, protected corn salad can extend the salad harvest for weeks at the beginning and end of winter. With protection, corn salad can grow right through the winter in Zones 5 and 6, and flourishes without any protection through the winter in Zone 7. In Zones 4 to 6, corn salad can be sown in fall like overwintering spinach, and harvested in spring. In areas with strong cold winter winds, consider adding floating row covers. In Zone 6, fall-sown corn salad will produce extra-early rosettes in late winter, if protected by heavy row cover. Or sow corn salad directly into cold frames in Zones 4 to 6 for late winter to early spring harvests, depending on latitude. Some growers in Europe, and now the United States, sow corn salad directly in flats in a cold greenhouse, and harvest the small rosettes without transplanting.

In the warm South, corn salad produces all winter long. Stagger plantings as you would mesclun, starting when the southern autumn becomes consistently cool. Corn salad also produces perpetually along the cool moist Pacific coast from Southern Alaska down to California. Flavor, however, is improved by light frost.

Because corn salad is a reliable self-seeder, home gardeners can make a self-perpetuating bed. Compost thoroughly, since the bed will produce for several years. Broadcast seeds about as thick as salt on a giant pretzel. Rake in, and keep moist until the seeds germinate, up to 2 weeks. Harvest thinnings for baby salad, leaving one plant every 6 by 6 inches. Allow the remaining plants to bolt and drop seeds, which will happen very slowly in corn salad. Remove the old plants and lightly rake the bed. Again, harvest the baby thinnings the following spring, leaving a seed rosette to mature every 6 by 6 inches. Every three years, transplant baby seedlings to a new bed, so the soil does not wear out.

In field plantings, sow 18 to 36 seeds to the foot, with 12 to 18 inches between rows. Germination takes 10 to 14 days. Keep moist, if possible. Thin to 6 plants per foot, using the thinnings as baby salad. Note that some varieties have larger seeds (10,000 to the ounce), recommended for spring and fall, while others have small seeds (28,000 to the ounce), more suitable for overwintering. Some newer varieties seem to be all-purpose. Generally you can follow the sowing dates for fall, overwintering, and spring spinach in your area.

Mache (Corn Salad)

Broadcast bands 4 inches wide will produce delicious very early baby salads. Otherwise, harvest whole rosettes at 45 to 50 days after sowing, when the leaves are 2½ to 3 inches long. Though corn salad is slow to bolt, flavor declines when rosettes sit too long in the field, especially in spring and fall.

Corn salad remains a minor crop in the United States, partly because it is unfamiliar; partly because of its penchant for the cooler springs and autumns of Europe. This will change, as market gardeners learn how to insert corn salad as a niche crop into the coolest margins of the year, and as a catch crop of any portion of the garden, cool greenhouse, or cold frame, that otherwise would lie empty through the winter. There's no question that corn salad will provide the earliest and latest green salad you've ever seen. And remember: always, always plant extra if your partner is pregnant.

Varieties

Corn salad (Stokes, 45 days), a minty-flavored large-seeded strain (10,000 seeds per ounce) for fall and spring sowing. Vert de Cambrai (45 days), an older small-seeded strain (28,000 seeds per ounce) for fall crops and overwintering. Vit (50 days), vigorous, mildew-resistant with nutty undertones for fall, overwintering, and early spring sowings.

- SEED: Large-seeded: 10,000 per ounce sows about 830 feet or broadcasts about 275 feet in 4-inch bands. Small-seeded: 28,000 per ounce sows 2,300 feet or broadcasts about 800 feet in a 4-inch band.
- GERMINATION: 10 to 14 days, 45 to 50°° F.
- VIABILITY: No information.
- DAYS TO HARVEST: 45 to 50 days.
- ROTATION: 3 years. Corn salad, as a member of the rarely planted *valerian* family, gives relief to the overused *composite* (lettuce) and brassica family rotations.
- BIODYNAMIC SPRAYS and PLANTING CALENDAR: Follow the schedule for spinach.

MELON

When does a vegetable become a fruit? This is a question that has troubled me time and again while I was trying to grow good melons in New England. I've heard the same story from market growers. They compost the field, lay down black plastic, set out the melon plants at just the right time, cover them with slatted plastic; and then, after a few weeks of cloudy and cool weather in August, they end up with an acre of cucumbers.

Not so in the central states. There I could always count on melons so uncannily sweet that the supermarket version seemed like a faint memory. Only readers who have feasted on such melons or wild ripe blackberries under a hot southern sun can get a sense of the flavor, more like a quality than mere sweetness. I've never managed this quality up north, though global warming is giving me hope. A truly ripe melon, still warm from the field, is like a condensation of high summer, as if the melon were a counter-image of the sun, rising slowly—just barely—above the vegetable horizon. In fact, it rises so slowly that one might mistake this slowly rising counter-image for the moon, lemon-skinned and cool. That might be part of the problem.

Slice open a muskmelon. Visually you can learn to tell something right away about the quality and taste. A perfect melon shows a striking contrast of complimentary color between the bright mint-green of the rind and the deep salmon or orange of the flesh. After a little practice, you can taste a good melon with your eyes. Poorly grown or unripe ones show a pale contrast at best. Eventually you might notice that the green rind is a melon leaf that has wrapped around a ball of sunlight. In the fruit, the leaf fulfills the promise it made in photosynthesis. In an unripe melon the leaf zone is never surpassed. The flavor is surprisingly similar to its close relative, the cucumber. The question is: how can you be sure you are going to get a melon with this intense contrast between the ethereal green of the rind and the deep salmon sweetness of the flesh? How can you transform a cucumber into a muskmelon?

Years ago Ruth Stout (the original no-till mulch gardener) came to the conclusion that warm summer nights were essential for high-flavored melons. She gave up in Connecticut. Today new types of plastic, better varieties, and close attention to the kind of plant the melon is, make good crops possible. Melon plants must be sufficiently advanced to ripen during the warmest nights your area offers. Ruth Stout's mulch method kept the soil too cool.

Melons are plants that lack both deep penetrating roots and upright stems. This is a basic characteristic of the squash family, and consistent with its subtropical origin. In the Middle East and India, melons don't need to strain for sun and warmth. Like many annuals, the melon is forced to grow quite far from its natural range where warmth permeates the whole environment. Cultural practice must compensate for this. The hill, the trellis, even an empty tuna can, lifts the fruit from the soil into the region of slightly greater warmth. A light sandy loam helps. A deep well of rotted compost beneath the hill allows for deeper root penetration. Here we compensate for the typical image of the squash family: fruits that are not quite fruits; fruits that are flotsam washed in from a sea of leaves.

The flavors in *Cucumis melo* are really extraordinarily complex. A range of flavor undertones combines with varying depths of sweetness that would require a wine taster to unravel. Each quality is concentrated by the summer sun and dry, warm nights, somewhat as pine resins are transformed into expensive perfume by desert heat. The well of the species is deep, and only recently have the complex waters of distant cousins been drawn to the surface. In optimum melon growing areas, these qualities can be captured with open-pollinated strains, but modern hybrids make true melon flavor possible in northern climates, at least in years with warm sunny summers.

Melons originate in Persia, and most melon varieties would prefer moving back—or at least to California and the Southwest. Choose melons proven for your climate. The breadth of selection is much broader in the mid-Atlantic states with their long summers and hot summer nights. Biodynamic friends in California grow persians, Mediterranean types, and crenshaws with comparative ease. New hybrids are pushing the south farther northward every year, but more than any other crop, melons make you remember where you live.

The oldest known muskmelon was carved on an Egyptian tomb about 2400 BCE, and for thousands of years melons did not extend beyond this region of arid heat: India, the Middle East, North Africa, and Spain. Yet even in optimal areas the combination of variety and culture was so tricky that it prompted a sexist Spaniard to observe in 1513: "If [a muskmelon] is bad, it is a bad thing. We say that good [muskmelons] are like good women and bad ones like bad women." Had he suffered New England summers, he would certainly have gone even further and compared our melons to bad men. Instead, the Spanish introduced melons to California in 1683, where they have continued to live happily to the present day.

Culture

Well-made hills are justified even with an acre of melons on sandy or medium clay loam. However, heavy compacted clay, peat, and muck soils are probably a losing battle. Melons love perfect drainage and warm soil (70°F). Home gardeners can compensate with deeply dug mounds augmented with organic detritus compost and sand. Some add a drainage well of sticks, detritus and sand 1½ feet below the mound. In well-drained medium loam, a hole the size of a bushel basket will do. Use a quarter to half a wheelbarrow of manure-based compost as back fill, alternating shovelfuls of compost and topsoil, mixing as you go. Spray the soil with horn manure (500) in early spring. A slight depression about 18 inches square can be made at the top of the hill to catch water. The calcium in animal manures is greatly appreciated by melons. Horse manure works well if not diluted by sawdust. Even conventional commercial growers have found that manure produces the best melons.

In marginal muskmelon areas a boxed bed works well, placed against the south wall of a house. This can increase your climate a whole zone. Some home gardeners hasten ripening by trellising the bed against the wall. Alternately, site your cold frame against a south wall, creating a microclimate two zones south of the actual latitude. Remember to open the frames by day during flowering for bee pollination.

In areas where un-hilled fields of melons can be grown, talk with successful growers, regardless of their growing method, organic or chemical. Ask what they've done and what worked best. Select the site carefully, since a south-facing field and light soil-type will be crucial to success. The fall before, the entire area should be thoroughly disked and sprayed with horn manure (500). On a field scale, watch the pH. Melons love lime and don't tolerate a reading below pH 6. Aim for 6.5 to 7. Gardens usually have that already from composting and manure.

Market growers can alter growing method according to soil type. Growers with sandy loam may need only to manure their field and set out plant pots every 2 to 3 feet in the row, 6 feet between rows. Growers with medium clay loam do better to plant in hills on 6-foot centers, a half bushel of manure compost per hill. Others manure the field and use a bed-making attachment to create field length beds, setting out posts at 2-feet intervals at the center of the beds. Still others use a single bottom plow to throw manured soil to the center from two sides to create a long hill.

Whatever method is used, melons are slow to colonize a field, leaving plenty of space for early crops of spinach or transplanted lettuce. Spinach happens to have the same soil and calcium requirements as melons. For intercropping I have used 7-foot centers with double rows of spinach in between. The spinach is cultivated once, cut twice, and tilled under.

Time melon plantings carefully for your region. In cooler climates, jumping the season may leave melon plants stranded in cool weather. Chilling means no crop. Though 3-inch pots are adequate, I've tried 6-inch pots just in case I want to delay setting out plants beyond the usual 4-week limit. Pots should be sown 4 weeks before expected soil temperature of 70°F. Use a soil thermometer. The transplanting date can be advanced up to two weeks if black plastic is used to pre-warm the soil, and row covers or slatted plastic tunnels are used. Some growers use the largest homemade soil cube size for melons, but peat pots cause less root disturbance, a crucial factor in handling. Melons with disturbed roots may not produce. For peat pots, a 50-50 mix of compost and sandy loam works well; so does an equal mix of 20% peat, 60% compost, and 20% sand. Biodynamic market growers sometimes use weed-free commercial mix watered with strong compost tea. Sift coarse homemade mixes through hardware cloth screen. Pack mixes lightly in pots, with no air spaces. Sow three seeds per pot, ¼ inch deep. Germinate in a very warm place (85°F) for seven days using a greenhouse heating pad, furnace room, or warm window. Keep moist but never soggy.

After the first true leaf appears, snip out (don't pull) the weakest of the three plants. Spray with silica (501) at least once indoors. Water or spray leaves and soil with equisetum tea against fungus. Strong light and good air circulation make strong plants. With commercial mixes continue to water with strong compost tea, organic liquid fertilizer, or fish emulsion. A week before transplanting, harden plants by reducing water and opening cold frames during the day. Cover at night and on cool days. Hardening is not as essential when plants will be placed under plastic or row cover.

Growers who jump the season pre-warm the soil for at least a week or two prior to planting, using black plastic. Use wire hoops and slatted plastic row covers or 7- to 10-foot wide polyester row cover. Use a soil thermometer to determine 70°F soil temperature. Set out two pots per hill, or a pot every 2 to 3 feet in rows, being careful to set exactly at soil level. Water thoroughly until plants root in garden soil. Growers in warmer areas direct-seed melons. Excellent soil preparation is essential, including—traditionally—up to 30 tons of compost per acre.

Be prepared for sudden attacks of cucumber beetles during the insect's first breeding period. Even in warmer areas where row cover is not needed to jump the season, it may be required to screen out cucumber beetles. These oblong yellow and green striped or spotted beetles can devastate a planting, either by eating seedlings or transmitting bacterial wilt. In open ground, biodynamic compost will improve plant vigor and reduce insect palatability, but unprotected plants should be sprayed with rotenone/pyrethrum prior to setting in the field. Bacterial wilt requires only one bite. Hubbard or zucchini seedlings may be used as a trap crop in separate mounds. This is not totally reliable, but sometimes then the beetles never touch the melons. In home gardens, strong herbs such as horehound, catnip, or lemon balm can be grown on the mound around the melon transplants. I've blended castor bean pods and leaves (frozen the previous year), applied every 4 days as an effective repellent and insecticide (ricinic acid). In the end I've returned to row covers and iron-based slug bait.

When female flowers appear, row covers should be opened daily so bees can pollinate fruit, increasing yield. Female flowers appear later than male flowers; the ovary is visible at the base of the flower, looking like a tiny fruit. (In the greenhouse you can use a paintbrush to transfer male pollen to female flowers.) Biodynamic growers spray silica at this time.

Silica can be sprayed at least once during vine growth, once at fruit set, and once during ripening. European biodynamic growers spray even more frequently. Where mildew has been a problem, spray equisetum tea weekly or use Safer's Mildew cure. Mildew is also controlled by variety, plant vigor (good mound preparation), and sufficient water. Drip is ideal. Over-watering during ripening will diminish sweetness and flavor. Growers in arid climates assure sweetness by withholding water during the ripening period.

Unmulched melons should be kept as weed-free as possible, but never disturb roots or move melon vines during weeding. Yields will be lowered. Organic mulches should never be used in the North; even in the South they will delay ripening. Home gardeners can improve ripening with the use of empty tuna cans. Open both ends and use the can as a pedestal for the fully formed green melons. This method also prevents damage from wireworms.

For experienced growers, harvest is visual. They can see the change in the muskmelon skin: a slight yellowing of the grey-green rind and a more corky quality to the netting. In true muskmelons the vine "slips" (separates) from a ripe fruit with a gentle push. In the new honeydew crosses, the vines may or may not slip, but the white rind takes on a yellowish blush. In a ripe charentais melon, the small green leaf attached to the fruit stem becomes pale. The stem must be snipped. Since shipped melons are "half-slip" at best, you can make a great local reputation by selling only full-slip melons. Fully ripe biodynamic melons unleash incredible consumer loyalty. Once people taste these melons, the ones from the store—even in season—seem like a winter memory, as faint as the memories of youth.

Varieties

In dry climates many open-pollinated strains produce disease-free vines. As humidity increases, the disease resistance of each variety must be noted, and sometimes hybrids should be chosen. Powdery and downy mildew on melon leaves can totally shut down sugar production. Areas with extensive cloud cover or short summers are more susceptible. In marginal melon climates, consult local growers and regional seed catalogs for the results of trials. Delicious 51 (77 days), for example, an early effort developed at Ithaca, NY, from the later-maturing Bender's Surprise. Delicious produces flavorful bred melons in the central states and in northern areas with fairly warm summers. Tolerant to fusarium wilt (race 1), Hale's Best (86 days), on the other hand, was bred for areas with long summers and drought late in the season. Hale's Best is resistant to mildew. Dry summers and drought concentrate its sweetness.

Sweet Granite (70 days), an open-pollinated strain developed in New Hampshire, will produce sweet, good tasting melons in short season areas, so long as vines grow vigorously and remain free of mildew. Spray weekly with silica (501), equisetum (508), and Safer's mildew cure. Pike (85 days) was developed in 1935 for less-than-optimal soils in cloudy Oregon. Plants are vigorous, disease resistant, and rival hybrids for flavor.

For hot humid areas and the mid-Atlantic South, the disease resistance of open-pollinated Edisto 47 (88 days, Southern Exposure Seed Exchange) rivals the hybrids. Edisto 47 resists alternaria leaf spot, downy and powdery mildew.

Remember that a highly flavorful variety subject to mildew on its leaves is worth less than a lesser variety that's mildew free.

Eden's Gem, also called Rocky Ford (89 days) is an 1881 heirloom melon from Colorado with sweet green high-quality flesh adapted to the central states. True Honeydew (100 days) with its extremely sweet green flesh and smooth pale green skin, requires a very long season to produce top quality fruits. Best for the Deep South, the Southwest, and California.

Nowadays winter melons are as rare as root cellars. Pioneers stored melons like these in sod houses through the winter and savored their sweetness and vitamin C through terrible February blizzards. One old homesteader sold his quarter to pan gold, and rather than leave anything behind, ate his entire supply of Christmas melons in one sitting. The story didn't say, but I suppose he died, since those old Christmas melons were 20 pounds apiece. A modern hybrid of Christmas melon called Lambkin (68 days) has white flesh and high sugar content, and stores for weeks in the fridge—several months in cold storage. Heirloom varieties are still available at Seed Saver's Exchange.

Winter melons are comparatively low in vitamins A and C. The deeper the orange color, the more vitamins A and C a melon contains. Deep orange muskmelons contain 3,400 international units per 100 grams, while honeydew has 40 and casaba 30. Vitamin C in deep orange melons is 33 mg, honeydew 23, Casaba 13. This may be one factor in your choice of varieties besides sweetness, which in some honeydews reach a brix (sugar content) of 12%.

Hybrid melons are sweeter, more uniform, higher yielding, and more disease-resistant than open-pollinated strains. In choosing varieties note brix, flavor, aroma, deep color, wide adaptation, disease resistance, and crack resistance. Sweet n' Early Hybrid (75 days) ripens high-quality medium sweet fruit in 75 days and continues bearing due to resistance to powdery mildew. Burpee Hybrid (80 days) is considered by many to be the most reliable and one of the best tasting muskmelons. Thick deep orange flesh, reliable high yields, a long harvest season, and vigorous vines. Burpee Hybrid also succeeds under glass. Ambrosia Hybrid (86 days) runs neck and neck with Burpee Hybrid, a favorite of home gardeners in all parts of the country; exceptional flavor, with vigorous, powdery mildew-resistant vines and small cores. Harper Hybrid (80 days), a honeydew muskmelon cross, has very sweet orange flesh with a tangy unique honeydew flavor and aroma, which holds for several days after picking. The newest generation of hybrids adds a strong tolerance to most melon disease, excellent taste and high sugar content. Sugar Cube (69 days, 14% brix); Primo

(79 days, 12% brix); and Jaipur (86 days). For small gardens try a compact hybrid such as Honey Bun (73 days) with very sweet orange flesh.

Previously, middle- and far-eastern melons were confined to optimal melon climates, but new hybrids have put these exceptionally sweet melons within reach of many sections of the country. Halona (73 days) is an improved eastern type with excellent flavor and resistance to fusarium race 2. Lilly Hybrid (78 days) is exceptionally early for a crenshaw, worth trying if melons are successful in your area. Light orange flesh is sweet and spicy. Burpee's Early Crenshaw Hybrid (90 days) matures at early ripening, has subtly flavored fruits 10 to 14 pounds with salmon flesh. When ripe, dark green skin turns yellowish; crenshaw melons are harvested by "forced slip."

Charentais are small exceptionally fragrant and delicious cantaloupes from France. For melon connoisseurs, their flavor and texture is indescribable—like flowers wrapped in gray-green skin. New hybrids will mature in the North and East. Unlike muskmelons, charentais stems do not slip away from the fruit at maturity. When ripe, the small leaf (attached to the vine at the same point as the melon stem) turns pale green. Charentais stems must be snipped rather than slipped. In most charentais, which have grey-green skin, the skin turns orange when overripe. Mature fruits weigh 2 to 3 pounds. Savor Hybrid (78 days) has deep orange flesh with classic sweet charentais flavor and texture, with resistance to fusarium and powdery mildew. Isabella (75 days) is probably a muskmelon's cross, with netted skin and charentais flavor and texture, as well as increased climate adaptability, disease resistance, and shelf life. Johnny's catalog describes Edonis (70 days) as "reminiscent of the pleasures of the gods in paradise," not the usual market grower's jargon.

Hybrid honeydews have pushed these normally long season melons northward, with increased adaptability to cloudy cool weather in Honey Yellow (71 days) and Honey Orange (74 days). Venus Hybrid (88 days) takes longer to mature but produces exceptionally sweet and flavorful green-fleshed melons in areas where muskmelons succeed. Harvest honeydews when the small leaf nearest the fruit yellows. Also learn to recognize the change in skin color from greenish to yellow in each variety as the fruit begins to ripen.

Newer galia-type honeydew hybrids have also improved adaptability (Arava, 77 days) and earliness (Diplomat, 71 days), both with resistance to powdery mildew. Galias have unique tropical aroma and green flesh, sweetest when rind begins to turn from green to yellowish.

At the beginning of this chapter I lamented the cucumber flavor of unripe melons. Exotic Asian melons such as Sun Jewel (68 days) look like lemon-yellow overripe cucumbers; they are actually very melon-like, sweet, and popular with melon-lovers. Another popular exotic is the ananas melon (San Juan Hybrid, 78 days), which looks like a muskmelon with cream-colored flesh and pear-like flavor. Skin turns mostly yellow-orange when ripe. Both Asian and ananas melon stems slip from the vine when ripe.

SEED: An ounce (1,125 seeds) will direct-seed about 600 feet of row. 100 seeds will produce transplants for 16 hills, at 2 pots per hill. An ounce of seed produces about 300 pots with 3 seeds per pot.

GERMINATION: 75%; 5 to 10 days, 75° to 85°F.

VIABILITY: 4 years.

DAYS TO HARVEST: 68 to 90 days from transplanting in the field.

MOON CALENDAR: All culture, including biodynamic sprays in fruit. When mildew is a problem, spray silica and equisetum in leaf.

ROTATION: 3 years for *cucurbitae* (squash, melons, cucumbers, gourds).

BIODYNAMIC SPRAYS: Horn manure (500) on field in fall and spring. Horn silica (501) at least once in the greenhouse, twice in leaf, once at fruit set, once during ripening.

COMPANION PLANTS: Aromatic labiates (mint family) and nasturtiums against cucumber beetles. Can be interplanted with spinach and lettuce; and in hot sunny climates interplanted with dry corn.

MUSTARD GREENS (AMERICAN STRAINS)

How is it possible I missed the "triangle of U" theory, which is such a vital piece of evidence for the plasticity of the *Brassica* genus? The theory is not new. In 1935 a Korean botanist whose initial was "U" postulated the interconnected hybrid origin of three very old brassica food plants: Asian mustard, Ethiopian mustard, and rutabaga. Even so, it took decades before genetic testing confirmed his theory. I did know about one ancient hybrid, which apparently occurred in Europe several centuries ago between two separate species of *Brassica rapa* (wild turnip) and *B. oleracea* (the wild precursor of cabbage and broccoli). The cross created a cabbage-flavored sweet turnip, the rutabaga. Ethiopian mustard (*B. carinata*), a green consumed mostly in North Africa, however, was not known to me at all. Ethiopian mustard is the second hybrid in the triangle; between *B. oleracea* and *B. nigra* (yellow mustard). And the truly ancient origin of the third mustard hybrid—*B. juncea*—was a complete surprise, though its place of origin was not. *B. juncea* is a hybrid of *B. nigra* and *B. rapa*. I'm used to thinking of hybrids—with some prejudice—as recent horticultural inventions, but the *B. juncea* hybrid appeared in the Himalayas more than 5,000 years ago! *B. juncea* cultivars quickly spread to China, the site of greatest variation; then to Japan, Southeast Asia, Africa, and finally the American South. In other words, a hybrid has been a backbone of Asian nutrition since the dawn of agriculture. Of course being brassicas, these three hybrids are not like most modern ones. They breed true from saved seed. Again, a testimony to the astonishing plasticity of the *Brassica* genus. The mustard of the American South is *B. juncea*.

Nutrition

When mustard greens are grown quickly, with ample compost and no gaps in moisture, they are among the tastiest and most healthful of greens. Only kale, collards, and Brussels sprouts exceed them in some respects (for lowering cholesterol and having an abundance of certain antioxidants that may help prevent cancer).

The anti-carcinogens sinigrin, gluconasturtiian, and glucotropaeolin, however, are unique to mustard greens. Cutting activates the enzymes; and leaving the chopped greens to sit for 5 minutes before cooking increases antioxidant value in all crucifer leaves. Light cooking also helps makes these crucifers' antioxidants and vitamins more available. Chopped baby mustard greens add zest to salads and spring mixes.

Mustard greens are extremely high in folates, which reduce homocysteines (a factor causing heart disease). Mustard greens are also high in vitamins A, E, C, and K, as well as calcium and trace minerals (selenium, iron, and zinc).

On the negative side, mustard greens are high in oxalates (that are also high in beet greens), which bind to calcium and may inhibit calcium absorption, possibly contributing to kidney stones in susceptible people when mustard greens are consumed as a staple. Mustard may also accumulate heavy metals such as cadmium, if greens happen to be grown in contaminated ground. This characteristic has proved useful in bioremediation, when heavy metals must be removed from contaminated soil.

Ethnic Recipes

In the Deep South, traditionally, mustard greens have become inseparable from pork drippings, but apparently a similar recipe was enjoyed by Indian Gurkhas long before America was discovered by Europeans. Adventurous cooks, however, may want to try more healthful Indian recipes. Typically, wilted greens are combined with garbanzo or kidney beans in a curry sauce and served over rice. One such sauce mixes a pound of mustard greens with 2 tablespoons each of fresh ground coconut and ginger,; and half-teaspoons each of cumin, nutmeg, turmeric, palm sugar (jaggery), salt, and black pepper. Lovers of traditional southern greens can also try a healthful version by substituting smoked turkey for the pork, and dressing the greens with garlic and balsamic vinaigrette.

Mustard greens seem to have for the most part bypassed European cuisine. A fourteenth-century Italian cookbook presents recipes for mustard greens; but I think fourteenth-century mustard greens may not have been mustard greens but actually wild rocket, raab, and arugulas. Mustard greens, however, are delicious when prepared in the Italian style—quickly sautéed in olive oil, garlic, and salt. Mustard greens also liven up a dish of workaday collards, when the two are steamed together.

Culture

Mustard greens germinate in very cool soil (45°F), which is fortunate, since they grow best in cool weather. Sow very early in spring, in early fall, and during the winter in the Deep South and on the West Coast. Gardeners in the South regularly overwinter fall-sown mustard from late September or October sowings, harvesting the leaves 30 days later. They sow again in January for a late winter harvest. Pests such as flea beetles, aphids, and cabbage worms, which trouble mustards in summer, are absent during the cooler months. Mustard prefers temperatures down to 20°F in preference to dry summer heat, when mustard rapidly bolts and bitters. Spring-sown crops should be timed to mature early. Sow 3 weeks before last spring frost and again 3 weeks later, ½ to 1 inch deep.

Mustard grows best in well-composted organic soil, with pH 5.5 to 7.5. Mustard benefits from any kind of composted organic matter. However, uncomposted manure will adversely affect flavor. If compost is in short supply, then add an organic fertilizer with 4 to 6 N before planting. Mustard greens are so intolerant of checks in growth (which are caused by poor fertility and gaps in moisture) that there's absolutely no point in sowing them unless you can meet their needs. Distracted home gardeners will probably do better sticking to kale and collards, which can better survive some neglect, hot weather, and delayed harvest.

Culturally, mustards should be treated like lettuce, sown and harvested successively. Always harvest when leaves are still growing vigorously. Notice the vital sheen, which fades when they are over-mature. Harvest window is short; never more than 3 weeks.

For farmers and market gardeners who have enough space in their gardens to rotate crucifers for at least three years (even better, five years), mustard greens have proved an excellent green manure. Washington State Extension reports farms that rotate potatoes and wheat with mustard cover crops suppress *Verticillium dahliae*, *Aphanomyces* (common root rot), and Columbia root knot nematodes. The effect is thought to involve the breakdown of mustard glucosinolates into organic soil chemicals, which have an action similar to soil fumigants. Mustard cover crops also increase the soil filtration rate and increase organic matter in the soil up to 9,000 pounds per acre. The downside is that shorter crucifer rotations may pass on mustard's susceptibility to club root.

Insects and Diseases

In hot spells, flea beetles may cause spring mustard greens to evaporate. Use floating row covers. Aphids tend to appear on older plants or plants stressed by heat or drought, especially in low humus soils. Correct the problem with better culture. For minor infestations use horticultural oil. Control cabbage worms and moth larva with *Bacillus* (Bt.).

To control disease, rotate three or four years and keep pH above 6.5. To prevent club root, raise the pH to 6.8. In club-root infected soils, raise the pH to 7.5. To prevent seed-borne infection, purchase hot-water-treated seed or soak seed yourself in 122°F water for 30 minutes prior to sowing. Higher pH also reduces rhizoctonia, sclerotinia stem rot, fusarium root rot, and white mold. Yellow leaf blotches are caused by downy mildew. If the crop has sufficient value, treat with an organic fungicide (either a beneficial bacterium or beneficial fungus). Mustards are also sometimes susceptible to turnip mosaic virus, which distorts the leaves. Control the aphid vector with horticultural oil.

Varieties

Besides the southern style mustards listed below (which also work well in Asian recipes) try the Asian mustards described under "Asian Greens." These include Red Giant (45 days) from Japan and Ruby Streaks (40 days), similar to Mizuna and Ho Mi Z (45 days), a slow-bolting spicy mustard.

Florida Broadleaf (45 days) is mildly tangy and sweet with large leaves, slow to bolt. Burpee's is first choice for flavor. Southern Giant (50 days) has a traditional spicy southern flavor, with curly crumpled bright green leaves.

Tendergreen (45 days), a much milder variety, is pleasant tasting, but with lower levels of the spicy antioxidants typical of the species. Green Wave (45 days) a spicy dark green curled mustard is reliable in warmer weather. Green Wave is fairly adaptable and slow bolting, a variety preferred by many commercial growers.

Both New Star Mustard (pungent) and Chinese Thick Stem Mustard (mild) show exceptional cold tolerance down to 12°F. For overwintering in Virginia and the Carolinas or for stretching the season farther north. For seed saving purposes, I am not certain of the genetic parentage of these mustards.

All mustards can be harvested in 21 days for baby greens or as a spicy addition to mesclun.

Mustard Greens (American Strains)

SEED: An ounce (15,000 seeds) sows about 1,000 feet. 2 grams (1,000 seeds) sows 90 feet. ½ gram sows 22 feet.

GERMINATION: 5 days above 45°F

VIABILITY: 4 to 5 years

ROTATION: 3 years minimum; 4 or 5 years where disease has been a problem.

MOON CALENDAR AND BIODYNAMIC SPRAYS: All practices in leaf. Follow the spray schedule for broccoli or cabbage.

OKRA

Even if okra (*Abelomoshus esculentus*) did not produce edible pods, gardeners might still plant okra for its beautiful hollyhock flowers. Red varieties such as Burgundy have striking red stems, red leaf veins, and red pods on large and impressive 5-foot plants. In central and southern states some varieties grow into fair-sized shrubs.

The things that have prevented more northerly gardeners from growing okra are shorter cool summers, high mucilage content of the pods, and unfamiliarity with the way half the world cooks it. Okra can be grown wherever melons succeed, using black or red plastic and row covers. Also take into account that climate zones (for better or worse) are getting warmer. (My zone recently changed from 5 to 6.) Newer short season varieties make okra growable as far north as Canada. Properly cooked, the mucilage itself is not a problem but an asset. The soluble fiber is so healthful that you may wish to follow the example of the huge swath of cooks from the southern United States across Africa, the Middle East, and into Southeast Asia, China, and Japan. In those areas okra has been a staple for centuries. Okra traveled to America during early colonial times with the slave trade. By 1748 okra was being grown as far north as Philadelphia.

Our word "okra" comes from the Nigerian *okuru*. "Gumbo" comes from a similar sounding Bantu word. Okra probably originated in the hot humid portions of Ethiopia, where many wild *Abelomoschus* species are still found. The only species not found in the wild is the one we eat, perhaps because edible okra (like Ethiopian mustard, Asian mustard, and rutabaga) is a natural hybrid of related species. The earliest mention of the edible pod is 1216 in Egypt; that is not ancient by the standard of garden species.

Okra shows unusual hybrid vigor and range of adaptability: soils can be wet, dry, rich, poor, light, or heavy. Although okra produces best in rich composted loam with plenty of water and high humidity, seedlings established by watering become one of the most drought-resistant of vegetables. Okra's adaptation to wet and dry may reflect its region of origin, where a rainy season alternates with long periods of drought; but it also must be due to allopolyploid hybrid vigor. Like other allopolyploid hybrids (Ethiopian mustard, and so forth), okra breeds true. Human-induced hybrid okras do not withstand drought, but many may be good choices for cooler climates.

The sliminess of okra is minimized by stir-frying, deep frying in cornmeal batter, or cooking with acid ingredients such as tomatoes, a bit of lemon juice, or balsamic vinegar. Gumbo is the foundation of Cajun cooking. Okra, tomatoes, onions, and hot peppers (to taste) are combined with either chicken, shrimp, sausage, or shellfish. In Japan, okra is used in tempura, the Japanese version of southern deep fried okra. In Singapore the pods are stuffed with fish paste, boiled with vegetables and tofu, and served with rice noodles. The very nutritious okra leaves can be eaten boiled, stir-fried, or added to soups as greens to thicken the broth. Young leaves are delicious added to mixed green salads. In many countries okra seeds are used to produce a healthful, fine-flavored cooking oil, high in unsaturated fats. Seeds can be used roasted as a coffee substitute.

Health

Although some people find okra too slimy, okra mucilage may be the most healthful fiber available. Okra's highly soluble fiber decreases the rate of sugar absorption in the intestine, and binds and lowers both cholesterol and bile acids. Okra fiber promotes regularity without irritating the intestinal wall, as wheat does. Okra fiber moderates conditions that may lead to intestinal cancer. Okra also appears to improve conditions for healthy intestinal flora, especially helpful following the use of antibiotics.

Okra pods are good sources of vitamins A and C, calcium, folate, magnesium, and potassium. Nutrients are even higher in okra leaves.

Culture

Since okra bears for a very long time, only one sowing per season is required. In the Deep South growers sometimes rejuvenate okra by cutting back a portion of the crop down to 6-8 inches, after the early summer crop is harvested. When there are 8 to 10 leaf nodes, growers side-dress with fertilizer for a stronger autumn crop.

Okra is direct-seeded when soil temperature is 65°F, as early as February in Florida and the Gulf Coast, and as late as June 1 in the central states. Even in states such as Alabama, the sowing date varies by a month from the southern to the northern part of the state. On the Alabama coast, seeds are sown on April 1; in the northern parts, May 1 (Alabama Extension). In the central states okra may be sown from February 1 to May 15 on the coastal plain; and from March 15 to as late as June 30 in the higher terrain (North Carolina Extension). In the North, okra should be sown in a 70 to 75°F greenhouse, 4 to 5 weeks before melon transplants are set in the field, with soil temperature 65 to 75°F.

Research has shown that black plastic mulch increases yields by 1 ½ to 2 times more than bare ground (Alabama Extension). Black plastic mulch must be snug to the soil and provided with drip irrigation or hand watered in home gardens. Infrared transmitting mulch (IRT) increases heat 10°F over black plastic (Iowa Extension) and may well tip the scale for successful northern harvest. The addition of heavy row cover may bridge early summer cool spells. Organic mulches cool the soil and are not recommended for okra.

Okra seeds require 27 days to germinate at 60°F, 13 days at 75°F, and 7 days at 90°F. Propagation mats can be set at 80 to 90°F. Use the same soil mix prepared for squash, melons, and cole crops. Three-inch pots will suffice, but the deeper 3 7/8- by 7 1/8-inch peat pots will better accommodate okra's long taproot, which hates to be disturbed.

Okra seed germinates faster when the seed coat is broken, by freezing overnight, abrading the seed lightly with sandpaper, or soaking the seed overnight in warm 90°F water. Sow 3 standard okra seeds or 2 modern hybrid seeds per pot. Using snips, thin to one strong seedling at first true leaf. Wisconsin Extension recommends transplanting okra under plastic slatted tunnels at third or fourth leaf stage on ground covered with infrared plastic mulch. They suggest pinching off the growing tip to stimulate lateral branching and increased pod set.

Okra favors pH 6 to 6.7 but tolerates 5.8 to 7.5. Avoid high nitrogen fertilizer, which promotes foliage at the expense of pod set. High potassium and phosphorus produce highest yields. Commercial growers break up nitrogen fertilization: some at planting time, with a moderate N side-dressing at pod set.

Okra's deep taproot, adapted to survive drought, establishes quickly with deep, 8- to 10-inch initial ground preparation. Full production in dry summers requires steady drip irrigation. Optimal soil temperature is 76°F. Long season varieties take up to 4 months to produce a full crop. Compact varieties, standard or hybrid, set pods in about 50 to 53 days. Like melons, okra requires warm night temperatures.

In long-season areas, okra can be direct-seeded 6 seeds to the foot and covered with ½ to 1 inch of soil. When plants are 6 inches high, thin compact varieties 12 to 15 inches to the row, 2 ½ feet between rows. Thin large varieties (some grow over 10 feet tall and require pruning to harvest) 2 to 3 feet apart with 5 feet between rows. Okra bears best when kept weed-free throughout the season, a problem solved by plastic mulch.

Okra will bear continuously, if pods are picked every 2 to 4 days. Plants shut down when unpicked, so remove over-mature pods. Use gloves for spiny plants that cause intense itching on bare skin. Note that when stems seem tough to snip, pods will be tough as well. Pods are ready 4 to 6 days after flowers open. Harvested pods don't keep much beyond a week, 10 days at best. Store at 50 to 55°F, 90 to 95% humidity. Below 45 to 50°F, pods may become discolored, pithy, and begin to decay. No point in growing more plants than you can use; 4 to 5 plants feed most families. Commercial growers know their market in advance.

Insects and Other Pests

Strong vigorous plants often outgrow insect attacks. Stressed plants may show aphids on the undersides of leaves. Use insecticidal oil. Thrips, which rasp the leaves like coarse sandpaper, are often found on plants stressed for lack of water and compost. Thrips hide in leaf axils; spray insecticidal soap or oil thoroughly into crevices.

Curled, distorted okra pods may appear to be the effect of a virus, but are caused by the salivary secretions of the brown (Say) or Southern green stink bugs. Stinkbugs are hard to control, but a growth regulator extracted from neem (Agroneem or Azatin XL) may work, if applied several times.

Caterpillar and moth larva may be controlled by *Bacillus thurengensis* (Dipel, and so forth). Cucumber beetles, Japanese beetles, and leaf miners can be controlled with pyrethrin/rotenone combinations.

Root knot nematodes are serious problems for okra in warm central and southern states. Pull stunted plants and look for root galls. Practice a 4-year rotation, which includes nematode suppressant grass crops (rye, corn, sorghum, and grain). Attacks are worse on poor land with no compost. Well-composted loam hosts fungi that disable nematodes. Root knot nematodes can be controlled with beneficial nematodes. Southern Exposure Seed Exchange notes that the deeper root systems of heirloom varieties are more nematode-tolerant.

Disease

Wet okra pods quickly become moldy. After pods dry, harvest promptly. Okra is susceptible to verticillium and fusarium wilts (VF). As far as I know, no VF tolerant varieties are available. Rotate three to four years between okra and other VF susceptible crops (nightshades, squash family, and sweet potatoes). Clean up infected debris. Compost with high-heat fresh manure or dispose of debris entirely.

Blossom blight on okra is caused by a cottony fungal growth tipped with black fungal bodies. Blossom blight is worse in hot humid weather, normal for summers in the Deep South. Okra grown in partial shade, in damp low-lying areas, or over-fertilized with nitrogen may also be susceptible. Overhead irrigation should be off by mid-morning (Alabama Extension). Biofungicides may help. Try spraying liquid copper before rain as a preventive.

Varieties

<u>Standard okra:</u>

Clemson Spineless 80 (54 days) produces abundant 3- to 4-inch pods on long-bearing narrow 4- to 5-foot tall plants. Spineless and easy to pick.

Burgundy (49 days) makes a fine total garden landscape subject: creamy flowers with maroon centers, 4-inch red pods, red stems and leaf veins.

Cow Horn (55 days, 1865) bears heavy crops of large 6-inch pods on 7-foot plants over a long season. May not be adaptable to the North.

Burmese (58 days) is an impressive plant from Southeast Asia with 16-inch leaves and pods that remain tender and spineless up to 10 inches. Pods are less slimy than other okra. May not be adaptable to the North.

<u>Modern Hybrid Okra:</u>

Annie Oakley 11 (48 days) produces abundant, tender 4½-inch pods in most regions.

Cajun Delight (53 days) is a widely adaptable hybrid of Clemson Spineless.

Millionaire (50 days) is a fairly large plant that produces well in the North. Strong vigorous plants are early maturing, but pods tend to get tough at larger than 4 inches. Keep harvested at 3 to 4 inches.

North and South Hybrid (49 days) is productive, early, and tolerant of cooler summers. Pods remain tender longer than many varieties. A reliable choice for all regions.

SEED: An ounce (about 500 seeds) direct-seeds about 80 to 100 feet of row, depending on variety and spacing; about 170 standard transplants or 250 hybrid transplants. 4 to 5 well-grown plants are sufficient for most households.

GERMINATION: 27 days at 60°F; 13 days at 75°F; 7 days at 90°F. Light abrasion of seed coat with sandpaper, overnight freezing, or overnight soaking speeds germination.

VIABILITY: 1 to 2 years. Purchase only one year's supply.

ROTATION: In the South rotate 4 years with grasses or sweet corn to suppress nematodes. In other regions 3 years may be sufficient. Rotate 3 years with all vectors of fusarium and verticillium (nightshades, squash, melons, and sweet potatoes.)

MOON CALENDAR AND BIODYNAMIC SPRAYS: Follow the schedule for melons.

ONION

According to the German Goethean botanist Gerbert Grohmann, the onion originates from the steppes of Central Asia, where brief periods of spring rain are followed by long dry summers. Onions aren't roots. Onions are sheaves of leaves that swell above the growing point, retaining water tightly under their dry skins. This enables the onion to retain a reservoir of wet weather from one season to the next and allows us to lift them entirely free from the earth, as if one were lifting and storing a portion of last year's atmosphere.

And what a pungent atmosphere it is, piercing the eater down to the soles of his feet! My Moldovan uncle enjoyed a raw onion every morning for breakfast. Uncle Izzy ate onions like normal people eat apples, washing his onion down with beer, and finishing his meal with an evil-smelling pierogi cigar. You can imagine how repulsive Izzy's odor was to little children, who unaccountably flocked around him like flies to molasses. We loved this sad-eyed refugee from Eastern Europe, who lived far longer than was logically possible. When I harvest onions I remember my great uncle, for whom these pungent reservoirs had the faint taste and smell of home.

Grohmann tells us that the onion is a "tunicated bulb"; this is an unfamiliar expression until one notices the word "tunic." A tunic is a loose-fitting garment, like a robe. The robes in the onion seem to have no end. The entire bulb consists of layers, each one enfolding the next. There are so many layers one feels like the peasant in the Russian folk tale who peeled an onion to find the soul, and ended up with nothing. Even the outermost layer is not like the skin of roots and fruit. The dry brown skin is a dry leaf tunic as well, while the wet inner layers are also just leaves. The onion bulb is entirely a watery leaf. However, if you cut an onion that is beginning to sprout, from the neck down to the root, you can see that the peasant was wrong. There is something at the center. Within the innermost layer one finds a small green flame. It is a beautiful green, extremely vital, a color present in plants only at the point of greatest meristematic activity. So the peasant missed that; something extremely precious is protected by all those robes, maybe even something as precious as a soul, who knows?

When gardeners cut an onion in this way, some may cry because it is so beautiful—or, for other reasons. But if you overcome yourself and meditate on the sheaves, you can see a solidified imagination of the waves of growth, as rhythmic as music, which surround the plant every year and bring it into being. Their movement reminds me of the veils of smoke when a candle flame is snuffed. I imagine the onion as a solid picture of these waves, extending outward, revealing the endless tunics surrounding our world.

In late summer these tunicated waves seal themselves off from the environment, and if not harvested, they will sit motionless, enchanted, in the frozen earth until next spring. When the earth thaws, the green flame will again be rekindled. New leaves appear, and from the center, a green stem begins to rise. This is the first time a stem has appeared in this plant, which previously was composed only of basal leaves and root hairs. The stem is like a hard hollow tube whose walls are nevertheless quite watery.

It is a strange image, which I would not take for granted. What was secretly present, invisible to us, to the peasant, and I suppose to my Uncle Izzy, rises as a hollow green tube terminating in a large bud. Our peasant was certainly Russian, since the bud looks like the onion dome of a Russian Church. The skin of this little dome bursts and the soul emerges, with a rhythm that mirrors the waves of leaves unfolding at the base. But here the image is reversed, because a mirror of forces is revealing itself. The flower stalks are not sheaths; they radiate outward, forming still smaller "bulbs" at the periphery of a sphere. These bud-bulbs also burst in a series of waves, surrounding the periphery in a garment of white stars, as if what poured inward to form tunic after tunic in the bulb below now bursts forth, freeing an image of itself for those who take the trouble to picture it.

Contemplate the entire image. Below, a "sphere," literally an oval, composed of concentric layers. Above, a radiating sphere bounded by a periphery of six-pointed stars. The center, a tube or pipeline between the two. Just as the plant is a reflection of the effects of the forces that surround it, so the upper and lower parts are a picture of this very relationship, a picture of strong direct forces passing from above to below—forces you can smell.

What I didn't mention during this observation is how my office has become completely permeated by the smell of sliced onion as I write. Even after I put the onion in the adjoining workshop, the smell continues to fill every corner of the building. It goes right through me. In other words, one can say that something arising out of this sheathing, raying, and interconnecting process created a scent capable of rapid permeation, literally permeating a living organism from its nose to the soles of its feet. This occurs almost immediately when you eat onion and garlic.

Ernst Kranich, another Goethean botanist, points out that the bulbs of the *Liliaceae*, of which the *alliums* are members, are actually leaf buds that have sunk into the earth. This bud, which is usually unfolding in the air, becomes enclosed within itself. It is a shoot, the part of the plant guided by the sun; but it is cut off from the sun. In this sense, the bulb is like the moon—it holds a reflection of the sun's light. Kranich says that bulbs remind him of the way an enclosed life is brought about within the reproductive organs of animals. This is an interesting conjecture, since as far as I know, the *alliums* are the only genus containing a plant version of the anti-inflammatory prostaglandin, a fatty acid connected to the animal reproductive system.

Although the prostaglandins take their name from the prostate gland, they perform wide-ranging anti-inflammatory duties in the animal organism. Like the penetrating odor of *alliums*, they permeate our bodies, affecting blood, heart, and muscles; even alleviating arthritis. A diet of raw onions is probably the reason Uncle Izzy lived so long (and also probably the reason he never married). You could say the same of the plant. The onion marshals forces usually reserved for reproduction and places them at the service of the entire organism. Its scent and taste perform a comparable function; it leads us by the nose into the depths of other foods, a sort of culinary and therapeutic Virgil, permeating even our fingers and toes.

I should admit here that I am building a schema that is part perception and part conviction. I believe that the shape and growth of plants is a picture of the forces that form them. Along with their particular biochemistry, the changing shapes as plants seem to me an infinitely slow series of dance movements; a sign language of formative forces; a performance in three or four dimensions (because it includes time) viewed by my mostly two-dimensional mind. Over the years I have become devoted to this choreography, become a camp follower of a barely visible arcane art form. Perhaps I delude myself in thinking I can read it, as if it were a language.

Take for example the strange polarity of onion seed and onion bulb. The bulb is a beautifully constructed water storage tank, both juicy and fiery with sulfur compounds at the same time. The seed looks more like pieces of charcoal than anything else, completely burned black as if the ripening seed incinerated and left only charred remains. Perhaps the onion could be seen as a biodynamic picture of the working of sulfur—the source of pungency in the bulb working right down into the watery element. Indeed the active therapeutic compounds of onion are sulfur compounds. The onion may help to make the sulfur process and its role in healthy protein formation more concretely visible.

Herbalists consider the onion to be a panacea, helpful for practically every condition: when the entire constitution has been weakened, when appetite has fallen off, for vitamin deficiency, for individuals prone to colds and repeated illness. Onions are said to strengthen the heart, the digestion, and to restore potency. At first this put me off, but when I thought about it, I decided not to dismiss it out of hand. It may be that onion as a complex is comparable to the antioxidants. When taken regularly over a long period of time, the onion may well significantly benefit the entire constitution.

Modern nutritional research has isolated some active therapeutic principles in the *alliums*. These include quercetin, an anti-carcinogenic substance; allicin, an anti-bacterial substance; and prostaglandin, which lowers blood pressure and fatty acids in the blood. These active principles are even stronger in garlic and wild *alliums*. In itself this may be an argument for using more green onions, wild onions, garlic chives, Egyptian onions, and so on.

Culture

Because the onion is all shoot, never forming flat leaves, but rather a cross between leaf and stem, the onion seems to grow best during the ascending sun. In the North, May and June are the months for strong growth; July is the time for filling out, and August for ripening and curing. Onions produce best when grown quickly, with no early checks in growth. Experiments have shown that plants kept fairly weed-free during early leaf growth will produce good yields even if later the field gets weedy. When young plants are not weeded, yield drops drastically. The same is true with insect attacks such as thrips. Plants set out early and growing vigorously are less harmed by thrips than those planted late or set back by poor fertility or early dry spells.

Onions appreciate a fertile medium loam that drains well, pH between 6 and 7, fairly rich in nutrients. Like the cabbages, onions have a liking for lime so long as pH does not exceed 7. They grow well on muck, rich sandy loam, medium clay loam that drains well, peat, or mineral soils. Specific onion varieties may do better on specific soil types. Commercial catalogs note the optimum soil type for each variety.

In areas with summer drought and midsummer thrip damage, sow seeds in a deep greenhouse bench or 5-inch deep flat from late January to middle February. Late winter sowings are good crop insurance even for winter storage onions, and essential for sweet Spanish types. Sweet onions get too pungent in summer, if sown in March or April. Since onion seed can germinate in very cold ground, additional heat may not be necessary so long as the earth is above freezing at night. In the central states a well-protected cold frame often thaws in the late February sun. A well-insulated solar cold frame may warm enough in late January. Soil for cold frame benches or flats should be at least 25% compost.

Onion seeds are easy to handle, and seedbeds should be sown carefully, four seeds to the inch in a furrow ¼ inch deep. Avoid a dense lawn of onion seedlings, since pricking out (that is, transplanting to wider spacing in a new greenhouse flat or bench) seems to set seedlings back too much. Careful spacing is also important when direct-seeding in the field; a dense seedbed will stunt the whole harvest even before the growing season has begun. In seedbeds or in cold frames, thick stands can be hand thinned 1 inch between plants, provided seedlings have not been shaded, abandoned, or blanched by crowding for a long time. If seed germination is poor or nil, the seed may be more than a year old or the potting mixture too acid. As with beet seed, a light dusting of lime over the seeds prior to closing the furrow may improve germination. Germination is also helped by covering the furrow with a ¼-inch band of fine-composted manure or a good quality bagged manure compost.

Onions look like grass when they germinate, but since they come up before most weeds, the seed row is easy to weed. I like the Cape Cod weeder for this purpose. If the stand looks too thick, thin them soon. Strong transplants pay back at every stage, including harvest. When the plants have ceased to look like grass and have a few rounded onion leaves begin sprayings of silica 501. Plants cramped in flats or benches for about eight weeks without change of soil benefit from compost/nettle tea, liquid seaweed, or fish emulsion. Checks of growth echo down to harvest. Plants should be timed so that vigorous growth can be maintained for the eight weeks prior to thawed conditions. Transplants can take some frost, but not hard freezes. Large solid plants take abuse better than spindly ones. Ideal size is halfway between a thermometer and a pencil.

Harden plants for a week when ground can be worked in spring. Lower the temperature, if possible, and water only enough to keep from drying out.

In the cold frame, expose plants to the spring sun during the day; leave cold frame open on frost-free nights. Move flats outside and cover only if threatened by sharp frost; in the central states, the end of March and farther north, sometime in April, depending on weather.

"Haircuts" are a question that I've never resolved. Some growers insist that keeping the seedbed cut to 4 or 5 inches produces stronger transplants. Others insist that haircuts lower yields. Extension websites insist haircuts are okay. I've tried both ways and haven't seen a difference. I know that when you transplant onion seedlings, the tops and roots must be trimmed: the tops get hopelessly in the way and the long original roots get stunted and cannot support large tops, until they re-grow from the base of the bulb. As a result, I cut leaves back to 4 inches and roots back to 2 inches. I lift whole handfuls at a time and cut tops and roots quickly with grass scissors, piling them in boxes as I go. The cut tops can be used as "chives."

In the garden make a furrow with a Warren hoe, the straighter the better as far as later cultivation is concerned. Lay the onions in the V with roots down, not half curled back. A whole row can be laid out before the furrow is closed and firmed. Don't plant too deep. The white of the onion should be above ground, the root plate just below ground level. Space 3 to 4 inches between plants for storage onions, 4 inches for Sweet Spanish. Rows can be a foot apart in beds or double field rows, with a tiller-width between each double row. Keep well watered during spring dry spells.

Keeping onion beds and field rows of onions weeded is a real chore, but essential for good crops. In home gardens thick mulch is ideal if the garden is free from perennial weeds. Mechanical cultivation never completely does the job, though precision rows and precision cultivators (often from Europe) help. There are no secrets that I know, just frequent use of the wheel or stirrup hoe before weeds emerge. Onion production is cut tremendously when the plants are overwhelmed by weeds in the early stages of leaf growth. Toward harvest, onion weeds are not so crucial. Bulbs become harder to find but do not diminish in size. Mulch is worth the investment when practical. Onions grow larger if soil is removed from around the tops of developing bulbs, or if initial planting was so careful that the root plate was only just below the soil surface.

Silica should be sprayed when the onions are growing vigorously, as described above, at third leaf and sixth leaf, during scallion stage, and once again at bulb formation. Side-dressings, compost, seaweed, or organic fertilizer can be applied when leaves are about 6 inches tall. Commercial growers also fertilize at the onset of bulb formation. This will increase yield, although high nitrogen may hinder keeping quality. Seaweed and nettle sprays are helpful at all stages.

Onion maggots plague some areas. Rotate crops and dust heavily around transplants with ground lime or wood ashes. Note this in your garden record, so as not to make rotated beds over-alkaline. Thrips are the scourge of many onion growers, cutting yields dramatically even in heavily sprayed fields, since thrips can lodge in protected leaf axils. In small gardens, herb interplanting and mixed culture helps. Getting plants onto the field as early as possible allows early growth before thrips breed. In this regard the faster growing hybrids give a significant edge over standard types. Many gardeners have thrip problems without knowing it. Thrips are barely noticeable to the naked eye, looking a bit like whiteflies. They rasp the onion leaves and make them look whitish, streaked, and old. What appears to be age is not so. Those bulbs never reach true maturity and don't store well. Safer's insecticidal soap and Ivory liquid detergent give some control. Studies have shown that Ivory liquid gives about as good control as pesticide. Use a few tablespoons per gallon of water.

Onion sets (miniature bulbs) can be grown mid-season by broadcasting a garden bed with seed about 1/8 inch apart in all directions. These will grow in a cramped manner making many tiny bulbs. Half-inch bulbs are the ideal size. Any variety will do the job, so long as it is a keeper. Stuttgarter has been reliable for generations, keeps well, and does not sprout in storage. Sets mature earlier than transplants, but do not keep as well as the best hard varieties grown in one season. Home grown sets must be cured in a warm, dry place for three weeks just like storage onions, then cured a second time after replanting, growing, and harvesting the following season.

In the North, growers direct-seed large amounts of onions as soon as the soil can be worked in spring. In the central states, I found that weeds, drought, and thrips overwhelm the field, when seeds are sown then. Direct-seed about ½ inch deep in light soil and ¼ inch deep in heavier soil, about 20 seeds to the foot. Remember that hybrid seeds nearly all germinate, but standard varieties have a lower germination rate. For small gardens a compost cover will demark the rows, increase the rate and speed of germination, and allow for skim cultivation prior to germination. Rows should be arrow-straight for ease of cultivation. Thin six plants to the foot for large bulbs. A little crowding will still make a crop. Spanish onions need more room, since each bulb is the size of a baseball, or in fertile soil, a softball.

Harvest for fresh use or market whenever the onions reach a good size. Of course, scallions can be pulled anytime, but they are usually a special variety, direct-seeded crop with no spacing or thinning. Fresh bulb harvest can begin when 25% of the tops have fallen. Final harvest begins when about half the tops are down. If the weather is dry the rest can be knocked down with a rake and left for a week or so. If wet weather prevails, it is better to pull the crop and cure in a hot dry shed for a few weeks. Onions can be braided on twine and hung to dry from rafters. Only thin-necked, completely mature, and well-cured onions store well. Onions require a near-freezing temperature for long storage, humidity at 65 to 70%. Onions re-sprout when stored at 40°F.

Varieties

Bulb maturity is tied to day length. Some varieties ("short-day") mature so early in the season that the seed is usually sown the fall before and overwintered to form bulbs the following year. Short-day onions, most of which are sweet and not for storage, grow best from subtropical latitudes (20°) as far north as southern California and southern Virginia (36°). "Long-day" varieties must be grown during longer northern days. Most long-day onions are hard storage types sown in the greenhouse or direct-seeded by early spring. Long-day onions are successful from Northern Virginia, the Midwest, and Sacramento (38° latitude) north through Canada to Southern Alaska (55° latitude). A third group are "day-neutral" and grow well anywhere in North America, regardless of latitude.

Northern gardeners who sow short-day sweet onions in the spring will be disappointed at the small size and pungency of the bulbs, because longer northern days prematurely initiate bulb formations. The effect of day length on the maturing onions is genetically tied to the date for water storage and dormancy. What previously expanded as leaf formation changes direction drastically, and becomes enfolded and enclosed within the bulb. A kind of inbreathing takes place, an ingestion of the sun's ascending and descending rhythm. The ingestion differs dramatically from north to south. Northern summer days (from 40° to 50° latitude) are much longer than southern summer days (30° to 38° latitude). Long-day onions (LD in some catalogs) are adapted to a summer cycle of very long days, while southern short-day onions (SD) are adapted to much shorter summer days. Unfortunately Johnny's Selected Seeds is the only catalog I know that is precise in this regard, since it gives the exact degree range for each variety. One variety, Ailsa Craig, (110 days) grows from 38° up to 60° latitude, which must be Scotland, since I cannot imagine it growing at Fort Churchill on Hudson Bay. Perhaps it grows in southern Alaska? Ailsa Craig produces Spanish-type onions in very cool seasons. Excellent fried with walrus steak.

Northern long-day onions start to bulb after day length has reached 15 to 16 hours, and then mature when day length decreases. Short-day onions bulb after day lengths of 11 to 12 hours. This means that short-day onions in the North will be triggered to bulb very soon after sowing. Short-day onions are usually sown in the fall or early in the New Year in the South. In the North, short-day onions must be greenhouse sown in January to get moderate yields and to maintain sweetness. Gardeners not too far north of 38° latitude who crave Vidalia-type sweet onions can greenhouse sow Granex Hybrid at this time, or try Candy Hybrid, which grows well into New Jersey. Otherwise, order plants from a southern plant company. Granex is marketed as "Vidalia" in the trade, although gourmet cooks believe a Vidalia onion can be grown only in Vidalia, Georgia.

Southern onions have at least one long-day rival from the Northwest, which gardening friends from Oregon consider the best onion of all. Walla Walla Sweet (300 days when sown in late summer and overwintered; 125 days when spring-sown in the greenhouse) is a widely adapted sweet onion that produces exceptionally fine tasting, mild sweet onions farther north (35 to 55° latitude). Walla Walla can be sown in late August wherever winter temperatures remain above -10°F, including coastal Zone 7 areas of New England and the Midwest. Spring-sown Walla Walla (January 1 in the greenhouse) will not be as large or sweet, but will still be very good quality.

Since Walla Walla doesn't keep, follow with Riverside Sweet Spanish (115 days), which can be sown in January or February or direct-seeded in April. Not as sweet as Walla Walla, Riverside keeps through December and is still one of the highest yielding onions. Sweet Spanish hybrids, such as Sierra Blanca (109 days, formerly called Super Star) are day-neutral for all areas and store 2 to 3 months, with high sugar content. Candy Hybrid (290 days overwintered, 110 days spring-sown) is also very sweet and day-neutral, but not as widely adapted (33 to 40° latitude) or as long storing.

A similar progression is found in red onions. The sweetest, mildest salad types are southern short-day, such as Southern Belle (115 days winter-sown or 300 days overwintered). Long-day versions include Bennie's Red, Mars (a hybrid of Bennie's Red), and the day-neutral Red Candy Apple Hybrid. Size and flavor fall between hard cooking onions and Sweet Spanish. Candy Apple is much sweeter than Mars, and stores for 2 months. Mars is sweet at harvest but grows increasingly pungent during its 4- to 6-month storage period.

Hard storage onions are mostly long-day types. Michigan, Ontario, and New York are areas well-known for hard onion production. Open-pollinated onions such as New York Early are quite hard and compete with the hybrids in storage. Other good open-pollinated keepers include Stuttgarter (the standard onion set), Early Yellow Globe, Ebenezer, and Southport Yellow Globe. Hybrids offer vigor, more disease resistance, and sometimes better storage qualities. In years past when I tried many varieties I found that hybrids were good at beating the main thrips infestation and were very high yielding, but not as easy to store. Choose hybrids with good resistance to fusarium, pink root, and perhaps leaf diseases such as botrytis and downy mildew. Note the soil preferences of each hybrid. One may perform well on muck (which is moist), another on dry or mineral soils. For muck soils choose varieties resistant to fusarium basal rot. For areas prone to wet weather choose varieties with tight necks resistant to neck rot. Some note "strong root system," a plus on any soil type. Onion breeding is active, so keep abreast as new varieties are developed. The only hybrid that's persisted for decades is Copra, which retains its sweetness during long storage and is always one of the last to sprout. Copra has a tight thin neck, less inclined to rot, and dries quickly in the field, the standard for all storage onions. Onions stored before the tops have fallen and dried naturally never keep well. Knocking them down with a rake is no substitute for natural ripening.

"Bunching onions," or scallions are onions bred to be harvested immature, at the leaf stage. Tender greens, white shafts, and miniature bulbs are eaten raw in soups, dressings, stir-fries, and garnishes. Green onion leaves are 4 times higher in iron, 5 times higher in vitamin C, and 100 times higher in vitamin A than bulb onions. They will become an increasingly valuable crop.

Japanese bunching types produce long white bulbless shafts that look like thin, miniature leeks. He-Shi-Ko (Hardy White Bunching, 70 days) is used both for summer crops and for sowing in fall, north and south. The hardiest bunching onion is not an *Allium cepa* but the perennial *A. fistulosium* (Evergreen Hardy White), mentioned under "Leeks, Welsh Onions, and Wild Onions." It can be sown in fall for over-wintering in severe climates, sown in spring, or divided the next summer as a perennial. Ishikura (66 days) has improved long-distance shipping qualities with long shafts for market growers. Ishikura is not hardy, but is used for spring and summer harvest. Tokyo Long White (68 days) is not winter-hardy, but is highly resistant to pink root, thrips, smut, and botrytis leaf blight.

In areas where swollen bulbs (as opposed to straight shafts) are desired as scallions, White Lisbon (60 days) is still very popular. White Lisbon is extremely early and usually must be harvested before the bulb swells too much, although swollen bulbs are fine for home use. Red-shafted scallions add color to salads and roadside stands. Newer varieties such as Red Barn (65 days) and others become red regardless of weather or temperature.

Oldtime gardeners in Europe and America also grew truly perennial bulb onions, called "multipliers." Multipliers may be an original form of *Allium cepa*, the modern onion. Like garlic and daffodils, multipliers reproduce themselves by natural bulb division. They include potato onion, shallots, and Egyptian onions. Once you buy them, they're yours forever, adapted to a wide range of climates north and south. Multipliers are available through seed exchanges such as Southern Exposure.

Potato onions, also called hill onion, mother onion, and pregnant onion, are the largest and most productive onions with clusters of bulbs, each 2 to 4 inches in diameter. A large 3- or 4-inch bulb may reproduce itself ten- to twelvefold. Cured bulbs keep for 8 to 12 months, green onions forced all winter. They are totally hardy and perfect for kitchen gardens.

Shallots are a more refined version of potato onions, renowned for their delicate flavor in French cooking, and are available as sets or seeds. Sets can be planted like garlic in the fall in fertile, well-composted soil or planted in spring. Press bulbs root end down, leaving the pointed sprout end above the soil surface, 6 inches between sets, at least one foot between rows in raised beds. Each seed will multiply up to tenfold. Shallot scallions can be forced in winter or harvested in spring from an autumn planting. Shallot seeds offer the possibility of selecting varieties for quality and long storage until next spring. Seeds are sown thickly in bands, similar to broadcasting lettuce, and covered with ½ inch of fine compost. If sown thickly, each seed will produce a single shallot; sow more thinly for sets to cluster and multiply.

Egyptian onions (also called top onion, winter onion, and walking onion) are more like garlic in size, habit, and strength of pungency. They probably have considerable medicinal value. Small bulbs are used in moderation in cooking and produce green onions through much of the year, right through the winter in mild areas. Like garlic, Egyptian onions produce small sets at the top of the flower stalk. Top sets can be planted, left to self-sow, or used in pickle recipes. These very hardy onions require a perennial bed of their own. Initial sets are available from Southern Exposure Seed Exchange.

SEED: Seed per ounce 7,000. A packet of 300 seeds sows 18 feet, or produces about 170 transplants. An ounce direct-seeds 300 to 400 feet but produces more than 4,000 transplants or 1,300 feet in the field.

GERMINATION: About 7 days.

VIABILITY: 1 year.

MOON CALENDAR: Sow in root or leaf. Cultivate and spray in leaf; or alternate between root and leaf. Harvest in root in the afternoon.

ROTATION: 3 years between onion family.

BIODYNAMIC SPRAYS: Horn manure (500) on seedbed and field. Silica (501) several times on seedlings. Compost-clay 500 dip for transplants. Silica in morning alternating between leaf and root days until bulb formation. When bulb forms, spray silica on root day in the afternoon.

COMPANION PLANTS: Alternate rows or interplant with carrots, lettuce, peppers, beets, chard, or cabbage. Chamomile and summer savory aid health and growth. Aromatic herbs repel thrips, as does nettle spray.

PARSNIP

It is hard to imagine, but before the advent of the potato, the parsnip (*Pastinaca sativum*) was a winter staple in central Europe. The herbalist Juliette de Bairacli Levy tells us that even today, lightly steamed parsnips served with white sauce and parsley are a typical French peasant dish; but generally, the potato has totally eclipsed parsnip as the "peasant root." The famous Russian author of the novel *Dr. Zhivago* must have had deep peasant roots since his patronym, Pasternak, is still the word for "parsnip" in Russia and Eastern Europe. The parsnip has so fallen from culinary grace that it might be good to review this odd member of the carrot family.

Its origin as a cultivated plant is uncertain. Wendell Camp (*The World in Your Garden*, 1957) believes that parsnips have been raised in gardens for more than 2,000 years. The Romans liked parsnips immensely and used them medicinally, but it is not clear whether they cultivated them, or only collected the roots from the wild. The Roman Emperor Tiberius was so fond of parsnips that he had the wild roots dug up each fall from the banks of the Rhine, thus beginning a long, sad tradition of importing winter produce instead of growing it at home. German peasants, however, carried the wild plant into their gardens at a very early date; the parsnip appears in a German gardening book in 1542. By 1550, the parsnip was also well established in England. By 1609, it was being grown by Virginia colonists. The colonists, in turn, passed the parsnip onto another people who sorely depended upon winter provisions, the Native Americans. In 1779, General John Sullivan campaigned to defeat the Iroquois in western New York by destroying their store of parsnips.

Apart from a round form of parsnip, which is grown in Europe, the parsnip we grow today hasn't changed much in 500 years. It may be larger, smoother in texture, and sweeter, but its unique hard-to-describe flavor still retains some of its wild origin. Before the so-called Age of Enlightenment, the parsnip was the "potato" of middle Europe. Parsnips and natural sourdough rye or sourdough wheat bread were the most common staples. I tried to follow the nutritional change that took place when these staples were replaced by potatoes and bread leavened with brewing yeast. Without sourdough fermentation, the new yeasted breads failed to break down phytate, a salt of phytic acid naturally found in cereal grains. The phytate in turn formed insoluble compounds with calcium, zinc, phosphorus, and iron, and interfered with their absorption; this was catastrophic among peasants, who lived on a limited diet. Bone malformation (rickets) and other deficiencies became epidemic across Europe.

It is a sad fact that the Age of Enlightenment, which brought so many improvements to industry and agriculture, increasingly came to regard the human being as a sack to be stuffed with substance. The potato seemed an ideal stuffing. In some countries its consumption was required by law. The potato, however, has seven times less calcium than parsnip, forty percent less phosphorus, four times less fiber, and six times less folic acid. Clearly, this trade was unfair. As noted in the *Encyclopedia Britannica*: "Undue dependence on ... root staples such as potatoes, yams [tropical white yam, not sweet potato], and cassava may produce not only vitamin deficiencies but also deficiencies of minerals and amino acids, the building blocks of proteins."

High levels of folic acid are formed in parsnip leaves and stored in the root. Folic acid is used in contemporary medicine to cure pernicious anemia and high white blood cell count. It works deep into the organism, making the high calcium levels in parsnip effective right down into the bone marrow, where blood and bone have their origin. The strong folate/potassium nature of this root is evident from the glossiness of its leaves. It provides structure without the rigidification that calcium alone would provide. "Calcium rigidifies us, while in potassium ...the fluid human being builds solid organs out of the coursing stream of liquids." (Suchantke, cited in Hauschka 1967) From the biodynamic point of view, potassium shows its dynamic nature not only in the rhythmic sequence of leaf nodes. When we eat parsnips the rhythms of leaf nature are transformed into the ebb and flow of cellular fluids regulated by potassium, reproducing the breathing of leaves at the cellular level, especially for the heart.

Parsnip is really typical of its *umbelliferous* kin. Parsnip's peculiar herbal undertones of flavor (reminiscent of chervil, coriander, parsley, and lovage) are condensed into a relatively bland root. Gerbert Grohmann reminds us of the fine line that exists in the *Umbelliferae* between the medicinal, the toxic, and the spicy, by pointing out that seeds of fennel, caraway, and archangelica are toxic to birds. I know some people who react that way to parsnips! For some people the taste goes right through them, shaking them with revulsion, as if it were some repulsive herbal tonic. Indeed the taste of parsnip is hard to describe, a combination of sweetness, herbal leafiness, and mineral undertone—a peculiar leafy herbal taste, which has been drawn down into the root.

And that seems to me the difference between parsnip and potato. In the brown skin of the potato the alkaloid-flavored leaf is fortunately denied—drawn down into the earth and canceled, drastically reducing folate levels in the tuber. In the parsnip, like most of its kin, the sunny dry airy temperate meadows of its origin are drawn down into the root. As a medicinal and culinary plant, it carries the effect of these airy meadows right through the winter, allowing some of the *umbelliferous* leaf nature to remain active until the sun returns in the spring. I should note, however, that Grohmann was right. The leaves of parsnip do contain an irritant, which in rare cases reacts with sunlight on the skin, producing a severe rash. This irritant does not seem to affect the root. Sensitive gardeners should wear gloves when harvesting and stripping leaves off parsnip.

Culture

Parsnip culture is similar to carrot, but much longer, slower, and much more frost-tolerant. Parsnips own the ground they grow in for the entire season. Most take 3½ to 4 months to mature. Since harvest should be after autumn frost brings out parsnip's full sweet flavor, count back 3½ to 4 months from October or November, depending on latitude. In the North and central states sowing takes place May 1.

Like carrots, parsnips like a medium or sandy loam with good drainage, moderately composted. Too much fertilizer or added nitrogen dressings will reduce quality and cause hairy roots.

Parsnips take forever to germinate, about 3 weeks. Seed covering must remain moist, which can be a pain in some years. Crusting clay will result in scatty stands. Home gardeners with crusty soil can use a sifted compost cover. Old timers sometimes place long boards over seed rows for 3 weeks to keep seeds moist. This works; but check under the boards daily during the third week and remove the boards immediately when the seeds germinate. Others soak the seeds overnight in compost tea. Drain the seeds, mix with dry sand (for handling purposes), and sow in ½-inch furrows about 15 parsnip seeds to the foot for club-sized Hollow Crown; 20 seeds to the foot for slender Harris Model types. Consider adding radish seed, 10 seeds to the foot, to mark the rows for skim-weeding. Cover with ½-inch friable soil or compost, tamp firmly, and water regularly (germination is difficult in dry weather). In home gardens hand weeding is required, but a light mulch helps.

The distance between rows can be 12 inches in beds or 18 to 24 inches in the field. Double field rows 6 inches apart are possible with a tiller space of 30 inches between the double rows. Single rows produce larger roots. Skim-weed the surrounding soil several times prior to emergence. The weed population will germinate three times before parsnips come up once.

When plants show true leaves, thin to 3 or 4 inches in the row, depending on the size parsnips you want. Biodynamic practitioners spray silica when plants show five true leaves, and several more times during parsnips' long four-month growing period. For better yields, keep well-weeded or mulch heavily. Most growers have few problems with insects or disease, but if celery blight affects your parsnips, practice at least a 3-year carrot and fennel rotation, and isolate from celery. If carrot fly is prevalent in your area, find out the egg-laying cycle from your extension agent, and plant later. Floating row covers can be used.

The taste of parsnips improves when frosted for a week or more, but young plants can be harvested. Large roots are very hard to dig and sometimes break, but they still seem to store well in the cold cellar. Some roots can be left in the ground for spring harvest. Parsnip tolerates 0°F soil temperatures, but lifting the roots becomes impossible in midwinter. For winter use, lift and store in a near-freezing, humid place. Larger roots store better and are less apt to shrivel. Perforated plastic liners or plastic-woven feedbags keep humidity high. Sand and leaves work well only if temperatures are close to freezing. If you have parsnips in the spring that you know will not be eaten as roots, try forcing the greens in a 60°F cellar. Pack in soil with the tops out and keep watered. Parsnip sprouts at 4 inches are delicious and unique in salads! Of course, the yield is very low. It's just a nice thing to do if you would be composting the roots at the end of the winter. Well-shaped sound roots can be replanted in spring to grow seed, or simply leave a few parsnips in the garden in fall. When most of the seeds on the umbel become ripe in late summer, dig the entire plant and hang upside down in a warm place. Place the seed stalks in a large paper bag when they are dry to catch the seed.

Recipes

French-fried parsnips: cut parsnips lengthwise into French fry-like sticks. Brush with oil and bake on cookie sheets at 400°F. Turn with a metal spatula when brown. Parsnip sticks become crispy on the outside, soft inside. Dip in ketchup at the table.

Stir-fried parsnips: slice thin discs of parsnip, sauté in oil with onions and grated fresh ginger. Add tamari when cooked. (Recipes thanks to Sherry Wildfeuer.)

Varieties

Varieties are fewer in America than in Europe, where even round forms of parsnips are available. Harris Model (120 days) is larger, more slender, and more gracefully tapered than Hollow Crown (105 days), which can grow into fair-sized wedge-shaped clubs. Harris Model types are favored commercially for smoothness, whiteness, and slenderness. Hollow Crown's fine texture, flavor, and bulk make it a better choice for root-cellaring. Andover (120 days) is a Harris Model type but sweeter (12% brix), with strong tops. Lancer (120 days) adds higher germination rate (notoriously low in parsnip) and tolerance to brown canker, the rusty patches on roots. The short to medium roots of Turga (110 days) have improved germination, adaptability, and vigor, and grow well in heavier soils. Check out new European varieties, which appear every few years. Hybrid parsnips offer higher yields and greater vigor, but that may not be essential in a niche crop like parsnip.

- SEED: An ounce of seed (average 6,000) sows up to 400 feet for large club-shaped Hollow Crown types, and 300 feet for slender Harris model types for market packs.
- GERMINATION: 60%; 21 days at 60°F.
- VIABILITY: 1 year (sometimes 2).
- DAYS TO HARVEST: 3½ to 4 months.
- MOON CALENDAR: All culture in root, including biodynamic sprays.
- ROTATION: 3 years for carrot family, *Umbelliferae*.
- MOON CALENDAR: Horn manure (500) before sowing. Silica (501) at first rosette, several times during leaf development, and when shoulders begin to swell. As root develops, spray silica in the afternoon.
- COMPANION PLANTS: An excellent deep-rooting companion. Interplant or alternate rows with cabbage family, bush and shell beans, and onions.

PEAS

Peas have been popular since the Bronze Age, perhaps even longer. Dried peas were found on the sites of Swiss Lake Dwellers and in prehistoric caves in Hungary. Peas were found in the ashes of Troy (c. 1200 BCE) and in more modern times as "green peas for Lent" in medieval England (which is, by the way, the first mention of peas in their unripe form). By 1536 the culture of both green peas and edible-podded peas was fully described in France. In England, Master Peas Blossom was so famous that he appeared briefly on the stage as a character in Shakespeare's *Midsummer Night's Dream*. By 1696 his popularity had increased to a gastronomic obsession. Earthy Master Peascod seemed to arouse ungovernable passion among the delicate ladies of the French Court. Thus Madame de Maintenon writes: This subject of peas continues to absorb all others! Some ladies, even after having supped at the Royal Table (and supped well too!), upon returning to their homes and at the risk of suffering from indigestion, will again eat peas before going to bed. It is both a fashion and a madness.*

Nor could the clergy ignore these uncontrolled passions! At some monasteries monks were forbidden to eat these pernicious vegetables because they were "so satisfying."

Since Master Peascod has turned up everywhere in gastronomic history, it seems odd that no evidence of *Pisum sativum* has ever been found in the wild. Did "pease craving" drive the last wild stands to extinction? Or was the species itself created by some prehistoric horticultural genius? Related species range from Ethiopia through Asia Minor to Northwest India, and in those places there is always a variety of *Pisum sativum* in the gardens of the local inhabitants, but no one knows how the cultivated species was developed. It may be that peas are the oldest garden plant.

The mystery of peas, however, goes even deeper in time than the Bronze Age. The mystery of peas is that they reflect a world in between the plant and animal world; a world that, according to Rudolf Steiner, has to be understood if we are to harness the forces of fertility in our present farms and gardens.

---

* This quote and other historical information is drawn from *The World in Your Garden*, 1957.

Peas are active representatives of one of the two primary poles of fertility discussed in biodynamics. They not only manufacture usable nitrogen; they also form a visible link between the atmosphere above the soil and the soil life beneath it. Nitrogen appears because legumes grow in concert with a living atmospheric stream, which should function in a farm or garden almost like an organ in an animal.

It may not even be accurate to say "present atmosphere of the earth," since peas and other legumes bear an atmosphere more albuminous and womb-like than present-day earth. Legumes may even recall an older, ancient earth, which has long since disappeared. Substances that today form inside the organs of animals are through the legumes generated outside just beneath the surface of the soil, as if the soil were a living animal organ.

The symbiosis between legumes and rhizobial bacteria is more comprehensive than (as is usually imagined) an opportunistic infection by bacteria. The connection is revealed, for example, in the uncanny biochemical resemblance of legume sap to animal blood. The seeds of *Phaseolus sp.* (snap beans, kidney, lima, mung beans, and so forth) and at least 60% of the legume family produce a large protein molecule (phytohemagglutinum) that clots certain human blood types. It provides a remedy for certain types of anemia, when a shortage of blood cells is due to the destruction of blood-forming tissues. It also deactivates certain tumor cells, just as a healthy immune system does. In other words, the same subtle healing forces we find otherwise only in human and animal organs have a corresponding life in wider nature as well. It might behoove us to try to discover the deep interrelationship that makes this connection possible, a relationship that Rudolf Steiner considered to be in itself a "huge organ" in nature's household. Farmers and gardeners ignore this to their peril.

The various species of *Leguminosae* (now called *Fabaceae*) are so closely united within this "un-plantlike" organ that as a family they seem to belong to a different order of plant being altogether. For this reason I have found it hard to understand how the *Leguminosae* is closely related to the rose order *Rosales*. In legumes, the upward-turning capacity of the rose to transform light and air into the fullness of fruit (the enclosing receptacle or covering of the seed) is either entirely missing or else turned upside down and plunged into the soil.

We eat the juicy receptacle in snap peas and snow peas; they are technically a fruit, but the fruitiness is suppressed, leaf-like. The gesture of the *Fabaceae* goes in the opposite direction from the rose and finds typical expression in the peanut. Once the flower has been pollinated, the forming fruit dives downward into the soil, somewhat like a larva. In the peanut the downward stream becomes visible. Like Pluto, it drags Persephone into the earth.

The pea becomes pregnant like no other plant. Pea leaves already grow like two insect wings on the stem, open to the light and present-day atmosphere of the earth. In the fruit, the two wing-leaves close and seal themselves off from the atmosphere. They swell and enclose a different atmosphere all their own. Goethean botanist Gerbert Grohmann even wonders if the air inside a swollen pea pod would be richer in nitrogen. Inside, a tiny embryo begins to grow, an embryo more proteinaceous than in any other plant group.

As it grows, the legume spreads its own albuminous atmosphere outward in the sphere of the roots, as if the pod were merely a small image of a larger enclosing structure. The soil life around the roots of a pea plant is extremely complicated, some of it directly connected to the roots, some indirectly. Azotobacter (an aerobic nitrogen-fixing bacteria), for example, is present even when legumes are not. It survives a secondhand existence saprophytically on decomposition products. *Azoto* means "nitrogen" in several romance languages, and Hauschka (2002, reprint) notes that the word derives from "azure," the blue of the sky. Azotobacter draws "the blue of the sky" down into the earth. Azotobacter may produce up to twenty-five pounds of nitrogen per acre per year. This probably accounts for the slightly revivifying effect of fallowing.

In the long run, however, old-time fallowing cannot maintain fertility. Alfalfa roots and their rhizobial bacteria, for example, add ten times more nitrogen than free-living soil bacteria; that's a three-year supply for non-leguminous plants. This is because the soil bacteria (Rhizobia) attached to leguminous roots find a direct connection to the atmosphere through the leaves. In the end, rhizobia and legumes build the most ecological pathway for nitrogen on the farm. The association is either symbiotic or science fiction, depending on your perspective. Rhizobia enter the root hairs and grow right through the cortex, then through the cells of the pericycle. Pericycle cells are stimulated to divide, producing a tubercle or nodule containing countless bacteria.

Bacteria are specific for various legumes. Peas and vetches share the same *Rhizobium leguminosarum*. Beans, however, require *R. phaseoli*, clovers *R. trifollii*, soybeans *R. japonicum*, and alfalfa/sweet clover *R. meliloti*. All rhizobia require fertile, well-drained, well-aerated, and nearly neutral soil. Most of them like lime. Inoculation of damp, poorly aerated acid soils is futile because in those soils denitrifying bacteria reverse the process of inoculation.*

Nitrogen exists in its non-living form in the atmosphere and in its most-living form in animal organisms. Legumes form the bridge between the two, ferrying nitrogen from its dead chemical condition above to a more living one below. For biodynamic practitioners the living form of nitrogen exists on the other side of this River of Forgetfulness, so to speak, almost like a memory of another world; or at least one that chemical agriculture has forgotten. The legumes play Charon—the ancient Greek ferryman between the living and the dead—to a process of remembrance.† The humble garden pea offers a mirror, if not for the ferryman himself, at least for the shape the living world acquires when it forms a pathway for nitrogen.

In a sense, getting to know biodynamics is the same as getting to know the pathways of nitrogen; how nitrogen is really bigger than its chemical form; how it never thrives in a living system in its inorganic form; how in its dead form it will invariably "explode," wrecking the water supply, wrecking soil life, and wrecking animal bodies. Nitrogen fertilizers not only pollute the water supply, but the fruit of excess nitrogen (over-production of grain) sometimes literally explodes in grain silos. This is not only a tragic accident, but also a picture of an over-nitrated agricultural system. The nitrogen of living systems may produce less grain, but it also will cause fewer long-term eco-tragedies.

In this way the reader may begin to sense the urgency with which Rudolf Steiner wanted farmers to understand nitrogen as a "being" belonging to and never separate from the living systems of the earth. In his *Agriculture Course*, he described nitrogen as being closely bound to the downward stream of atmosphere/legume/soil—a truly living organ. The earth needs this being in its totality,

---

* The biodynamic preparations, especially horn manure (500), and the compost preparations have been developed to activate a network of soil life closely related to legume rhizobia. The network is exceedingly complicated. To merely scratch the surface, we might add: bacteria called Nitrosomonas (and others) convert free ammonia in the soil to nitrates, whether the ammonia has been injected by farmers or appears as a product of decomposition (in much smaller amounts). Since nitrites are toxic to plants and animals, it is fortunate that other bacteria (Nitrobacter, etc.) can convert the toxic nitrites to usable nitrates. Sulfur-oxidizing bacteria make sulfur available as sulfates for the synthesis of protein. Acid-producing bacteria make rock or bone phosphorus available to plants. Other bacteria synthesize plant growth hormones (indole-acetic acid). Legume roots in turn give off malic acid, pentoses, and phosphatids, substances useful to soil life. Even under anaerobic conditions Clostridium bacteria make some nitrogen available.

† In classical mythology the river Styx ("forgetfulness" in Greek) formed the boundary between the living and the dead. Charon was the ferryman who rowed departed souls across.

like an essential memory of its own formative childhood; perhaps as a continuation of those forces of its childhood that have not died, and which increasingly will require the knowledge and cooperation of human beings to sustain.

Culture

In biodynamic culture, peas follow horn manure (preparation 500) as surely as spring follows winter. Captured by the soil metabolism as peas are, they stir the earth's vitality just after and in concert with horn manure. Legume activity and horn manure are like separate incarnations of a similar process. As such, ground sprayed with horn manure and planted with peas provides an important first cover crop of the season.

Early crops are sown when frost is still in the ground. Sandy loam is most easily worked after a thaw. It drains well; important, because peas are injured by poor soil drainage. Clay loams bear later, but produce more peas. Very heavy soil types that drain poorly, are low in humus, and have a pH lower than 6 or higher than 6.8, produce poor crops. Largest crops are produced in soils with high humus, pH 6.5, with ample supplies of potassium and phosphate and small amounts of nitrogen. Composted garden soils need no additional fertilizer. If organic fertilizer is added, do not apply in seed drills; it may cause seeds to rot.

For home gardens, peas may be soaked, drained, and pre-germinated at 65°F in a pail of water with a few handfuls of compost and a pinch of horn manure per pail of seed. When the radical (rootlet) begins to emerge in about four days, the seeds can be dusted with *Rhizobium leguminosarum* and planted in rows or broadcast in beds. Pre-germinated peas can be sown two weeks later than un-soaked peas. They emerge very quickly. Since peas germinate slowly at 50°F soil temperature and much better at 60°F, this method produces more even rows more quickly. If you happen to forget your pail of peas until they ferment, sow them anyway. I've done it a few times, and they always grow. Indications for sowing snap peas and snow peas are the same as for English peas.

Un-soaked peas should be sown 10-15 seeds to the foot, or 6 seeds to the foot if you pre-germinate. Sow at soil temperature of at least 55°F. Cover with ½ to 1 inch of soil, or fill the furrow with compost. Be sure no peas are visible on the soil surface. These become a flag for birds. When sowing seed mechanically, experiment on a tarp to determine seed rate. Seedbed should be prepared finely and only when soil is friable. I know that some folks sow peas as thickly as rain, but a well-prepared seedbed germinates much better.

In beds, peas can be broadcast, sown in 2 rows, 1 foot apart, or in 3 rows, 6 inches apart. In the field, peas can be sown in double rows, 5 inches apart, with 2 feet between double rows. In either case, pea plants from 16 to 28 inches tall will hold each other up. Broadcast beds should be mulched, since weeding is too difficult. Rows of peas should be cultivated lightly after emergence to catch germinating weeds. I like to skim them quickly with a stirrup or wheel hoe once a week.

Spray peas with horn silica (501) when leaves and tendrils appear and again at flowering. In areas subject to mold and mildew, try the leafless types (Novella II and Curly) and spray equisetum once a week. Identify problems, and plant resistant varieties. "Pea failure" is caused by a too-short rotation. If wilt or root rot prevail, plant only once in five years in each bed or portion of the field. Pea aphids have never been a problem for me. Usually aphids appear on soils deficient in nutrients and humus, or on plants that have been held back by cool soil temperatures.

The problem with late summer plantings is not soil temperature but soil moisture. Keep water on the seedbed and seedlings, and peas will yield well in October. For Progress types, count back 70 days from first expected fall frost.

Harvesting peas is an art I've never learned really well. I test my visual guesses by feel and tasting. Once I get the knack, I pick quickly only by eye. Aging English peas get lighter green and wrinkled. Snap peas are good until peas have filled the pod, but sweetest when the peas themselves have just begun to fill the pod. Snow peas must be harvested at the flat stage, but size will depend upon variety. Tasting as you pick will inform your eye.

Dry seed saved for soup or sowing should be dry heated for five hours at 120°F if holes from pea weevils are visible in the peas. If temperature is held precisely, seed viability will not be affected.

At any time peas can be used as a cover crop, but attention should be paid to pea failure due to root rot (fusarium or other organisms). If peas tend to go brown from the ground up, practice five-year rotation.

Varieties

I find it harder to distinguish pea varieties than, say, carrots. For years my sole criterion was to harvest a large crop of peas, till the ground, and put in the fall carrot sowing. Burpeana Early was the only pea that made this possible where I lived at the time (Southeast Pennsylvania). It tasted good and froze well, but peas followed by carrots won't work in shorter New England summers. Now I try a new variety every year, followed by bush beans, salad greens, or beets. One catalog made a distinction between bright green peas, such as Green Arrow, for use in canning, and dark green peas, such as Frosty, for freezing. Green Arrow, a time-tested English heirloom, freezes fine. The biggest problem is taking the time and trouble to pick the peas at just the right stage of development—not too young, but especially not too old. For each variety, a random checking will tell you when to start picking. In the future, breeders may come up with a super-sweet pea. But as far as I know, there isn't even a hybrid pea available. Who cares? Most people cannot even get all the old fashioned ones picked. Progress #9, around for decades, is still a "processor standard."

The short-vined varieties (most of which are offshoots of venerable Laxton's Progress) require no fence, mature early, are easy to clean after harvest, and allow for succession crops. Maturity averages 58 days. Tall varieties are trouble to fence and clear away, but produce far more peas in a smaller space over a longer period of time and with far less strain on the back. Tall types mature late, beginning at 70 days, but their quality is exceptionally good, certainly a consideration for home gardeners.

Most of the short-vined types range from 16 to 24 inches tall. Laxton's Progress matures in 55 days on 16- to 18-inch vines and is good quality, similar to Burpeana Early and Progress #9. Little Marvel, another progress pea, is sweeter than its forebear, 18 to 20 inches tall, 60 days to maturity, and is popular with early markets. Knight is an early large-podded progress type, a strong grower with considerable disease resistance (common wilt, pea enation virus, bean yellow mosaic virus, and powdery mildew). In areas where rotation has not been practiced, disease resistance is an essential.

Next in size and time of harvest are the Lincoln/Green Arrow types. They are easier to deal with when staked, but hold themselves up fairly well in a wide row. Some gardeners use a brush fence with them, but I find the clean-up a tangle. Lincoln (30 inches, 67 days), the standard for generations, is a main crop pea, and still as good as its younger competitors. It bears late, even into July, when other peas are scarce. Green Arrow (28 inches, 68 days) is a true old English pea that offers exceptionally heavy production of very long pods (more than 4 inches). Resistant to downy mildew, wilt, and leaf curl virus. Green Arrow sets peas near the top of the plant for easier harvest. Frosty (30 inches, 64 days) also sets near the top, is wilt resistant and especially recommended for freezing.

Tall types are worth the trouble in small gardens, city gardens, against walls, or where late production is useful. Chicken wire or trellis works well and looks great covered with pea vines. Tall Telephone (40 inches, 70 days) produces long pods with a lot of peas. Alderman (48 to 60 inches, 72 days) is taller still, with enormous pods and heavy set.

Later still is Wando (30 inches, 68 days), the only hot-weather pea I know of. In Pennsylvania I wasn't impressed with its heat resistance, but gardeners in the North claim good crops in midsummer. Useful for gardens with a very late start or for late summer sowing for fall harvest.

Although new varieties appear every year, peas seem more resistant to change than other vegetables. There are no hybrids, but heirloom peas are always in circulation; new types such as the patented "leafless pea" never quite take off. Replacing many leaves with tendrils improves pod visibility, ease of harvest, air circulation (where pod mold is a problem), and yield (3 times the average). Gourmet cooks also like using the tendrils for garnishes, but at present only one catalog offers a leafless pea. For growers the biggest benefits of breeding are disease resistance, more compact growth, upright branching (to hold pods high up), and increased yield.

I've always loved Asian flat-podded peas, but the quality of the ones I've grown (Mammoth Melting Sugar, Oregon Sugar Pod, Little Sweetie, and Dwarf Grey Sugar) didn't measure up to the ones I found in Chinese restaurants or Asian markets. Part of the difference must be soil preparation and climate, but I appreciate improved strains: Oregon Giant (30 inches, 60 days) has higher yields of larger 4½-inch very sweet pods and is tolerant to pea enation, mosaic virus, powdery mildew, and common wilt. Snow Sweet (24 inches, 60 days), with unusually tender sweet 3½ to 4-inch pods, tolerant to fusarium and powdery mildew, is probably the closest (so far) to an ideal stir-fry snow pea.

Snap Peas (full-size peas with edible pods) are still in the process of development. Found by chance in a field of peas, the first variety, called Sugar Snap (5 to 6 feet, 72 days) was good eating, but seemed to want to grow beyond itself. Its nodes were stretched out like a plant struggling to reach the light. Even with good fencing there weren't enough nodes and tendrils to hold fast against the wind or weight of the crop. Like the older varieties of string beans, the strings of snap peas must be removed. Even so, they were a pleasure to eat raw with a dip or lightly stir-fried.

Sugar Ann (24 inches, 52 days) a compact version of Sugar Snap, shortened the nodes and is resistant to common wilt; it has held its own for several decades. Very sweet and crisp. Sugar Sprint (24 inches, 58 days) is the first almost stringless snap pea, with excellent quality, fresh or stir-fried. High yielding and an improvement over earlier stringless snap peas, which were not as flavorful as the original strains.

Last we must mention the mother of all peas, the smooth-seeded type used for soup. They are probably similar to the original Bronze Age peas. Not sweet like the English green pea, heirloom varieties include Alaska (green split pea), Century (yellow split pea), and Holland Capucijner (gravy-colored split pea). The latter produce attractive violet-red and pink flowers. Dried peas are sown in early spring and harvested in July or August, depending on latitude. Support is not necessary. Some gardeners also let English peas dry on the vine, for saving seed and making soup in the winter. They are not as soupy, however, as smooth-seeded peas.

SEED: Seeds per pound; 1,500 to 2,700; packet (200-375 seeds) sows 13 to 25 feet. A pound sows 100 to 150 feet. Recommendations per foot or per acre vary from 10 to 25 seeds to the foot, a range of 100 to 270 pounds of seed to the acre. Check with local growers and extension agents. Depends also on size of plants, density of rows, and soil.

GERMINATION: 80% depending on soil type and temperature; 5 to 8 days at 50 to 60°F.

VIABILITY: 3 years.

DAYS TO HARVEST: 60 to 75 days.

MOON CALENDAR: Sow in fruit, cultivate in leaf or fruit. For cover crops alternate leaf and root.

ROTATION: 3 years; 5 years if pea failure has been a problem.

BIODYNAMIC SPRAYS: Horn manure (500) before sowing. Compost tea with 500 to soak and pre-germinate seed; silica (501) when tendrils appear and when flower buds appear. For seed saving, spray silica on ripening pods when the moon is in Leo.

COMPANION PLANTS: Early dwarf types before carrots, with early corn, with potatoes, among fall cole crops, on tomato fences prior to tomatoes. Peas are said to be inhibited by the onion family.

PEPPERS

In an English botanical garden I once came upon a collection of unusual *crassulas*. The *bryophyllum* or piggyback plant is one common *crassula*, sometimes grown as a houseplant. (Other common *crassulas* include sedum, *sempervivum,* and kalanchoe.) Johann von Goethe was quite impressed by *bryophyllum*. Its succulent leaves produce tiny plantlets directly from the leaf-margins. Tiny roots form in the air even before the plantlet is released and falls to the earth. It seemed significant to Goethe that genesis took place from the leaf region of the plant, and fell down. It seemed to demonstrate his theory that the leaf contains all the primary formative forces underlying plant development.

The unusual *crassulas* do not give such a simple impression as *bryophyllum*! Only readers who have looked closely at the internal organs of animals will have some idea of the strange appearance of these plants. Some were grey, some flesh-colored, others a sickly pale purple. The leaf forms were bulbous, fleshy and irregular, unrecognizable as leaves; more like kidneys, intestines, and parts of diseased organs. The fluid, elegant form that we expect from plants was not present at all. Something from the inside, perhaps akin to animal organs, was expressed on the outside. I should also add that the flowers were quite anemic: small, pale, milky stars.

The pepper plant (*Capsicum annuum*) has very sleek regular leaves, smooth to the touch, all very similar, showing little obvious metamorphosis. The plants show a normal branching — nothing strange or organ-like. The fruit and seeds are more interesting. The fruit cavity is like a dry tomato, a tomato that lacks juiciness. Inside, pepper seeds are suspended like shelf mushrooms. Normally seeds have a slightly embryonic form, but pepper seeds, which germinate inside the developing fruit, look like tiny animal embryos. You don't see these forms in every pepper, but once you do, you notice that this form persists in the outer form of the fruit as well.

What Goethe and later botanists have pointed out is that irregular or abnormal plant development displays archetypal features concealed within the integrated whole. My impression is that something akin to animal development suddenly stands out; something connected within the fruiting process. It happens in the pepper without the animal being visible. It also occurs in plants inhabited by reproducing insects in the form of fruit-like galls. The insect is able to initiate the fruiting process in the leaf or stem because the insect secretes fruit-inducing hormones. In the case of the galls, the insect larva becomes the seed at the center of the animal-contrived fruit.

Most gardeners have noticed how disagreeable the taste and smell of an immature green pepper can be. Nothing else in the garden rivals it for acridity. Its scent is similar to the lower portions of the plant, as if the normal filtering process of metamorphosis were insufficient. The scent is similar to rank weeds in wet places. Gardeners do all they can to carry the process further to create mature green fruits (which still contain some acrid flavor) or richly colored sweet ones. But even when the pepper becomes colored, sweet, and superbly flavored, it is still hard to consider it a fruit. Rather, it reminds me of a fruit gall, as if the herbaceous part of the plant were inhabited by an invisible insect. It is a surprise akin to discovering that the innocent fern, so completely chastely leaf-like, which in fact originated before fruit existed, reproduces using motile sperm.

Immature peppers still contain small amounts of the toxic alkaloids found in leaf and stem, which is probably what makes them so disagreeable. "Fruiting" hasn't filtered them out yet. Light and heat do. Mature green peppers have the highest vitamin C content. As the fruit turns red, C goes down a touch, but vitamin A gets very high and alkaloid content dwindles.

Culture

Peppers are less tolerant of late spring chill than tomatoes, prefer a lighter soil, and grow much more slowly than tomatoes in the seedling stage. Sow seeds 8 weeks prior to transplanting peppers into outside soil temperature of 70°F. Count back from the date you can confidently direct-seed bush beans. In the South, some gardeners count back from the average date the dogwood blossoms fall. It is a waste of effort to jump the season with peppers. In cold spells the pepper blossoms drop; plants become stunted and produce late, or never. Plants chilled in the field (below 50°F in June) throw all their energy into leaf production. The few late fruits that develop may appear only during the first September frost.

Poorly drained and heavy soils also fruit poorly and invite pepper diseases. Heavy soils in garden beds can be double-dug to improve drainage. Crushed stone can even be added to the bottom trench. Also consider raised beds. Peppers do best in a muskmelon-type soil, a loam high in silica that warms up quickly in spring. They like fair amounts of phosphorus and calcium, but prefer a pH below 7.

It is worth the time to sow pepper seeds in flats or cells, seed by seed, using tweezers or a moistened toothpick. Peppers appreciate the breathing space, both for air circulation and root development. Also, new hybrid pepper seed is expensive. Be sure to use a seedflat mix that drains well, half finished-biodynamic compost and half sandy-loam. Spray the mix with horn manure (500). Maintain soil temperature at 80°F during germination. Professional growers use a greenhouse heating mat with a thermostat. Germination takes several weeks, often twice as long as tomato.

When true leaves appear, transplant to large cells, 2- to 4-inch peat pots or standard flats. In flats be sure the grid is generous, with at least 3 inches between plants. Large peat pots produce the stockiest earliest producing plants, with the least transplant shock. Seedlings that struggle for root space and light never fully recover.

Provide full sunlight, including backlight if possible. Window-grown seedlings often become leggy and unproductive. Avoid the north side of attached greenhouses. Like eggplant, peppers depend upon high light levels and constant warmth. Day temperatures should reach 70 to 75°F and fall cooler than 60°F at night only during a narrow window of time. According to Johnny's Selected Seed Catalog, growers can lower night temperature to 55°F, but not below 53°F, for 4 weeks after pepper transplants have 3 true leaves; this can increase fruit set. Thereafter raise night temperatures to 65 to 70°F.

Never over-water seedlings. Better to let potting soil dry slightly before watering, but never to the point of wilting. Nettle, equisetum, and seaweed sprays are good tonics for peppers at this stage.

Harden seedlings a week before setting plants in the garden by reducing moisture, but do not chill. Because the time for setting out varies from year to year, it is difficult to do so at the optimum stage, which is just before flower buds have opened. If the season is slow to warm, keep seedlings under glass for another week.

Gardeners in the North sometimes pre-warm an area with black plastic several weeks before setting out. Flowering peppers exposed to chill (below 50°F) produce poorly; early crops can be somewhat protected with floating row covers or slatted plastic. In cold areas, slatted plastic over hoops and black plastic mulch is sometimes the only way to generate enough heat for peppers. Growers in central states have found that peppers produce best with no mulch of any kind. In southern and dry western states, organic mulch should not be applied until soil has become thoroughly warm. Cooling pepper roots during early growth delays fruiting. Silver plastic mulch has produced the highest number of marketable peppers and reduces insect-borne virus. (Penn State Extension).

To produce abundant sweet fruits, peppers require moderate amounts of nitrogen and potassium, with generous amounts of phosphorus and calcium, which also help to prevent blossom end rot. Biodynamic compost (made from manure, leaves, and weeds in equal amounts) is usually sufficient for home gardeners, but may not be enough for market growers. Market gardeners should test their soil and add phosphorus to the compost if necessary, and possibly nitrogen. Phosphorus sources include rock phosphate (38%), bone meal (22%), fish meal (6%), cottonseed meal (3%), chicken manure (2.8%), wood ashes (1.8%), and grape pomace (1.5%). But remember that too much phosphorus enlarges fruit while reducing nutrient value. High nitrogen (fishmeal and chicken manure) may produce mostly leaves. Apply side-dressings and liquid feedings only after plants blossom in the field.

Unlike tomatoes, peppers are usually planted at the same depth they grew in flats, cells, or pots. Florida Extensions had better results burying stems up to the first true leaf. Penn State did not. Deeper may be better in high drainage soil. Never cultivate deeply since shallow root systems will be damaged. Skim, using a stirrup or scuffle hoe. Spray horn silica (501) when plants are established in the field, when blossoms open, fruits begin to develop, and when the first fruit reddens.

Since peppers are set out in the field late, they make a good succession following spinach. When the soil is thoroughly warm, harvest whole spinach plants every 12 to 18 inches, and then plant the peppers. Spacing depends on variety. The older O.P. cultivar Staddon's Select requires 18 to 20 inches between plants; hybrids can be packed 12 inches in the row. Rows can be 20 to 36 inches apart. Northern growers have found that packing plants 12 inches in the row, so that the roots touch sooner, stimulates lateral rooting and earlier production.

Cutworms can be foiled with paper collars or a thick layer of wood ashes sifted around the base of the plants. Aphids can be controlled with insecticidal soap; this is important since aphids are vectors of the many viruses that affect open-pollinated and some hybrid strains. Pepper diseases are aggravated by heavy soil, cool wet conditions, and poor drainage. If open-pollinated varieties don't work, choose hybrids resistant to tobacco mosaic, pepper mottle, cucumber mosaic, and potato virus Y. Keep the greenhouse aphid-free and avoid planting peppers near aphid-attracting plants in the greenhouse, such as lettuce. Rotate nightshades every four or five years if viruses persist.

When the first peppers reach full size, harvest promptly before they redden. If early fruit is prevented from getting red (or orange, and so forth), total yields will increase up to 25%. Harvesting takes some practice, since careless picking often breaks off entire branches. Use pruning shears to snip stems. Fresh peppers don't keep long, but ripe peppers dry beautifully and can also be pickled, frozen, and made into salsa. Those warm rainbow colors look great against a background of winter snow.

Varieties

Peppers have been popular with South and Central Americans for thousands of years. Their surprising range of color looks as if an ancient Indian blanket were giving birth to pigments, revealing colors hidden in the deep fabric of the species. The colored antioxidants in sweet red pepper have already shown specific anti-carcinogenic properties. The new rainbow varieties may reveal a still greater spectrum on the verge of discovery. For chefs these colors have become a new art form, igniting salads and stir-fries with crimson, brick, tangerine, orange, gold, yellow, lavender and lilac, and a dark purple. The strangest of all are white-skinned varieties, as pale as soap and probably not great nutritionally. Others, however, go through stunning changes, like fledgling birds that molt and emerge as newly colored adults.

Peppers range from lilac (Lilac Belle, 81 days) to dark purple (Purple Beauty, 72 days), passing from lavender to lilac to deep red with no green phase. Islander (81 days) changes from lavender through a parrot display of violet, then yellow-orange streaked, and finally turning dark red. Orange bells pass from green to a very sweet juicy orange. Bright yellow varieties also become very fruity and sweet, while the unusual strange chocolate brown (Sweet chocolate, 78 days) conceals brick red flesh under brown skin.

The specific varieties of these multi-colored bells change from year to year with improved disease resistance and adaptability. These may include resistance to tobacco mosaic virus, bacterial leaf spot, phytophthora root rot, cucumber mosaic virus, blossom drop, pepper mottle virus, and potato virus. Disease worsens with less than a 3-year nightshade rotation (eggplant, tomato, potato, and so forth.). Harris Seeds has the clearest chart for exact disease resistance. Stokes and Johnny's also note disease resistance with each variety.

Reliable open-pollinated varieties include King of the North (80 days), a sturdy cold-tolerant plant with prolific fruit set; Yankee Bell (80 days) also cold-tolerant, sets fewer fruit but a larger number of mature marketable fruit. The most reliable hybrids for me have been Ace (70 days) and Lady Belle (71 days), both producing in cooler adverse conditions when others fail.

Another dependable pepper includes Italian ramshorn or bullshorn (Corno di Toro), which has higher sugar content than bells at maturity. Sweetness, disease resistance, and wide adaptation are reasons why Jimmy Nardello's Italian frying pepper (78 days) has been grown for more than one hundred years. Nardello's Italian caramelizes beautifully when roasted. Another Italian, Carmen Hybrid (72 days), is also sweet, intensely flavored for roasting, and widely adapted. There are many other ramshorns, all of them delicious and easy to grow, especially in warm, moderate climates.

Among the delicious group of peppers called pimentos, Lipstick (73 days), which many consider the tastiest pepper of all, stands out for high yields of 4-inch-long, thick-walled bright red fruits. Easy to grow, even in cool climates and cool years. Cheese pimentos are similar, but larger and often used for stuffing. Round of Hungary (75 days) is deeply ribbed, deliciously sweet, and reddens early. Topepo Rosso hybrid (90 days) is in a similar class, shaped a bit like a tomato with thick sweet peppery flesh. Plants are vigorous and high yielding.

Sweet Banana peppers (72 days) produce huge numbers of 5-inch yellow horns (8 inches in hybrids), which turn sweeter as they redden. Open-pollinated sweet Bananas are incredibly productive and ripen early in any area where peppers can grow. Some new hybrids (Sweet Spot X3R, 71 days) produce up to 35 extremely sweet 3-inch fruits per plant, even in rainy humid climates, with added disease-resistance. Hungarian Hot Wax is identical in every way to Sweet Banana except for its heat, which varies from mild chili to hot cherry in intensity. Great for salsa, pickles, and frying.

The heat of hot peppers is measured on the so-called Scoville scale. The complete scale, which ranges from 400 to 450,000 Scovilles units, can be found online or in the Harris Seed Catalog. There is enormous variation even in similarly named types. Mildly hot pimentos rate 500; an average chili rates 1500; Hungarian Wax, cayenne, cherry, and jalapeno all rate from around 3,000 to 5,000. Serrano del Sol is hotter still, but Asian peppers such as Thai Hot are 26 times hotter than chilies, at 80,000 Scoville units, while habaneros burn the rafters at 250,000. The hottest of all is Caribbean Red, used in Jamaican jerk sauce, 450,000 units. But don't knock the heat: apparently antioxidant lycopenes rise along with Scoville units.

For lovers of some heat, well-balanced with sweet flavor, try Mariachi Hybrid (66 days), a mildly hot pimento (600 Scovilles units) for use fresh, roasted, stuffed, or pickled, with resistance to tobacco mosaic. Krimzon Lee (82 days) is a large sweet moderately spicy paprika for grilling, roasting, and salsa. Tiburon hybrid (85 days), an ancho pepper, combines raisin-like sweetness, mild spiciness, and resistance to bacterial spot and tobacco mosaic virus. Ancho-poblano type peppers, which combine mild spiciness and raisin like sweetness, are usually stuffed green with cheese, meat, or raisins and nuts, and fried into *chile rellenos*. Used green, this type of pepper is called *poblano*; when red or dried it becomes *ancho*. Anchos are combined with unsweetened chocolate in mole sauce. Hybrid anchos such as Tiburon (85 days) add resistance to bacterial spot and tobacco mosaic virus. Holy Mole (85 days) a pasilla pepper, with a nutty, tangy bite, is also used in mole sauce. Finally, for those who crave the smoky, savory flavor of habanero with only mild heat (100 Scoville units), try Zavory (90 days).

Cayenne peppers, the ones tied and hung in decorative *ristras* from the rafters of Mexican homes, have a long history in cuisine and natural medicine; they have been used as an antiseptic, to improve circulation, and as a general tonic for young and old. Long Slim (75 days) and its descendants are the standard for dry *ristras*. Others with thicker walls dry too slowly. Early cayenne hybrids ripen earlier in short season areas; they have a stronger stem structure to hold fruit off the ground.

Jalapeños are generally hotter than cayenne. Early Jalapeño (60 days) ripens quickly in cooler regions. Hybrids such as El Jefe are more widely adapted, with good disease resistance to bacterial leaf spot (races 1, 2, and 3) and potato virus *y*. Although serrano peppers are hotter still, their flavor is also characterized by how their distinctive tanginess bites the tongue. Serrano requires a long season. Even in Mexico, jalapeño far out-produces serrano.

Heat in peppers varies not only with type, but also increases with sun and length of season. But no matter how you grow or measure their heat, habaneros are unbelievably hot. Many are considered Asian, even by older taxonomists, but the name (*Capsicum chinensis*) is an error. Traders brought habaneros to India and China from Central America in the seventeenth century. Their use has become so wedded to Indian, Southeast Asian, and Sichuan Chinese cuisines that it's hard to imagine Asian cooking before the habanero arrived. Previously, Asian dishes were flavored quite differently with local spices.

Thai Hot (50 days, 80,000 Scoville units) decorates a beautiful ornamental plant. One very hot chili pepper, Numex Twilight (85 days) begins purple (not green) and ripens to yellow, orange, and finally red. Kung Pao (85 days, 10,000 units) is a good pepper for Sichuan stir-fries with excellent flavor and aroma. Kung Pao looks like cayenne and can be braided into *ristras*. But a word of caution in handling and preparing the super-hot peppers. Their sting is agonizing, if you accidentally rub your eyes or other sensitive parts of the body. Caribbean Red (95 days) is off the charts in this respect.

SEED: About 4,000 per ounce. A packet of 100 standard seeds produces about 55 plants.

A packet of 30 hybrid seeds produces about 22 plants. An ounce produces 2,250 or more plants. 5 ounces will produce an acre of transplants.

GERMINATION: 55% standard; 75% hybrid. 14 days at 70°F. 10 days at 80°F. Night temperatures above 60°F, except during cold treatment.

VIABILITY: 2 to 3 years. Days to harvest: 60 to 75.

MOON CALENDAR: All practices, including biodynamic sprays, in fruit sign. Sow before full moon with other practices during ascending moon.

ROTATION: 3 years for peppers and other members of tomato family; longer in virus-infested areas.

BIODYNAMIC SPRAYS: Horn manure (500) on bedding soil and on garden. Silica (501) on plants in flats after established, with equisetum (508) weekly if disease is a problem. Compost-clay 500 dip on roots of transplants. Silica a week before and after first blossoms with valerian (507) added during fruit formation and ripening, during morning hours.

COMPANION PLANTS: Interplant among spinach, carrots, beets, and onions.

POTATO

A plant's character is its destiny.
~ (Adapted from Ralph Waldo Emerson)

The potato (*Solanum tuberosum*) belongs to a closely related group of *solanaceous* plants that are found abundantly along the slopes of the Andes, often at fairly high elevations. Potato breeders still scavenge these wild strains, many not edible in themselves, for new and desirable traits. They need to, since potatoes are susceptible to more plant diseases than any other commercial vegetable.

The people who developed the potato had a social order that was an unusual mix of egalitarian social practices and rigid hierarchy. In the center stood the Sun King, who was priest and monarch, a kind of pharaoh. Yet unlike the pharaohs of Egypt or the sun kings of France, the Inca monarch belonged to a hive-like social order that was truly generous. For them, the monarch was the center of their universe, but not in the grotesque egotistical sense that caused so much suffering in Europe. In the Inca culture, for example, it was actually against the law to starve. In fact, indifference to hunger would have violated a widely practiced sense of social etiquette.

The potato was a staple for these people and played a primary role in their food program, although the varieties were so different from modern commercial types that dietary comparisons are impossible to make. According to Wendell Berry, who reconnoitered the original areas of potato culture some years ago, the Andean strains are smaller, drier, and more concentrated in flavor than our best baking types. *Ensminger's Nutritional Encyclopedia* also points out that the diet of South American people who remained healthy on a "potato diet" included amaranth greens (pigweed) and *chenopodium* greens (lamb's quarters). They also included the high-protein amaranth grain (achita) and the chenopod grain (quinoa), both of which equal or exceed the European grains in food value. Even today the Andean Indians are among the hardiest and long-lived of peoples.

The next people to carry the potato forward on its historical journey were men of opposite constitution from the Incas. I don't need to describe to what length the conquistadors carried human egotism. Leave it to say that the conquistadors drove humanity at sword point into a new era, whether anyone wished to go or not. The potato sailed along as a kind of stowaway.

The conquistadors took the potato back to Europe at the very moment when the whole continent was experiencing a vast upheaval in consciousness. Yet for nearly one hundred years the potato slept like a plump sleeping beauty, biding its time, grown mostly as an ornamental novelty. The peasants of Europe realized at once that the potato was a close relative of the deadly nightshade, and decided potatoes must be poisonous as well. Those who did venture to cook them, did so in ways that seem bizarre to modern taste, such as steeping potatoes in wine or making them into a sweet preserve.

As a staple, the potato was exceedingly slow to gain popularity with working people. At first potatoes were far more popular with people who believed themselves to be rationalist thinkers. In the seventeenth century, people began for the first time to consider food in terms of bulk. From the point of view of bulk, the potato appeared to be nothing less than a nutritional savior. Imagine a plant that could easily out-produce wheat, rye, and barley by 20 times! Imagine huge crops that would grow vigorously in cold, damp conditions where wheat would invariably fail. Imagine a plant that was easy to propagate, easy to store, and (seemingly) so unfussy that it would grow even in peat. As soon as food shortages appeared in parts of Europe, counselors hurried to advise their monarchs about the benefits of potato culture. If the people would not be convinced, they said, his majesty should appear on the balcony savoring a platter of boiled potatoes. Potatoes should feed the people by decree.

And so they did. During the Age of Enlightenment, potato consumption grew very rapidly. Hindsight tells us it grew far too rapidly, displacing traditional crops such as barley, especially in Ireland. Around the mid-sixteenth century, potatoes appear to have gained a toehold in Ireland, where the moist, cool climate and sour soils had always been hit and miss for grains. By 1700, the potato had become both bread and meat for poor cottagers.

Yet, even on a small scale, monoculture brings misery in its train. And it was no exception for the potato. Beginning in 1817, late blight increased year by year. Potato fields were wasted; infected haulms (tops of the plant) passed the fungi from field to field. The use of other grains had fallen into neglect. By 1847, three-quarters of a million Irish people had starved, and well over a million others fled the country to America. The potato was hard at work. Some even credit the potato for Irish independence, since those who remained behind were politicized in the highest degree. The IRA probably remembered that it was the Royal Society of London that encouraged the planting of potatoes in Ireland in 1663 "as a safeguard against famine."

It seems ironic that the potato should have been promoted by rationalist thinkers, since excessive consumption produces the opposite qualities from clear thinking. But who knows? Perhaps they had just that in mind. Perhaps they thought a sleepy, earthbound populace would be easier to rule. Those rationalist philosophers might have done well to read the *Lippincot Farm Manual* (1913), which gives the following advice about feeding potatoes to poultry: "Care should be used to regulate the amount, as their extended use is apt to make poultry lose their appetite, become dopey and out of condition." In other words, the chickens become more obedient but produce fewer eggs.

Nutritionally, potatoes fill the intestine without really invigorating it. Both the internal structure of the tuber and its mode of growth show a plant that is moving away from the effects of sunlight. This is evident even from its nutritional profile. The potato has about four times less protein, carbohydrates, vitamins, and minerals than the grains. The starch cells are enlarged, anonymous, and amoebic in structure. They do not radiate, but expand aimlessly. The radiations of a carrot, on the other hand, are orderly and show an inverse reflection of the leaf rosette above the root. This leaf activity cannot be reflected in the potato tuber because the tuber is itself a leaf-bearing stem; the seed eyes are nodal points for leaves. I once watched in amazement as a novice garden apprentice completely buried the leaves of onion transplants upside down, with the root sticking in the air, but who in the world could have imagined this as the basic gesture of a plant species?

I wonder how the Yaqui Indian seer Don Juan would characterize the potato? Don Juan apprenticed himself to another nightshade, that distinctly poisonous lady of the night, *Datura stramonium*. A noxious weed in some areas, the unattractive leaves of *Datura* unfold mercurial, lovely trumpets—not just lovely, but bewitching in their beauty. The bud is folded into a five-rayed spiral, sending forth an intoxicating fragrance that would seduce even the most wary. Once she draws you in, however, the toxins in *Datura* drive a spike into the pit of the stomach, likened by some to the pains a Templar must have felt as he was tortured by the Inquisitor. Aching rheumatic pains wrack the body. The head is buried under an immovable weight, nearly bursting. The eyes feel contracted, full; the breathing oppressed. The soul is overwhelmed by fear; frightful visions arise. If you cannot locate *Datura,* you can get a similar high from a salad of green potato skins, but such a journey is not recommended. There is enough solanine in a few fully green potatoes to kill a horse.

In order for the potato to be edible we have to suppress the stem's leaf activity entirely. We hill the stems; an odd practice if you think about it—as odd as an apprentice burying onion leaves. I have wondered if the potato's tendency toward a legion of leaf diseases has its origin here. Perhaps the development of leaf substance below the ground displaces vital forces normally active in the light and air. Perhaps it is because the stem is growing out of its element that the potato cannot maintain internal form, neither budlike (as in bulbs), conical and radiating (as in carrots), nor spheroid (as in beets). Potato leaves are also visually unusual. The green is deep, but not vital, and the texture is puckered like curly top virus; leaf metamorphosis is unpronounced.

Nutritionally the potato is also incomplete—part root and part grain, but in both cases only part. It corresponds roughly to the starch portion of the wheat. Bakers, incidentally, have exploited this partiality by using the potato starch and its enzymes as a basis for yeast culture. I bake potato rye bread, which is absolutely delicious when made in the Eastern European style. The rye counterbalances the potato; the potato gives texture and flavor to rye. Rye also balances the potato in the field. Rye cover crops give the soil a cleansing following potatoes, helping to reduce the persistence of potato diseases in the rotation.

From what I've written, readers might imagine that I don't like potatoes. Not true. I like them very much, I but don't eat them as often as I once did and no longer regard them as a staple. As a staple, they fill the space of the intestine to the exclusion of plants more vitally needed by the human constitution. At the present I regard the potato as a less frequent and much enjoyed addition to my diet.

Culture

Potatoes are subject to more innovative culture than any other garden plant. Many of these methods have given me much pleasure to use; and some go a long way toward offsetting problems with disease, insects, and fertility. Each method has a specific function and produces results for different conditions.

The traditional furrow and hilling method is the most common, but actually produces the least potatoes and the most insect problems. It is the standard practice for field culture. Potatoes are cut into pieces, each of which contains an "eye." A furrow is made about 3 to 4 inches deep and potato pieces are dropped every 10 inches and covered with soil. Thereafter, as the shoots rise above the ground, the soil is hilled up several times around the leaves, since the potatoes form off the new stems above the old eye potato.

A higher yielding variation is the trench method. Here a trench 8 inches deep is dug. The potato piece is planted at the bottom, and a mixture of soil and compost is used to fill the trench as the stems shoot up. Thereafter the stems are hilled with soil. This is more work, but yields twice as many potatoes, and of much higher quality.

The third method involves a shallow furrow like the first, but hills exclusively, with some form of organic mulch, up to a foot deep. I use maple leaves because they're available from fall cleanup. This method produces high yields and the fewest insect and disease problems.

A Scottish gardener described the lazy-bed method to me. She merely puts potato pieces on her peaty ground surface and covers with more peat. This method works well in American gardens, too. After the soil is tilled, lay potato pieces in rows or in a 12-inch by 12-inch grid over a bed and cover with 6 inches of leaves; when the shoots rise above the mulch, add another 6 inches. If you have the mulch, this method is the least work and produces high yields and few insect problems.

Still another method is to plant potatoes in the fall under a foot of mulch. Although not often practiced in New England, this method produces very early potatoes. Gardeners may have noticed that un-dug potatoes sprout the next spring in almost any climate, even without mulching. The downside may be rodent predation.

Disease and insect problems are fewest when the root systems are kept cool, moist, and protected. Sandy loam with good drainage is the best soil type, fairly high in organic matter with a pH of 5.5 to 6.5. Common scab cannot grow below pH 6, but thrives above 7. Vegetable composts low in manure are best. Fresh manure and horse manure especially are high in calcium, and they raise pH. Humic acids in mature compost seem to offset the problem and strengthen plants dramatically. Excessive nitrogen aggravates the unbalanced growth inherent in potatoes and attracts insects.

Biodynamic practitioners plant potato sets shortly after spraying biodynamic horn manure preparation (500). Many also prepare a slurry dip for sets composed of 5 gallons of water, a shovelful of compost, a half shovelful of local clay, and either a pinch of preparation 500 or a quart of the stirred preparation. Mix well and stir for an additional 15 minutes, as you would for other biodynamic sprays.

If it is small, the whole seed potato may be used for planting, but larger potatoes may be cut into plum-size pieces with at least one eye. Too many eyes produce a jungle of undersized potatoes. Allow cut pieces to callus for a day or two prior to planting. Sets are placed 10 to 18 inches apart in the furrow, with 2 to 3 feet between rows. 2 feet for heavy mulch; 3 feet allows for hilling. In mulched beds, 8 inches x 15 inches is possible. Sowing dates can vary from February in the milder states to early April in the central states, to late April in the North. Potato plants sown too early are occasionally wasted by frost. Tops will re-grow, but maturity will be delayed, perhaps stunted, if the shoots and leaves were very large.

Since I've started following one hilling of soil with a deep mulch of hardwood leaves, I don't side-dress or use foliar fertilizers. Some growers find liquid seaweed effective. Others spray a strong cold steeped tea made from nettles fermented with comfrey. And still others spray a dilution of blended fresh alfalfa leaves. The growth enzymes in alfalfa work best in high dilution: no more than a cupful of leaves per 10 gallons of water increases potato yields. Foliar sprays can be used frequently, since enzymes stimulate vitality above ground, which is very important to the potato. Biodynamic growers spray silica solution at least twice, sometimes in combination with equisetum tea.

Biodynamic practices, a four-year rotation, high organic matter, good drainage, and mulches minimize disease and insect problems. Again, I've found that a mulch of hardwood leaves eliminates insect problems. Flea beetles, leafhoppers, and Colorado potato beetles have not been a problem with leaf-mulched plants. Colorado potato beetles used to be legion on my unmulched plants. If you are using pesticides, try to change your cultural practice. Purchase certified disease-free sets. Maintain levels of phosphorus and potassium, best supplied by compost and earthworms. Follow potato crops with rye, and increase the nightshade rotation to five years. If vines still show signs of disease, burn the haulms after harvest. Rudolf Steiner also suggested rejuvenating seed by cutting out eyes and planting in flats. This reduces the area of disease carryover and allows the forces in biodynamic compost to predominate. A few years ago I gave a local biodynamic farmer a bushel of potatoes, which had been raised biodynamically here and in Kimberton, Pennsylvania, for ten years. Grown side by side with varieties from other sources, the biodynamic sets were the only ones free of late blight.

For areas where carryover disease is a major problem, tissue-cultured stock might help. Each mini-tuber produces about 3 pounds of potatoes. Tissue culture (which I've never tried) claims 20% increase in yield. Elimination of disease may require a full year of rye, followed by two years of non-vector crops (no nightshades, etc.). True potato seeds are rarely listed in seed catalogs, but are also completely disease free. They provide an alternative to avoid tuber-borne diseases or to get a jump on the season. Greenhouse culture is similar to tomato, but cooler (60°F), with an acid (peaty) potting soil and 6 weeks more work than tubers. I've noticed, however, that in the few places I see seed marketed, nothing is mentioned about cooking qualities or taste, so they probably are useful only where disease is endemic.

Some biodynamic growers rejuvenate their own stock by planting tiny eye pieces in 3-inch peat pots, ½ inch deep in a 50-50 compost peat mix about seven weeks prior to the date for transplanting tomatoes outside. Dip eyepieces in compost-clay 500 prior to sowing, and then dip the entire pot prior to setting in the field. Grow at 60°F in a sunny greenhouse or cold frame. Transplant deep, with only the shoot sticking out, in a garden soil free of nightshades for five years. Bailey's *Horticulture* notes that one grower, by dividing eyes successively, as one would in eye culture, got over 2,500 pounds of potatoes from one pound of seed potatoes!

The bright light method produces early high yielding crops. Expose seed potatoes to bright light at 65°F for three weeks prior to the date you sow tomatoes in flats. Skins will green like above-ground stems. When potatoes sprout, cut apart carefully and plant in peat pots. In general, exposure of seed potatoes to bright light at 60°F for two weeks prior to planting creates hardier, stockier plants. Light activates the latent enzymatic activity of the stem to promote strong, early growth. It works so well just because the potato is a closet stem.

In the Deep South in areas of great summer heat and high humidity, potato culture is often so difficult that the word "potato" means sweet potato. Sweet potatoes were born for the South; the Irish potato was not. Southern gardeners sometimes plant two crops of Irish potatoes, one in early spring and another in summer for a fall crop.

Early potatoes can be harvested with mid-season peas by loosening the soil a bit and pulling out a few tubers per plant. The rest can be left until July. Potatoes kept for more than a week should be left in a dark, warm (70°F) place for a week to harden the skin. However, early crops keep only four to six weeks at 65°F, so don't plant more than you can eat or sell. For storage crops, use late varieties and wait to dig until the root cellar is cold, even a month after the vines have died. Potatoes store poorly above 45°F; 38°F is ideal. Potatoes from diseased vines don't store well at all, since the plants need to go through a normal shutdown process to prepare for dormancy. Some home gardeners extend the keeping life of potatoes by rubbing off seed eyes in January and again in late winter. They remember, of course, to save enough un-rubbed, disease-free potatoes for seed.

Varieties

When the original potato varieties radiated out from the Andes in the seventeenth century, they lodged in foreign ports and became isolated, with little communication. In Germany in 1972 I was served unfamiliar yellow potatoes with a rich almost creamy flavor. At the Salvation Army in Reykjavik where somehow in my youthful wanderings I spent Christmas one year, I was fed fingerling potatoes that had a completely unfamiliar taste and texture. Gradually, small fingerlings emigrated from Scandinavia with their waxy, creamy texture and sweet taste, so different from American white potatoes that they might belong to another species entirely. Some almost do. Blue and purple-skinned types (*Solanum tuberosum* var. *phureja*) and knobby russet types (*S. tuberosum* var. *andigena*) still seem to have Peruvian dirt clinging to their skins. Sweet small pink and yellow potatoes from Sweden, France, and Russia with their full-bodied yellow flesh have now become the standard for gourmet cooks. It makes you wonder how much more remains to be discovered; what textures and qualities may still be hidden in remote Andean valleys.

A few decades ago most Americans wouldn't have even recognized fingerlings as potatoes; but in fact, fingerlings are much closer to the Andean original. French Fingerlings have pink skin and rich golden flesh streaked with red. Swedish Fingerlings are round finger-sized waxy yellow potatoes, the color and texture of butter, with excellent taste. Medium-sized at maturity, but often harvested early as gourmet baby potatoes; excellent keepers. Finnish fingerlings with their yellow waxy flesh and nutty taste are gourmet favorites; excellent for summer potato salad. Russian Banana is also a waxy yellow fingerling, resistant to scab and somewhat resistant to late blight; early harvests have exceptional quality.

European breeders have developed larger yellow-fleshed varieties of fine quality. Carola is the highest yielding of the yellow-fleshed varieties, oval, with very good flavor, medium dry, not waxy. Others such as German Butterball are best-flavored when small to medium sized. Keep abreast of new European types as they appear in catalogs. Yukon Gold was developed because Canadian growers of European descent wanted a yellow potato adapted to North America. In this case the Canadian breeder crossed an indigenous yellow Peruvian potato with several North American types. The result is considered by many to be the best eating potato of all. Fine textured, medium dry yellow flesh with superior taste; stores for long periods, but no scab resistance.

All Blue is a russet potato with Blue Peruvian ancestry. Deep blue skin, lavender blue flesh, with a tasty, unusual flavor and flaky flesh. Many Peruvian blue and purple potatoes seem to be too lumpy and irregular in shape to market in seed catalogs. These and other heirloom potatoes can be searched out from seed savers and small suppliers. Caribe is a well-shaped early purple-skinned potato with snow-white flesh; large oblong, flavorful; it keeps well for a summer potato and is useful as a "new potato." Scab resistant.

Red potatoes are commonly grown for early summer use. Red Norland is early, dry textured for baking and frying. Scab-tolerant, not a good keeper. Red Pontiac has thin rosy red skin, a traditional favorite for boiling in the skin, served with green peas. Matures mid-season, produces in heavy soils, and keeps well. Red Gold with orange-red skin and yellow flesh yields well for summer use, but does not keep. Resists scab, verticillium wilt, and late blight.

Russets have been the leading baking potatoes since Luther Burbank developed his special strain in 1874. Russets all have brown skin with dry flaky white flesh, and they require more space than other potatoes, from 14 to 18 inches between sets. All keep well. Mostly grown commercially in the West, but now largely absent from seed catalogs in favor of other heirlooms and newer varieties. Gold Rush is a very good quality russet with excellent disease resistance against scab verticillium and black spot bruising, with tolerance to hollow heart.

White Cobbler is also popular for baking in summer because of its dry texture and earliness; not a good keeper. Onaway is an early, good-flavored potato that keeps well; suitable for short season in northern areas, resistant to scab and late blight. Kennebec remains a reliable, high yielding, all-purpose late-keeper with good flavor and good disease resistance to mosaic, late blight, blackleg, and wart; but no scab resistance. Very thin-skinned for a keeper;

scrubs off easily without peeling. In warmer areas where nematodes are a problem, look for nematode-resistant plants, such as Daisy Gold, an all purpose deep yellow potato or Beltsville (also scab- and verticillum-resistant). Also remember that in potatoes a deep interior color indicates higher vitamins A and C. (The color green, however, indicates toxic alkaloids.)

- TUBERS: Consider greening seed potatoes by exposure to light for 3 weeks prior to planting. One day before planting, cut seed tubers into 1- to 1 ½-inch pieces with at least one eye (growing point) per tuber. Let pieces cure in a dry place for a day or more. Potato pieces (sets) are placed from 8 to 18 inches apart in the row, depending on variety. For most varieties order a set per foot of row. When purchased by the pound, expect about 10 sets per pound in large potatoes and 20 per pound for fingerlings.
- SEED: True potato seed has never really taken off, except for breeders. Seed per ounce 50,000. A packet produces 40 plants, an ounce 20,000 plants.
- GERMINATION: 75%; 12 days at 68°F, but erratic above 75°F. Grow at 55 to 60°F. Set out when nights are frost-free.
- DAYS TO HARVEST: 90 to 120 from date of transplanting.
- GERMINATION: Cool ground, early spring, after ground is 50°F.
- DAYS TO HARVEST: 70 to 120 days
- MOON CALENDAR: Sow and plant in root; moon apogee is also possible. Against blights, spray silica (501) and equisetum (508) in leaf in ascending moon, for tuber formation spray silica in root during descending moon.
- ROTATION: 3 to 5 years depending on disease problems.
- BIODYNAMIC SPRAYS: For indoor plants, spray as for tomatoes, but on root days. Use silica (501) in combination with equisetum (508) for fungal problems. Compost-clay 500 dip for transplants, roots, and seed pieces. Horn manure on field before sowing. Silica and equisetum several times before flowering, once after flowering, and at least once during tuber formation. Later sprayings should be done in the afternoon.

COMPANION PLANTS: In the potato patch interplant early peas, broad beans, early cole crops. Early bush beans in mid- or late potatoes allegedly deter Colorado potato beetle, which would be great since potatoes are alleged to deter Mexican bean beetle. Mulch certainly increases deterrence. Don't try to dig potatoes until bush beans are harvested, since bean roots are disturbed. Alternate rows of beans and potatoes are easier to manage.

Marigolds inhibit nematodes. Dead nettle (*lamium*), sainfoin, and nasturtium aid growth. The latter repels insects. Mint family repels insects. Caraway, dill, chervil, and coriander aid growth and attract beneficial insects.

Potatoes allegedly are weakened by nearness to apple trees, sunflower, cherry, raspberry, tomato, and squash family. But I get huge crops by placing rows of potato sets between rows of winter squash. The potato leafs out long before the squash vines overwhelm the patch.

Potato ground can be cleansed of pathogens both before and after by planting dense stands of rye. Early potatoes can be followed by legume crops, a legume rye mix, or a pasture rotation. Virginia growers sometimes follow with cowpeas in summer and spinach in fall.

PUMPKIN

Novice seed savers discover soon enough that pumpkins cross freely with other members of the *cucurbita pepo* species. Even after gardeners figure out how to keep them from crossing on the sly, the activity of selection becomes an education in itself. Seed savers quickly learn that the gardens are not composed of things, but qualities. "Qualities" become a way of looking at the world; no longer staring blankly at creation or walking around in a spiritual coma as we were taught to do in school, but investing each perception, each change of plant color and texture with its full endowment of life. Genetics is abstract only in school. The biggest secret your biology teachers never told you is that the distinctions of "alive" vary in every hair, in every filament along every stem. Abstractions are the proverbial scales that need to fall from your eyes. A genus is really a slowly changing cloud of qualities. A species is an immersion, an initiation into the elemental life that seethes beneath the surface of perception. In seed-saving you have to know the genetic rules, but to know what you're seeing—to play the game—you have to immerse yourself in the life that qualities represent. Pumpkins are a good place to start, since more than one species is involved. But the actual work is done by closely observing, each day more intensely than the day before.

"True" pumpkins belong to the species *Cucurbita pepo*. They cross freely with other members of the species, including summer squash, acorn squash, delicata, and sweet dumpling. When true pumpkins (such as Connecticut Field, New England Pie, Small Sugar, or Jack o' Lantern) cross with zucchini or yellow summer squash, the offspring invariably become ovoid and elongated, with anemic orange rind and pale stringy flesh. Crosses between the closely related delicata and sweet dumpling, however, have good-tasting, sometimes "improved" offspring, despite unorthodox form.

Extremely large pumpkins are usually *Cucurbita maxima* squash, the same species as the superb quality buttercup, kabocha, and hubbard. Somehow maxima "pumpkins" have completely lost maxima eating quality, and are grown exclusively to impress children and judges at state fairs. It may be that quality and huge size are inversely connected, and that a limit to form has been exceeded. Atlantic Giant (250 to 500 pounds) is the record-holder, followed by Big Max (100 or more pounds). Both seem a lesson in plant breeding: every garden fruit has an optimal size beyond which quality falls like a stone. Maxima pumpkins lack the long swan's neck stem handles of true pumpkins. Their stems are fleshy, similar to hubbard, but not useful as handles, which makes no difference since no one could pick them up anyway. They also lack the clear orange skin color characteristic of true pumpkins; the color is sodden. Their skin is slightly hubbard-textured, their shape ungainly, squat and off-center, and their color and flesh a peculiar saturated orange, as if pigment had leaked from over-expanded pumpkin cells.

For texture, flavor, and color a better choice is Red Hubbard, the deep orange *Cucurbita maxima* preferred by pumpkin pie-makers and pie factories. I remember the first time I pulled up to Mrs. Smith's Pie Factory just before Thanksgiving. Acres of semi-trailers were lined up, loaded with warty red hubbards for her famous "pumpkin" pie. Apparently the Red Hubbard can be pureed whole, with no telltale flecks of skin, and it tastes far better than pumpkin. Red Hubbard is not a pumpkin even in appearance, but an orange-skinned strain of Blue Hubbard (which also makes a better-than-pumpkin pie). Red Hubbard totally lacks the traditional pumpkin shape. The so-called Japanese pumpkin, called orange Hokkaido or Red Kuri, is a smoother creamier version of *C. maxima*, with sweet nutty flavor for puree and pie.

Finally, one sometimes finds a pumpkin-shaped butternut squash, a charming oddity with pumpkin shape and butternut (*C. moschata*) skin and flesh. Not carvable, but a good baker and keeper. Other *C. moschata* used for "pumpkin" pie include Quaker pie, Japanese pie pumpkin (not the *C. maxima*) and Cushaw pumpkin. Another cushaw, Green Striped Crookneck, has been used for pies in the South and belongs to another species, *C. mixta*.

To save seed, the pumpkin crop must be isolated from kindred species. *Cucurbita pepo* is especially vulnerable, since it includes so many incompatible members. *C. moschata* (butternut, and so forth) is an unlikely cross and is usually (but not one hundred percent) safe to grow with *C. pepo*. *C. maxima* pumpkins will seriously damage the offspring of *C. maxima* squashes (buttercup, hubbard, Hokkaido). And these squashes, in turn, will alter the size and shape of *C. maxima* pumpkins, although they might improve the quality of their flesh—but not enough. Since dry squash and pumpkin seed lasts up to six years, it is possible to forego saving the seed of certain species in given years and thus isolate *maxima* or *pepo* varieties one year in every five to collect seed.

The question "What is a pumpkin?" obviously depends more on use than species. Celebrators of Halloween have insisted on the *C. pepo* shape ever since Washington Irving sent a headless horseman raging down Main Street, pumpkin in hand, in the nineteenth century; but the original meaning of pumpkin refers to culture, not species. The old French *pompion* means "cooked by the sun"; and sun is what these Central American natives require to be full and fine tasting, whatever the species used.

Nutritionally, pumpkins are an excellent source of vitamin A. At 6,400 international units of vitamin A per 100 grams, pumpkins compare favorably to Swiss chard (6,500), bok choy (3,100), broccoli (2,500), collards (6,500) and butternut squash (6,400). The amount of vitamin C in pumpkin is not enormous, but it would be enough to get you through the winter if that were all you had to eat. And even if you don't care to eat pumpkins as a vegetable, they provide superior winter-feed for livestock, both flesh and seeds.

Pumpkin seeds are remarkably nutritious and have significant nutritional therapeutic value. Seeds contain 29% protein; 46% very high quality oil (non-cholesterol and an excellent source of vitamin E); 51 mg (per 100 grams) calcium; 1,144 mg phosphorus; 11 mg iron; twice the vitamin B of many vegetables; and several important trace minerals. Note that the iron present in pumpkin and winter squash seeds is not only outstanding in the vegetable kingdom (5 times more than kale), but even surpasses beef liver (8.8 mg)! That means these seeds are really valuable for people tending toward anemia, especially pregnant women and adolescents. Non-traditional medicine also recommends pumpkin seeds for the maintenance of the prostate gland in men, although I am not aware of studies confirming this. The seeds of all pumpkin varieties can be eaten, but some varieties produce seeds with no hulls: Triple Treat is larger than Small Sugar, good for pies, and keeps well.

Culture

All pumpkins require at least 100 warm days to mature. Giant pumpkins require more than 4 warm months. Culture and insect problems are the same as for winter squash. In areas with vine borer infestation, hybrid vigor and early maturity may be helpful. All *C. Moschatas* are vine borer-resistant. As with squash, deep wells of compost solve many problems, including plant vigor, productivity, disease- and insect-resistance, and availability of moisture late in the season.

Semi-bush plants can be packed similar to zucchini. Others are long and trailing (12 feet) requiring 6 feet between mounds. Giant pumpkins must grow unimpeded over mounds that resemble excavations. Giant vines grow 25 feet; for prizewinning specimens, only one pumpkin can be matured per mound. In many areas pumpkins are left to cure in the field after the vines have died. For long storage, don't let fruits take more than very light frost.

Varieties

Most traditional pumpkins for carving Jack o' Lanterns are *C. pepo* and range from 12 to 20 pounds. Traits to consider are color, uniformity, strong handles, size yield, and sometimes disease resistance. Open-pollinated cultivars include Connecticut Field (110 days), directly descended from the colonial pumpkin first grown by Native Americans. Like many plant types able to survive the climatic changes over millennia, Connecticut Field is extremely diverse in size and shape. Its descendant Howden (110 days, c. 1970) has a stronger handle and better color, but suffers reduced yield in cool summers. Young's Beauty (104 days) is better formed, with good-quality flesh. Tom Fox (110 days) has an unusually strong handle, uniform size (10 to 16 pounds), and good yield. Charisma PMR (98 days) adds powdery mildew resistance, which increases yield and quality.

White pumpkins are mostly decorative, but have edible orange flesh. The hybrid Lumina (110 days, 12 pounds, *C. Maxima*) is a novelty Jack o' Lantern with milk-white skin and delicious orange flesh. For the best decorative white, sacrifice flesh quality and harvest slightly immature. Valenciano (110 days) is a flattened *C. Maxima* white "pumpkin" with edible orange flesh. The Silver Moon (110 days, 12 pounds) is a hybrid *C. Maxima* with resistance to powdery mildew and mosaic virus.

For pies and storage, Small Sugar (100 days, 6 pounds, *C. pepo*, also called New England Pie) is still the standard, with dense, sweet, dry, stringless flesh that stores up to 4 months. Although pumpkin seeds are always edible, the naked seed varieties offer hull-less seeds. Baby Bear (100 days) offer hull-less seeds, fine-grained flesh, and good storage up to 4 months. For greater production of large hull-less seeds plant Styrian Naked Seeded Pumpkin (100 days), an heirloom from Austria. Styrian pumpkins are ripe when the mostly green skin shows some orange. It needs to cure 2 weeks before extracting, washing, and fan drying the delicious seeds. Flesh is suitable only for livestock.

The most visually satisfying pumpkin is an heirloom *C. Maxima* from nineteenth-century France. Rouge Vif d'Etampes (115 days, 20 pounds), is called Cinderella because it looks like the heavily ribbed bright scarlet orange carriage in the fairy tale. The flesh is deep orange with winter-squash quality for baking, soups, and pie. Traditionally used for a non-sweet squash pie in France. Jarrahdale (100 days, 8 pounds) is another attractive deeply ribbed *C. Maxima* "pumpkin," hubbard-grey in color with very good flavor, texture, and storage qualities. Musque de Provence (125 days, 10 pounds), marketed as Fairytale, is a third deeply lobed "pumpkin" of the *C. Moschata* cheese type. Flesh and long storage similar to butternut.

Probably the oldest known squash is Seminole (95 days, *C Moschata*), already being grown in Florida by the Seminole when the Spanish arrived in the 1500s. Seminole is cheese-shaped, similar in flavor and color to butternut but sweeter, and stores for up to a year. Like butternut its hard stems are resistant to vine borer. Well adapted to the hot humid South.

For SEED, BIODYNAMIC SPRAYS, and COMPANION PLANTS, consult the corresponding species under Winter Squash.

RADISH, BLACK SPANISH AND DAIKON

In the Western world, radishes (*Raphanus sativus*) are mostly "catch crops" (fast-growing crop used between plantings of others). In the East, however, as daikon, they have become a staple. If radishes disappeared in the West, few consumers would notice, but in Japan more daikon is consumed than any other vegetable. Daikon is sometimes eaten raw, but more often stir-fried, cooked in soup, mixed in rice dishes, or pickled in brine to produce the Asian version of sauerkraut. Daikon leaves are also eaten as a green, steamed, stir-fried, or made into Korean kimchee. Special varieties have been bred for leaf tenderness and flavor.

Daikon roots have good quantities of vitamin C, and fair quantities of typical brassica antioxidants. Daikon roots have a delicate flavor and light texture, never meaty like rutabaga. The leaves are far more intense, nutritionally and therapeutically. When any brassica is chewed, typical crucifer enzymes (myrosinase and glucosinulates) are transformed into antioxidants (allyl isothiocyanates); but another antioxidant, glucoraphasatin, is unique to the radish species. Glucoraphasatin has been shown to be antimutagenic (may prevent cancerous mutations); apoptotic (may promote cancer cell death); antifungal and antibacterial. While daikon is in the garden, it reduces nematode populations, as well as (negatively) repelling earthworms (cited by Montaut, et al. 2010). Daikon and radish leaves are very high in antioxidants, vitamins A, C, and K, folate, iron, potassium, and calcium.

In the West, radishes are small and quick growing, maturing in as little as three weeks from sowing. The exception is Black Spanish (50 days), a large black radish the size of a turnip, which can be root-cellared for the winter. Black Spanish is the western equivalent of daikon; it can be grated raw in salads, cooked like turnip, or pickled as sauerkraut. Black Spanish also contains the highest levels of the unique antioxidant glucoraphasatin, which has been shown to increase the detoxification enzyme in cancerous liver cells (Hanlon, et al. 2007). The effect is strong: only 1 mg of aqueous extract of black radish is required (Agricol, National Agricultural Library). High levels of glucoraphasatin are associated with the spicy heat of Black Spanish.

Although Black Spanish dates to the sixteenth century and enjoyed wide popularity in nineteenth-century France, England, and other parts of Europe, this valuable vegetable has almost disappeared from gardens. Devotees of daikon should give this even more healthful version a try.

Black Spanish works in any recipe calling for daikon, or any Western recipe calling for cabbage. One Mediterranean salad recipe combines peeled thin-sliced Black Spanish with sliced fennel, blanched sliced carrots, and fresh arugula, topped with grated pecorino cheese and vinaigrette.

Finally, some radish varieties are grown for seed pods (siliques), which are used as a spicy condiment in Europe. Their spiciness indicates high levels of radish antioxidants. Rat-tailed radish, a variety brought to Europe from Asia produces huge 8-inch seedpods, which have been pickled in Europe since the seventeenth century. One German variety, Munchen Bier, is served as a beer snack.

Culture

Small Western radishes germinate so quickly (3 to 7 days at 45 to 50°F) that some gardeners use sparsely-sown radish to mark rows of slow germinators such as carrot or parsnip, allowing close skim-weeding in just a few days. Germination and growth are most rapid in well-composted sandy loam, pH 6.5 to 7. Rows can be tight, 5 to 8 inches apart, 15 seeds to the foot; or broadcast in 2- to 3-inch bands, 35 seeds to the foot. Home gardeners can intercrop radishes between newly sown crucifers, or sow rows of early radishes 18 inches between rows, and interplant radish rows with other crucifers.

Western radishes should be sown and harvested quickly, or the crop discarded. As Bailey's *Horticulture* points out: rapid growth promotes crispness, the prime criterion of radish quality. Bailey also cautions that fresh manures ruin taste and texture. Medium-sized radishes such as Black Spanish, smaller daikon, and round watermelon daikon (Red Meat), can be sown 7 to 10 seeds to the foot and thinned to 3 or 4 radishes to the foot. Black Spanish can be sown when soil has warmed to 60°F. Early spring cold temperatures trigger bolting. For winter storage, Black Spanish can be sown from late June in the Northeast to late August in the mid-South. In the Deep South and along the Pacific coast, roots can be overwintered in the ground. Beds planted with long daikon should be dug or tilled deeply—even double-dug down to 16 inches, with 2 wheelbarrows of compost per 30-foot bed. Deeply friable soil will produce larger, more uniform roots, and fewer broken roots during harvest.

Daikon should be sown thinly, 6 seeds to the foot, and thinned to 4 to 5 inches between plants, depending on desired harvest size, from large carrot to fair-sized club. Allow 18 to 24 inches between rows. In Japan some daikons grow to 40, 50, even 90 pounds, but most are harvested the size of large carrots.

Radishes become pithy, hot, and tough in poor soil and under stress from heat, drought, and deficiency of compost. Stressed plants also seem to trigger a feeding frenzy from flea beetles, which adore radish leaves anyway. Organic pesticides are not cost-effective for this crop. Plants fertilized with compost made from cow manure and/or maple-leaf compost weather attacks better. I use row covers, also effective against cabbage root maggots and other crucifer insect pests. Gardeners sometimes plant radishes close to other crucifer transplants as a trap crop for flea beetles. Row covers protect both crops.

Harvest Western radishes promptly, beginning 20 days after sowing and ending a week later. Short harvest window is another good reason for home gardeners to intercrop small sowings between long-standing crucifers. Washed harvested radishes in perforated plastic bags last up to 1 month under refrigeration. Commercial growers store at 32°F.

Daikon must be harvested even more carefully than parsnips. Roots are very brittle and break unless lifted slowly with a spading fork. Push the fork down until it disappears a few inches to the side of the row, hold the fork in place with your foot and lower the handle toward yourself. Use broken, insect-damaged, and scored roots as soon as possible. To store perfect fall-harvested roots: cut the tops 2 inches above the crown and wash (never scrub), pack in perforated plastic-lined boxes, and root-cellar or refrigerate as close to freezing as possible for 1 to 3 months. The high humidity of perforated plastic prevents desiccation.

Varieties

Open-pollinated Western radishes:

French Breakfast Improved (25 days), a rose-scarlet heirloom with white tips and mild pungency. Still enjoyed in Europe sliced raw on buttered bread.

Champion (20 days) a large bright red radish, crisp, sweet, flavorful, with vigorous tops. Young tops excellent and highly nutritious for salad or stir-fry.

Cherry Belle (24 days) ¾-inch roots all season long. Resists pithiness.

White Icicle (30 days). Harvestable as a Western-style radish and 5-inch carrot-sized daikon, which it is. Mild flavored, resistant to pithiness and summer heat.

Hybrid Western radishes:

Perfecto (25 days) remains crisp up to golf ball size. Young greens are an excellent pungent addition to salads or stir-fry.

Cheviette (25 days) is a hybrid of Cherry Belle, with good heat tolerance, sweet pungent taste and crisp texture, even when large. Slow to become pithy.

Red velvet (27 days) has unusual stability and disease resistance. Resists cracking, pithiness, and summer heat. Tolerant to rhizoctonia and powdery mildew.

Easter Egg (30 days) is not a variety but a colorful mix of red, purple, and white radishes. For roadside appeal and children's gardens.

Black Spanish radishes:

Black Storage (53 to 80 days) is a large (up to 6 inches) heirloom, very pungent, suitable for winter storage.

Nero Tondo (50 days) is slightly smaller (up to 5 inches), very slow bolting with better uniformity. Very pungent. Stores well.

Open-pollinated daikon:

Watermelon or Red Meat (50 days) is a 3½-inch round Chinese heirloom, white with rose-colored flesh, excellent mild flavor, extremely sweet.

Misato Rose (60 days) produces a 5-inch round with green and white skin, rose and white flesh. A very adaptable daikon, which grows well even when "crowded or thinned late" (Southern Exposure Seed Exchange).

Miyashige White (50 days) a traditional premium Japanese daikon for fall storage, 12 to 18 inches long, 2 to 3 inches in diameter. Blunt tips. Sow from late July in the North, late August to early September farther south for fall harvest. Mature roots stay crisp, juicy, and tender.

Sunkyo Semi-long (32 days), a Chinese radish, not really a daikon, with 4- to 5-inch crisp pink roots, very pungent, nutty and very sweet. Use like western radishes or stir-fry. Attractive edible leaves with pink stems. An excellent all-purpose choice for use as a Western radish, daikon, and green.

Hybrid daikon:

April Cross Hybrid (60 days). Very slow bolting daikon for late spring or summer harvest, though April sowings may work only in regions with consistently warm stable weather. Crisp mild sweet roots, 8 inches long and 3 inches wide.

Alpine (55 days) a shorter 5- to 6-inch daikon, suitable for shallower or stonier soils, bolt-tolerant for spring and summer sowings.

Minowase Summer Cross #3 hybrid (50 days) a pungent succulent daikon for fall harvest, 16 by 2 inches. Tolerant to mosaic, fusarium, and heat. A variety flavored by growers for late harvest.

Omny Hybrid (60 days), a slow-bolting daikon, 16 by 2¾ inches, for late spring to fall harvest with tolerance to soft rot, mosaic, and black rot, but not partial to heat.

SEED: Precision-graded Western radish seed will produce stronger more uniform crops; available from commercial seed catalogs. An ounce of Western radish seed (about 1,500) sows from 60 to 125 feet, depending on seeds per foot (12 to 24). Still higher density can be achieved by broadcasting 3-inch bands, 35 seeds to the foot, especially good for home gardens. High-density radish plantings succeed because the crop matures before weeds take over.

A small packet (3.5 grams, about 300 seeds) will sow 20 linear feet at 15 seeds to the foot, or about a 12-foot band at 25 seeds to the foot. A half ounce (625 seeds) of Western radish seed will sow about 40 linear feet at 15 seeds to the foot, or 25 feet broadcast in a 3-inch band at 25 seeds to the foot. An ounce of daikon or Black Spanish (average 1,500 seeds) sows about 215 feet of row at 7 seeds to the foot. A ¼-ounce packet of daikon or Black Spanish (about 375 seeds) sows about 54 feet of row at about 7 seeds to the foot.

GERMINATION: 3 to 7 days at 45 to 50°F. Black Spanish may bolt when sown under 60°F.

VIABILITY: 5 years.

ROTATION: 3-year minimum. Be careful not to overtax your crucifer rotation with this quick-growing crop.

MOON CALENDAR: All practices in root, unless radishes are being grown for their leaves.

BIODYNAMIC SPRAYS: For Western radishes, one spraying of 501 as roots begin to swell. For daikon and Black Spanish, spray 501 twice, first at full leaf rosette, next as roots begin to swell. Otherwise follow practices for cabbage family.

RUTABAGA

Botanically the *Brassica* genus seem to specialize in a plant version of "neoteny." In animals such as dogs and humans, neoteny means that offspring retain youthful plasticity, lengthening the period when social bonding and learning can take place. In brassicas a whole genus retains the juvenile plasticity of the meristem (the most vital tissue at the growing point) throughout the plant, allowing even a single species (*B. oleracea*) to form countless variations with an unusually strong antioxidant profile. The rutabaga or "swede" is an extreme, even ironic example of this. On the one hand, the swede seems archaic, out of date, a relic of a bygone era when refrigeration and rapid transportation did not exist. Generations of small landholders in parts of Europe, Russia, and North America were saved from extinction thanks to the rutabaga. They were saved from starvation because rutabaga encloses brassica power in a meaty root that sits happily in a cold cellar for 4 months. Yet, old fashioned as it seems, rutabaga is probably the most recently created garden vegetable.

Rutabaga appears to be a naturally occurring hybrid of cabbage (*B. oleracea*) and turnip (*B. rapa*), formed, it seems, without human intervention. Some sources say rutabaga was discovered wild in Sweden in 1620. Others (University of Wisconsin website) claim rutabaga was first cultivated at the same time in what is now the Czech Republic and spread across northern Europe, Russia, and Scandinavia, where it is still a winter staple.

Botanists don't classify the rutabaga as a typical hybrid, but as a new species, *B. Napobrassica*. This is not a random genetic occurrence. A similar event took place in Asia 5,000 years previously to produce mustard *B. juncea*, a cross between *B. rapa* and *B. nigra*. The parents of rutabaga (turnip and cabbage) have 20 and 18 chromosomes respectively, while the rutabaga possesses 38. Rutabaga is the envy of hybridists because its offspring do not revert wildly to parent types. Normally hybridists radically inbreed the parents of a future hybrid, drawing each successive genetic line into a tighter, narrower, and more specialized genetic rift. Inbreeding augments special traits and vigor. The original plant species, however, has strong opinions against this procedure. Offspring usually spring back violently to the broad watercourse of the species, displaying breadth rather than narrowness. Brassica crosses are different. They breed true, doubtless the result of their intrinsic plasticity.

Nutritionally, rutabaga combines, and in some aspects augments, the virtues of its parents. Rutabaga is 45% higher in calcium than turnip and 34% higher than cabbage. Turnip root has only trace amounts of vitamin A; cabbage has 130 units, while rutabaga has 550 units per 100 grams. In vitamin C, rutabaga has more than turnip and almost as much as the 47 mg of cabbage (as a leaf, cabbage has even more than orange juice). Other common winter storage crops have far less C: carrots (3 mg) and beets (6 mg). Also interesting is the substantial drop in sodium in rutabaga: 4 mg as opposed to 34 mg in turnips and 14 mg in cabbage. In taste as well, the rutabaga is a hybrid, with the pungency of turnip made sweet and mellow by cabbage, yet curiously more substantial than either.

One can readily understand why in the scurvy-prone North, especially Scandinavia, rutabaga is a staple winter crop. The name "swede," or Swedish turnip, also suggested to some writers that Sweden might really be the country of origin. *Rotabagge* itself is a Swedish word. Presently, rutabagas are a common winter food throughout northern Europe, but have only a small following here because Americans have forgotten the art of root-cellaring. This may change, however, since rutabagas carry "brassica power" right through the midwinter. Don't underestimate them. As my elderly mother said after the October 2008 financial collapse, "I can't believe I'm going through the depression twice!"

Culture

The common name "swede" indicates the favored climate for rutabaga. In this continent, Canada is the largest producer, although rutabagas grow well anywhere north of the Mason-Dixon line. Culture is the same as late cabbage or brussel sprouts, also scions of northern Europe. In the North, rutabaga puts on size in September and October; in the central states it may keep growing into December if the weather is mild. Rutabaga suffers from prolonged heat, irregular supplies of water, and summer drought. Insects are worse at those times. A cabbage soil produces the best quality roots: pH 6 to 7, medium clay loam, and moderate compost. Sandy soils produce smaller roots with more insect problems. In lighter soils add more compost and spray liquid seaweed as a foliar feed if unsure of soil fertility. The University of Wisconsin reports that rutabaga seed drilled into sod has no insect problems. Organic clove-based herbicides might provide sufficient knock-down of weeds prior to drilling (conventional growers use Round-Up).

Sow rutabaga seed at least 90 to 100 days before regular fall frosts, June 1 to July 15, depending on latitude. Seed may be direct-sown or started in a seedbed and transplanted like cabbage. Biodynamic growers spray horn manure 500 during the previous fall and again in spring, and before planting dip transplant roots in a slurry of compost, clay, and horn manure 500. Seeds are usually direct-seeded no more than 10 seeds per foot, or 6 with a precision seeder in rows 2 to 3 feet apart. In moist ground, depth can be ¼ inch, but in midsummer during hot dry weather sow as deep as ½ inch. If soils tend to crust, home gardeners can use a ½-inch compost cover in the seed furrow for better germination and stronger, more insect-resistant seedlings. Roll and tamp the compost well for good soil contact. My older mechanical seeder tends to drop too much seed. Test on newspaper for even spacing and less thinning, around 6 inches per plant. Market growers can purchase sized seed.

In dry weather and sandy soil, flea beetles may wipe out seedlings. Flea beetles don't even wait for full emergence, but destroy the seed leaves as they break the surface. Either dowse with rotenone at emergence (not 100% effective), or use floating row covers until a full rosette of leaves is established. Since row covers are expensive and time-consuming, rutabagas may not be a practical market crop in certain areas. Market crops require moist "English" conditions, with cool summers or long cool autumns. Rainless heat waves in July and August really set rutabagas back, although often they survive and put on flesh in September and October.

Thinning is essential for this substantial plant. They really need at least 6 inches. You can see the future size of each rutabaga plant at seedling stage, quite visible in the stockiness of the stem and the size and color of the leaves. For this reason, thin only after the plants are well established and showing vigor (unless you have over-seeded). Choose the stockiest seedlings, even if spacing becomes uneven. Biodynamic growers spray horn silica (501) after thinning and once again as the roots begin to swell (which in rutabaga is inseparable from the stem). Keep well weeded. As in cabbage, some soil can lay against the stems so long as the growing point remains unburied.

Insect pests and diseases are the same as cabbage. Cabbage worms don't seem to favor rutabaga leaves, but can be controlled with Bt (Dipel). Cabbage root maggot is worse on non-clay soils with low humus. In smaller gardens the egg-laying of the fly can be prevented with row covers or a layer of wood ash or lime the size of a dinner plate, dusted around the stem. Plantings timed to mature just before hard frost usually miss the root maggot. Note the egg-laying cycle in your area.

Rutabaga is subject to many cabbage family diseases. Black rot (soil-borne bacteria) proliferates in wet weather, causing yellowing, wilting, and finally rotting. Soft rot, a soil-borne fungus encouraged by humid conditions, causes the same soft decay common in broccoli. Black leg (soil- and seed-borne fungal dry rot spread in wet weather) appears as black spots on leaves and stems. Turnip anthracnose is seed-borne, producing characteristic water-soaked spots on leaves. Interior brown rot is caused by boron deficiencies, not usually a problem in composted gardens and usually curable by the addition of leaf mold or leaf compost. Club root, a soil-borne fungus, apparently impossible to eradicate once established, causes hideous distortions of the roots resolved only by 6-year crucifer rotation. Otherwise, practice the normal 3-year crucifer rotation.

Many of these bacteria and fungi are present in garden soils. As more and more desirable brassicas appear on the market, the 3-year rotation becomes challenging! Consider separate crucifer debris compost for use in flower gardens, shrubs, and fruit trees. Discard infected refuse. The inherent vigor of organic and biodynamic plants helps to overcome the presence of these pathogens. Even club root can be overcome sometimes using "extremely" vigorous seedlings that have been grown to rosette stage in peat pots, although this is not a likely possibility for rutabaga. Gardeners with chickens or cattle can use leaves and culls as high protein-fodder. In fact, swede protein is so high that ruminants need time to adjust. Never use as stock feed in breeding season or when the seeds are in flower (U. of Wisconsin).

Rutabagas do their best growth in the fall, when light levels are declining, day-length shortening, and the biochemical message is being sent to store nutrients and sugars in the root. At all latitudes, September and October are therefore important times for biodynamic gardeners to spray horn silica (501), on root days in the afternoon when the life in the leaves is descending into the earth.

Rutabagas can take regular light nighttime frosts. Autumn sweetening even requires some frost to trigger the final maturing process. Harvest after at least two white frosts and before hard frost sets in. It has been my experience that the stem necks of rutabaga can be cut without causing rot in the stored roots. Roots can be stored all winter in sand, leaves, wood shavings, or perforated plastic bags, so long as the temperature is near freezing and high humidity is maintained. Rutabaga is one of the best-keeping roots, wonderful in soups, stews, stir-fries, or cut into French fry-sized pieces, lightly oiled and baked. Swedes are delicious mashed half and half with potatoes, a traditional Scandinavian midwinter staple. Scandinavians sometimes add mashed carrots for color, which increases nutritional value.

Varieties

The standard variety, Purple Top Yellow (90 days), not to be confused with Purple Top White (a turnip), is still widely planted north of the Mason-Dixon line. When well composted, Purple Top Yellow grows huge, ranging from softball to muskmelon in size. Commercial growers, especially in Canada, favor Laurentian (90 days), similar to Purple Top Yellow but more uniform in size. Both are fine-grained and substantial with sweet yellow flesh. Johnny's Selected Seeds has offered a hybrid of the hybrid (Helenor, 90 days) for high yield, with light orange flesh and sweet flavor. Open-pollinated strains usually exceed the demand of most markets.

- SEED: An ounce, about 9,000 seeds, direct-sows about 1,400 feet of row, 6 seeds per foot; or produces at least 6,000 transplants, up to 3,000 feet of row, 6 inches apart. ¼-ounce packet sows 175 feet to 350 feet.
- GERMINATION: 75%; 7 to 14 days at 70°F; but germinates at 50°F so long as moisture is available.
- DAYS TO HARVEST: 90 to 110.
- MOON CALENDAR: All practices, including biodynamic sprays, in root signs, especially during descending moon.
- ROTATION: 3 to 6 years depending on cabbage diseases.
- BIODYNAMIC SPRAYS: Horn manure (500) on field before sowing. Silica (501) in morning when rosette of leaves develops and several times thereafter until root development begins in fall. As root develops, spray silica in afternoon on root days during waning moon.
- COMPANION PLANTS: Beans, peas, fall spinach, celery, lettuce. Strong herbs deter flea beetle. See cabbage for other possibilities for interplanting where a root crop is appropriate, such as with *umbelliferous* herbs and seeds.

SALSIFY

My first encounter with salsify was not the purple-flowered *Tragopogan porrifolius*, the oyster plant that is occasionally grown in gardens. It was the yellow-flowered *T. dubius* that I knew as goatsbeard, which is found in open dry woodlands, fields, and waste places. Both plants have long narrow foliage whose wider base wraps around the leaf stem. They are edible as salad or cooking greens early in spring. In both cases the name *tragopogan* ("goatsbeard" in Greek) refers to the bristly seed spheres, similar in structure to dandelion but twice the size. The seed spheres are geometrically so complex, utterly magical in morning light, that it never would occur to me in two millennia to compare them to the beard of a goat. Each seed hangs from a feathery parachute, which I suppose reminded some ancient goatherder of a beard, since salsify has been cultivated in the Mediterranean for more than 2,000 years (Spellenberg 1979).

The mature cultivated root looks like a parsnip, up to a foot long, 1 to 2 inches in diameter at the shoulder, and tastes somewhat similar to an oyster, with the added inulin sweetness typical of other composite roots (scorzonera, burdock, Spanish oyster plant, and so forth). The earthy oyster flavor especially comes out when the roots are sliced and french-fried.

Seeds are sown in spring about the same time as carrot or parsnip. Sow 15 to 20 seeds per foot in rows 2 to 3 feet apart and thin 3 to 6 inches between plants. An ounce (2,100 seeds) sows from 140 to 170 feet; a mini packet (145 seeds) from Johnny's Selected Seeds sows 10 to 14 feet. The only available variety, Mammoth Sandwich Island, an heirloom grown since 1894, matures in 4 months.

Roots can be harvested in fall, with some left in the ground for late winter and early spring harvest. Roots stored in a cold cellar or refrigerated must be kept humid with perforated plastic. Like parsnip, cellared roots put forth tender salad shoots in early spring when storage temperatures rise in the high 40°sF.

Roots left in the ground will send up flower stalks in the second year, producing saveable seed. When seed spheres have fully formed, cut the stalks and hang upside down in a dry place in paper bags to catch the seed. Seed viability is one to two years (Fitz, 1978), but germination and viability are strongest in the first year after harvest.

The Spanish oyster plant (*Scolymus hispanicus*) is another salsify relative with a milder oyster flavor and roots almost twice the size of salsify. According to Bailey's *Horticulture*, the seeds are much easier to handle and sow, if you can find them. Leaves of Spanish oyster plant are very prickly, but tender shoots and young leaves are eaten like cardoon in parts of Spain.

> SEED: An ounce (about 2,600) sows about 130 to 170 feet at 20 to 15 seeds to the foot. A packet of 100 seeds 5 to 7 feet.
>
> DAYS TO MATURITY: 4 months.
>
> VIABILITY: 1 to 2 years. Biennial plants produce seed in the second year.
>
> MOON CALENDAR and BIODYNAMIC PRACTICES: All practices for roots on a parsnip schedule.

SCORZONERA

The perennial *Scorzonera hispanica*, is also called black salsify or black oyster plant because the skin of the root is black and because it shares a common earthy oyster-like, artichoke-like flavor with the biennial salsify (*Tragopogan*). Both plants are native to the Mediterranean region, but wild salsify is found in dry fields and waste places, while wild scorzonera prefers damp grassy meadows. Both reflect their native ecosystems: Scorzonera leaves are more lush, broad, and upright; salsify leaves are narrow, lean, and grass-like. Both share high levels of diabetic-friendly inulin. Scorzonera gets its name from *escorza near* ("black bark" in Spanish), referring to the black corky skin (Stephens, Florida Extension). The corky skin helps scorzonera hold up well in the root cellar.

Although barely known in the U.S., scorzonera has been widely cultivated in Europe since the seventeenth century. Belgium began commercial production not long after, followed by Holland, France, and Germany. In Europe peeled scorzonera is often cooked with peas and carrots; served like asparagus with a white sauce; or parboiled, battered, and french-fried. A more Mediterranean recipe parboils peeled roots in water with a 1/8 cup lemon juice or balsamic vinegar, seasoned with coriander, thyme, a bay leaf, and peppercorns. Drained roots are then browned in olive oil with fresh thyme added at the last minute.

Culture

Scorzonera grows best in cool to moderately warm temperatures (55 to 75°F). Growth is poor above 85°F and below 45°F. Seeds can be sown in spring and harvested 3 to 6 months later, or sown in early autumn and harvested the next summer. The British leave the roots in the ground for two years to increase root size.

Scorzonera roots prefer a light, deeply prepared carrot soil, with low nitrogen and moderate phosphorous and potassium. If compost is needed elsewhere, scorzonera will produce well in fertile garden soil with no additional fertilizer. Roots, however, are not tolerant of heavy, compacted, or stony soils: roots become short and forked. In very deep friable soil, longstanding roots may reach 3 feet long and an inch at the shoulder, although the brittleness of scorzonera makes extra-long roots a chore to harvest.

Scorzonera seeds are huge—up to ½-inch long. Viability is two years with better germination the first year after harvest. When soil temperature is about 60°F, sow seeds ½ inch deep, 10 to 14 seeds to the foot in rows 18 to 24 inches apart. Thin plants 3 to 4 inches apart.

Scorzonera is fairly insect- and disease-free. Sometimes new seedlings damp off. White rust (albugo) blisters may appear on mature leaves, sometimes causing plant death. Apply copper hydroxide as soon as blisters appear.

Older varieties include Hoffman's Schwarze and Improved Einjahrige. Both have consistent long roots. The newer variety Belstar Super has 9- to 11-inch roots, ¾ inches in diameter. All varieties have black skin and white flesh.

SEED: an ounce (2,600) sows 120 to 160 feet at 20 to 15 seeds to the foot. A packet of 100 seeds sows 5 to 7 feet.

DAYS TO MATURITY: 3 to 6 months, or 2 years for extra large roots.

VIABILITY: 1 to 2 years. Perennial plants produce seed in the second year and annually thereafter.

MOON CALENDAR AND BIODYNAMIC PRACTICES: All practices in root on a parsnip schedule.

COMPANION PLANTS: Scorzonera is said to repel carrot fly. It's worth a try to sow a row of scorzonera between 2 rows of carrots, or in home gardens to mix carrot seed with 25% scorzonera.

SPINACH

Live in each season as it passes. Open your pores and bathe in all the tides of Nature in all her streams and oceans... a true panacea of all remedies mixed for your especial use... Do not resist her.

~ Henry David Thoreau

Have you noticed that spinach tastes different in spring than it does in fall? If you didn't know otherwise, you might believe that the varieties are different, and that one is a special French variety rarely found in the States. But no, they both grow from the same seed on the same ground. The only change is the time of year. Spring spinach tastes exceptionally clean, fresh, and invigorating. It is light and tender in texture, a natural for salads. Fall spinach is surprisingly sweet. It may also be tender, but seems more substantially nourishing. Perhaps the protein content is also higher, I don't know, but certainly the sugar is.

It is amazing how a different aspect of the plant predominates during each part of the growing season. In spring we welcome the first green haze that covers the forest. Fruits don't appear in spring; the "extra-early" varieties lack the sublime nectar of late summer. Early peaches taste "shipped-in." You have to wait until late July or August for the true sweetness of peach and muskmelon. Maybe it has to do with where the sun is, or how much warmth has accumulated in the earth as the season progresses. That would certainly say something about melons and peaches. But even in a plant like spinach, which grows from seed so quickly, the leaves from a late summer sowing taste like fruit.

I think this is because spinach is what Johann von Goethe called "pure leaf." It is very impressionable. It takes up the influence that surrounds it very quickly. This not only makes it taste good in two distinctly different ways, it also teaches us a lot about the varying conditions under which it grows. Spinach is the quick instructor of garden culture.

With a little practice, a gardener can see not only the shortage of nitrogen in pale yellowing leaves and stunted quickly bolting plants, but also high nitrates when the leaves go beyond a certain depth of greenness, also becoming watery and saturated, and begin to lose form. Commercial growers often apply a lot of nitrates to spinach, too much. Sometimes not only for high yield; but also to keep rabbits off. Rabbits are very sensitive to excess nitrate levels. Humans often lack rabbit sensibilities and regularly poison themselves with nitrates. But with the help of spinach we can become more aware of this problem. Notice this carefully when growing spinach under glass! I've grown winter greenhouse spinach that was very large and had no taste; it seemed shut off from the right balance of earth and sky. How to create a biologically active soil in a greenhouse instead of a mere nutrient composition is an essay unto itself, but spinach can give you the clues. In midwinter there is not enough sunlight to prevent nitrates from accumulating.

The next soil property that spinach reveals is tilth. Spinach grows best in soils with high porosity. Spinach loves the silica fraction of the soil. If you've tried to grow spinach in both sandy loam and clay loam, you know that given adequate compost it does better in soil with more sand. I've also noticed that spinach in clay is more prone to soil-borne fungi. It may be that spinach was originally a coastal plant (like its close relative, the sea orach) and that a bit of sandy coast still clings to its roots. You can partially approximate the lightness of sandy loam by increasing organic matter. Besides finished compost, rotted silage, hay, and leaves are excellent. Un-rotted manures and high organic fertilizers pump spinach and spoil flavor. Develop a little rabbit awareness and you will reject the result.

Spinach picks up its environment so quickly that it serves to put you in touch with the environment as well. It is a wide-open creature of the rising and falling light, and through it you can read the weak points of your garden culture. Through it you can even taste the spring and the fall on the tip of your tongue.

Culture

Spinach is even more versatile in the crop rotation than lettuce. Any ground that is idle and waiting for heat lovers can be planted with spinach. With very little planning, tremendous spinach catch crops can be taken from a squash or melon patch. Just think of the space wasted between squash mounds! I have often put two rows (sometimes double rows) of spinach between rows of squash. Leave room for one or two cultivations. Spinach can also be sown where peppers will be grown. When the pepper transplants are ready, just hoe out spinach at the right spacing. Do you have tomato fences? What use are those 2- to 3-foot gaps between plants? Sow spinach in early spring where tomatoes will be planted later; or better yet, sow spinach the October before. Many varieties easily overwinter. When the soil is warm enough (about 65°F) chop out spaces for tomato plants. Spinach can also follow midsummer heat lovers like bush beans, or any other crop that is harvested by August, such as onions. Although late summer germination is sometimes poor, autumn spinach produces right into cold weather. Commercial growers in lower New England overwinter late sown spinach (before hard frost) without protection. In colder sections, plantings are covered with floating row cover. Both produce a crop next spring almost before you've finalized your garden plan.

The culture of spinach is not similar to its cousin the beet. Except for a common love of calcium, spinach needs higher soil fertility (nitrogen), more water, and a looser, sandier loam. Clay soils, which regularly produce huge beets, need work before they grow good spinach. A "muskmelon-type" soil, one that warms up quickly in spring, is ideal for spinach. A southern exposure is good. Problems with virus and mildew can often be traced to heavy, sodden soils.

Spinach germinates best when sown while nights are still frosty and the days about 40°F. Later sowings don't germinate nearly as well. For this reason consider preparing the ground for spinach the fall before. Apply generous amounts of compost, prepare the seedbed, and give the soil a spray of biodynamic horn manure. Sow in late winter or very early spring as soon as the ground has thawed. For decades I used my old Plant Jr. Seeder set at plate-hole #11, two settings lower than the recommended #13. Cup seeders are more accurate to eliminate thinning. Try a practice run on newspaper. Aim for 10 seeds to the foot. I also dust the seed in the hopper with a handful of dolomitic limestone to improve germination. Spinach loves neutral pH—6.5 to 7.5—which is not available naturally in many areas of the Northeast. If you have trouble germinating beets, chard, and spinach, dusting the seed with lime will help. Never use hot hydrated lime.

The essential thing is to beat spring heat. In the Deep South spring heat arrives like a steamroller and cuts germination substantially, so late fall sowing may be the only alternative. Depth of sowing depends on soil: about 1/2 inch for light soils, 1/4 inch for clay loam. Be sure the seed is lightly firmed to insure good soil contact. For hand sowing in smaller gardens, sifted compost cover is good, especially for late summer and early fall planting when germination is more difficult.

One of my goals for spinach has been to see how little work I can do and still get a good crop. On land not too infested with weed-seed, I get away with just one skim cultivation. I often plant double rows, since beyond the plant's early stages I stop weeding. Some growers pack the rows very tightly, closer than a foot between rows. Given a biologically active soil, spinach is so prolific I tend to plant too much. I've never lost much sleep over that, as spinach makes a quick meal for earthworms and a great addition to the diet of hens and pigs.

However, if yields are too low, the gardener may be tempted to use liquid feedings. Just remember that spinach is impressionable. Spinach pumped up with fertilizer tastes empty and always contains residual nitrates. Use compost or nettle/seaweed tea, if need be, twice during early rosette stage, but not within two weeks of harvest. Biodynamic growers spray silica (501) just as the plant begins to form a rosette.

In southeast Pennsylvania I never achieved a large consistent stand of autumn spinach. Heat, crusting, and dryness were hard to overcome. Spinach had to be sown just when those amazingly sweet melons were ripening, hardly in accord with the near-frost conditions favored by spinach. I always kept water on the seedbed, using overhead irrigation. In Massachusetts, where nights in late August are much cooler, for late sowings I find bed culture better than field. I try to plant only what I can care for, since one good dry-out during emergence can wipe out all seedlings. Biodynamic silica can be sprayed at rosette stage along with late carrots or cole crops.

To overwinter spinach in the field, sow seeds from late September to middle October, depending on latitude. Keep the seedbed moist. Further south, spinach can be sown in November and harvested through winter. Some gardeners take one cutting before hard frost and again in March. This worked in Pennsylvania. Younger plants sown late seem to weather frost better.

Spinach can also be sown in a cold frame sometime in October. Plant only in finished compost. Soak seeds overnight, drain, and dust with lime to make them easy to handle and to improve germination. Sow at 1/2 inch, tamp, and keep them moist. To avoid overheating, leave frames open until hard frost. Even then, closed frames sometimes heat above 100°F, which may trigger bolting.

If you suffer from cold frame-forgetfulness syndrome, you might consider Asian greens, Green Ice lettuce, and Batavian lettuce. These take a greater range of heat than spinach, although none endure the cold as well.

Cold frames and greenhouses not only shut out wind and cold, they also shut out a good percentage of the environmental and cosmic forces. This is something you can taste. Biodynamic growers have found that silica (501) helps the plant better utilize scant sunlight. Horn manure (500) and the compost preparations promote balanced, less watery, uptake of nutrients.

A tightly insulated cold frame will produce for a long time, but even if your frame freezes, spinach re-grows in late winter, unless plants are too old. Four leaf cuttings are about the limit. In late winter, cold frame or cold greenhouse sowings could be made again, but remember to rotate. Every few years replace cold frame soil down to 8 inches.

Varieties

Spinach varieties vary in quality and yield, but not so dramatically as they vary in when and how they are grown. The same variety grown in different areas will respond differently in terms of yield and susceptibility to disease. Soil type, humus, drainage, and disease resistance are closely intertwined. Gardeners with heavier soil should choose varieties of spinach with high resistance to downy mildew and spinach blight (mosaic virus). In many areas, downy mildew, the bane of muskmelons, is also the bane of good spinach production. Much of the high yields and ease of culture in hybrids are due to disease resistance, which is noted precisely in market-oriented catalogs. Note also bolt resistance (for warm weather), fast growth rate (for young salad), and success when overwintered. Some growers consider how easily a variety can be cleaned due to leaf shape and texture: some varieties are smooth, some highly savoyed (ruffled); Asian varieties have a clean, smooth shape.

Sometimes varieties of spinach are bred for local conditions. A Missouri gardener once showed me his spinach trials. He had a local variety, Ozark, growing next to a French variety prized by Alan Chadwick. To me, the Ozark tasted richer and much sweeter. Many gardeners consider French spinach second to none, but it's worth testing varieties for your region. The heirloom Monstreux de Viroflay (sounds a lot better than "Monster of Viroflay," 45 days) and its descendant Butterfly (45 days) have great vigor and excellent rich flavor.

The old standard Bloomsdale (47 days) still performs well for early and main crop planting. Extremely savoyed, dark green leaves are slow bolting and heat tolerant with mild salad quality. Withstands extreme cold. Winter

Spinach

Bloomsdale (47 days) grows well in autumn. Young plants overwinter, even in the North. Resists downy mildew and mosaic. Cold-Resistant Savoy (45 days) is still the longest standing spinach variety, blight-tolerant for late summer, fall, and overwintering in cold climates.

Many seed catalogs, even some committed to organic agriculture, offer only hybrid spinach seed. Hybrid spinach grows faster, bolts more slowly, and offers significant disease resistance. Mildew makes plants unmarketable. The durable hybrid Melody resists mildew (races 1 and 2), while newer hybrids are resistant to 11 races of mildew. I suspect increased resistance runs parallel to monoculture, shorter rotations, and build-up of mildew from squash, cucumbers, melons, pumpkins, beans, and peas; perhaps also from pushing spinach into hot moist weather.

A hot-weather spinach substitute, which really tastes like spinach, is a sort of chard called perpetual or spinach beet (55 days). This great plant, sometimes hard to find in seed catalogs, produces all season long from a single sowing. Other midsummer alternatives include the tropical Malabar spinach (*Basella rubra*, 35 days), also called climbing spinach; a somewhat mucilaginous plant adapted to extreme heat. Seed germinates slowly, 10 to 12 days at 80°F. Malabar Spinach needs lots of water; not drought tolerant. Nichol's Seed Catalog recommends adding shredded Malabar Spinach leaves to chicken broth with ginger and tofu. New Zealand spinach (*Tetragonia expansa*, 60 days) germinates even more slowly, up to 28 days, but is highly drought tolerant. To speed germination, soak seed overnight before planting.

A third warm-weather alternative is vegetable amaranth (*Amaranthus tricolor*, 50 days), which has a more spinach-like taste. Amaranth leaves are not only high in vitamins, minerals, and protein, but also are extremely decorative. Amaranth requires warm soil (at least 70°F) to germinate, and moderate amounts of water. Also called hinn choy, tampala, and red calaloo. Harvest young leaves and quickly steam or stir-fry.

SEED: An ounce of spinach seed (about 2,500) sows about 250 feet.
1 packet (1/6 ounce) sows 40 feet.

GERMINATION: 60%; prefers cool soil 40 to 50°F. Lower germination in late summer and early fall. Keep seedbed moist and use more seed. Dust seed with powdered agricultural lime.

VIABILITY: 3 years.

DAYS TO HARVEST: 40 to 55; if longer, something is wrong with culture or conditions.

MOON CALENDAR: All practices in leaf, ascending moon, including biodynamic sprays.

ROTATION: 2 to 3 years, between beets, chard, and spinach, and other mildew-prone crops (squash family and legumes).

BIODYNAMIC SPRAYS: Horn manure (500) on land before sowing. Silica (501) at least once when true leaves appear, sprayed in the early morning.

COMPANION PLANTS: A beneficial catch and pre-crop. Sow very early, preceding tomatoes, peppers, squash, melons, and eggplant. Interplant by harvesting every third spinach plant. Interplant with first year strawberries, or alternate strawberry rows with spinach and onions.

STINGING NETTLE

Stinging nettle (*Urtica dioica*) is one of the centerpieces of biodynamic gardening, as a compost preparation, compost ingredient, and liquid manure. In very early spring young nettle leaves provide the earliest greens of the season and probably the most nutritious; they are very high in vitamins A, E, D, C, and K, chlorophyll, iron, and other minerals. Nettle leaf protein is off the charts for a non-legume, 25% (Hughes, 2006); this makes nettle a valuable and under-utilized fodder crop for poultry, livestock, and people. Margareta Leuder, my garden teacher, said that during World War II she owed her life to nettle. Nettle is one of the most healthful and therapeutic of all vegetables.

Therapeutic Value

The sap of stinging nettle bears an uncanny biochemical resemblance to human blood, not only the similarity of chlorophyll to haemoglobin, but numerous other blood chemicals as well. Nettle sap, however, is a wild blood, very wild, unconfined by a closed circulation, totally open to the cosmos. Imagine if the blood trapped in the dark vessels of our bodies were suddenly able to evade all alarms and guards and iron gates, and escape into wider nature. I would like to follow it tumbling out of my aorta, disappearing into wider nature, into a completely alien circulation. I have no doubt I would become infused by something akin to the origins of human blood. I sense that this uniquely nutritious and annoying plant holds a key: that the walls of these two circulations are not impassible, but composed of an extraordinary permeable membrane between the human being and the world of plants.

Nettles are rich in anti-inflammatory antioxidants (kaempferol, quercetin, isorhammetin and scopoletin) that reduce the risk of heart attack and cancer (Ahmed 2007). Nettles also contain coumarin, an aromatic flavinoid that is blood thinning, antifungal, anti-tumorous, and causes appetite suppression. Coumarin is responsible for the sweet smell in new mown hay, sweet clover, and cinnamon. Nettle hay has been grown for cattle and poultry fodder in Sweden and Russia because it significantly increases egg and milk production.

Nettle has been shown to lower blood sugar and blood pressure and increase insulin resistance (animal studies cited by University of Maryland Medical Center). Nettles reduce pain symptoms of arthritis by reducing inflammatory cytokines, thereby lowering the required dosage levels of NSAID's (ibid). Nettles also increase free testosterone in aging men by suppressing globulins. Globulins cause prostate cells to divide and grow too rapidly (Popa 2005).

The catch to this remarkable plant is its bee-like sting and unrelenting invasiveness. The hairy spines contain a close biochemical equivalent of bee sting (histamines, acetylcholine and serotonins, also basic constituents of human blood). Mature hairs cause angry welts on exposed skin, even stronger reactions in sensitive people. The trick is to harvest young leaves before the sting develops. Emerging leaves are so sting-free, some foragers eat them as salad, a pleasure I leave to others. But I do harvest the youngest leaves barehanded to use as greens in stir-fries, curries, and soups. After a week or so I prefer to use rubber gloves. The sting compounds are completely neutralized by cooking; no need to use two waters. I tend to stop harvesting new growth before plants flower. After flowering, nettles form cystoliths, which irritate the urinary tract. Harvested early, nettles have a rich nutty flavor worth incorporating in many recipes. I even saw a recipe for spinach lasagne where the spinach was actually nettles!

Culture

The problem with nettle is where to grow it! Nettle spreads uncontrollably by root and seed, and gravitates like a magnet to the rotted manure around barns, gardens, and homesteads. Never plant nettle near your garden, let alone in it. Some gardeners have been fairly successful building a deep-boxed bed. I prefer not. Nettles have a way of getting around most barriers. Better to banish nettle to a far corner of the property. Keep the stand cut to prevent seed dispersal. Use the cut leaves for fermented compost tea. Also add cut leaves to the compost pile. Protein and enzyme content is so high that nettle can create an excellent vegan manure when real manure is not available. High nitrogen, high protein, and high enzymatic activity make nettle a proven and potent compost activator. Pile heat should prevent seed dispersal, but cut nettle at or before flowering.

Nettles are easily propagated by root pieces and divisions. Use gloves. Seed can be collected as well; seeds are nutty and intensely nutritious. Nettle also feeds hosts of butterfly species.

SUMMER SQUASH

Seeds of summer squash (*Cucurbita pepo*) from prehistoric caves in Mexico date to around 8000 BCE, making summer squash as old as any *Ur*-crop found in the Middle East. (Hancock, *Plant Evolution* 2004). Colonial accounts attest that Native American varieties, culture, and culinary use have remained basically unchanged from ancient times to the present. An early visitor to Florida (1650) found many varieties of summer squash growing in Native American gardens: "A fine variety of colors...agreeable to taste. Planted in April, the fruit is fit for eating in the middle of June. [The Indians] do not wait for it to ripen but gather them and place them immediately in the fire." (Austin, *Florida Ethnobotany* 2004). According to colonist Roger Williams (1643) the Narragansett Indians in New England ate squash very young as salad. Their word for squash, *askuta,* means eaten uncooked (ibid).

So, in my home, summer squash continues its tradition as one of the oldest fast foods, the first fruit I grab on summer nights when I arrive from working, late and sweaty, with no time even to shower. Who can't be grateful for a 10,000 year-old healthful fast food, braised and on the table faster than you can peel potatoes?

Culture

Summer squash grows best at 65 to 75°F, pH 5.8 to 7, in heavily composted rows or hills, ½ bushel of compost per hill. Squash requires moderate nitrogen with high levels of phosphorus and potassium, optimally. Though commercial growers may apply 8-24-24 with a shot of nitrogen at 9-inch growth, organic and biodynamic growers get better flavor with composted manure or mixed compost fortified with an organic fertilizer. When soil temperatures are 70°F at 4 inches down, sow 3 seeds to the foot, ½ to 1 inch deep in rows 5 feet apart; 6 feet for large plants such as yellow crookneck and costata romanesco. For hill culture, sow 6 to 8 seeds in a 10-inch circle and thin to the 2 or 3 strongest on hills 4 feet apart in all directions.

Seeds germinate in 6 to 12 days; 6 days using black poly and row cover. Black poly with drip and slatted row cover may raise air and soil temperature

10 to 20°F. In warm climates black poly may drive temperatures well above the optimum 75°F. Silver-colored plastic mulch generally reduces non-beneficial insects and aphid-borne mosaic (California Extension), while increasing *Hymenoptera* (bees, ants, wasps, etc.) (Alabama Extension). I get very early crops using heavy row cover and baited iron phosphate for slugs in Zone 5, with no black plastic and only one watering before the squash leaves crush against the rebar hoops. I then remove row cover and mulch with leaves. Market growers supply 1 to 2 beehives per acre for adequate pollination.

Summer squash is monoecious—both male and female flowers grow on the same plant. Male flowers are not as full, with thin stems. Female flowers have larger stems and fuller flowers, which are swollen at the base where the fruit is forming. Costata romanesco is often harvested this way. When harvesting flowers for salads and frying, harvest many, but not all, of the male flowers on each plant.

Summer squash has a shallow but extensive root system and no tolerance for compact soil. In heavy, poorly drained soils use raised rows, beds, or high mounds. Home gardeners will have excellent results following mound instructions for cucumber. Deeply prepared mounds have never required irrigation from me; and they will greatly reduce water needs in arid climates. Plants are more vigorous and produce longer than in row culture. But even in row culture, seedlings are not water-greedy. The Florida Extension recommends as little as one seedling irrigation per week. Organic mulch increases yield and may eliminate watering altogether, but it retards early harvest. Delay mulching until plants are well established. In lean soils, seaweed nettle and compost teas can be applied at full leaf rosette. For biodynamic practices follow the schedule for cucumber.

Harvest

Summer squash matures in 5 to 7 days from flower set. Skin should be shiny and tender; the rind should mark easily with a fingernail. Dull rinds too hard to mark should be discarded; leaving gargantuan fruit on the vine instructs the plant to stop bearing.

Harvest size varies with market. Traditionally zucchini and crookneck have been harvested at 5 to 6 inches in the western U.S., and 7 to 8 inches in the East, but gourmet markets everywhere are demanding smaller fruits, as little as 3 or 4 inches. Check before you deliver, even to your partner's kitchen. Scratching and bruises from careless handling reduce market value and shorten window of viability for sale.

Fruits must lose field heat (cooled below 50°F, but not below 42°F) within an hour of harvest. Zucchini tolerates refrigeration for 2 weeks; 10 days for other summer squash. Summer squash has low to moderate sensitivity to ethylene (from apples, etc.), a natural gas that hastens ripening and reduces storage life.

Insects

Use row covers until flowers appear, to prevent early damage from striped and spotted cucumber beetles (which also transmit bacterial wilt), flea beetles, squash bugs, and vine borers.

Vine borers are the death of summer squash, though the problem decreases with large field stands. Some growers spray the lower stems early in the season with pyrethrins to prevent the vine borer moth from laying eggs inside the stem. Spray late in the day to avoid killing bees. Once the moth larva is feeding, the entrance hole becomes an open wound, messy with frass. Home gardeners sometimes hook the larva out with a bent wire or penknife and bury the damaged stem, which may root. Home gardeners plagued by borers might consider Tromboncini, a *C. moschata* summer squash whose tough butternut-like stems are resistant to vine borers.

Squash bugs at nymph stage (yellowish-green larva with dark abdomen and thorax) are easy to control with insecticidal soap. Adult squash bugs are so well armored they are almost impossible to control. Squash bugs are far worse on black plastic, and no problem at all using organic mulch. Southern Exposure Seed Exchange has success using Black Beauty zucchini, a variety especially favored by squash bugs, as a trap crop for hand-picking adult squash bugs.

Arkansas Extension notes that control of leafhoppers may help break the mosaic virus cycle, along with prompt composting or plow-down of refuse. Spray thoroughly with insecticidal soap. Aphids tend to congregate on the undersides of leaves, usually on stressed and aging plants. Use insecticidal soap or oil. Aphids are repelled by silver mulch.

In light Southern soils root knot nematodes (visible as root galls) cause serious damage. Flowers appear, but never fruit. Control with parasitic nematodes. Rotate infested land with grains, especially rye or corn.

Seed corn maggots (Delia) sometimes feed on squash seeds. Cutworms destroy young seedlings at soil level. Cardboard collars (cut from cereal boxes) wrapped around seedlings and buried a few inches above and below the soil level will protect seedlings; also against wireworms. Promptly plow down or compost end-of-season plant debris.

Diseases

Summer squash is affected by three mosaic viruses: watermelon mosaic virus (wmv), zucchini yellows (zymv), and cucumber mosaic virus (cmv). Vigorous, well-composted plants are less susceptible. Mosaic viruses are spread by leafhoppers. Compost all debris and rotate *cucurbits* for three years.

Mildew covers leaves with white or grey mold, blocking available sunlight and reducing yield. Downy mildew occurs early in the season in cool damp weather. Powdery mildew lowers yield in hot dry weather, especially in fall, as plants begin to age. Plant late successive crops to maintain vigor in the fall, or use potassium bicarbonate or copper fungicide spray.

Blossom end rot in squash, a disorder also well known to tomato growers, is caused by poor uptake of calcium during dry spells. It won't occur on well-composted hills or with organic mulch. It is sometimes precipitated by poorly drained stagnant soils, which limits nutrient flow. Use raised beds.

Poorly drained soils also invite phytophthora rot on root, crown, or fruit. Spores are spread by rain, producing a white to gray mealy growth (Massachusetts Extension). When soil moisture is low, the fungus causes little if any disease, but spores are extremely long lasting—up to ten years (ibid). Rotate affected crops (*cucurbits*, nightshades, and snap beans) at least three years with non-susceptible families such as corn or grain. Plant on well-drained land. Organic market growers spray newly affected plants with copper hydroxide solution. Septonia and anthracnose leaf spots, which may cut production, are also controlled by copper hydroxide. As a home gardener I accept whatever the plants give, and then let them go.

Varieties

Old, open-pollinated (O.P.) and hybrid varieties are divided by a sizable gulf. Heirloom varieties have superior flavor and texture. Hybrids yield twice as many fruits and offer substantial disease resistance. Growers who stick to heirloom varieties should stagger plantings every few weeks to keep stands vigorous. Calculate your latest possible sowing for fall harvest or plant a mix of O.P. and disease resistant hybrids.

Some varieties confer natural disease resistance, others are bioengineered; the difference is impossible to discern from seed catalogs. Some varieties are called "precocious"; that is, the appearance of disease, watermelon mosaic virus (wmv), for example, may remain latent longer. Also note resistance to zucchini yellows mosaic virus (zymv) and cucumber mosaic virus (cmv). Powdery mildew (pm) resistance is significant since it severely reduces fall production.

Open-Pollinated Zucchini:

Costata Romanesca (62 days), a highly valued Italian heirloom with half the yield and twice the flavor and texture of most hybrids. Large vigorous plants. Fruits are traditional Italian—medium green body with pale green ribs.

Dark Green Zucchini (50 days). Vigorous, productive, concentrated early yields. Mottled green with pale green flesh.

Fordhook (57 days) a reliable, vigorous bush plant with dark green fruits.

Hybrid Zucchini:

Italiano Largo Hybrid (59 days) retains stronger and nuttier flavor from its O.P. forebear in a productive hybrid plant.

Green Tiger (57 days), also a striped Italian-type hybrid with fine taste and appearance. Rated best tasting by Burpee.

Butterstick Hybrid (50 days) small golden zucchini with good taste and texture. A single vigorous stem makes fruits easy to pick.

Open-Pollinated Yellow Crookneck and Straightneck:

Yellow Crookneck (55 days) has been a favorite for millennia. Buttery, corn-like flavor with good texture. Best eaten before 6 inches, but I like the immature seeds. Bright yellow, warty skin, large long-bearing vines.

Saffron (53 days). High yields of very tasty yellow straightnecks.

"Patty pan" or scallop squashes have been popular with the Latino community for more than 10,000 years. O.P. Golden Bush Scallop (68 days) very productive over a long season with better flavor than other patty pan squash. Matures late. Harvest at 4 to 5 inches.

Hybrid Patty Pan:

Sunny Delight (45 days) early yields of creamy, nutty yellow fruits. One of the best-tasting summer squashes.

Starship (53 days) medium green scallops with good taste and texture. Fruits look like immature kabocha.

Flying Saucer (50 days) combines dense texture and nutty flavor with the roadside appeal of an ornamental gourd. The fruits look like an unfamiliar species of starfish, with white and yellow arms and green stripes at the blossom end. High summer temperatures reduce color contrast.

Specialty Summer Squash:

Sweet Gourmet Hybrid (50 days), a Lebanese type with unique flavor and light green zucchini shape. Yields 50 to 70% more fruit than other zucchini. A good choice for home or market.

Tromboncino (80 days *C. moschata*) is a late season summer squash from the same species as butternut. The only summer squash resistant to vine borers and many other insects. Mottled green fruits taper to a trombone bell at the blossom end. Long vigorous vines are best trellised. Fruits are harvested at 8 inches. Bears much longer than *C. pepo* summer squash. Seed savers note that Tromboncino will crossbreed with butternut.

SEED: An ounce of zucchini, about 188 seeds, sows 27 hills or 63 feet of row. An ounce of yellow summer, about 280 seeds, sows 40 hills or 93 feet of row. An ounce of patty pan, about 300 seeds, sows 43 hills or 100 feet of row. A packet of 30 seeds sows 6 hills at 5 seeds per hill or 15 feet of row.

GERMINATION: 6 to 12 days at 70°F. 2 weeks at 60°F.

VIABILITY: 4 years.

DAYS TO HARVEST: 48 to 62 days.

MOON CALENDAR: All practices in fruit.

ROTATION: 3 years for *cucurbit* family (squash, melons, and cucumbers).

BIODYNAMIC SPRAYS: Follow the schedule for cucumbers or melons.

SWEET POTATO

Many a Southern family has maintained health in the face of poverty solely due to the sweet potato and its homesteading companion, the collard. I believe George Washington Carver was the first to point out that sweet potato provides more nutrition per square foot than any other crop. Carver developed an optimum warm soil rotation for the southern grower. He knew that sweet potatoes were ideal for the leached, low-nutrient soils common on homesteads in the South. For a pioneer crop he planted cowpeas, also called black-eyed peas or crowders, a southern legume that thrives on land that is losing heart. He followed cowpeas with sweet potatoes, and would allow small-holders to plant cotton only after the land had been, in his words, "rested, refreshed, and enriched." In this way Carver hoped to restore the failing health of the large body of impoverished rural African-Americans. In 1905 he wrote: "I saw hundreds of squalid, ramshackle cabins tenanted by forlorn, emaciated, poverty-stricken Negroes who year after year struggled in cotton fields and disease-laden swamps, trying to eke out a miserable existence. When day was done they came home to rest in the crude one- or two-room log cabins of rough pine. Often the families numbered more than a dozen persons, ranging from infants in arms to the old and decrepit."

Carver had the idea that by using only rotation and the compost scraps from the homestead, the small farmer could establish a self-cycling entity. The plants he proposed were cowpeas, corn, sweet potatoes, peanuts, and collards, with cotton for the cash crop. The animals were pigs and chickens. In this rotation, two soil-building crops, peanuts and cowpeas, were combined with two "heavy feeders," collards and corn. Sweet potatoes fit in as a crop that could pick up whatever was left and produce more than its share of nutrition. Peanuts, peanut hay, and cowpea hay were used to fatten hogs. Some corn was used for finishing. Carver's creed, "Start where you are, with what you have; make something of it," is the basis of his concept of the self-cycling homestead. For a particular climate and soil type the sweet potato was one pillar of this vision.

Baked sweet potatoes provide a substantial portion of a meal, including dessert, with very little input beyond labor. They provide more vitamin A than collards (8,100 international units per 100 grams, versus 7,800 in collards).

Collards, however, supply three times more vitamin C (76 mg, versus 22 in sweet potato) and 5 times more calcium (188 mg, versus 40 in sweet potato). In a pinch young sweet potato leaves, which are steamed as greens in Southeast Asia, easily make up the difference. The leaves are high in C and A and, especially, lutein. You never know when hard times will strike again. Sweet potato also has less than half the carbohydrates found in grains—32 grams per 100 grams versus more than 70 in grain. The sugars in sweet potato are beneficial for diabetics, stabilizing blood sugar and lowering insulin resistance.

In my years gardening in Pennsylvania I had been looking for a rotational break in my garden. I was overusing the land, producing tons of carrots and cole crops; and when bok choy, Chinese cabbage, and other brassicas became more popular, the crucifer problem got worse. I needed a crop that wasn't related to anything else, covered the soil all season like a green mulch, didn't require much work, and didn't eat up the compost needed for heavy feeders. You might think that such crops exist only in dreams, but since I've given the clues away already, you know I mean sweet potato.

My garden friends disagreed. They insisted that market crops were confined to the long summers and sandy soil along the Jersey Coast. If I hadn't bumped into an old local grower who happened to have an extra bushel of slips (rooted sweet potato shoots), I never would have tried. The slips were unbelievably productive. And when I looked into it, I discovered sweet potatoes were grown right across the central states, especially by the Amish. Home gardeners grow them as far north as Michigan. For years, Cornell University in Ithaca, New York, has developed new varieties for short-season areas. Market gardeners with moderately light soil and warm nights in September will do well. Home gardens with a well-worked clay loam will grow sweet potatoes, so long as the soil is not too rich and drains well.

Sweet potatoes (*Ipomoea batatas*) are a morning glory. Being in the family *Convolvulaceae*, they conflict with nothing else in the rotation, unless your garden happens to be infested with bindweed (Convolvulus). Sweet potatoes thrive in a lean, well-drained sandy loam. Extra nitrogen, even in the form of compost, will produce bloated and cracked roots that don't cure or keep. I found this out the hard way when part of my crop grew below a manure heap. The vines grew 15 feet long from the leached nutrients, re-rooting and sprouting sweet potatoes at every leaf node. The bloated roots, each as large as a football, were useful only as pig fodder. Although phosphorus and potassium are appreciated by these plants, the residues from previous compostings are all they need. Commercial growers use a 2-8-10 formula, which gives some idea of the plant's needs. Gardeners sometimes add wood ashes to the planted ridges to provide potassium, which raises the pH, but produces chunkier potatoes of good flavor. Sweet potatoes also tolerate a wide pH range (5.2 to 6.7). Lime is used only to counteract high aluminum soils, which are toxic to sweet potatoes.

Culture

Once you've grown your own sweet potatoes, you can grow your own slips. (Sweet potatoes from the supermarket may have been sprayed with maleic hydrazide, a sprout inhibitor and suspected carcinogen). In the fall select smooth, chunky potatoes free of corky scurf, pits, cracks, discoloration, and signs of rot or physical injury. Set these aside until about 6 to 8 weeks before melon transplanting time for your area (minimum soil temperature of 70°F). To check internal quality, a piece can be cut off the pointed end of the potato. The flesh should be deep orange (depending on variety) and free of greenish-black streaks.

The North Carolina Sweet Potato Commission notes that small roots produce as many slips as large ones. They estimate 15 slips per bedded tuber, but claim that pre-sprouted tubers yield 2 to 3 times more. To pre-sprout, store roots at 75 to 85°F with 90% humidity for 2 to 4 weeks until sprouts appear. Pre-sprouted tubers require only 4 to 5 weeks in a hot bed to produce twice as many slips, reducing care time and energy use.

Market growers can create 24-inch hot beds for sprouts in a greenhouse by covering the soil with clear plastic; pre-heat the soil to 85°F. Remove plastic and plant sweet potatoes with 1- to 2-inch spacing between tubers, covering with 1 inch of soil (3 inches will cause rot). Re-cover with plastic, with air hole punctures in 4-inch squares to prevent heat and carbon dioxide build up. Monitor desired 75°F temperature with a soil thermometer. Remove plastic when sprouts appear uniformly throughout the bed. Fertilize with composted nettle and/or seaweed tea. Most productive sprouts are 8 to 10 inches tall with 8 or more leaves.

In late winter, home gardeners can plant tubers indoors in 6-inch-deep flats. Use sandy loam and 1-inch soil cover. For clay loam, add half sand. Keep flats at 75°F in a boiler room or on a germination mat. Check temperature using a soil thermometer. Keep moist but never wet. When shoots rise about soil level, move to sunny location (70°F). Add an inch of soil when sprouts are 3 inches tall. Fertilize as above. Pull for planting when slips are about 8 inches tall and outside soil temperature is 70°F, whenever melons are planted in your area.

Last fall in a sunny window I placed a few potted green sweet potato plants with the big roots removed and tops pruned back. They sprouted slowly, somehow survived 50°F winter nights and by early spring produced 6 vines. I then buried the nodes (but not the terminal shoots) in four adjacent pots, producing dozens of vigorous slips.

In climates where melons are marginal, warm the growing area for 2 weeks with black plastic. Biodynamic growers spray the soil with horn manure (500) prior to laying plastic. In my medium loam, I raise long ridges 1 foot high, 2 feet wide, and 3½ to 4 feet apart. Ridges warm up faster and should run east to west, if possible, to form a southern slope. In chancy areas try slatted plastic tunnels. Sweet potatoes stop growing below 60°F, and rot below 50°F. They prefer a soil temperature above 70°F.

Slips are fairly tough. Homegrown slips will take off faster and produce more tubers earlier, but I've never seen even really badly wilted shipped crates of slips fail. In the central states I dipped purchased slips in compost-clay 500 slurry prior to planting, but the North Carolina Potato Commission cautions that even dipping in a common water bucket may spread disease if any slips are affected. Slips can be spaced 12 to 18 inches in rows 3 to 4 feet apart. Keep the slips watered until they perk up. Except in drought, sweet potatoes don't need more water.

When the vines start to run, biodynamic growers spray silica (501) on a root day. Since they grow all season, sweet potatoes can be sprayed on a schedule convenient with other root crops. Keep the patch well weeded in the early stages of growth. Later on, when the area is a sea of heart-shaped leaves, weeds will not affect yield. Vine tips can be used as a pot herb without damaging the plants, but don't bother digging for potatoes until late September, at least not north of Virginia. Sweet potatoes form late in the season, when summer days begin to shorten. In late August or early September, spray silica in the afternoon, during descending moon if possible. Valerian (507) helps the sweetening process.

Sweet potatoes need to be harvested promptly after the first frost nips the vines. Vines should be cut to prevent frost-spoiled juices from damaging the roots. Vines make excellent fodder for cattle, pigs, and goats, as well as first-rate vegetable compost. The best way I've found for digging sweet potatoes by hand is to stand on the north side of the ridge, grasp the central stem with one hand and push a spading fork into the north side of the ridge a foot behind the stem. Lift the fork and pull the stem at the same time. Since most potatoes form on the south side of the ridge, this causes the fewest injuries. Market gardeners sometimes adapt an old white-potato digger. In commercial sweet potato areas, specially designed diggers can be bought or borrowed.

Handle gently. Skins are tender. Cull and consume small, speared, and cut roots as food or fodder within three weeks. For about 10 days after harvest, cure medium to large undamaged roots in a warm, humid place (80° to 90°F) with some ventilation. I use the same place I cure winter squash. Curing heals scratches, and tightens and toughens the skins. Sound, uncured potatoes keep about a month; cured ones keep until spring or later. Sweet potatoes will not keep in a root cellar. They require a dry, warm place (55 to 60°F) to keep well. Store with winter squash. They will sweeten as the months roll by. Save smaller evenly shaped, chunky roots for sprouts in the spring.

Varieties

In North America, sweet potato and yam are the same plant. Both are *Ipomoea batatas*. The true yam (*Dioscorea*) is a memory of a tropical tuber never grown in the United States, whose name is used by southerners for some sweet potatoes. The important distinctions in variety selection are color and quality of flesh, and moist or dry.

Moist-fleshed potatoes include Centennial, Jewel, Garnet, Georgia Jet, Beauregard, and Puerto Rico. Centennial is widely grown, reliable, stores well, and has resistance to cork and wilt. Jewel, an improved Centennial, is my favorite variety. Flesh is rich, sweet, and deep orange, indicating high vitamin A. Both Jewel and Centennial are excellent, flavorful keepers. Georgia Red is very moist (a bit mushy for my taste) but adaptable to some northern locations. Beauregard's early maturity makes it well adapted to the North. Resistance to nematodes makes it valuable in the South. Fine eating quality. The plant-protected (PP) variety Evangeline grew well for me in the North, although not as well as my home-started slips; and you can't propagate it. The external sweet tubers are nematode-resistant. Puerto Rico is another good variety, available as Running Vine and Short Vine (Bunch) for small gardens. Vardaman is a soft fleshed, high-yielding variety with compact vines. Garnet is rich, sweet, and internally smooth, excellent for pie and popular in organic markets, grown widely in California. In Virginia, Baker is favored.

So-called dry-fleshed sweet potatoes include Jersey Orange and Nemagold, resistant to nematodes. It is a matter of taste and regional preference whether you choose a moist or dry type, but remember that White Yam, Jersey White, White Bunch, and Japanese White, although temptingly sweet, are unfortunately low in vitamin A. Japanese White is the most delicious sweet potato variety: dry, sweet with wonderful flavor and texture. When I bake orange-fleshed varieties I always add a few Japanese for pure eating pleasure. Japanese White Murasaki is resistant to nematode and fusarium root rot. Before choosing, search your local university extension on the internet, and talk to local growers for best regional varieties.

Sweet potato plants are available from many seed companies and wholesale growers that ship bare root plants; usually, a hundred-plant minimum. Market growers should confirm that plants are certified disease free. States where slips are grown extensively may suffer from monoculture and disease buildup.

SEED: 80 to 100 slips needed for a 100 foot row. 3 bushels of slips plant an acre.

GERMINATION: Plants do not grow well below 70°F. Sweet potatoes set in sandy loam will sprout in 2 to 3 weeks at 80°F.

DAYS TO HARVEST: 4 warm months.

MOON CALENDAR: All cultural practices, including biodynamic sprays, on root days, descending moon, if possible.

ROTATION: 3 years.

BIODYNAMIC SPRAYS: Horn manure (500) on land before setting out slips. Silica (501) when vines begin to run, sprayed several times during descending moon. In late August and early September, spray silica in the afternoon during the root formation. Spray valerian (507) during extended cloudy weather.

COMPANION PLANTS: Alternate rows of sweet potatoes with cowpeas, peanuts, and *umbelliferous* plants; in alternate mounds of corn; or beds of vertical plants such as the *Umbelliferae*. Avoid interplanting with rich soil lovers such as cole crops.

SOURCES: Many seed companies ship bare root bunches. For larger orders search online for wholesale suppliers in Tennessee, Alabama, or other southern states.

TOMATILLO

Tomatillo (*Physalis ixocarpa*, also called husk tomato) is a tomato-like nightshade wrapped in a beige papery husk, which apparently predates the tomato. The fruit is used green to make *salsa verde*, a Mexican hot sauce. Ripe tomatillos may be yellow, red, or purple, but are usually harvested green, when the fruit is still firm with tartness reminiscent of lemon or green apples. Tomatillos lack the juicy cavity of the tomato, making them easier to prepare as raw or cooked salsa.

Salsa verde can be made by simmering tomatillo for 5 minutes and then adding raw chopped onions, fresh cilantro leaves, fresh lime juice, fresh chopped hot peppers, sugar, and salt. Another method simmers all ingredients together. A third chops all ingredients raw and serves the raw salsa within the hour. To make a spicy tomatillo relish or jam, simmer tomatillos, chilies, garlic, fresh ginger, vinegar, sugar, and salt for 40 minutes until thick. In India tomatillos are added to curries. Raw tomatillos add zest to salads.

Nutritionally, tomatillos may be significant not only due to the usual suspects, but because instead of the usual tomato pepper antioxidant lycopene, tomatillos contain withanolides, which appear to show distinct anti-tumor and anti-inflammatory activity.

Culture

Tomatillos are not self-fruitful; two or more are needed for pollination. Once established in warm climates, tomatillo spreads invasively. In Kenya it is the major weed of agricultural land. Plants grow 4 to 5 feet with the ranginess and rankness similar to cherry tomatoes, but without tomato hairs. The small pointed smooth leaves are more like pepper leaves. Tomatillo produces good crops in most soils, but requires fairly good drainage and near-neutral pH. Culture is similar to tomato, but requires a much longer season. Most cultivars are not suitable for northern summers. In the North, even with short season varieties, follow a planting schedule for melons. In very hot dry climates tomatillo may also suffer. The ideal climate would be a long, warm, but not scorching summer.

In the central states, sow indoors in the greenhouse about 4 weeks before last frost, when melons are set out, soil temperature 70°F. Kentucky Extension recommends sowing indoors 3 to 4 weeks before last frost. New Jersey Extension recommends 4 to 6 weeks before last frost. In the North, Johnny's Selected Seeds catalog recommends setting out 4- to 5-week transplants 1 to 2 weeks after tomato transplanting. Sow the tiny seeds with tweezers, 3 seeds per 3-inch peat pot and thin to the strongest seedling. Set in the field 2 to 3 feet apart, 4 feet between rows.

In Mexico, tomatillos sprawl between rows of corn. In cooler climates, black or red plastic pre-warms the soil. Cage or trellis the vines; prune like tomatoes to control size. California Extension recommends plastic tunnels followed by staking to avoid fruit rot. Commercial growers apply moderate 9-8-8 fertilizers, which is high by organic or biodynamic standards. Drip irrigation is preferred to overhead to avoid powdery mildew late in the season when fruits are ripening.

Tomatillo is sometimes subject to tomato, cucumber, alfalfa, and potato mosaic viruses. Control aphid vectors and proximity to susceptible crops. Saved seed may transmit virus.

Insect pests include the huskworm in the South. Southern Exposure Seed Exchange suggests planting tomatillo as early as possible to avoid this pest. Potato beetles can be controlled with Spinosad.

Tomatillo is usually harvested green, when the husk begins to split. Fully ripe, the fruits fall to the ground. Fruits store for 2 to 4 weeks at 41 to 45°F.

Varieties

Toma Verde (60 days) is an early fruit variety, most likely to produce well in the North; it has large green to greenish-yellow fruit. De Milpa (70 days) has a strong pungent tomatillo flavor. Fruits are green and purple; it stores well. Purple (65 days) has attractive green husks with purple veins and deep purple fruits. Everona Large Green (90 days, long season) is a Mexican heirloom with 2-inch berries. It produces well in the hot southern summers, during periods of drought, and even in heavy clay soil. Pest resistant.

SEED: Tomatillo seed is half the size of tomato, about 17,000 to the ounce.
BIODYNAMIC PRACTICES: follow tomato schedule.

TOMATO

The history of the tomato is short—it is the most recently introduced staple food—and resistance to its introduction was initially very strong. Early explorers considered this fruit, which was called *tomati* or *tomatl* by native Mexicans, a curiosity, not a food. Tomato leaves are quite toxic; and since related alkaloids were already well known to Europeans from henbane (*Hyosycyamus niger*) and deadly nightshade (*Atropa belladona*), they called the tomato *Lycopersicon esculentum*, the edible wolfpeach. Not a very appetizing name.

I was surprised to learn that the tomato was not even eaten in the United States until the nineteenth century, despite Thomas Jefferson's inclusion of the tomato in his garden plan of 1781. The Italians were the first Europeans to consume the tomato in quantity, and it is difficult to imagine Italian cuisine without it. Although, indeed, pasta made its way north from a ninth-century Arab settlement in Sicily, the tomato only arrived from the New World centuries later, in 1590. Elsewhere in Europe the tomato was not grown for food until the mid-eighteenth century; and then it really took hold only as a greenhouse crop, due to cool cloudy summers.

The tomato still has its skeptics. Macrobiotics considers the extreme acidity (yin) to be unhealthful. The acrid taste of green tomatoes and immature green peppers correctly indicates the presence of alkaloids, which, however, does not mean that green tomato alkaloid (tomatine) is bad. Far from injuring test animals, tomatine bound to cholesterol and lowered LDL. Test animals had reduced incidence of liver and stomach cancers (Friedman 2007).

Many Europeans have believed that the tomato is carcinogenic. Indeed, the tomato is an easy target for the old natural philosophic tradition of the "doctrine of signatures," in which a plant's visual similarity to an organ indicates an imagined diagnostic connection; or in the case of the tomato, a warning. Indeed, many heirloom tomatoes do resemble animal organs or organs distorted by a disease such as cancer. The rank, formless habit of growth doesn't help either; nor does the peculiar acrid smell of the sticky, toxic sap in the leaves and stems that stain your hands as you tie the vines.

Despite these impressions, no clinical study has ever demonstrated that tomatoes cause cancer. Quite the opposite; populations such as Italians, who consume tomatoes in quantity have fewer cancers than those who eat them less frequently (American Cancer Society, 2010). Tomatoes are now thought to protect specifically against cancers of the cervix and prostate, when used as a regular part of the diet. Tomatoes may be important to the diet just because they are so different. Both tomatoes and red peppers produce a special form of pre-vitamin A called lycopene. This form of carotenoid, not found in other garden vegetables (but found in red grapefruit and watermelon) has been shown to be highly anti-carcinogenic in laboratory tests. Lycopene in tomatoes increases as the fruit ripens and deepens in flavor.

But that's just what's so frustrating about tomatoes. For a staple, they have an annoyingly narrow window of peak flavor. In New England, gardeners prepare the whole season for a race that's over in a matter of weeks. In some years (for example, the summer following the eruption of Mt. Pinotuba) true tomato flavor just doesn't arrive at all, especially in blight years and years with excessively rainy summers. Cherry types such as Sweet 100 are more flavor-reliable, but less useful in sandwiches, cooking, and canning. In all varieties, peak favor will be determined by choice of variety, early leaf development, and plant protection. These prepare the plant for its peak ripening period.

Tomato Diseases

I have always suspected that plant diseases increase as a plant is pulled farther and farther from the growing conditions where it first evolved. I think it likely that the so-called cold treatment of tomato seedlings to increase fruit set—where young plants are exposed to 55°F nights and 75 to 85°F days—harkens back to the origins of the tomato on the slopes of the Andes in Peru. There is no evidence, however, that Peruvians ate tomatoes; there are no pictures of tomato on ancient pottery, for example, even though eight wild species of tomato still persist in the Andes as weeds. The tomato first appears as a vegetable thousands of miles north in prehistoric Mexico, where almost no wild progenitors have been found. The jump of ecosystems into Mexico was not huge. The altitude of the central Mexican plateau is high, the nights cool, and days warm; but the jump to Europe and North America was an "eco-stretch."

Northern growers continue to stretch the tomato away from optimal conditions, and away from optimal flavor. The conventional greenhouse tomato is the most extreme example, more like a hospital than a garden. In conventional greenhouse culture, tomatoes are virtually removed from all normal earth and environmental contact. Growers fumigate the soil regardless of the disease resistance of the tomato variety. Commercial greenhouses can't be located where tomatoes or peppers are still growing, or near compost piles, lest airborne fusarium be sucked through greenhouse vents. Antiseptic footbaths prevent people and pets from tracking in soil pathogens. In other words, the soil, the earth itself, is no longer an ally, but the enemy. The greenhouse becomes, in effect, a space station.

There are many lessons here. (1) Disease increases with the distance from the optimal tomato-growing season. (2) Even with resistant varieties, disease prevention is to a great extent related to the same growing conditions that produce taste. (3) Every change you make in growing conditions can be tasted. (4) Don't jump into organic and biodynamic tomato forcing until you've learned the pitfalls, practiced a few seasons on a small scale, and evaluated the market without stars in your eyes. (5) Finally, remember the peculiar goal of greenhouse growers: their idea of a very good forced tomato is—so far—very mediocre in taste.

Fungus diseases in tomatoes grown outside follow a similar pattern. Most fungi appear when weather strays from optimal "tomato climate," becoming too hot and too moist. Likewise, when soil drainage is poor; when the plant is carrying too great a fruit load; or when the plant is grown under too great a pressure from large amounts of fertilizer. Disease is reduced by increasing plant vigor through biologically active soils, organic mulches, increased high-quality composted organic matter, nightshade rotation, avoidance of monoculture, increased use of leguminous cover crops, and use of biodynamic soil and compost inoculants.

Alternaria solani, the cause of tomato early blight, one of the most destructive tomato diseases, may first appear in the greenhouse, causing the damping off of seedlings. It may appear again as stem canker, collar rot, or leaf blight. Leaf blight first affects the oldest leaves, then works its way upward. Brown spots become target-like. Leaves turn yellow, wither, and drop from the plant. Plants with stem canker may retain wilted leaves but produce few fruits; leaf blights tend to be worse when plants are loaded with fruit. Alternaria then infects the fruit as sunken lesions.

Since alternaria may always be present, the best solution is to keep plants growing vigorously, starting in the greenhouse. Use compost-based potting mix, don't crowd seedlings, and use fans for good air circulation. Water early and let plants dry by late afternoon. Give liquid feedings of fermented nettle/compost tea, liquid seaweed, or fish emulsion. Tomato cultivars tolerant to early blight include Mountain Fresh, Juliet (plum), and Defiant. Cornell Extension also lists Old Brooks, a large warm-season heirloom as resistant to early and late blight.

Biologically active soils confer some resistance. Keep the soil fed with compost made with manure, leaves, and plant refuse (not from nightshades). Use legume and rye cover crops to increase nitrogen and organic matter. Rock phosphate strengthens stems and improves fruit quality. Packing tomatoes tightly in the row cuts air circulation. Determinate plants (see following section on varieties for definition) sprawling on the ground invite infection; so do wounds caused by insects. Shot holes from flea beetles allow entrance of fungal spores. Protect young plants with row covers. Some organic growers spray copper fungicide prophylactically before symptoms of fungus disease appear, but copper fungicides may adversely affect beneficial soil organisms. Monitor soil levels of copper to avoid toxicity, which gives another reason for at least a 3-year rotation. Seed savers should kill residual fungus spores from alternaria and anthracnose by soaking seed in hot water (122°F) for 22 minutes.

The fungus that caused the Irish Potato Famine, *Phytophthora infestans*, caused havoc in the Northeast and Midwest tomato crop in 2009. *P. infestans* causes late blight in tomatoes and potatoes. Late blight presents as purplish-black lesions on stems or leaves, with whitish spore growth appearing on the edges of the lesion in humid weather, especially on the undersides of the leaf. If white spores fail to appear, place an infected leaf and a piece of damp paper towel inside a clear plastic bag. After 12 hours the appearance of white spores will confirm diagnosis. Spores are airborne and flourish with high humidity, rainfall, and overhead irrigation. Immediately destroy infected plants, including potato haulms and nightshade weeds by bagging or burning. There is no cure once symptoms appear. Some organic growers spray copper fungicides or the biocontrol Serenade prophylactically, although Cornell Extension points out that late blight occurs too sporadically to justify prophylactic sprays. Matt's Wild Cherry appears to be late blight-resistant. Likewise, Legend, Mountain Magic, Plum Regal, Juliet (plum), and Defiant Ph R. are somewhat resistant.

I find tomato wilt diseases hard to tell apart. Bacterial wilt is caused by ralstonia *(Pseudomoneas solanacearum)*. It occurs more frequently in warmer climates, at high temperatures, high soil moistures, high pH (above 7), and on land infested with nematodes. At first, lower leaves wilt on a hot day but recover at night. A few days later, the entire plant wilts suddenly. Cut stems that are squeezed or placed in water emit slimy yellow, green, or gray ooze. Unlike bacterial canker there is no yellowing of leaves (chlorisis). Bacterial wilt cannot be controlled directly; other than maintaining plant vigor with biologically active soils and organic nitrogen, and by controlling root-knot nematodes (using beneficial SF nematodes).

Fusarium causes plants to wilt more slowly than bacterial wilt. Sometimes the entire plant yellows and wilts; at other times, fusarium may wilt the lower leaves on only one side. Fusarium-infected stems show a drier, firmer rot. Root-knot nematodes also exacerbate fusarium wilt. Control nematodes and use fusarium-resistant varieties, designated (F). Fusarium lasts a long time in the soil and requires a 6-year rotation to suppress.

Verticillium wilt favors cooler weather than fusarium, which grows stronger the farther south you go; but otherwise, verticillium symptoms often appear similar to fusarium. However, just to confuse you, verticillium sometimes just yellows and dries, but doesn't wilt. Bag or burn infected plants. The only controls are resistant varieties (V) and a 5-year rotation with corn or grasses.

Other tomato diseases that limit production include septoria leaf spot: small watery spots appear scattered thickly over the leaves in wet weather and under heavy fruit load. Control with copper fungicide or Serenade. Rotate tomatoes three or four years. Grey leaf spot causes small dark spots on the underside of older leaves, which yellow and drop. Bag, burn, and rotate tomatoes three to four years.

Curly-top virus is common on beets, some varieties of peppers, and on tomatoes. It is precipitated by excessive sun stress and poor leaf cover, causing twisted, curled leaves, and the stunting of the entire plant.

Tobacco mosaic virus (T) affects all nightshades. Avoid rotation with eggplant, peppers, potatoes, petunia, tobacco, and flowering tobacco, as well as weedy fields containing jimson weed, ground cherry, and horse nettle. Tobacco mosaic first appears as malformed leaflets, mottled older leaves, and grayish appearance. Young leaves tend to be long and stringy, pointing upward. This is often a problem in greenhouses; pruning knives and scissors should be dipped in household bleach between plants.

Blossom drop and blossom end rot are not diseases but disorders arising from adverse growing conditions. Blossom drop can be caused by low moisture, hot winds, night temperatures below 55°F, or day temperatures above 95°F. Temperature above 90°F seriously limits seed germination and prevents fruit set. Blossom end rot, also a cultural disorder, reminds us that the tomato is really a small red balloon. It swells with availability of nutrients and rain, and shrinks when these diminish, leaving a brown leathery area opposite the stem. Calcium increases nutrient availability (manure composts are usually sufficient), and mulch maintains an even supply of water.

Biodynamic growers spray horn silica (501), which works internally in the plant to strengthen resistance to fungi. Silica sprays can begin from the first true leaf through to the ripening stage. Equisetum, on the other hand, works from the outside, on the surface of the leaf, making it less favorable to fungal growth. Spray equisetum liberally over the seedbed after sowing and during germination. Spray with silica (501) weekly after the first true leaf and, especially, at first flower bud formation; at first fruit set, several times during the green stage, and when fruit begins to color.

Insects

Tomato hornworms, fruit worms, and other caterpillars sometimes bother tomatoes. *Bt* (*Bacillus thuringiensis*) controls feeding caterpillars, as do *braconid* and *polistes* wasps. Egg cases on the backs of hornworms are the work of the braconids. Encourage wasps with flowering *umbelliferous* plants (dill, fennel, archangelica, and so forth). When fruit worms look sick (shriveled, poor color), they can be blended and used as a spray to spread a disease against caterpillar, nuclear polyhedrosis virus.

Flea beetles go into a feeding frenzy during reproductive periods. Floating row covers can protect young tomato plants; older plants are usually past harming. Cutworms can devastate transplants on new ground, especially ground that was formerly sod. Use cardboard collars 1½ inches below ground and 3 inches above. Colorado potato beetles sometimes eat tomato leaves. Heavily mulched plants are often unaffected. Bt San Diego, marketed as M-One, is an effective control of larvae.

Whiteflies, a problem in overheated greenhouses, look like flying dandruff. Let temperature drop to 55°F at night. Yellow boards coated with Vaseline or tanglefoot work as a trap. If released early during a greenhouse infestation, the tiny parasitic wasp *Encarsia formosa* provides adequate control. In summer, vegetable oil sprays are an easy, non-toxic way to suffocate white fly adults, nymphs, and eggs. Many growers have observed that inadequate nutrition severely augments insect attack. Commercial greenhouse mixes are "hollow" from a biodynamic point of view. Whiteflies are rarely a problem outdoors.

Nematodes (N) are extremely minute, sightless, worm-like creatures. The fungi nurtured by good compost and leaf mold produce an astounding arsenal of lassos, glues, and harpoons that help eliminate nematodes. In the South where heat is high, frost is shallow, and organic matter low, nematode resistant varieties may be necessary, but don't underestimate your invisible allies. They ask only to be invited by biodynamic compost and organic cultural practices.

Culture

The sweetness and interior quality of tomatoes depends upon adequate supplies of potassium, phosphorous, and calcium. Compost is often enough. Wood ashes add a measure of sweetness. Rock phosphate can be added, if phosphorus tests low. Calcium (provided by wood ash and lime) and steady supplies of water are needed to prevent the irregular spurts of growth that cause blossom end rot. Lime may also be used to raise pH to the optimum 6 to 6.5, which the Hawaii Extension says may also lower fusarium in the field. Even so, organic growers find that high levels of organic matter allow for a much wider range of pH, from 5.5 to 8.5. Tomatoes, however, are fairly tolerant of pH.

Compost can either be fully or half-rotted. Raw manures and high nitrogen organic fertilizers produce excessive leaf growth and poor fruit set susceptible to fungi. Organic and biodynamic growers get good yields with low incidence of disease using only compost and legume cover crops. The USDA at Beltsville, Maryland, and many northern growers recommend hairy vetch; others use fava beans (a cold soil legume) and various clovers. Calley peas also tolerate cool conditions and more acidic soils. In warmer climates crimson clover, Austrian winter peas, bell beans (a field fava), and many other legumes provide ample nitrogen and organic matter. The USDA at Beltsville has developed a complete program for planting tomatoes into fall-sown hairy vetch, which could be modified for organic growers.

Traditional biodynamic growers isolate tomatoes, leaving tomato fences in the same place for seven years and feeding tomatoes their own composted haulms. These practices have never made sense to me. They sound like a recipe for disease buildup and soil depletion. Better to rotate like other crops, at least three years between nightshades; six years where disease is a problem. Better to interplant with legumes, lettuce, spinach, corn salad, herbs, and the onion family.

Extra-early indeterminate tomatoes can be started in a heated greenhouse or sunroom 8 weeks prior to last expected frost. Low light levels produce leggy, unproductive plants that often sunburn and stunt. Large potted determinate tomato plants can be permanently stunted if transplanted to cool conditions after fruit set. These should be protected until outdoor soil temperatures exceed 50°F, or transplanted outside under plastic.

For mid-season crops, those timed to fruit at the season of peak flavor, sow no earlier than 6 weeks before last expected frost. Tomato seeds are big enough to sow thinly, one at a time, using a tweezers or wet toothpick. Cells or flats sown with just the amount of seed needed for sturdy plants will repay in time saved. Tomato seeds have a high germination rate, even after many years.

Most organic gardening experts recommend soilless mixes for flats and cells to prevent transmission of soil-borne disease. I've known this for 35 years, but because I always want to recycle organic materials at hand, I've used only compost and unsterilized garden soil. Both biodynamic compost made with about 25% cow manure and compost made from maple leaves have produced vigorous growth and seem to eliminate damping off. The biodynamic approach is to enhance soil life, not eliminate it. In my experience, plant vigor is a huge factor in overcoming soil pathogens.

Whatever mix you choose, maintain temperature from 75 to 85°F, usually from a greenhouse heating pad. When seed leaves appear, flats should be moved to a bright, sunny location. Keep flats from drying out, but never overwater or water late in the day, which may encourage fungi. Sow seeds 1 inch apart, 3 or 4 rows to the flat; or 1 seed per cell in special germination flats. Transplant after the first true leaves appear and plants are about 1½ inches tall. Transplant to cell flats, 2- to 4-inch peat pots, or put 12 to 24 seedlings in a standard flat.

Extension research has shown that tomato plants can be made more productive if seedlings are allowed to cool down to 52 to 56°F at night for 10 days to 3 weeks after the first true leaf appears (not the seed leaf). Day temperatures can rise to 80°F, so long as nights are cool. I call this "the Andes Treatment," an eco-memory of conditions from their natal habitat.

Extra-early indeterminate plants can be transplanted again to 1- or 2-gallon plastic pots and staked in the pot. Rock phosphate can be added to improve fruit quality. Side-dressings include fermented nettle plants, compost/tea, liquid seaweed, and fish emulsion. Biodynamic growers spray both equisetum tea to inhibit fungus Horn Silica (501) when a few true leaves appear, and thereafter every two weeks.

A week prior to setting plants in the field, cut back watering to the minimal and expose flats daily to direct sunlight. Outside soil can also be pre-warmed by covering tomato beds with black plastic for a week prior to setting out. Soil for early crops benefits from compost fortified with rock or coral phosphate. Otherwise, dust beds with rock phosphate in spring. Avoid planting outside until night temperatures exceed 45°F. Row cover over arcs of rebar or #9 wire eliminate wind and raise ambient temperature. "Walls of Water" (plastic tubes filled with water that surround the plants) are expensive but protect tomatoes to as low as 16°F. Home gardeners sometimes wrap tomato cages in plastic until the weather warms.

Strong transplants can always be planted more deeply than they grew as seedlings, but if the plants become leggy, tomatoes can be buried at a 30° angle leaving only the top 5 inches of leaves and growing point above the soil. Peat pots not fully buried may wick water from the root ball. If cutworms are a problem, wrap the lower portion of the main tomato stem with waxed paper. If you use plastic mulch for weed control, consider red plastic, which increases yields up to 20% and reduces early blight (Penn State Extension).

How close tomatoes are planted depends on the tomato type, the method of support, and whether the plants will be pruned. Support is important, since fruit ripens poorly on the ground and tends to rot. Heavy mulches of oak or maple leaves minimize soil-borne decay for unsupported plants, but staking increases flavor and early ripening. Determinate plants don't need pruning but still benefit from staking. Determinate plants can be set 1 to 2 feet apart in rows 3 feet apart. Indeterminate single-stem can be set 1½ to 2½ feet apart with 4 feet between rows. Double stem on grape wire, or cattle fence can be set at 2 feet apart. Un-pruned plants supported by heavy-duty wire cages need 2 feet between each cage.

Single-stem pruning produces larger, earlier fruit, but in some varieties results in more cracking and less leaf cover against sunscald. To prune single-stem, remove all side shoots that grow in the leaf axils, leaving only the terminal growing point. Tie the main stem with twine loosely to a stake or fence. Continue to tie weekly, or spiral the main stem around the twine as it grows. For double-stem, allow one axial branch to grow in addition to the main stem and tie to the fence as above. In either case, fencing should be fairly sturdy, with posts 6 feet above the ground, 8 to 10 feet apart; but not so deeply set that they cannot be easily moved in the fall. Some growers find a single line of heavy wire is sufficient; others prefer cattle fence, with more places to tie.

Wire cages must be strong. Most purchased cages are not. If you have space to store them, using cylinders of concrete reinforcing wire will work. Years ago, I saw one garden with cylinders made of fencing too small to reach through; the ripe fruit was growing inside, just beyond reach! Paste tomatoes need some sort of cage, although I have often tied them to cattle fence. The worst mistake is to stop pruning and tying halfway through the season. Dozens of useless stems appear and the weight of the fruit will break stems, using earlier ties as gallows.

Varieties

Tomato varieties are either determinate or indeterminate. Determinate types set most of their fruit at once and grow very little thereafter. They are a good choice for canning and paste, since the fruit ripens all at once. Many are subject, however, to early blight (alternaria), a problem in extra-early tomatoes. Indeterminate plants grow in all directions even after fruit has set. Their vigor sometimes makes them more disease-resistant, denoted by the letters listed after the name (V for resistance to verticillum wilt, F for fusarium wilt, T for tobacco mosaic virus, N for nematode resistance, and so forth).

Extra-early tomatoes are nearly all determinate. Their quality is so mediocre that if I lived in an area that couldn't ripen main season tomatoes, I'd rather return to the earlier Italian cuisine, before the tomato arrived, and eat my pasta with greens, garlic, and olive oil. Whatever the variety, the season is too early to develop classic tomato flavor; many are too acid. The best, such as Moskvich (60 days), have been developed for colder climates such as Siberia, Sweden, or the Ukraine, where they have no choice. One variety, strangely named Sophie's Choice (55 days, determinate), really sums up the problem. Was the breeder imagining trading her children for an early ripe tomato? Or was the breeder implying that extra-early tomatoes are a choice no one should have to make? Whatever you decide, put down black plastic for 2 weeks prior to transplanting. Follow with heavy protective row cover or Walls of Water, and so forth.

With early hybrids the story is the same. They tempt you with increased yield and disease resistance, but to me they taste "store bought." Fourth of July (49 days, indeterminate) is probably the earliest hybrid you can grow.

Mid-sized fruits are firm, juicy, and fairly tasty. Many gardeners favor Early Girl hybrid (59 days, indeterminate or bush, V, F1 and 2) but I find the flavor slightly green and too acid. Some descendants of Early Girl have improved taste and disease resistance.

Long-season heirlooms have set the standard for tomato flavor, which is so various that it requires years of exploration. The downsides are a brief flavor window (optimal only 3 to 5 days after harvest), short shelf life, and almost no disease resistance.

One of the earliest tomatoes with classic tomato flavor is the heirloom Super Lakota, also called Super Sioux (75 days indeterminate). Super Lakota is both productive and adaptable to cooler, wetter tomato seasons. Most heirlooms require a long sunny season with moderate warmth (70 to 85F). Many consider Brandywine (85 days determinate) the reigning queen of flavor, but Brandywine's shortcomings (low yield and no disease resistance) urge you always to plant a mix of varieties. Other contenders for the tomato crown include Prudens Purple (75 days, indeterminate), which is similar to Brandywine in flavor, but 10 days earlier, more productive, crack-resistant, and more widely adapted. Also Cherokee Purple (80 days, indeterminate), with deep purple color and tangy "unmatched" classic tomato flavor. And Pineapple and Big Rainbow (both 90 days, indeterminate) produce colorful golden yellow "beefsteak" tomatoes streaked with red. Each are rated "best ever," but may fully ripen too late in the season for northern growers. Italian heirloom Costoluto Genovese (78 days, indeterminate) also needs a long season. It is best for warm central, southern, or western states. This large beefsteak sets well in heat from midsummer far into the autumn, with delicious complex flavor and some disease resistance. Arkansas Traveler (89 days, indeterminate) is more widely adapted and sets highly flavorful fruits, not only in heat and drought, but also in the cloudy Northwest. Fruit is crack-resistant and keeps well. The Spanish heirloom Valencia (76 days, indeterminate) is a beautiful sweet orange tomato with classic flavor and texture. Heirlooms work best for home gardens and roadside stands.

Hybrid tomatoes were created to improve disease resistance, yield, and firmness for shipping. For more than fifty years classic tomato flavor and nutritional value have declined in market varieties. The conflict between flavor and shipping has never been resolved, but many hybrids have good flavor for home and local market. Better Boy (70 days, indeterminate, VF, NA) has proved its reliability and disease resistance for decades, especially where nematodes are a problem in the South. In areas with a long growing season, Burpee's Big Boy (78 days, indeterminate, VF) comes close to classic tomato flavor. A reliable producer of large deep red beefsteaks. Big Beef (73 days, indeterminate) adds an even more complete package of disease resistance to very good flavor. Celebrity (70 days, indeterminate, VF1 and 2, TMV, NA) is a compromise: very widely adapted, vigorous, high yielding, and crack-resistant with large fruit of good quality. Some of the newer crosses such as Pink Beauty (74 days, indeterminate) come closer to balancing firmness and disease resistance with excellent flavor. Country Taste Hybrid (90 days, indeterminate, VF1 and 2, TMV) combines heirloom beefsteak flavor with high yield, retention of freshness after harvest, and disease resistance. Others such as Brandy Boy (78 days) are earlier, more productive and highly flavored hybrids of heirlooms.

For the taste of a possibly original meso-American tomato, plant a few of Matt's Wild Cherry (60 days, indeterminate), a different species of tomato altogether. Collected from the wild in Mexico, these unique plants are vigorous and somewhat blight-resistant with small very sweet (11% brix) soft red fruits, not high-yielding. Fine by me, since most cherry varieties produce more fruit than home gardeners can handle.

Cracking is a perennial problem for cherry tomatoes. Chadwick's Cherry (90 days, indeterminate), for example, is sweet, flavorful, and prolific. It almost makes up for a lack of crack resistance in sheer volume of fruit. In some years and for some varieties half the fruit cracks after a rain. Market growers note crack resistance when they purchase seed. The German indeterminate Gardener's Delight, also called Sugar Lump, bears very sweet, crack-resistant cherries from mid-season to frost. Sometimes, unique color, such as the dark purple of Black Cherry (70 days, indeterminate) trumps other traits with sheer novelty and exceptional heirloom taste. Golden Gem (65 days, indeterminate) also pairs well with Chocolate Cherry in color, though it surpasses it in sweetness (10% brix), crack resistance, and high yield. Market growers increase sales by offering boxes of mixed colors—purple, yellow, orange, and red.

Hybrid doesn't guarantee crack-resistance, either. The popular Sweet 100 types crack easily. Supersweet 100 (65 days, indeterminate) is a high vitamin, disease-resistant cherry tomato with a brix so high it could be stacked on a candy counter; but it cracks easily. Sweet Million (60 days), however, offers increased crack- and disease-resistance. Also consider planting Marcellino (65 days, determinant), a tasty cherry that retains texture and quality a month after harvest. Sun Gold (62 days, indeterminate) is an extremely popular orange supersweet, crack-resistant with exceptional flavor. Black Pearl (65 days, indeterminate) offers a new flavor for salads: when chilled, fruits taste like grapes. Grape tomatoes, however, have no grape flavor, though many are highly crack-resistant. Juliet (60 days), for example, makes excellent salad, sauce, and salsa, with very strong disease resistance. Look also for resistance to late blight in grape varieties such as Red Pearl (58 days).

Paste tomatoes have less juice and more body to boil down quickly for sauce. Heirlooms such as Myona, Amish Paste, and San Marzano (all about 85 days, indeterminate) are highly productive with superior old-fashioned tomato flavor. I took a gallon of sauce I made from my San Marzanos on a school canoe trip, and those teenagers couldn't believe the flavor! Even "gourmet" sauce from jars tastes washed out by comparison. Unfortunately, heirlooms often succumb to leaf disease late in the season. Roma (76 days, determinate, VFN) is the only reliable disease-resistant heirloom I know of; it makes very good sauce. Viva Italia (80 days, determinate, V, F1 and 2, A, N, and so forth) is a hybrid of Roma with increased yield vigor and disease resistance. It is excellent for the South, where nematodes are a problem. Margherita Hybrid (75 days, determinate, VF), like San Marzano, is multi-use, excellent for sauce, salads, and roasting. Finally, Health Kick Hybrid (75 days, determinate, VFA) is not only a high-yield pasta and salad tomato, but also produces 50% more lycopene (thought to reduce cancer risk) than any other tomato.

- SEED: About 8,000 per ounce: an average of 128,000 per pound. A packet of standards contains 125 to 200 seeds and produces 90 to 150 transplants. A packet of hybrids contains about 40 seeds and makes about 30 transplants. An ounce of seed produces at least 6,000 transplants. An ounce of seed carefully sown will transplant an acre.
- GERMINATION: 85%; 7 to 14 days at 80°F. Except for cold treatment grow at 60 to 68°F.
- VIABILITY: 4 years.
- DAYS TO HARVEST: 50 to 75 days.
- MOON CALENDAR: All culture, including biodynamic sprays in fruit, ascending moon, if possible. In areas with leaf blight, spray silica and equisetum on leaf days.

ROTATION: At least 3 years between nightshades (tomato, pepper, potato, eggplant); 6-year rotation where disease has been a problem. Follow nightshades with a rye cover crop, if possible.

BIODYNAMIC SPRAYS: Horn manure (500) on potting soil and on field. Silica (501) on growing transplants at least once; equisetum (508) if fungus is a problem in the greenhouse. Compost-clay 500 dip on transplant roots when planting. Silica frequently when plants are established, both before flowering and during fruiting. Equisetum and valerian (507) in cloudy weather. Spraying should done be in the late morning. Tomatoes benefit from stinging nettle spray and liquid seaweed.

COMPANION PLANTS: Tomato is considered a loner by some biodynamic growers. Tomatoes can be planted in the asparagus patch in association with basil and parsley. Nettles (a stinging invasive plant!) grown nearby are said to improve growth and improve internal quality. So also parsley, basil, borage, and marjoram. Marigolds, calendula, and nasturtium repel some insects and nematodes. *Umbelliferous* plants (celery, dill, chervil, parsley, and so forth) are good companions; other nightshades are not. Onions, garlic, and shallots are compatible. Intercrop with fast-growing spinach and salad. Interplanted legumes increase yield.

TURNIP

Why is there such an enormous difference in nutritional value between roots and leaves? Turnip roots (*Brassica rapa*), for example, have barely a trace of vitamin A, and 36 mg of vitamin C per 100 grams, while turnip leaves skyrocket to 7,000 international units of A and 139 mg of C, 2¾ the C of orange juice. Likewise beets, which rise from 20 units of A and 10 mg of C in the root to 6,000 and 30 in the leaves. Only the carrot holds its own in the root, although, I suspect its mere 8 mg of C must be vastly higher in the leaves.

The reason is that the leaf is the biological center of life on earth. The leaf is actually a place, an exact location, which—without exaggeration—is as exotic as Paradise. Imagine a site inaccessible to GPS because it is never static, always moving, as if the air were broken into a billion shifting points of growth, a constantly changing window of stained glass, spread horizontally over the earth. Leaves spread from growing tips into a vast plane. They are minute meeting points of earth and sky, thin as a slice under an electron microscope, as broad as a continent. I totally agree with Goethe, the German poet and leaf morphologist who said that if you can't begin to perceive this constantly shifting location, if you can't begin to grasp that the leaf is the primary agent of the metamorphosis of plants, "you will wander forever a sorry guest upon the earth." Biologically, the temple of our existence is built out of leaves. For us as gardeners, leaves are the litmus test for everything we do.

The leaf is not merely a static Euclidean plane with the top part facing sunlight and the bottom part facing dark earth. A leaf is not a thing; it's a rhythm, which taken as a totality — its coming into being in the meristem, its spreading outward in the horizontal plane and its final fading downward—is the breathing organ of our planet. I think of the leaf as a continual exchange between earth and sky, where the invisible seams that sew the world together are made visible—hourly, daily, seasonally, year after year.

Over the years I've learned more by sight than by science whether a leaf is growing well, and whether it will keep us well. For every plant and variety there is a right tone of green, neither oversaturated nor chlorotic, and a corresponding depth of flavor, which provides a key to garden culture and nutritional value. With the precipitous decline in the nutritional value of commercial crops, this has become essential to learn. Turnip greens are a good schooling in this regard. Their wild pungent *cruciferous* flavor is evidence of unusually high antioxidant level. Turnip greens have twice the calcium of broccoli. This would have been no news to instinctive gardeners such as the ancient Romans, who according to Pliny, considered turnips second in importance only to beans and grains.

Brassica rapa shares the strong antioxidant profile of other brassica leaves. *B. rapa* leaves are high in isorhamnetin, exceeded only by Chinese chives (*Allium tuberosum*), dill weed, and parsley. Antioxidant levels are highest in flower buds, the tiny green sepals that wrap around the flowers. Buds from bolted turnips and Chinese greens (also *B. rapa*) add pungency to salads and as a last-second addition to stir-fries. I graze on bolted buds every chance I get.

In lab experiments isorhamnetin has inhibited several cancers (Universities of Minnesota and Seoul 2011; East China University 2006). Isorhamnetin reduces HDL cholesterol (Sichuan University 2007), detoxifies the liver in lab rats (Yamagata U. 2008), inhibits adipose fat cells (Seoul National U. 2009), functions as a vasodilator, reducing the risk of cardiac incidents (U. of Granada 2007), and reduces serum glucose in diabetics (Toyama Medical U. Japan 2002).

Whether you like to eat turnip greens and roots depends partly on how young and well grown they are. The first turnips I ever tasted were old winter stored roots, bitter as sin. I avoided them for years. I should note, however, that some people are genetically twice as sensitive as others to bitterness in turnip leaves and roots (Monall Center 2006). The key to growing flavorful not-too-bitter greens and sweet, fine-grained, tender roots is quick growth, which means ample water, plenty of compost, cool temperatures, and early harvest. In the South, turnips are fall-sown and harvested well into the winter. Ice Bred White Egg is hardy down to 6°F. Their winter hardiness was one reason Pliny recommended them.

Harvest turnip greens young, when roots are 2 to 3 inches in diameter. For storage turnips, stay with rutabaga. Young 2-inch turnip roots are delicious raw, diced in salads. Young leaves can be stir-fried or steamed with garlic, onions, and olive oil; or, traditionally southern, with a few strips of bacon. Many southern recipes call for 30 minutes of boiling, even a change of water to remove bitterness; but this refers to older greens. Better to harvest roots at 2 inches while both greens and roots are tender and sweet. Spring-sown turnips have to be watched closely, lest hot dry spells ruin their quality. Europeans grate turnips to make sauerkraut. In Asia turnips are pickled, especially scarlet varieties.

Culture

Given moist cool weather, turnips grow well in any soil that produces good cabbages. The quality of the turnips below is always indicated by their greens above. If greens are yellowed, shot with holes, or lack a vibrant green characteristic of rapid growth, the turnips below will be sharp, bitter, and pithy. The need for organic matter increases as the season warms and dries. In light sandy soils, insect problems, especially flea beetles, often increase to the point of ruining the crop; best to sow and grow under floating row cover.

In most areas, midsummer crops should be avoided unless irrigation, row covers and high-organic matter soils are available. Usually an early spring sowing and a late summer sowing are more successful. Turnips are direct-seeded, sown as soon as soil can be worked in spring, 12 to 24 seeds to the foot, ¼ to ½ inch deep, in rows 12 to 15 inches apart. In soils that tend to crust, cover the garden furrow with ½ inch of fine compost instead of soil. Seeds germinate faster and seedlings are more vigorous with compost cover; this is obviously practical only in home gardens.

Seeds germinate quickly, usually in a week to 10 days, given 65 to 70°F daytime temperatures. In some areas flea beetles make seedlings disappear the day of emergence. Biodynamic compost, medium clay loam, and horn manure (500) increase cation (ion) exchange capacity (uptake of nutrients), and decrease insect predation; but many growers rely on row covers to prevent flea beetles and cabbage maggots from reaching the plants. Bury the edges of the row cover the same day you sow. During flea beetle feeding frenzy, pesticides never provide sufficient control for quality greens.

Horn silica (501) can be sprayed once for small bunching turnips (thin to 1 inch between plants), since these are ready not long after the spring radishes. Storage turnips (thinned to 2 to 3 inches) can be sprayed twice with 501 and fed with liquid seaweed or compost/fermented nettle tea when plants have formed a full green rosette. Make visual observations and taste tests for the optimal harvest time of greens and roots: usually 30 to 50 days from direct sowing, depending on conditions. Neither roots nor greens hold well in the ground. When growing for greens, irrigation is desirable in most areas. Greens can be cut and re-cut again. Roots can also be left in the ground in the fall for re-cut greens, but the roots themselves will not be edible. Storage roots can be tennis ball- to softball-sized, but lack the sweetness and internal quality of rutabaga.

Varieties

The large aging turnips I learned to hate were Purple Top White Globe (55 days). This old variety is really very good at 3-inch maximum. In areas with mild winters Purple Top can be left in the ground for greens and harvested all winter. Ice Bred White Egg (45 days) is fast growing and frost tolerant (to 6°F) with very tender roots. Tokyo Cross Hybrid (35 days) is even faster—35 days for 2-inch roots, 70 days for 5-inch roots of good quality. Harukei Hybrid (38 days) is grown for sweet, fruity 1- to 2-inch baby turnips for bunching with dark green hairless leaves. White Lady Hybrid (35 days) produces mild sweet roots with smooth tender tops; widely adaptable and bolt tolerant.

Seven Top (45 days) is an old variety grown exclusively for greens but, again, must be harvested young. The root is woody and inedible. Mostly used in the South during cool weather.

Amber Globe (63 days), a fall crop and 5-inch storage turnip with sweet yellow flesh, probably higher in vitamin A. Also used for winter greens in areas with minimal frost. Ohno Scarlet (55 days) is used in Asia for red turnip pickles.

SEED: An ounce (about 8 to 13,000 seeds) sows an average of 350 feet.
   1 gram (160 to 450 seeds) sows 15 to 41 feet at 11 seeds per foot.

GERMINATION: 80%; 10 days at 70°F.

VIABILITY: 5 years.

DAYS TO HARVEST: 35 to 60 days.

MOON CALENDAR: All practices in root signs, descending moon, if possible, unless plants are used for greens, then leaf sign.

ROTATION: 3 years; 6 years if root maggot or cabbage diseases are persistent problems.

BIODYNAMIC SPRAYS: Horn manure (500) before sowing. Silica (501) in morning and leaf sign if greens are used, later when roots begin form spray in afternoon, root day, descending moon.

COMPANION PLANTS: Chard, lettuce, celery, peas, leeks, spinach, and mixed. See cabbage for other brassica companion plants. Strong herbs and highly diverse mixed culture deter insects.

WATERMELON

It has been four decades since I had my first lesson in biodynamics. The teacher was old; the lesson (to me) was new; the occasion unpremeditated. Margareta Leuder, my first gardening teacher, was slicing open a watermelon for her great-grandson and recalling her childhood in the Sonoran Desert. Although still an active biodynamic gardener at the time, she had not grown that particular watermelon. She might have been grumbling about that fact, muttering discontentedly under her breath that shipped-in fruit had no value. In her opinion it was better to eat weeds—which in fact she did, nearly every day. The big problem as she saw it was to convince her adult grandson—really an impossible task, since he was even more headstrong than she was, and had no taste for weeds whatsoever. Not that she didn't try. She even froze weeds from the garden for her great-grandchildren to eat in winter. But her efforts were not particularly appreciated.

When the knife cut through the rind, the huge watermelon fell into two halves. Inside were black seeds and red flesh glistening in the sunlight, swirling into three red streams, strangely like an embryo, a giant red embryo. She tapped the rind with her knife and continued her grumbling monologue about the desert, about the Mexican Indians at the turn of the century, about the lack of water.

"You don't know what water is," she complained. "I can tell you've never even been thirsty. You don't appreciate it—either the streams outside this watermelon or the ones inside it."

She said this with a force that was completely unexpected, beyond anything I could imagine. She described how, as a five-year-old living in the Sonoran Desert in 1905, she had learned the value of water. She described how the rich landowner upstream cut off their water supply to force them to sell. She described a child's pain as she dragged bucket after bucket to her father's precious peach trees, which he considered more valuable than gold. She watched them die one by one. The desert, she said, taught her about death; but she also learned that the water bubbling up from the rocks was completely different from the water swirling within the red embryo of the watermelon. The local

Indians, expressionless and silent to white people, taught her how to grow that magic red water, and taught her to value it.

"You cannot imagine what this red globe really is!" she exclaimed. "You cannot know yet what makes it different from sugar and water and red food coloring. But I'll tell you what I learned then: this is water that the sun has drawn into itself."

If Margareta Leuder was a mystic, she was a very down-to-earth mystic. She believed the water in melons had special value, perhaps in the way winter meltwater really has greater value than well water. As I remember it, however, my "First Lesson in Biodynamics" was not only about the therapeutic value of watermelon. It was really how inorganic elements become transformed when taken up within living systems. Within the living system, they reveal their true face. Something hidden becomes visible, comes to life.

As you watch a three-year-old soak his overalls to the skin with melon water, it may be hard to believe that watermelon doesn't really have more water than other fruits. My children never got half so wet eating cabbage, but they were too young to read the *USDA Agricultural Handbook No. 8*. Both cabbage and watermelon contain approximately the same amount of water, about 92%. Makers of sauerkraut already know that cabbage holds a lot of water. Why does watermelon seem so much wetter? Is the difference between cabbage and watermelon the way in which the water is held within the plant? If one compares cross sections, the shape of flow in cabbage is bound to the growth sequence of leaves, whereas the flow in watermelon appears to be purely fluid dynamic.

Were this not the case, Central Africans could not use wild watermelon as a life-saving water supply. In areas of Africa plagued by drought, several forms of *Citrullus vulgaris* grow wild; some sweet, some intensely bitter. Both look identical, apparently to dissuade marauders, and the natives must taste each fruit before carrying it off. Natives also cultivate the sweet type as a water source and have done so since prehistoric times. Watermelons seeds were found in King Tut's tomb; they had spread to all the hot, dry lands from India to Spain before recorded history.

Whether the Ancients placed any special value on watermelon beyond its refreshing sweetness I do not know, but Margareta Leuder's claims have been proved correct by contemporary research. Her point was that all water taken up by plants becomes therapeutic—she would even say sacred. In watermelon the known therapeutic agents are lycopene and citrulline. Population studies and biochemical research suggest that lycopene, also found abundantly in peppers and tomatoes, protects against aging, cardiovascular deterioration, lung, stomach, and prostate cancer, diabetes, osteoporosis, and male infertility.

Lycopene is very high in watermelon, and its levels of citrulline are the highest of all fruits or vegetables. Citrulline has been called "Vegan Viagra" because of its effect on blood vessels (Cormio et al., U. of Foggia Dept. of Urology 2011); but citrulline does much more than Viagra. It strengthens the circulation and immune system as a whole. It helps to remove toxic compounds from our bodies and may help reduce obesity and diabetes. Citrulline improves total cardiovascular function, reducing hypertension (Figuera et al., Florida State 2010); and it increases aerobic performance in athletes, reducing fatigue (Takeda, E. et al. 2011). Plenty of citrulline is present in watermelon pulp, but even higher concentrations are found in the white rind. In Asia the white rind is stir-fried with oil, onions, and garlic. In the southern United States the white rind is made into pickles.

Culture

Most supermarket watermelons are shipped north from hot dry areas; sometimes from desert areas watered with timely irrigation early in growth, then withheld during ripening to develop sweetness and flavor. Although these watermelons can be shipped north, the hot dry conditions cannot. Hotness and dryness appear more briefly in northern and central areas, usually in July and August. Quality will depend on maintaining intense vitality during June and July, not always easy to do!

Culture for watermelon is similar to muskmelon; but watermelon has always seemed to me fussier, requiring faultless ground preparation to outgrow susceptibility to disease. Watermelons are intolerant of heavy clay soils; poor drainage invites disease problems. Plants require fast-draining sandy or silt loam, and a southern exposure not shaded by trees at any point during the day. Watermelons are more tolerant of low pH than other melons, as low as 5.5, with best growth from 6 to 6.8. The USDA recommends one beehive per acre for O.P. and normal hybrids; three hives per acre for triploid seedless. Home gardeners with clay soils can lighten planting mounds with 20% sand, 40% compost (especially made with hardwood leaves), and 40% native soil. Poorly drained clay or hardpan can be corrected with 6 inches of gravel that is dug into the subsoil below the mound. Field watermelons also benefit from raised rows or beds running east to west, with generous applications of compost. In the North pre-warm the soil with black plastic 2 weeks before transplanting. Use drip irrigation, to minimize water on leaves, reducing spread of disease.

Sow watermelons on the same dates as muskmelons, about 3 weeks prior to expected transplant date, when soil temperatures are at least 70°F. For O.P. varieties sow 3 seeds per 3- or 4-inch peat pot. For expensive hybrid seeds, sow one seed per pot. Germination takes 5 to 10 days at 75 to 85°F. Use the same potting mix made for squash and other melons. I've used either equal parts sandy loam and manure compost, or more recently, equal parts leaf compost and garden loam. Many organic growers use soilless mixes to minimize disease. Consider spraying the soil surface weekly with equisetum (508) or "Mildew Cure" to suppress soil fungi. Biodynamic growers spray with horn silica (501) and equisetum after true leaves appear. Remove the weakest of three seedlings with scissors. Fertilize with nettle/compost tea, seaweed tea, or fish emulsion.

Seedless watermelon requires two sowings. Stokes Seeds suggests sowing the pollinator "Side Kick" a week earlier than the seedless variety, using normal sowing temperatures, and so forth. Sow one pollinator for every three seedless watermelon plants. The seedless triploids, however, require a higher 90°F germination temperature. Pre-warm the starting mix to 90°F. Using a propagating mat, water the mix, and allow it to dry for 24 to 48 hours at 90°F. Germination soil that drips when squeezed is too wet; squeezed soil that falls apart is too dry. Seeds germinate and transplants grow best when seeds are set with pointed (radical) end facing up or sideways, never down. After placing one seed per pot, keep trays at 90°F for 48 to 72 hours. Mist flats only; no overhead irrigation! After one-third of the plants germinate, reduce temperature to 70 to 80°F. Keep pots moist (not wet) by misting. When transplants fully emerge and unfold, watering and temperature can vary slightly; but high temperatures create tall, spindly plants. Over-watering is the primary cause of hollow heart and many other failures of seedless melons.

Watermelon seedlings dislike being handled and moved around. Transplant carefully so as not to disturb roots. Never move vines around to weed or hoe. Undersides of leaves suffer when exposed to sun.

When garden soil is 70°F, set plants in the field at 4-foot spacing for compact types; 6 feet for longer vines and larger watermelons. For seedless varieties, place one pollinator then three seedless, since bees tend to graze single rows up and down. Never plant separate pollinator rows. In northern areas protect plants from the cold and cucumber beetles using black or red plastic with row cover and #9 wire hoops to prevent abrasion of the leaves. Water transplants until established, and then withhold water for 2 weeks to promote deeper rooting. Thereafter trickle irrigate weekly when rainfall is normal, daily in dry spells.

When vines begin to run, give plants feedings of liquid seaweed or biodynamic compost/nettle tea. Spray soil and leaves with equisetum and organic mildew control (Mildew Cure, and so forth) to prevent leaf mildew. Leaf mildews block sunlight from penetrating the leaves, and the plants never attain full ripeness and sweetness. Biodynamic growers spray 501 on a muskmelon schedule. Remove any fruit (using shears) that appear shriveled or decayed to reduce stem end rot, but avoid handling vines. To assure ripeness of fruits in August, remove small immature fruits that have no chance of ripening. This will direct the plant's vitality to those that remain. Withhold water again when melons are full size (ripening). Some home gardeners place ripening fruit on tuna cans (with both ends of the can removed) to prevent rotting from ground contact. This method also makes it easier to see the belly of the melon, whose color is one indication of ripeness. The belly is whitish-green when unripe and yellowish when ready to pick. Also, the surface of the fruit begins to dull; the rind becomes more resistant to penetration by the thumb and rougher to the touch. The tendril closest to the melon stem becomes dry and brown. Finally (and least reliably), the melon makes a "punk" sound when flicked with your fingers, rather than "pink" or "pank."

Varieties

Open-pollinated watermelons include a host of heirloom varieties, some available in mainstream catalogs, most others only from seed-savers' exchanges. Moon and Stars (100 days, 25 lbs.) was rediscovered by Ken Wheatley of Seed Savers Exchange, and since has been reselected by many plant breeders into many variants. Fruits are thin-skinned with bright sweet red flesh suitable for home and local market. The yellow moon and star patterns against a very dark green rind get a lot of attention at farm stands. Even the leaves are covered with yellow stars. Older varieties, such as Charleston Gray (85 days, 35 lbs., with high levels of citrulline in USDA tests) and Georgia Rattlesnake (90 days, 30 lbs.), require a typical long hot southern summer. Charleston has some resistance to anthracnose and fusarium wilt.

Crimson Sweet (90 days, 10 to 25 lbs. also high in citrulline) has been a reliable producer of very sweet melons in the North and South for nearly 50 years. Its wide adaptability is no doubt due to good disease resistance (to anthracnose 1 and 3 and fusarium 1 and 2). Southern Exposure Seed Catalog notes that crimson sweet "promotes beneficial soil fungi that inhibit fusarium wilt."

Sugar Baby (76 days, 6 to 12 lbs. high citrulline) produces many icebox melons on 6-foot centers. It has been extremely popular since 1959, reliable North and South, widely adapted and drought tolerant, with classic southern melon sweetness and texture. The hard crack-resistant rinds turn almost black when ripe. Bush Sugar Baby is a still more compact, 10-pound version for home gardens with short 3½-foot vines. Early Moonbeam (76 days, 7 lbs.) also has short vines, sweet crisp yellow flesh, and thin rinds for home and local market.

I found it interesting that of the top 20 watermelons tested by the USDA for highest levels of citrulline only 4 were hybrids; no hybrids were in the top 10 (USDA Ag. Research Lab 2011). Also interesting: OP watermelon bred for low sugar had the least citrulline, 4 times less than top contender O.P. "Tom Watson."

Older hybrid watermelons are diploid and self-pollinating. Little Baby Flower (70 days, 3 lbs.) is unusually prolific for a watermelon, producing 3 to 5 fruits per plant (most watermelons produce 1 or 2). Fruits are high in sugar, with crisp texture and excellent flavor. Sweet Favorite (79 days, 11 lbs.) ripens early in the North, producing bright red sweet fruits on anthracnose- and fusarium-resistant vines. Sorbet Swirl (77 days, 10 lbs.) displays its embryonic swirls in red and yellow; it produces in both cooler and warmer years with excellent sweetness and texture. The bright orange flesh and sweet taste of New Orchid (80 days, 8 lbs.) make it an excellent choice for home and fresh market. Burpee reports that Big Tasty Hybrid (85 days, 7 lbs.) won their taste test over 50 other varieties.

The newest hybrids are seedless (triploid); and contrary to the general rule of hybridizing, are less vigorous than open-pollinated or conventional hybrids. Triploids require special germination, and the planting of a separate pollinator variety. Some seed companies include the pollinator; others sell them separately. Plant one pollinator for every 3 seedless transplants. Pollinators such as Side Kick or Ace produce small vines and very small inedible fruit. According to the Stokes catalog, Side Kick should be sown a week earlier than its seedless companion. Other pollinators such as Jenny Hybrid (8 lbs.) produce tasty super-small seeded melons (SSS), an edible but perhaps confusing companion.

Choose seedless varieties carefully. Some, such as Orange Sunshine (85 days, 18 lbs.), are super-sweet (12% brix) with exceptional flavor, and hold up well for shipping. Others, according to the Harris Seed Catalog, leave a metallic aftertaste. Also consider what may have been lost in breeding. It seems possible that hybridization of watermelons decreases therapeutic nutritional value. I also wonder if the tendency to hollow heart in seedless melons, which breeders are struggling to overcome, indicates that seed removal has eliminated something essential? Is the fruit the same? Is the water the same water?

- SEED: Size varies from 600 to 900 per ounce, which sows 300 to 450 feet of row. Get to know each variety individually. Packets of O.P. may contain 20 to 50 seeds while fancy hybrids contain 10 to 15 seeds. A packet of non-hybrid will sow about 5 to 12 hills at 4 seeds per hill; a packet of hybrid will sow 4 to 7 hills at 2 seeds per pot.

- GERMINATION: 70%; 5 to 10 days at 75 to 80°F. Open-pollinated seed lasts 4 to 5 years.

- DAYS TO HARVEST: 75 to 100 days from transplanting.

- MOON CALENDAR: All practices in fruit, ascending moon, if possible.

- ROTATION: 3 years for squash, melons, and cucumbers.

- BIODYNAMIC SPRAYS: Horn manure (500) on potting soil and field. Silica (501) on transplants. Compost-500 tea at transplanting. Silica when vines run, again before flowering, and once more during fruit development. Use valerian (507) in less than optimal climate and weather. Spray equisetum (508) before mildew appears, if mildew is a problem in your area.

- COMPANIONS: Sow aromatic herbs on hills to deter cucumber beetles when row cover is not used. Plant trap crops of zucchini between hills. Allow nasturtiums to grow freely on sides of hills. Grow with dent, flint corn, or any other melon-squash family companions, so long as watermelon vines are not disturbed.

WILD SALADS

Amaranth, Dandelion, Lambs Quarter's, Miner's Lettuce, Orach, Plantain, Purslane, Sorrel, Upland Cress, and Watercress

My first garden teacher had no tolerance whatsoever for hunting. She wouldn't even wear leather shoes. But she was almost prehistoric in her daily round of foraging wild greens. The first time I spotted her foraging in half-light, I mistook her for a small animal shuffling between garden rows. For Margareta Leuder, foraging was never a back-to-the-land fancy, as it was for me. But of course I wasn't born on a wagon train in 1899 travelling to a remote homestead in Sinaloa, Mexico. Margareta couldn't remember whether her first words were Spanish, Polish, German, or Huatl. She guessed Huatl, since she remembers spending more waking hours in the fields with native women than she did with her Polish mother. She claimed that by age six, her back was permanently bent from hoeing. The Indian women taught her which weeds were food and which were medicine. They taught her how to survive on almost nothing, which in some years was all they had.

Compared to her respect for weeds, Margareta had a low respect for garden vegetables. Whenever it was her turn to cook, she fed us weeds. She blended them daily for her infant great-grandson. She began the season with ramps (wild onion) and steamed nettles, followed by chickweed, lambs quarters, and purslane in salads; then purslane, lambs quarters, and amaranth as steamed greens.

Margareta never collected wild seeds, or tried to make wild greens more tender with compost and water, although we certainly preferred the tender lamb's quarters growing on the compost heap. She was deeply suspicious of efforts to alter and hybridize wild plants. I can still see her eyes narrow and harden, staring at us through the window of another era. She saw all of us as descendants of Esau, trading a bottomless well for mere size and tenderness. I guess she would be pleased that wild plants have been granted a small but respectable niche in the mesclun market, although she was so born to the wild, it's hard to say.

Amaranth

Species of amaranth have been grown as greens and grain since prehistoric times. *Amaranthus* tricolor (Joseph's coat) has been used as greens in Mexico (as tampala), in Africa and the Caribbean (as calaloo), and in China (as hinn choy). Amaranth seed (*A. candatus*, love-lies-bleeding) has been grown for grain for more than 6,000 years in Peru; and more recently adopted by farmers in India and Nepal. Indians flavor steamed amaranth with cumin, red chili, and salt, while the Greeks season steamed *A. viridis* with olive oil, salt, and lemon juice. Somehow amaranth was closely connected to the ancient Greek Ephesian Mysteries and their goddess Artemis, hence the meaning of amaranth, "undying or never fading," in another word "immortal"!

Whether the Greeks knew something astonishing or goddess-like about amaranth, I can't say; but I do know that its undying vitality has become the nemesis of no-till agriculture. Wild pigweed (*A. retroflexus*), the one so loved by Margareta Leuder, has become completely immune to the chemical herbicide Roundup, overwhelming tens of thousands of acres. Farmers accustomed to subduing fields with tractors designed for alien invasion have been reduced to hiring hand weeders. It's a great show, which I wouldn't miss for anything: little David amaranth flinging stones in the eye of the giant Goliath, Dupont!

With a plant named "Immortality," I expected to discover unusual anti oxidants in amaranth. Researchers at National Taiwan University have isolated "a novel immune-stimulating protein from *A. spinosus*, which stimulated B lymphocyte activity in vitro" (Bi-Fong, Lin et al. 2004). Researchers at the University of Guelph in Canada found that amaranth species contain "several times the amount of phytosterols as other plants" (Marcone et al. 2003). Amaranth reduces blood glucose and improves lipid profile (*Indian Journal of Pharmacology* 2011). And so on. In fact I found that potential therapeutic possibilities for amaranth fairly match its panacea-like use in traditional Asian medicine.

On the negative side, amaranth contains high levels of oxalic acid (which can cause kidney stones in susceptible people) and nitrates. Excess feeding of amaranth leaves has been shown to lower hemaglobin in pigs. Even the high level of antioxidant and anti-inflammatory agents in amaranth may have negative effects if consumed in excess amounts (Lehmann 1992). Enjoy these greens intermittently.

In Pennsylvania I was plagued with pigweed. It popped up everywhere almost overnight. I never minded it. Amaranth provided an instant cover crop, breaking up hard soil and producing a huge harvest of organic matter. We quickly weeded the luxuriant plants before they produced seed, and layered moistened plants with manure to make the best compost ever. I swear that the heating pile smelled to me like baking bread! I really mean it; it smelled delicious!

When planting *A. tricolor* (50 days) for greens (much more attractive than pigweed!) remember that this species is a warm season subtropical, so wait to sow the tiny seeds (47,000 to the ounce) until soil temperature is 70°F. Consider diluting the seed with baked dry sand to prevent over-sowing. Aim for a dozen seeds to the foot and thin to 6 inches apart. Force side branching by snipping terminal buds, and harvest leaves individually. The leaves of *A. tricolor* are so beautiful that this species can be used ornamentally in the flower border.

Dandelion

Dandelion (*Taraxacum officinale*) has become a pernicious weed only since the rise of the great American lawn. Otherwise dandelion's long history is unimpeachable. The greens have more vitamin A than carrots and kale; and they are high in vitamin C, minerals, and the antioxidants lutein, luteolin, and caffeic acid. Dandelion leaves stabilize blood sugar and detoxify the liver. The old English name "piss a bed" refers somewhat crudely to dandelion's strong diuretic and kidney cleansing effect. Note that "Italian Dandelion," another excellent semi-wild plant, is actually a chicory (*Cichorium intybus*).

Dandelion root exudates promote soil life and penetrate deep into the C horizon (soil level four layers down), breaking up hard soils and raising minerals from the depths. Dandelion's ability to promote soil life makes it an important biodynamic compost preparation. I also have unlimited praise for that bane of the lawn industry, the radiant dandelion seed head. Dandelion flowers are lovely, but the seed heads are one of the most sublime examples of geometry in nature, as if everything to be noticed about the geometry of plants had congealed into a single ecstatic moment.

Dandelion is a very hardy perennial; once established, greens can be cut for many weeks, although leaves tend to become too bitter by the beginning of summer. Because of its unusual hardiness, dandelion can be sown from spring to fall, or sown in seedbeds and transplanted after a few true leaves appear. Seeds are very small (45,000 to the ounce), so mix with dry sand to prevent over-sowing. To produce small leaves for mesclun mix, sow in wide 4-inch bands and cover very lightly with fine soil or sifted compost. Otherwise sow like lettuce, 8 seeds to the foot, and thin to 8 inches apart. Leaves for salad mix are harvested young, no longer than 4 inches. Larger unblanched leaves can be steamed and dressed with balsamic vinaigrette. The rosettes of large French varieties are usually tied when the rosette is half-grown to blanch the centers, and make the leaves less bitter and more tender. Cut most or all of the flower stalks before too many of those magical seed heads scatter seed across the garden.

French broad leaf varieties of the dandelion are somewhat self-blanching, which reduces bitterness. The variety Vert de Montmagney is mild, even without blanching

Lamb's Quarters (Magenta Spreen)

Magenta spreen (*Chenopodium gigantium*, 30 days) is a kind of lamb's quarters (*C. album*), but larger and covered with glistening magenta crystals of oxalic acid. Both are close relatives of spinach. Magenta spreen is a colorful and piquant addition to salad mixes and stir-fries. Seeds are exceedingly small (56,000 to the ounce), three times smaller than lettuce, and difficult to sow precisely. Again, try mixing the seed half and half with baked dry sand. Broadcast lightly in 3-inch bands, with a thin compost covering. Keep surface moist but not sodden until germination, and then water regularly. Leaves are more tender in well-composted soil. Harvest by shearing when plants are 6 inches tall. Mesclun growers reseed bi-weekly. Home gardeners should note that abandoned plants grow up to 8 feet tall in fertile soil and spread thousands of seeds over the garden.

High levels of oxalic acid in Magenta spreen, as well as orach, sorrel, and spinach, may contribute to kidney stones in some people.

Orach

Red orach (*Atriplex hortensis*, 40 days) is another chenopod related to lamb's quarters. Orach leaves are deep purple with abundant bright purple crystals of oxalic acid on the undersides of leaves. Orach is high in both oxalates and salt, which it accumulates. In Australia orach is called Old Man Saltbush because it tolerates high sodium soils. Sheep favor saltbush, and meat from sheep grazing on orach is equal in quality to grain-fed stock, with high levels of vitamin E (Wikipedia).

At 6,000 seeds per ounce, orach seeds are 9 times larger than spreen and 9 times easier to sow and space. Sow 1 to 2 inches between seeds with ½ inch of soil or compost cover. Seeds germinate in about 9 days. Thin to 8 inches between plants. Begin harvesting when plants are about a foot tall. Because of oxalic acid content, limit use to about 5% of salad mix.

Plantain

One plant Margareta never convinced me to love was broad-leaved plantain (*Plantago major*). She was so committed to weeds that it really didn't bother her if leaves were somewhat fibrous and unpalatable. Research papers show that *P. major* has promising anticarcenogenic (Chaing 2003) and anti-inflammatory (Ozaslan 2007) potential, and high vitamin content; but it's just no fun to eat. So I was glad to discover that a fiberless plantain (*P. coronopus*, 50 days) suitable for salads was available from Johnny's Selected Seeds under the name Minutina. *P. coronopus* is also called buckhorn plantain because of the antler-like shape of the leaves. The Italians call it *Erba stella;* and besides using it as a crisp salad, they sauté it in olive oil and garlic, sometimes adding anchovies or Italian bacon (pancetta).

The seeds are exceedingly small (120,000 per ounce), so mix with dry sand to sow in succession. Small rosettes can be cut like mesclun or thinned to 5 inches.

Purslane

Purslane (*Portulaca oleracea sativa*, 50 days) was revered by Margareta Leuder more than any other vegetable except stinging nettle. She ate it as much as possible, and even froze purslane for soups in the winter. I know this flies in the face of "seasonal eating," but weeds were more important to Margareta than consistency. She fondly remembered *verdolaga* (Spanish for purslane) from her childhood in Mexico, where it is cooked with tomatoes, onions, hot peppers, and cilantro. Cooked in this way, the natural mucilage in the stems becomes useful as a thickener, as it does also when added to vegetable soup.

Purslane was the first weed Margareta learned to forage at her parents' remote homestead in 1902. When she was four, the local Indian women taught her to gather the fleshy leaves and stems from between the cornrows. Margareta claimed that collecting wild greens, much more than gardening, is what taught her to taste nutritional intensity, which is really the goal of biodynamics. Margareta tasted almost nothing from civilization until their homestead was turned to dust in her late teens, thanks to the diversion of their water supply by (she said) Sears Roebuck and Company. When her father shipped her back to relatives in Poland, she felt as if her insides were carved out by the loss of those native women and their Hualtl language. She was miserable in Poland until she began dating a young Count named Keyeserlingk, whose father hosted the first biodynamic farm. She never abandoned her conviction that the real origin of biodynamics was weeds.

Margareta would not have been surprised that purslane has more omega-3 fatty acids than any other leaf vegetable; it has 4 times more than spinach, and more antioxidant glutathione than any other plant except asparagus and avocado (Simopoloulos et al. 2002). She would have nodded her head as I listed its high vitamin content or high potassium, and would have been interested that purslane's high calcium is reduced by oxalates that are even higher than those in spinach (USDA). But that's not really how she looked at plants. Her attitude was a kind of primordial piety or gratitude; in the end (she said it often) she felt unworthy to inherit this astonishing green planet.

To me purslane stems look strangely like some deep sea invertebrate, crawling across the ocean floor, somehow re-emerging on nearly every continent. Purslane has been eaten everywhere from ancient Greece (apparently sowed in Greek gardens before other Europeans had gardens) to aboriginal Australia, where they use the tiny seeds (65,000 to the ounce) in protein- and oil-rich cakes. The minute seeds (3½ times smaller than carrot) really benefit from mixing with 3 parts dry sand before sowing.

Margareta always left a cover crop of purslane growing in the corn rows, removing most other weeds. She contended that purslane shaded the soil, conserved water, and penetrated hard soil—which it does, allowing the corn roots to travel deeper. Massachusetts Extension notes that purslane is not a problem for corn and beans, but does compete with low-growing crops. Competition will also depend on whether ample composting over many years has left a sufficient residue of nutrients to deal with the extra plant load. Many growers, however, believe that constant soil cover has greater long-term value in protecting the soil from leaching and oxidation than slight loss in yield.

Red purslane "Gruner" (50 days) is similar to the wild form with small leaves and red stems. Golden purslane "Goldberg" (80 days) is much larger.

Sow after all danger of frost is past, about 15 seeds to the foot with a thin cover of friable soil or fine compost. Thin to 4 inches for red, 6 inches for golden. Harvest crisp salty young shoots for salads and whole plants down to 2 inches above the growing point for greens.

Miner's Lettuce

Miner's lettuce (*Montia perfoliata*, 40 days) is also called Claytonia or winter purslane, for its juicy leaves, stems, and membership in the purslane family. Miner's lettuce is native west of the Rockies, and like European corn salad, could be foraged when nothing else was available and scurvy was knocking at the door. Miner's lettuce can be foraged wild on the Pacific coast (British Columbia to Baja), and east to Arizona and Utah. Plants are similar in hardiness to corn salad; Zone 7 winters unprotected, and Zone 5 in a cold greenhouse.

The round leaves are actually two leaves that grow together, with a stalk of small white flowers at the center. The seeds are very small, 45,000 to the ounce, so dilute with baked sand to prevent over-seeding. Sow 10 to 15 seeds to the foot and cover with ¼ inch of sifted compost or fine soil. Thin to 2 or 3 plants to the foot, a foot between rows. Harvest leaves several times above the growing point during the season.

Sorrel

Sorrel (*Rumex acetosa*) also called spinach dock, is another wild sour green, often grazed by children. The French brought sorrel into the garden centuries ago to make a lemony soup and salad ingredient. My grandmother often made schav, a Jewish soup made from sorrel with chopped egg, sour cream, and scallions, served cold. As a child I dreaded the visits when schav was served. To my child's eye schav looked like a stagnant algae covered pool; that would have been fine, except that it lacked painted turtles. I know this because I slowly dragged my spoon through the soup, and all that came up was boiled egg. Sour cream apparently helps to mute the intense oxalic acid, but nothing could alter the fact that my *bubba* was a terrible cook.

Sorrel is less dominant used as flavoring in vegetable soups and stews, and adds a lemony flavor to baked fish and fish soup. Red Veined Sorrel (*R. sanguineus*, 55 days) adds the same lemony zest and color to mesclun mixes. Both French and Red Veined Sorrel can be grown as perennials in the herb garden or sown as annuals, 8 inches apart with 12 inches between rows. Seeds are small, about 28,500 per ounce, so dilute half and half with baked sand.

Harvest lower leaves until the rosette is fully established. Cut the entire rosette 6 inches above the growing point for continuous harvest. To rejuvenate unharvested plants, cut flower stalks as they appear and all the leaves above the growing point. Plants can be divided in fall or early spring. Sorrel grows well in cool weather for early spring and late fall harvest.

Upland or Early Winter Cress

When I first collected wild greens as a teenager, I didn't distinguished between common winter cress (*Barbarea vulgaris*) and early winter cress (*Barbarea verna*). I called both "yellow rocket," a name still used for both in some parts. Common winter cress has only a few pairs of lobes below the rounded main body of the leaf. Early winter cress has 4 to 10 pairs of pinnately divided lobes. Both wild species taste enormously strong! Even my untutored 17-year-old palette sensed something powerful lurking in these leaves, something nearly absent in garden crucifers. Gathering early winter cress was once a late winter ritual among Italian immigrants, whose taste for bitter greens like raab exceeds the average American's by several orders of magnitude. This ritual goes back to Italy, where the native Mediterranean cress has been foraged since ancient times.

Both *Barbarea* greens are most palatable in the cold months of the year, from late winter to early spring; and then again during the spring-like flush in October, which I call second spring, due to similar light levels. Frost improves flavor, which is mustardy, sweet, and bitter; late fall heat spells and bolting make the leaf bitterness intolerable. The flower buds, however, which look like buds of broccoli raab, add a wonderful mustardy bite to mixed salads and stir-fries.

Because of extremely high levels of vitamin C, early winter cress is also called scurvy grass, following its long history of curing winter C deficiencies. Country people marked where it grew to harvest it from under the snow. In England early winter cress had already come under cultivation in the seventeenth century. The *Barbarea* in the genus name refers to the date when rural people began harvesting the rosettes: December 4, St. Barbara's Day (Angier 1974). In the American South, *Barbarea verna* is called creasy greens, colloquial for cress.

Barbarea verna not only has high levels of vitamin A, minerals, and C (3 times more than orange juice), but also is one of the richest sources of gluconasturtiin, the precursor of a potent anti-inflammatory and anti-carcinogenic isothiocyanate (Dey 2006). Lab tests have shown promise in possible treatment of ulcerative colitis, rheumatoid and osteoarthritis, irritable bowel, and colon cancer. (ibid) Gluconasturtiin is found in other members of the crucifer family, but levels in wild *Barbarea* are unusually high.

In Florida early winter cress is sown from September to December, and harvested as a winter crop (Florida Extension). In the warmer parts of North Carolina, early winter cress is sown in mid-August and harvested from January to March (North Carolina Extension). In the northern states where summers are not intensely hot, early winter cress can be sown from mid-spring (Johnny's Selected Seeds). Northern sowings are slower to bolt in cooler climates. In the Pacific Coast and Northwest, sow in early fall and harvest all winter. In general, sow whenever spinach would be successful.

Early winter cress responds to added organic nitrogen, but nutritional and therapeutic values will be better with compost. Plant in well-drained loam, pH 5.5 to 6.5 (North Carolina Extension). Seeds are small, averaging 20,000 to the ounce; about 1,600 seeds sow 100 feet. Seed germinates more slowly than other cruncifers. Home gardeners may wish to cover with ¼ inch of fine compost to increase germination, 16 seeds to the foot in rows 12 inches apart. Thin plants 4 to 6 inches apart. After 50 days when leaves are 4 inches long, either harvest individual leaves above the growing point, or cut the entire rosette as you would a loose-leaf lettuce. To maximize the transformation of gluconasturtiin into usable antioxidant, chop the fresh leaves for salad; or leave the chopped leaves to sit for 5 minutes before stir-frying.

North Carolina Extension reports that unlike other cruncifers, early winter cress is highly insect-resistant. The only recorded problems were some cases of root aphids in the South.

Watercress

Less than a mile from my home, a strong underground spring feeds a shallow pool before it flows through an abandoned pasture. Watercress (*Nasturtium officinale*) grows there year round in Zone 5 because the babbling spring is a constant 50°F. Conditions for watercress are perfect: clean spring water descending from a wild State reservation. The bed of the pool is high humus, limey, high pH.

Few gardeners have access to a stream suitable for watercress, and those that do, probably don't take advantage of it. Watercress in the United States doesn't command the enormous sales it does in the United Kingdom. Recent research may change that, and may also change gardeners' attitude toward planting watercress in their gardens.

The father of western medicine, Hippocrates, thought so highly of watercress he built his first hospital near a watercress spring. The ancient Greeks revered watercress as a cure-all, and fed the greens to their soldiers before they went to battle. Renaissance herbalists valued watercress as a blood cleanser; and they were right, although the cleansing proved to be deeper than they ever imagined. By the nineteenth century, watercress was the British national salad, for rich and poor alike. I can't imagine American steelworkers carrying watercress sandwiches to work, but watercress is widely consumed by the British working class. The consumption of watercress in the United Kingdom has risen astronomically every year (University of Ulster 2010).

Recently, University of Ulster scientists conducted a trial test of 30 men and 30 women that intentionally included 30 smokers of both sexes, since smokers as a rule have significantly higher levels of blood cell DNA damage. One bowl of watercress per day reduced damage to lymphocytes 22.9% and reduced blood triglycerides 10%. The therapeutic agent, as with Upland early winter cress (*Barbarea verna*) was phenylethyl isothiocyanate (Hoffman 2009). Blood levels of lutein, which may lower risk of cataract and age-related macular degeneration, rose 100%; beta carotene rose 33%. There was a significant rise in vitamins C, E, folate, and fiber as well. In all participants—especially the smokers—blood cell DNA damage was significantly reduced. Researchers noted, "blood cell DNA damage is an indicator of whole body cancer risk." (ibid). The University of Southampton (England 2010) also showed that regular consumption of watercress inhibited breast cancers from forming new blood vessels, an effect similar to new targeted cancer therapies.

Watercress is more of a challenge to grow than its therapeutically equivalent cousin Upland cress. The bulk of United States production (very small compared to the United Kingdom) is located in Central Florida, where the drainage basin is apparently still sufficiently clean (Florida Extension). Plants are grown partially submerged in un-shaded shallow pools.

James Stephens of Florida Extension suggests a home garden alternative. Replicate a shallow pool by digging out a basin 6 inches deep and lining it with plastic. Cover the plastic with 2 inches of compost or potting mix. Seeds can be lightly broadcast with ¼-inch compost cover when outside temperatures are 50 to 60°F, and kept constantly moist. Otherwise seeds can be started in peat pots or cells, set in water-filled trays, changing the water daily. Transplant cells to the basin at 2 inches, with 4 inches between plants. Fill the basin with water as the seedlings grow. The shortcoming of this method is lack of outflow and the likelihood of stagnation during the 6 weeks remaining before harvest.

Watercress can also be grown in garden soil (pH. 6.5 to 7.5), if heavily supplied with organic matter and regularly irrigated to the point of saturation. If possible, choose a depression or low-lying area with slow drainage. Sow the incredibly small seeds (147,000 to the ounce) diluted with 5 parts baked sand, ¼ inch deep, about 24 seeds to the foot. Thin to 4 inches. Alternatively, sow as above in peat pots or cells. Keep the area constantly moist. Leaves and stems taste best if harvested before flowering and high heat. Between Zones 6 and 9 the bed can be perennial. New beds can be established by transplanting cuttings.

White flies can sometimes be found on the undersides of leaves. Use insecticidal soap. Spider mites cause flecking discoloration and scorching (Utah Extension). Use insecticidal oil. Plan to control snails and slugs with baited iron phosphate. Watercress seems to have few disease problems.

WINTER SQUASH

Saving seeds for winter squash has taught me so much about garden culture that I regret not doing it consistently for every vegetable. As I pass the squash patch, I look at the fruits differently, capturing the shape and vigor of whole plants more quickly and concisely. I notice connections between field and fruit that I missed before. The shade of green in every leaf seems to rise more clearly from something I did, or something omitted. Whole seasons become condensed in the color and quality of rind and flesh in a single squash. At harvest, I carry the color of the season out of the garden. If I've managed to build my squash mounds right, their orange color is so intense it makes the squash from our co-op look anemic by comparison.

Throughout the winter, my family eats the previous season critically, bite by bite. They taste what I did in every carrot, in every potato, in every bag of frozen corn and peas. The teenagers, especially, show little gratitude for all the work they didn't do. Their remarks are less thorns than beggar ticks, but I still have pick them off one by one; and they force me to recreate the season again, bite by bite. Even the successes leave me discontented. Will I be able to duplicate this flavor and color the following year? In my first forays into seed saving nearly 40 years ago, *Cucurbita pepo* got me into trouble. I cannot remember how it went, exactly. It was like a soap opera. Yellow crookneck (*C. melopepo*) coupled with pumpkin (*C. pepo*), patty pan with acorn, Delicata with spaghetti. Everyone ended up in the wrong bed; every match ended in divorce. *Cucurbita maxima* mix-ups were better: buttercups, Sweet Mama, Chestnut, Black Forest, Hokkaido, even hubbards crossed into tasty, if somewhat unorthodox, offspring. Fortunately that bloated slob, Big Max, has never grown in my garden. His offspring would have reduced legendary maxima quality to cattle fodder. Only the butternuts (*C. moschata*), like Benedictine monks, kept entirely to themselves. They bred true no matter who else was around.

Had I looked carefully at the stems, I could have easily recognized the species and avoided trouble. All *Cucurbita pepos* have the smaller or larger swan-neck handles found in true pumpkins. The stems of *C. Moschatas* are short and hard, while *C. Maximas* are corky and very thick.

When I cut through the skin of a squash in midwinter, cut through the orange flesh, cut through the seed coats themselves into the oily germ, it seems as if I am cutting through the layers of time, like cutting through the growth rings of a tree. My knife cuts through these jackets like memory. Immature and poorly developed fruits are the memories I like least. Immature fruits do not taste good, do not keep long, and produce seeds of poor viability. Seeds from immature fruits also seem more susceptible to insect attack at the cotyledon stage (my anecdotal impression). The skin of mature butternut is a deep, even tan, free of pale green undertones. The stem end should be full, rather than appearing slightly under-inflated. Flesh should be a rich, even medium orange, almost ruddy, without stringy pockets or white flecking. Acorn squash should be dark Lincoln green, almost black, with full, well-defined ridges and flesh as golden as possible for the type, slightly nutty, fine-textured, and without strings. The flesh of buttercup, kabocha, and hubbard, along with many other maximas should have dry, sweet deep orange flesh, even better tasting than sweet potato when well grown, deliciously nutty and substantial. Try to select squashes large and full for the type, ones growing from the most vigorous vines with large, strong leaves. In all species, vigorous leaves are the key to good flesh and seed formation. Finally, I prefer not to save seed from a squash I have not eaten.

Eventually, your eye will begin to see a connection between skin color and flesh, and good fruits for selection and storage will pop right out of the field. I always divide the harvest three ways: immature, mature but damaged culls, and perfect mature. Damaged culls last a month or so and can be eaten or fed to stock. Immature go to stock or compost heap. Perfect mature maxima and moschata squash get cured for ten days in a warm attic or boiler room to harden their skins and shrink them somewhat. Most keep for the winter; butternut until next April. *Cucurbita pepo*, which should not be cured, I use first: after a few months, the skin yellows and the flesh loses quality. *Cucurbita maxima* vary. They are very susceptible to the development of small rotten spots on the skin or stem. Some people wipe them with a cloth and vegetable oil, but they may still go downhill by midwinter. Moschata squash can last until spring, but they become spongy and fibrous by April. Storage temperature for all squash is 55 to 60°F with low humidity. Some very dry basements might do for storing squash; a poorly heated room might work; an attic rarely; a root cellar never. If you are designing a country home, that old-fashioned cool larder is a good idea.

Culture

I've never seen squash finish well if it didn't start quickly and strongly with large deep green leaves and vines. This begins with germination. Cotyledons respond immediately to biodynamic compost. This first growth affects their whole future development. I have gotten the strongest results from lightly packing 4-inch peat pots with pure compost, but seedlings also grow fine mixing compost with half soil. Even when I direct seed hills, I get stronger seedlings covering seeds with 1 inch of compost. They take off fast and, since I put any amount from a bucketful to a quarter-wheelbarrow of compost per hill, they keep growing strongly right until harvest. A well of compost makes irrigation unnecessary in all but the driest climates. Squash from inadequately composted ground never develops full sweetness, substantial texture, or deep orange color; and vitamin content is drastically reduced. Side-dressings or liquid feeding may give a boost to a failing crop, but mound preparation very early in the season (when you have less work to do anyway) pays off in quality, yield, and reduced insect predation. The less compost used, the worse cucumber beetle attacks get. They are greatly reduced by good mound prep, though I still protect cotyledons with row cover.

Although black plastic warms soil early and prevents weed growth, I have found that black plastic increases insect attacks, especially squash bugs. For those who use plastic, metallized silver might be better; but I've never tried it. Colorado Extension has shown that silver mulch repels aphids, white flies, and leafhoppers, thereby controlling insect-borne viruses, as well as flea beetles. But I could find no research on cucumber beetles or squash bugs. In my gardens, organic mulches, especially hardwood leaves, have totally eliminated predation by squash bugs. Blue plastic mulch significantly increases yield in muskmelons and zucchini; and likely it will improve winter squash, since the blue spectrum increases photosynthesis (Penn State Extension).

The cucumber beetle (yellow with green stripes or spots) is small but voracious during the spring breeding season. They feed insanely on *C. maxima* and zucchini seedlings, and only slightly less insanely on other family members. Large (4-inch) peat pots, manure-based "cowpots," or hand-made soil blocks give a jump on the insect season along with the use of floating or heavier grade row cover (which significantly increases growth rate).

Plan sowing no earlier than 4 weeks before outside soil temperature is above 65°F (usually June 1 in the North, May 15 in the central states, and still earlier in the South and on the West Coast.) In the North, consider applying black plastic 2 weeks before planting to warm the soil, and covering transplants with heavier weight row cover for extra warmth. Early gambling on winter squash seems pointless. For earlier harvest, plant bush varieties. Plants that sit in pots longer than 4 weeks may be permanently stunted.

Sow three seeds per pot, ½ inch deep. Germinate at 75 to 85°F on a greenhouse heating pad or in a very warm room. After germination grow in a warm (65 to 85°F) sunny spot free of draft. When the first true leaf appears (not the rounded seed leaves) snip out (don't pull) the weakest of the three seedlings. Keep pots damp but never sodden. If commercial potting mix is used, feed with compost tea or fish emulsion twice a week for the next two weeks. For the week before setting out withhold fertilizer, reduce water, lower temperature, and expose to full sunlight, without glazing, if day temperatures are above 65°F.

If night temperatures are still flirting with frost on the expected planting date, use row cover. In the North, I favor heavy row cover for spring cucurbits and crucifers. The heavy grade not only significantly increases plant size and growth rate (probably due to increased temperature and CO_2, but also lasts much longer, up to 10 years if handled and stored carefully (keep rodent-free). Heavy row cover works best supported with #9 wire hoops or rebar. For added vigor, dip peat pots in a solution of compost/nettle tea. Roots are drawn quickly through the pot and take off faster. For plants not protected by row cover, spray leaves with a kaolin clay solution (marketed as Surround) against cucumber beetles.

Because of poor drainage in spring, I always plant squash in mounds or raised rows, 6 feet between groups of plants. Never plant where water may collect in wet weather, which may lead to phytophthora crop failures.

Direct-seeding matures good crops even in New England, but seedlings need to take off quickly. I excavate bushel-sized holes and remix soil with at least a quarter-wheelbarrow of half-mature compost. Since the hills are large, I sow 6 seeds 8 inches apart per hill with a sprinkle of organic slug bait. I weigh down the edges of row covers with stones. I lift the cover once to weed, water, and add organic slug bait, but otherwise leave them alone until the vines frantically press against the fabric trying to get out.

Unidentified squash seedlings pop up all over a compost heap in early spring. This gave me the idea to sow my own seeds very early, 9 seeds per hill, at 50°F soil temp. I even have a notion to try sowing squash mounds in late fall. Saved seed is so abundant. Overwintering a few dozen seeds per hill might select for vigor and cold-hardiness.

In some years I have transplanted volunteer squash seedlings from the compost heap in spring. Butternut, buttercup, and kabocha squash make vigorous and tasty volunteers. Acorn or delicata, as mentioned before, which produce worthless crosses with summer squash. One year, when I isolated summer squash behind the barn, the volunteer delicatas were the best ever.

Insects and Diseases

Squash seedlings attacked by cucumber beetles may succumb to bacterial wilt, which is transmitted by the beetles. Maximas fare the worst. Moschatas (Butternut) usually keep growing. In maximas, bacterial wilt becomes evident when the vines begin to run. Vines wilt suddenly and severely, like punctured balloons. They never perk up. To protect from beetles, keep vines under row cover as long as possible, until leaves press on the fabric.

On the other hand, if vines wilt in the morning after they've run to full length, the problem is probably vine borer. Again maximas go down and moschatas keep going. Butternut stems are harder for the moth to bore into. Borers reveal their presence by greenish frass exuding from holes in the stem. In zucchini the whole stem looks as rotten as the back of sin in a medieval sculpture. I've read that injections of Bt or nematodes (Gardens Alive! catalog) kill the larva, but I've never had the time or patience to try it. Some home gardeners slit the vines, remove the larva with a penknife, and rebury the vine. Generally, if the vines are growing vigorously early in the season, they mature fruits. If not, the fruits never develop color and flavor, and don't keep well. Next time plant earlier, in 4-inch peat pots, make the mounds deeper than ever, and keep plants protected during early growth. The larger the vines spread before insects arrive, the less damage. Spray seaweed and biodynamic horn silica (501) weekly for three weeks after row cover is removed, then silica at key growth points: when first flowers appear, when first fruit sets, and when the first fruit begins to get its mature color.

Downy mildew appears in cool damp weather and powdery mildew appears in hot dry weather. Both ruin the crop by coating the leaves with a dilute talcum powder of spores, which cuts down production of chlorophyll. Spray equisetum and Safer's Mildew Cure weekly before mildew appears. Gummy stem blight, also a problem on watermelon, produces the sunken brown spots on stored squash and brown scab on butternut. The Cornell Extension website notes that control of mildew will significantly reduce infections of gummy stem blight.

Phytophthora rot may appear at any stage of growth, usually when soils are waterlogged, or during extended warm, wet weather. Seedlings may damp off, leaf crown may collapse, roots may rot if water table rises, and fruit may rot from ground contact. Illinois and other extension sites note total loss of commercial cucurbit crops from phytophthora in some years. Practice strict 3-year rotation; not just with other cucurbits (squash, cukes, melons, watermelons) but also with other vectors including all nightshades (tomato, pepper, potato, and so forth) and lima beans. The British Columbia Ministry of Agriculture reports that preventive sprays of fungicide to control powdery mildew before symptoms appear may help to control outbreaks. Avoid overhead irrigation.

Fruit from vines that have wilted or whited out before the end of the season have no flavor and won't keep; the same with late-setting fruit. Learn to distinguish by eye the storable mature fruit for each variety. Immature fruit will also produce non-viable seed for seed savers. Skin color should be strong and deep for the type; it tends to get less shiny when fully mature. Size should conform to the variety. Skin and flesh of immature squash looks pale compared to its mature brethren. Seeds from immature squash are useless for seed savers. Immature fruit looks under-inflated, especially in mature butternut, where stem ends look incompletely inflated and tan skin looks pale. Light tan outside means tasteless and colorless inside, fodder only for livestock. Unfortunately, most butternuts I see in produce isles (even in organic co-ops) are pale and fairly tasteless.

Squash can be left in the field until the first frost. Repeated or deep frost will damage fruit, leaving watery or glassy patches that will not keep. Leave 1 inch of stem on each squash. Separate out salable and storage squash. Consume damaged squash, or donate culls to livestock, or compost. Till under or compost all plant residues to reduce disease and insects. If your autumns are hot, field-cure maximas and moshatas in the sun for a week. In cooler autumns cure in a dry greenhouse, warm shed, attic, or boiler room for a week to toughen the skins. Curing pepos reduces quality. Squash stores best around 55°F with fairly high humidity and good air circulation—conditions hard to achieve for home gardeners. Eat the pepos and maximas first, leaving the moshatas for winter. Check weekly for sunken lesions,

Varieties

Once the botanical groups are known, it's easier to decide if an unfamiliar squash might become a new favorite. Even if the catalog doesn't identify the species, each species bears a family resemblance. The gray-green hubbard squashes are the largest of the *C. maximas,* 10 to 15 pounds each, too large for most households. They seem to have originated during the era of extended families, which included grandparents, uncles, apprentices, and farm hands. Grown well, hubbards swell to the size of Thanksgiving turkeys and make a tasty stuffed "bird" for vegetarian households. New England Blue Hubbard is back-breaking to harvest at 15 to 20 pounds each. Baby hubbards, such as Baby Blue, are much the smaller and earlier, not much bigger than the largest buttercup. Golden or Red Hubbard is orange, but otherwise similar to the 10-pound Warted Hubbard. Golden Hubbard has been the staple of the pumpkin pie industry for decades, since no green flecks discolor the puree. At Mrs. Smith's Pie Company I saw acres of bright orange hubbards piled high as barns for her signature "pumpkin" pie. Apparently she never uses pumpkins. Maximas have better taste and the orange skin blends with no flakes.

Hubbard flavor is truly exceptional. When grown well, it is hard to stop eating it; even the skin is delicious! It is nutty, dry, sweet, and unforgettable. It requires a good memory, however, because hubbard is so inconsistent. As one long-time biodynamic gardener from California remarked, "When hubbards are great, there is nothing like them; but I have never figured out exactly what growing conditions—sun, humus, and moisture—make the difference." Probably one difference is the variability of the strain. There appear to be considerable differences of size and internal quality in most sowings. Another factor is maturity. Even slight immaturity produces disappointing fruit, its rich sweetness diluted beyond recognition.

With large hubbards, it is best to leave only one fruit to mature per vine, or two fruits for the smaller ones. That means a lot of vine for a low yield, practical only when a gardener has land to spare. If mature and well cured, maxima squash maintain excellent quality in storage. If not mature and not well cured, they rot like fish. They even smell like rotten fish.

Burgess buttercup was invented to solve this problem. Flavor and quality are comparable to the best hubbard, and so rich and sweet they need no butter. Many claim Burgess is still the best tasting squash. However, Burgess buttercup is low yielding, usually only three well-matured fruits per plant. About

25% less squash than butternut, with 25% more flavor. Unfortunately, buttercup shares other major *C. maxima* weaknesses; its seedlings are susceptible to cucumber beetles. Full-grown plants fall to viral wilts and stem borers. Fruits are only fair keepers.

Buttercup is dark green, with silver streaks and a grey cup at the bottom, usually 3 to 4 pounds, sometimes larger. Buttercup hybrids such as Bon Bon (90 days) are larger, more uniform, and yield more fruits per plant, up to 5 per vine. Bon Bon has some resistance to powdery mildew. For smaller gardens, Autumn Cup Hybrid (95 days) grows in compact semi-bush plants.

Japanese squashes are similar in appearance to buttercup, but lack the grey cup at the base. Flesh is rich, dry, flaky, and with a distinct sweet flavor that is preferred by macrobiotic customers. Open-pollinated Black Forest is a medium dry kabocha squash with 4 to 5 fruits per vine. Sweet Mama Hybrid (80 days) is fusarium wilt-resistant and stores up to 5 months, if kept very dry. Grey-skinned hybrid kabocha, such as 13 lb. Grey Ghost (100 days), also store very well, with unusually fine maxima flavor and sweetness.

Sunshine Hybrid (95 days) with its brilliant red-orange fruits has extraordinary curb appeal and fine quality bright orange flesh. Terrific for farm stands; for Halloween and Thanksgiving. Red Kuri, also called Orange Hokkaido, is the Japanese version of Orange Hubbard. It produces fleck-free puree, as smooth as baby food, the silken tofu of squashes. A highly decorative red-orange squash, useful for pie and pumpkin pudding.

The flesh of most varieties of *Cucurbita pepo* is not as fine textured, sweet, or nutty as *C. Maxima*. Pepos are related to pumpkins and have the same curved swan's neck stem. For some, nothing tastes better than a well-grown acorn squash (*C. pepo*), baked with butter, honey, and cinnamon. Others find acorn squash anemic and do not care for their stringiness. They argue that baked maximas supply the butter and honey for free. To taste their best, acorn squash must be well composted and fully mature.

Table Queen (80 days) has been around since the Civil War and, when well grown, can produce very good quality *C. pepo* fruits with sweet, fine textured flesh. Table Queen also stores fairly well for an acorn. The acorn hybrid, Honey Bear (85 days) has even better eating quality, more substantial and sweet. Honey Bear fruits are single serving, half the size of standard acorn. If powdery mildew has reduced the quality and yield of your acorn squash, look for a PM-resistant variety. Some are semi-bush vines suitable for smaller gardens or high-density plantings.

Delicata or Sweet Potato squash, (*C. pepo,* 100 days) have better taste and texture. Delicata is long, oval-shaped, cream colored with long, green stripes, with still very fine flavor, increasingly popular in fancy markets. Sweet Dumpling (100 days) is higher yielding with similar coloration and flesh, shaped somewhat like a small pumpkin. The gourd-like coloring of Carnival Hybrid (95 days) has nice roadside appeal but not as high quality flesh as other delicata. Like other pepos, the delicatas do not require curing for storage, but last longer than acorn, up to 4 months.

The *Cucurbita moschata* group is the easiest to grow, the most reliable producers, and the easiest to store for long periods. As far as I can tell, all butternuts and their kin taste about the same. They are sweet, even-textured with tan skin and give a lot of flesh for the size. They also appear to be the only species resistant to the vine borer, a real problem in southern and central states; less so as you go north. The largest butternuts, such as Ultra HP Hybrid (90 days), weigh up to 10 pounds each, with high yield and good quality. The smallest, such as Butterbush (75 days), produce 1½-pound fruits on 4-foot bush vines. Most gardeners choose a butternut in the mid-4½ pound range, such as Waltham (100 days), still the standard for the type. Waltham is fairly uniform, blocky, with deep orange flesh and very good taste. If cured for a week, Waltham keeps all winter and sweetens in storage, lasting in edible condition until spring.

Again, the value of hybrids is primarily powdery mildew resistance. Vigorous mildew-free vines and leaves significantly improve fruit quality and sweetness (also achieved by ample high-quality compost). Metro PMR (105 days) is also more compact, with smaller 2½-pound fruits. Early Butternut Hybrid (75 days) is useful in short season areas with vines one-third the size of Waltham, fruits 2½ pounds, maturing a month earlier than other butternuts.

> SEED: Seed size varies from 125 to more than 400 seeds per ounce. An ounce of Hubbard or Kuri (125 seeds), sows 20 mounds, 6 seeds per mound. An ounce of acorn (250 seeds) sows 40 mounds at 6 seeds each. An ounce of buttercup or kabocha (150 seeds) sows 25 mounds, 6 seeds each. An ounce of butternut (345 seeds) sows 57 mounds, 6 seeds each. An ounce of Delicata or Sweet Dumpling (430 seeds) sows 71 mounds, 6 seeds each. (Seeds per ounce averaged from Stokes and Johnny's seed catalogs.)

GERMINATION: 75%, seven days at 80°F.

VIABILITY: 4 years.

DAYS TO HARVEST: 90 to 110 days.

MOON CALENDAR: All practices, including biodynamic sprays, in fruit, ascending moon, if possible. For mildew, spray equisetum on leaf days.

ROTATION: 3 years for members of the squash, cucumber, melon family. Best not to follow nightshades.

BIODYNAMIC SPRAYS: Horn manure (500) on soil for peat pots and on field. Compost-500 tea on transplants when setting out. Pre-soak seeds overnight in compost-500 tea before sowing for direct-seeding in mounds by hand. Dip transplants in compost-500 tea to transplant water when sowing in dry periods. Spray silica (501) at least once in greenhouse, when vines begin to run, flowering, fruit set, and ripening. Spray silica in the morning. Valerian (507) may be added during ripening of winter squash.

COMPANION PLANTS: For cucumber beetles, interplant with radishes and strong scented herbs such as oregano, lemon balm, catnip, horehound, nasturtium, and marigold. Vine borers are repelled by wormwood, but since wormwood contains growth suppressant toxins, plant only at side of hills or sprinkle cut wormwood leaves over squash stems. Southernwood, rosemary, sage, santolina, mint, and tansy also repel borers. Tansy can also be cut and shredded over squash stems. Squash bugs are repelled by nasturtiums and attracted by black plastic mulch. Squash can be interplanted with corn, pole beans, and shell beans. Allow 8 feet between mounds to prevent shading.

Appendix: COVER CROPS

Since the plow destroyed the sea of grass covering the Great Plains, soil organic matter has declined 60% (Norton, University of Wyoming). Extreme aeration has burned up the humus, threatening the world's greatest reserve of organic matter—possibly even threatening agriculture itself there and in many parts of the world.

Nothing—not even ample composting—replaces rest years under pasture mix. A durable soil structure and long-lasting humus—one soil scientist told me these humus compounds may last hundreds of years—can only be established when undisturbed by tilling. Ideally this should redirect alternative agriculture toward permaculture, where all crops are produced from a perennial green base. I know some market growers in tropical areas who achieve this, but the rest of us barely use cover crops at all, and that's what I'd like to address here.

Many biodynamic growers describe the soil as a living organism, but it really isn't like a cow, or even an earthworm. A better analogy would be a colonial sea creature, such as the man o' war. The man o' war is really a colony of different polyp animals that act together like a single animal. Each organ—the helmet, the stinging tentacles, the grasping digestive tentacles, and the reproductive organs are conjoined separate species. Soil is like that, an invisible colonial animal under our feet, connected to the air and sky by the magic carpet of plants we remove at our peril.

To understand the soil you have to imagine it in time-lapse photography, changing as slowly as a plant grows, in response to the same seasonal cycles. When we dig it up, it looks static, but in fact soil life makes Tolkein's world seem unimaginative, so diverse and strange are its creatures, with their lassos and hoops and ghostly mycelial fingers. There is not even living and dying as we understand it, but more like the tumbling interchange of cells and substance inside an animal's body.

When we plow down a cover crop, durable plant compounds such as gums, resins, and waxes, which served specific roles on the surface or interior of leaves, become the binding foundation for soil structure, just as gluten binds the crumbs in bread. White threads of fungal mycelia sew a ghostly organic fabric between the crumbs, increasing water retention and suppressing parasites (nematodes).

Trails of mucus and slime from earthworms and other soil organisms create a durably moist crumb. The organic whole creates plants highly resistant to disease and drought, increases antioxidants and nutrient content, and helps prevent erosion and leaching of nutrients into the water table. If you examine the clods closely, month by month, a well developed loam might remind you of whole grain bread. This is a good standard of tilth, if you remember that every clod is only a single shot of a changeable flow, a change of seasons under the earth.

The Ancients imagined a giant, called Atlas, holding up the earth, which against all odds seems to be still struggling under our feet, under increasingly difficult conditions. According to 100 years of statistics, what holds up the earth today is about as well fed as some of the poorest parts of Bangladesh.

Cover Crop Solutions

Market gardeners with land to spare divide their crops into 4 parts, rotating vegetables with a grass and legume pasture mix as a rest crop. Others transplant certain vegetables with perennial ground cover, such as subclover or hairy vetch. Others overseed hairy vetch between rows of sweet corn or other longstanding crops during the last cultivation, or follow fall-harvested crops with winter rye to increase organic matter, suppress a wide range of pathogens, and prevent winter erosion.

Rye is widely used as a winter cover crop because it grows later in the fall and earlier in the spring than legumes, offers almost as much nitrogen as crimson and berseem clover, and has a good carbon to nitrogen ratio (14 parts C to one part N). Rye also deposits 25% more biomass than its closest legume competitor.

With the lowest germination temperature of all cover crops, rye can be planted fairly late, even during light frost. Rye establishes best when sown 4 weeks before killing frost. In late spring the stand of rye can be killed by mowing during pollination phase: notice when dusty pollen begins to fall. Wait 2 to 3 weeks after plowdown of grasses to plant new crops.

Rye also has significant allelopathic residual effects, suppressing plant diseases and soil pests such as nematodes.

A low carbon to nitrogen ratio is extremely important following higher CN crops such as corn (66 carbon to 1 part nitrogen), which requires nitrogen to break down. This is also the case with extreme CN rations such as sawdust bedded manure. Sawdust has such a high CN ratio (over 250 to 1) that it not only negates the value of the manure, but it ties up all available nitrogen in the soil. If you use sawdust bedded manure, compost it with fresh garden weeds and green legume forbs for a full year before application.

Legumes are the best cover crop source for nitrogen. Roughly half of legume nitrogen becomes available the year following plowdown. The other half continues to feed successive crops over the next 2 years. Hairy vetch, sweet clover, and Austrian winter peas have very high N values. Be sure to add the correct rhizobial bacteria for nitrogen nodule formation for each legume species. Rhizobial bacteria will persist in the soil for several years after application and may continue to be sufficient for future crops. Rye can also be mixed with Austrian winter pea preceding vegetable crops. In Oregon State University tests the rye/Austrian winter pea mix reduced nitrogen fertilizer applications 125 pounds per acre for broccoli and 150 pounds per acre for sweet corn. Rye alone caused a 10% decrease in yields (Burket, Oregon Extension 2003).

Spring sown clovers sown between row crops—4-foot tomato rows—produce nitrogen all season long and leave a substantial nitrogen legacy for N hungry crops (crucifers, etc.) the following season. Clovers include crimson, alsike, yellow sweet, white, berseem, and red. Some clover types may be preferable in warmer, colder, drier, or wetter climates. Alsike, for example, tolerates wetter sites (as does rye), as well as areas of low fertility. Clovers also vary in fertilizer value: sweet clover offers 40% more nitrogen and biomass than berseem. White clover fares poorly in dry soil. Crimson clover prefers cool, humid weather and is only moderately shade tolerant—thereby producing weak stands in corn (Oregon Extension). Birdsfoot trefoil (a legume, but not a clover) is also tolerant of low fertility and can be sown with pearl millet or barley under those conditions.

Deep-rooted legumes act as subsoilers. Blue lupine, red clover, and alfalfa chisel down 5 to 7 feet into the subsoil. Crown vetch, yellow sweet clover, and black medic drill down 3 to 5 feet. Hairy vetch and white clover, 1 to 3 feet. Deep rooted cover crops draw up soil minerals otherwise unattainable: organic acids break down minerals from deep insoluable rock (Sullivan, National Sustainable Information Service). Root chiseled passages are then open to successive garden crops. Deep-rooted brassicas provide the same service. Turnip, field radish, rape, and mustard penetrate just as deep as the legumes, with excellent biomass, but are somewhat limited by our usual overpacked crucifer rotation. More often these cover crops are used by farmers.

The advantage of brassica cover crops is how quickly they provide weed suppression and large biomass. Brassicas also suppress many plant pathogens and root rots (Abawi, quoted in Michigan Extension). Brassica cover crops should never be used where club root has been reported.

For home gardeners the most attractive and practical cover crops double as food crops. These include broad beans (and their smaller cousin, bell beans), green soy beans, garden peas, cowpeas, bush beans, and green shell beans. Fertilizer value and value to soil organisms will be greatest if tops are tilled under when leaves are vital and not aging. This still allows for several pickings. Sow peas and beans in rows 1 foot apart to create greater biomass.

Mixing winter squash and pumpkins with undersown legumes also allows for both production and cover crop. Vetches and low growing clover can be broadcast between mounds and raised rows. Vines will ride the vetches and clover, and fruit may be harder to find than on mulch, but the benefit to successive crops will outweigh the inconvenience.

Buckwheat is the only grain (really a seed) that could be harvested in a home garden, since it matures quickly in almost any climate. As a cover crop, however, seed is broadcast thickly in fall and left to be killed by winter frost. In spring the buckwheat residue will be transplant-ready as a malted mulch. Be sure to use iron-based slug bait.

Lastly, I want to mention the USDA trials planting tomatoes into hairy vetch. Plots and controls were planted in both Binghamton, NY, and Raleigh, NC. Hairy vetch was sown 2 months before winter, August 24 in Binghamton and October 18 in Raleigh, using the proper rhizobial bacteria. The vetch grows into a dense mat before winter and by tomato transplanting time next spring will be 2 feet deep. On a dry afternoon when the vetch is flowering, reduce the stand to mulch using a high speed flail mower. The USDA planted tomatoes directly into the mulch, using half the recommended fertilizer for tomatoes. Tomato diseases were reduced by 50% on the vetch mulch (as opposed to bare soil and black plastic controls). Vetch cover increased tolerance to disease and delayed plant aging. Production costs for the vetch tomatoes were slightly higher, but net profits were 40% higher. Weeds and pests were suppressed by vetch at all stages. Summer water loss was also reduced. Fertilizer values for the vetch ranged from 3 to 5,000 pounds of organic matter per acre and 120 to 200 pounds of nitrogen per acre. Oddly, the study did not mention the additional dollar value of residual nitrogen biomass and bioactivity in successive years. This method can also be used for corn, pumpkin, squash, and cucumber, and possibly crucifers and peppers.

Index

Abelomoschus, 230
Ace (peppers), 267
Achard, Franz Karl, 112
achita (amaranth grain), 270
acorn squash, 360, 366
aesthetic-therapeutic, 11
Afghan Purple (carrot), 89, 96
aflatoxin, 133-134
Age of Enlightenment, 248-249, 271
agretti, 20-21, 32
Ailsa Craig (onion), 244
Ajo Rojo (garlic), 168
Alaska (split pea), 261
Alderman (peas), 260
alfalfa, 32, 37-38, 255, 275, 322, 371
alfalfa tea, 24, 33, 124, 139, 275
alkaloid, 22-23, 116, 146, 263, 279, 323
All Blue (potato), 278
Allium, 164, 168-169, 191-194, 196-197, 238-239, 245-246, 338
Alpine (daikon), 290
alternaria, 83, 91, 95, 126, 148, 221, 325-326, 332
amaranth. *See* Wild Salads, Amaranth
Amaranthus, 305, 349-350
Amazing (cauliflower), 100
Amber Globe (turnip), 340
Ambrosia Hybrid (melon), 222
American Hybrid Storage No. 4 (cabbage), 84
Amish Paste (tomato), 335
Anasazi Bush (bean), 46
ancho-pablano peppers, 268
Andover (parsnip), 252
Annie Oakley (okra), 234
anthracnose, 44, 47, 141, 209, 294, 312, 326, 345-346
anti-carcinogen/carcinogen, 23, 60, 193, 213, 226, 239, 266, 317, 323-324, 352, 355
anti-inflammatory, 118, 164, 238, 307, 321, 349, 352, 355
antioxidant, 15, 23, 28, 30-31, 69, 101, 117- 118, 146, 173-174, 225, 239, 266, 268, 286, 291, 307, 337, 349, 353, 356, 370

Antriplex, 351
Anvenue (lettuce), 205
Aphanomyces. See common root rot
aphids, 26, 51, 58, 73, 104, 150, 200, 202, 227-228, 233, 238, 258, 265-266, 310, 311, 322, 356, 361
Apple Green (eggplant), 151
April Cross (daikon), 289
Arava (melon), 223
Archangelica, 10, 249, 328
Arctium lappa, 76
artichokes/cardoons, 22-27, 111
Arkansas Traveler (tomato), 333
arnica, 179
Aristotle, 111
Armoracia, 173
arugula, 28, 226
  as wall rocket, 28
Asian Brassicas, 15-18
Asian flat-podded peas, 260
Asian Guy Lohn (broccoli), 70
Asian mustards, 17, 18, 225, 228, 230
asparagus, 30-37, 298, 336, 353
  as Sparrow Grass, 30
asparagus bean, 46-47
  as yard-long, 46-47
asparagus beetles, 35, 38
asparagus rust, 36
Atlantic Giant (pumpkin), 281
Atomic Red (carrot), 96
Aunt Ada's Italian (bean), 45
Aunt Molly's Ground Cherry, 172
Autumn Cup Hybrid (buttercup squash), 366
Autumn King (carrot), 97
Azotobacter, 255
Baby Bear (pumpkin), 284
Baby Blue (squash), 365
Bacillus (Bt), 26, 64, 82, 92, 109, 125, 150, 175, 183, 228, 233, 293, 328, 363
bacterial blight, 209
bacterial wilt, 139, 141, 149, 220, 311, 326-327, 363
bacterium, beneficial 228

Bailey's *Horticulture*, 23, 33, 35, 55, 276, 287, 297
Bandit (leeks), 196
Barbarea, 355-357
barilla (agretti), 21
Basella, 305
Batavian escarole, 118, 154-156, 205, 206
Batavian lettuce, 201-202, 205, 303
bean, 12, 44, 54, 59, 91, 98, 104, 137, 160, 197, 252, 295, 305
  bush, 34, 38-42, 47, 85, 105, 110, 115, 127, 186, 212, 252, 254, 257, 259-260, 263, 280, 302, 353, 372
  pole, 42-45, 47, 134, 137, 201, 212
bean beetle, 40-41, 42, 47, 210, 280
Beauregard (sweet potato), 319
beefsteak tomatoes, 333
bees, 11, 35, 140, 179, 211, 218, 220, 310, 311, 344
beets, 20, 48-54, 111-113, 114, 149, 181, 226, 240, 292
bell beans, 329, 372
Belstar (broccoli), 67
Belstar Super (scorzonera), 299
Beltsville (potato), 279
Bennie's Red (onion), 244-245
Berry, Wendell, 270
Beta vulgaris, 52, 111
Better Boy (tomato), 333
Bianca Riccia (endives), 156
bibb lettuce, 204
Big Beef (tomato), 334
Big Mama (lima bean), 211
Big Max (pumpkin), 282
Big Max (winter squash), 359
Big Rainbow (tomato), 333
Big Tasty Hybrid (watermelon), 346
Big Top (Asian carrot), 97
Big Top Western (horseradish), 176
Bilko (Chinese cabbage), 126
bindweed, 33, 316
biodynamic, 3, 5, 8-9, 11, 27, 47-49, 59, 68, 80-81, 88, 93, 99, 121, 123, 139, 148, 169, 181-183, 193, 199-200, 205, 217, 219-221, 232, 251, 254, 256-257, 265, 275-276, 297, 322, 325, 328-330, 339, 341-342, 345, 350, 352-353, 361
  sprays, 19, 25, 38, 47, 54, 59, 68, 75, 77, 85, 98, 101, 105, 110, 115, 121, 127, 143-144, 152, 157, 166, 170, 176, 180, 186, 191, 195, 197, 206, 212, 215, 224, 229, 235, 247, 261, 275, 280, 285, 290, 295, 306, 314, 320, 336, 340, 347, 368
bioremediation, 20, 226
birdsfoot trefoil (legume), 371
Black Beauty (eggplant), 151
Black Beauty (zucchini), 311
Black Bell II (eggplant), 150
Black Cherry (tomato), 334
Black Forest (winter squash), 359, 366
black heart (a boron deficiency), 50, 104, 175
Black Iroquois/Black Mexican (corn), 134-135
Black Magic (eggplant), 146
black oyster plant, 298
Black Pearl (tomato), 335
Black Pride (eggplant), 149
black rot, 82, 83-85, 189, 190, 290, 294
black salsify. *See* scorzonera
Black Seed Simpson (lettuce), 204
Black Spanish radish, 286-287, 290
Black Storage (radish), 289
black tip, 26
Black Turtle (bean), 47
blackberries, 179, 216
black-eyed peas, 315
Blau Greuner Winter (leeks), 196
Blood Butcher (corn), 134
Bloomsdale (spinach), 304
blossom blight, 234
blossom drop, 140, 207, 266, 327
blossom end rot, 265, 312, 327-328, 329
Blue Curled Scotch (kale), 185
Blue Hubbard (pumpkin), 282
blue lupine (legume), 371
Blue Thunder (cabbage), 84
Blue Wind (broccoli), 67
blueberries, 161
Bohemian/Maliner Kren (horseradish), 176
Bolero (carrot), 95, 97
bok choy, 154, 178, 189, 283, 316
bolting, 3, 10, 17, 18, 28, 51, 70, 104, 108, 110, 113, 114, 115, 119, 120, 124, 125, 126, 127, 181, 198, 338
  (in lettuce), 203, 205
Bon Bon (butternut squash), 366

Borlotto (bean), 46
boron deficiency, 99-100, 109
Boston (lettuce), 204
botrytis leaf blight, 58, 245-246
Brandy Boy (tomato), 334
Brandywine (tomato), 333
Brassica, 15-18, 22, 34, 60, 69-72, 78-80, 124-127, 151, 182, 187-188, 215, 224-225, 286, 291-292, 294, 316, 337-338, 340, 371, 372
breathing diaphragm, of the soil, 49
Bright Lights (chard), 115
Brilliant (celeriac), 105
Brinial (eggplant), 145
broad bean (fava), 55-59, 127, 207, 280, 372
Broad London (leeks), 196
Broad Windsor Long Pod (fava), 55, 59
broccoli, 3, 15, 17-19, 40, 60-65, 78, 99-101, 134, 182, 189, 225, 229, 283, 337
broccoli raab, 26, 69-70, 355
Bronze Age (peas), 261
Bountiful Gardens Seeds, 59, 114
brown bead, 67
brown canker, 252
brown (Say) stink bugs, 233
Brown Tempest (garlic), 169
Brussels sprouts, 15, 71-75, 77, 99, 181, 225, 292
Bryophyllum, 262
buckwheat, 32, 88, 179, 372
bud rot, 26
Bull's Blood (beet), 53
Bullshorn (pepper), 267
bunching onions. *See* scallions
Burbank, Luther, 129, 161, 278
burdock, 76-77, 141, 296
Burgess (buttercup squash), 365
Burgundy (okra), 230, 234
Burmese (okra), 234
Burpeana Early (peas), 258
Burpee Hybrid (eggplant), 151
Burpee Hybrid (melon), 222
Burpee Pickler (cucumber), 140, 142-143
Burpee's Best (lima bean), 211
Burpee's Big Boy (tomato), 334
Burpee's Beananza (bean), 44
Burpee's Early Crenshaw Hybrid (melon), 223

Burpee's First White (cauliflower), 101
Burpee's Tender Pod (bean), 43
Bush Blue Lake (bean), 43
Bush Sugar Baby (watermelon), 346
Butterbush (squash), 367
buttercrunch lettuce, 120, 204, 205
butterbeans, 207-208
buttercup squashes, 281-283, 285, 359-360, 363, 365-367
Butterfly, (spinach), 304
butterflies, 92, 308
butterheads (lettuce), 201, 204, 205, 206
   Dutch, 204
butternut squashes, 282, 283, 285, 360, 363-364, 367
Butterstick Hybrid (zucchini), 313
"button up," 61, 67, 99, 100

cabbage, 4, 15, 19, 40, 47, 62, 72-73, 78-85, 86, 99-100, 105, 110, 115, 183-186, 188-189, 191, 206, 225, 229, 247, 252, 287, 290-293, 295, 339, 342
   wild, 22
cabbage flies/worms, 64, 73-74, 80, 82, 125, 175, 183-184, 227-228, 288, 293, 339
Cajun Delight (okra), 234
Calabrese/Calabria (broccoli), 66
calendula, 179, 336
Camp, Wendell
   The World in Your Garden, 248
cancer, 28, 146, 165, 173, 193, 225, 231, 286, 307, 323, 324, 335, 338, 343, 356, 357
Candy Hybrid (onion), 244
Cape Gooseberry (ground cherry), 172
Capitane (lettuce), 204
Capsicum, 262, 268
caraway, 10, 68, 75, 82, 85, 91, 127, 160, 186, 199, 249, 280
Cardinal Hybrid (cabbage), 85
cardoon. *See* Artichoke/Cardoon
Caribe (potato), 278
Caribbean Red (hot pepper), 268-269
Carnival Hybrid (winter squash), 367
Caroflex (cabbage), 83
Carola (potato), 278
carotene, 18, 95, 96, 357
carrot, 7, 10, 49, 51, 59, 62, 86-98, 102, 105, 106, 122, 127, 160, 180, 183, 197,

199, 206, 247, 250-252, 272, 292, 299, 303, 337
carrot fly/worm, 25, 91-92, 95, 98, 197, 251, 299
Carver, George Washington, 182, 315
casaba (melon), 222
cassava, 207, 249
castor bean, 144, 220
caterpillars, 10, 64, 82, 92, 210, 233, 328
catnip, 68, 75, 85, 91, 98, 127, 144, 186, 220, 368
cauliflower, 15, 22, 60-61, 66, 67, 78, 81, 84, 99-101, 109, 182, 188
cayenne peppers, 267-268, 269
Celebrity (tomato), 334
celeriac, 47-48, 102-106, 127, 170, 199
celery, 21, 31, 32, 47, 59, 85, 103, 106-110, 127, 159, 170, 186, 197, 199, 251, 295, 336, 340
celery blight, 251
celtuce (stem lettuce), 203
Centennial (sweet potato), 319
Century (yellow split pea), 261
cercospora leaf blight, 91
Chadwick, Alan, 55, 87, 138, 304
Chadwick's Cherry (tomato), 334
Chadwick's French Intensive Method, 138
chamomile, 68, 75, 85, 186, 247
Champion (collards), 184
Champion (radish), 288
Champlain, de, Samuel, 178
Chantenay (carrot), 87, 96-97
chard, 51, 54, 62, 85, 111-115 186, 306, 340
  Swiss, 51, 111-112, 181, 183
Charleston Gray (watermelon), 345
Charentais (cantaloupe), 221, 223
Charisma PMR (pumpkin), 284
Charmant (cabbage), 83
Cheddar Hybrid (cauliflower), 101
Chenapodium, 181, 270, 351
chenopods, 20-21, 181, 270, 351
Cherokee (lettuce), 205
Cherokee Purple (tomato), 333
cherry. *See* Ground cherry
Cherry Belle (radish), 288
chervil, 127, 199, 249, 280, 336
Chestnut (winter squash), 359
Cheviette (radish), 289

Chichiquelite (huckleberry), 162
chickpeas, 55
chickweed, 348
chicory, 27-28, 91, 98, 116-121, 156, 199, 350
chile peppers, 268
Chiko (burdock), 77
Chinese cabbage, 17-18, 62, 123-126, 154, 156, 184
Chinese chives, 338
Chinese Lantern (ground cherry), 171
Chinese leek, 192-193, 194, 196-197
Chinese Thick Stem Mustard, 228
Chinese tsai shim (pac choi), 17
chioggia (beet), 51, 53, 119
  as Dolce di Chioggia, 53
Chioggia Red Preco (radicchio), 119
chitin, 9
chives, 91, 98, 105, 110, 169, 338
chlorisis, 327
Chocolate Cherry (tomato), 334
chocolate spot. *See* botrytis
choy sum. *See* Chinese tsai shim
Christmas (lima bean), 211
Cichorium, 118, 156, 350
cilantro, 59, 321, 352
Cimmaron (lettuce), 205
citrulline, 342-343, 345, 346
Citrullus, 342
Classic (eggplant), 149, 151
Claytonia (miner's lettuce), 354
Clemson Spineless (okra), 234
climbing spinach (spinach), 305
clover, 73, 255, 307, 329, 370-372
club root fungus, 62, 83, 294, 372
Cocarde (lettuce), 204
Cold-Resistant Savoy (spinach), 305
cole crops, 26, 79, 189, 197, 200, 261, 302-303, 316, 320
collards, 7, 71, 78, 106, 181-184, 188, 190, 225-227, 283, 315-316
Columbia root knot nematodes, 227
Colossus (Conover's Colossal beans), 36
common root rot, 227
Compositae (daisy), 117, 178
compost tea, 24, 64, 100, 120, 124, 140, 143-144, 147, 195, 219, 241, 292, 304, 310, 326, 331, 344, 347, 368
Connecticut Field (pumpkin), 281, 284

Index

Conquistador (celery), 110
Contender (bean), 43
Convolvulacae, 316
copper hydroxide, 299, 312, 326
Copra (onion), 245
coriander, 38, 48, 59, 68, 127, 160, 280
corn, 41, 44, 121, 128-137, 178, 224, 261, 313, 315, 353
corn borer, 26, 133
corn earworm, 133
corn salad. *See* Mache
corn smut, 130, 132
cos (romaine), 205
Cosmic Purple (carrot), 96
Costata Romanesca (squash), 309-310, 313
Cossack Pineapple (ground cherry), 172
Costoluto Genovese (tomato), 333
cotton, 315
cottonseed meal, 50, 265
cottonseed oil, 150
cotyledons, 78, 86, 92, 108, 182, 201, 360, 361
Country Gentleman (corn), 135
Country Taste Hybrid (tomato), 334
cover crops, 369-373
Cow Horn (okra), 234
cowpeas, 46, 137, 280, 315, 320, 372
Cranberry Bean, 46
creasy greens (winter cress), 355
crenshaw (melon), 217, 223
Crimson Sweet (watermelon), 346
crookneck squash, 309
Crosby Egyptian (beet), 52
crotonaldehyde, 165
crowders (peas), 315
crown rot, 26
crown vetch, 371
cucumber, 138-144, 220, 224, 305, 314, 347, 364, 368
cucumber beetles, 139, 224, 233, 311, 345, 347, 361-363, 366, 368
cucumber mosaic virus, 141-143, 265, 266, 312, 313, 322
Cucumis melo, 143, 217
Cucurbitae, 137, 139, 143, 149, 152, 220, 224, 281-283, 309, 312, 314, 359-368
cumin, 55, 58, 160, 226, 349
cup plant, 179
curly dwarf virus, 26

curly endive, 118
curly top virus, 273, 327
Cushaw (pumpkin), 282
cutworms, 26, 35, 151, 202, 265, 311, 328, 331
Cylindra (beet), 48, 53
Cynara, 22-23
daikon radish, 286-290
Daisy Gold (potato), 279
dandelion. *See* Wild Salads
Danvers (carrot), 87, 91, 93, 96-97
Danvers Half Long (carrots), 96
Dark Green Zuccini (zucchini), 313
Dark Lollo Rosa (lettuce), 204
Datura, 272
deadly nightshade, 146, 271, 323
Deadon (cabbage), 84
De Cicco (broccoli), 66
deer prevention, 35-36, 168
Deer Tongue (lettuce), 204
Delicious (melon), 51, 221
Defiant (tomato), 326
Delecata (squash), 281, 359, 363, 367
Delphic Oracle (ground cherry), 173
De Milpa (tomatillo), 322
dent corn, 44, 129, 134
Desoto (the person), 134
Detroit Dark Red Medium Top (beet), 52
Detroit Short Top (beet), 53
Diablo (Brussels sprouts), 75
dill, 10, 38, 48, 59, 68, 75, 82, 85, 91, 127, 144, 160, 186, 199, 280, 328, 336, 338
Dioscorea, 319
Dipel (Bt), 26, 35, 82, 92, 109, 125, 133, 175, 183, 233, 293
Diplomat (melon), 223
Diva (cucumber), 142
Dottenfelder Storage (cabbage), 84
double digging, 32, 87, 208
downy mildew, 65, 67, 99, 139, 141-142, 199, 204, 205, 209, 211, 221, 228, 245, 259, 304-305, 312, 363
Dragon (carrot), 89
Dumpling (squash), 367
Dusky (eggplant), 150
dwarf English peas, 91

EA Special Strain (celery), 110
Early Girl Hybrid (tomato), 333

early blight, 148, 325, 326, 331, 332
Early Blood Turnip (beet), 53
Early Butternut Hybrid (squash), 367
Early Fall Rapini (broccoli), 70
Early Flat Dutch (cabbage), 84
Early Jersey Wakefield (cabbage), 83
Early Moonbeam (watermelon), 346
Early Purple Sprouting (broccoli), 66
Early Purple Vienna (kohlrabi), 190
Early White Vienna (kohlrabi), 190
Early Wonder (beet), 52
Early Yellow Globe (onions), 245
Earth Tones Dent (corn), 134
earthworms, 88, 91, 102-105, 122, 199-200, 206, 275, 286, 303, 369-370
Easter Egg ((radish), 289
Eastland (lima bean), 209, 211
Ebenezer (onions), 245
Edamame, 57
Eden's Gem (melon), 222
Edisto (melon), 221
Edmonson (cucumber), 142
Edonis (melon), 223
eggplant, 145-152, 200, 264, 266, 306, 327, 336
Egyptian onions, 239, 246-247
elephant garlic, 167-169
endive, 98, 117-118, 153-157, 199
English peas, 257-258, 261
Ensminger's Nutritional Encyclopedia, 270
Epic (eggplant), 149-150
equisetum tea, 41-42, 47, 83, 85, 91, 98, 105, 108, 110, 121, 132, 139, 140, 144, 152, 166, 189, 202, 206, 219- 221, 224, 258, 264, 269, 275, 279-280, 328, 330, 335-336, 344-345, 347, 363, 368
Erba stella, 352
Erbette (chard), 115
ergot, 130
Ermosa (lettuce), 204
erucin, *28*
Eruca sativa, 28
escarole, 27, 91, 98, 117-118, 153-157, 199, 205
etheric oils, 48, 106
Ethiopian mustard, 225, 230
Evangeline (sweet potato), 319
Evergreen Hardy White (onions), 245
Everona Large Green (tomatillo), 322

Fabaceae, 254
Fairy Tale (eggplant), 151
Fairytale (pumpkin), 285
Farao F1 Hybrid (cabbage), 84
fava. *See* broad bean (fava)
favism, 57-58
fennel, 10, 40, 64, 68, 82, 91, 158-160, 249, 251, 328
fiberless plantain, 352
field garlic, 193
field mice, 52
fingerling potatoes, 277-279
Finnochio (fennel), 158
fish emulsion, 24, 147, 166, 219, 240, 326, 330, 344, 362
Flagrano (bean), 47
flea beetle, 16, 28, 65, 69, 73, 82, 124-125, 133, 144, 150, 152, 162, 175, 183, 190, 227-228, 275, 288, 293, 295, 311, 326, 328, 339, 361
flint corn, 129, 135. 347
Floriani Red Flint (corn), 134
Florida Beauty (eggplant), 149
Florida Broadleaf (mustard green), 228
Florida Market (eggplant), 149
Flowering Mustard (guy lohn or *kai lan*), 17
Flying Saucer (squash), 314
folic acid, 249
folates, 226
fool's parsley, 88
Fordhook (lima bean), 211
Fordhook (zucchini), 313
Fordhook Giant (chard), 114
Fourth of July (tomato), 332
Fremont (cauliflower), 101
French Batavian (lettuce), 205-206
French Breakfast (radish), 288
French Chicory (Pan de Sucre or Sugar Loaf), 118
French Dandelion, 117-118
French Filet (bean), 43, 44, 47
French Flageolet (bean), 47
French Horticultural (bean), 46
Fresh Pick (bean), 43
Friar's beard (agretti), 21
Frosty (peas), 259-260
fruit galls, 262-263
Ful medames, 55

Index

fusarium rot (wilt), 32, 35-36, 83, 110, 126, 209, 221, 223, 228, 234-235, 245, 258, 260, 320, 325, 327, 329, 332, 345-346, 366

galias-type melon, 223
"gambler's period," 61, 131
Garden of Eden (bean), 45
garden huckleberry, 161-162
Gardener's Delight (tomato), 334
gargeer, 28
garlic, 54, 68, 75, 85, 91, 105, 110, 121, 145, 163-170, 186, 193, 206, 246, 321, 336-337
garlic chives, 91, 169, 183, 192, 196-197, 239
Garnet (sweet potato), 319
Garrison's Pineapple (ground cherry), 172
Genuine Cornfield (corn), 45
Georgia Green (collards), 184
Georgia Jet (sweet potato), 319
Georgia Rattlesnake (watermelon), 345
Georgia Red (sweet potato), 319
German Butterball (potato), 278
German Extra Hardy (garlic), 168
German Porcelain (garlic), 168
ghibberellic acid, 24, 26
Giant Fringe Oyster (endive), 118
Gigant (kohlrabi), 191
glasswort, 21
Glatter Silber (chard), 114
globe artichoke, 22-24
goatsbeard (salsify), 296
gobo (burdock), 76
God's earth, 128
Goethe/Goethean, 130, 181, 187-188, 255, 262, 300, 337
  his way of observation, 49, 147
Gold Mine (wax beans), 44
Goldberg (purslane), 353
Goldberry (ground cherry), 172
Golden Acre (cabbage), 83
Golden Bantam (corn), 135
Golden Beet (beet), 53
Golden Bush (squash), 313
Golden Frills (mustard greens), 17
Golden Gem (tomato), 334
Golden Hubbard (squash), 365
gophers, 36
gourds, 224

Graffiti Hybrid (cauliflower), 101
Granat (Chinese cabbage), 126
Grandmother Stallard (bean), 46
Granex Hybrid (onion), 244
grasshopper, 125
Green Arrow (peas), 259
Green Gita (asparagus bean), 46
Green Glaze (collards), 184
Green Globe (artichoke), 26
Green Goliath (broccoli), 66
green onions, 192, 239, 245, 246
Green Sprouting, Italian (broccoli), 66
Green Striped Crookneck (pumpkin), 282
Green Tiger (zucchini), 313
Green Towers (lettuce), 205
Green Wave (mustard greens), 17, 228
Grey Ghost (squash), 366
Grohmann, Gerbert, 236, 249-250, 255
ground cherry, 171-172, 327
Gruner (purslane), 353
gumbo, 230-231
gummy stem blight, 363-364
guy lohn, 17-19Gypsy (broccoli), 67

habanero peppers, 267-268, 269
hairy vetch, 329, 370-372
Hale's Best (melon), 221
halo blight, 47, 209
Halona (melon), 223
Hanlon (radish), 286
Hansel (eggplant), 151
Happy Rich Hybrid (broccoli), 70
hardnecks, garlic, 168, 169
hardening-off, 24, 81, 109, 219
Harper Hybrid (melon), 222
Harris Model (parsnip), 250, 252
Harris Seed Catalog, 134, 156, 266-267, 347
Harukei Hybrid (turnip), 340
He-Shi-Ko (hardy white bunching onions), 245
head rot, 61, 65, 67
Health Kick Hybrid (tomato), 335
Helenor (rutabaga), 295
Helianthus, 178
hemlock, poison, 88
henbane, 323
Henderson Bush (lima beans), 211
Hickory King (corn), 44-45
hill onion, 246

Hinn Choy (spinach), 305
Hippocrates, 357
Hiroshima Green (mustard greens), 17
Ho Mi Z (mustard green), 18, 228
Hoffman's Schwartze (scorzonera), 299
Hokkaido (squash), 282, 359, 366
Holland Capucijner (split pea), 261
Hollow Crown (parsnip), 250, 252
hollow heart, 278, 344, 347
hollow stem, 67
Holsteiner Platter (cabbage), 84
Hon tsai tai (Brassica), 17
Honey Bear (squash), 366
Honey Orange (melon), 223
Honey Yellow (melon), 223
Honey Bun (melon), 222
honeydew, 58
honeydew melons, 221-223
horehound, 91, 98, 220, 368
horn manure, 4, 47, 50-51, 54, 62, 68, 75, 79, 80, 85, 88, 98, 105, 109-110, 113, 115, 122, 124, 127, 131, 137, 144, 152, 155, 159-160, 166, 170, 180, 186, 189, 191, 195, 197, 200, 202, 206, 218, 224, 247, 252, 256-257, 261, 264, 269, 274, 279, 293, 295, 302, 304, 306, 318, 320, 336, 339, 340, 347, 368
hornworm, tomato, 328
horseradish, 173-176
Howden (pumpkin), 284
Hubbard (squash), 220, 281-282, 285, 359-350, 360, 366, 367
huckleberry. See garden huckleberry
hummingbird, 46
Hungarian Hot Wax (pepper), 267
huskworm, 322
Hybrid Orion (fennel), 159
hyssop, 91

Ice Bred White Egg (turnips), 338, 340
Iceberg lettuce, 203, 205
imaginative perception, 9
Imperator (carrot), 95-97
Imperial Star (artichoke), 26
Improved Einjahrige (scorzonera), 299
Inchelium Red (garlic), 169
infrared transmitting mulch (ITM), 232
insecticidal oil, 26, 51, 58, 150, 175, 202, 233, 265, 358

insecticidal soap, 58, 104, 150, 168, 210, 311, 358
inula, 179
Ipomoea, 319
Irene (eggplant), 149
Irish potato famine, 326
Irish potatoes, 276-277
Ishikura (onion), 245-246
Italian bush (flat beans), 44
Italian dandelion, 117-118, 121, 156
Italian lacinato (kale), 185
Italian raab, 17
Italian Sprouting Broccoli (guy lohn or kai lan), 17-19
Italian Largo Hybrid (zucchini), 313
Ivory liquid detergent, 242

Jack o' Lantern (pumpkin), 281, 284
Jacob's Cattle (bean), 47
Jade (bean), 43
Jade Cross (Brussels sprouts), 75
Jade Pagoda (Chinese cabbage), 127
Jaipur (melon), 222
jalapeno peppers, 267
January King (cabbage), 84
Japanese beetles, 233
Japanese or Chinese Lantern (ground cherry), 171
Japanese horseradish, 174
Japanese knotweed, 179
Japanese leek, 194
Japanese pie pumpkin, 282
Japanese White (sweet potato), 320
Japanese White Murasaki (sweet potato), 320
Jarrahdale (pumpkin), 285
Jefferson, Thomas, 323
Jenny Hybrid (watermelon), 347
Jericho (lettuce), 205
Jersey Giant (bean), 37
Jersey King (beans), 37
Jersey Orange (sweet potato), 319
Jersey White (sweet potato), 320
Jerusalem Artichokes, 178-180
Jewel (sweet potato), 319
Johnny's Selected Seeds (catalog), 24, 45, 59, 69, 120, 134, 205, 223, 243, 264, 267, 295-296, 322, 352, 356, 367
Joseph's coat (amaranth), 349-350

Index

Juliet (tomato), 326, 335
Jumbo (bean), 44
Juwarot (cabbage), 89

kabocha (pumpkin), 281, 360, 363, 366-367
Kaitlin (cabbage), 84
kale, 3, 40, 71-72, 78, 84, 112, 181-186, 190, 225, 227, 283, 350
Kaleidoscope Mix (carrot), 97
Katzen, Mollie
 Enchanted Broccoli Forest, 178
Kennebec (potato), 279
Kentucky Wonder (bean), 44-45
Kermit (eggplant), 151
Keystone (endive), 156
King of the Garden (lima beans), 211
King of the North (pepper), 267
King Richard (leeks), 196
Kinko (carrot), 87
Knight (peas), 259
Kohlrabi, 54, 160, 182, 187-191
Komatsuna (Brassica), 18
Kossack (kohlrabi), 191
Kranich, Ernst, 238
Krimzon Lee (pepper), 268
Kung Pao (pepper), 269
Kurado (carrot), 95-97
kyona (Brassica), 18

Lactuca, 198
Lady Belle (pepper), 267
lamb's quarters. *See* Wild Salads, lamb's quarters
Lambkin (melon), 222
Lancer (parsnips), 252
Large American Flag (leeks), 196
Large Speckled Calico (lima beans), 211
Large Smooth Prague/Giant Rooted Prague (celeriac), 105
lavender, 28
Laxton's Progress (peas), 259
leaf blight/spot, 91, 95, 126, 221, 325
leafhopper, 210-211, 275, 311
leaf miner, 51, 54, 112, 115, 233
leeks, 47, 54, 98, 105, 110, 192-194, 196, 340
Legend (tomato), 326
legumes, 62, 137, 254-255, 329, 336, 371-372

Leguminosae, 254
lemon balm, 91, 98
lettuce, 16, 27, 34, 40, 44, 62, 71, 85, 91, 98, 105, 117, 118, 120-121, 154-157, 186, 198-206, 213, 215, 219, 224, 246-247, 266, 295, 301, 303, 329, 330, 340
L-dopa, 57
Leuder, Margareta, 7-8, 12, 307, 341-342, 348-349, 352-353
Levy, Juliette, de Bairacli, 165, 170, 248
Liliacene, 238
lima beans, 55-56, 207-212, 254, 364
lima bean pod borer, 210
lime, 21, 49-51, 63-64, 74, 80, 113, 124, 138, 218, 239, 240, 242, 253, 294, 302, 303, 305, 317, 329
Lilac Belle (pepper), 266
Lilly Hybrid (melon), 223
linamarin, 207
Lincoln (peas), 259
Lippincot Farm Manual, 272
Lipstick (pimento peppers)
Little Baby Flower (watermelon), 346
Little Leaf (cucumber), 143
Little Marvel (peas), 259
long-day onions, 243
Long Island Improved (Brussels sprout), 74
Long Island Seed Project, 161
Long Slim (peppers), 268
Loose Heads (lettuce), 204, 206
lovage (levisticum), 10, 106, 199
love-lies-bleeding (amaranth), 349
Lucullus (chard), 114
Lumina (pumpkin), 284
Lutz (beet), 48, 123
Lutz Green Leaf (beet), 53
lycopene, 324, 342-343
Lycopersicon, 323
lygus or tarnished plant bug, 211

mache /corn salad, 213-215, 330, 354
Magdeburgh/Sicilian chicory, 118
Magenta (lettuce), 205
Magenta Spreen (lamb quarters), 54, 351
maize, 128-131
Mariachi Hybrid (peppers), 268
marjoram, 75, 186, 336
Marketmore (cucumbers), 142
Malabar (spinach), 305

malaria, 57
Marcellino (tomato), 335
Margherita Hybrid (tomato), 335
marigold, 144, 152, 280, 336, 368
Mars (celeriac), 105
Mars (onion), 244
Marvel of Four Seasons (lettuce), 204
Mary Washington (bean), 36-37
Matchless (lettuce), 204
Matt's Wild Cherry (tomato), 326, 334
Maturity (peas), 259
Maverick (carrot), 95
Maxibel (bean), 44
Maxima (pumpkin), 282, 365-366
Maxima (squash), 360, 363-364
Mediterranean cress, 355
Mediterranean thistle, 22
meer rettichi. *See* horseradish
melons, 32, 137, 139, 145-146, 180, 200, 216-224, 230, 232, 235, 300, 301, 305-306, 314, 317-318, 322, 343, 347, 368
meristem, 78
mesclun/baby lettuce, 203, 228
metamorphosis, 2-3, 15, 23, 49, 60, 72, 78-79, 102, 129, 158, 174, 182-183, 187-188, 254, 262-263, 273, 337, 342, 256
Metro PMR (squash), 367
Mexican bean beetle, 40
Michihli (Chinese cabbage), 125-126
Mild French Silver Skin (garlic), 169
mildew, 41, 43, 65, 61, 95, 139-142, 199, 200, 202, 204, 205, 209, 211, 215, 220, 221-223, 228, 245, 258-260, 284, 289, 302, 304-306, 312, 313, 322, 344, 345, 347, 363, 364-366, 368
Millennium Hybrid (bean), 37
Millionaire (okra), 234
Minestra Nero (broccoli), 70
Minicor (carrot), 97
miner's lettuce. See Wild Salad, Miner's lettuce
Minowase Summer Cross (daikon), 290
mint, 68, 75, 85, 141, 144, 186, 224, 280
Minuet (Chinese cabbage), 126
Minutina (plantain), 352
Misato Rose (daikon), 289
mites, 26, 41, 150, 210358
Miyashige White (daikon), 289
mizuna (mustard green), 17-19, 228

mold, 4, 42, 44, 141, 149-150, 167, 228, 234, 258, 260, 312
Moneta (beet), 53
monoecious, 142
Monstreux, de Viroflay, (spinach), 304
Monterey (celery), 110
Montia, 354
Morris Heading (cabbage-collard), 184
mosaic free, 204
mosaic virus, 41, 43, 47, 228, 259, 266, 268, 279, 304-305, 310-313, 322, 327, 366
Moschata (squash), 360, 363-364
Moskvich (tomato), 332
Mother onions, 246
Mountain Fresh (tomato), 326
Mountain Magic (tomato), 326
Mrs. Smith's Pie Factory, 282, 365
Muir, John, 193
Multipliers (onions), 246
Munchen Bier (radish), 287
muskmelon, 95, 216-218, 221-223, 263, 343-345, 361
Musque de Provence (pumpkin), 285
mustard greens, 17-18, 225-229, 291, 372
mycorrhizae, 131
myona (tomato), 335

Nadia (eggplant), 149-151
Nagoya Red Garnish (kale), 185
Nantes (carrot), 53, 93-94, 96-97
Nantes Half Long (carrot), 94
Napa cabbages, 126
Nardellos Italian (pepper), 267
Narragansett Indians, 309
nasunin, 146
Nasturtium family, 356
nasturtiums, 144, 224, 280, 347, 368
Natacha (escarole), 156
Natura, 9-10
Nelson (carrot), 95
Nema Green (lima bean), 209
Nemagold (sweet potato), 319
nematodes, 150-152, 183, 209-210, 233, 235, 279-280, 286, 311, 319-320, 326-327, 329, 332
Neon Lights (chard), 115
neoteny, 291
Nero Tondo (radish), 289

Index

nettle tea, 7, 33, 64, 73, 79, 83, 91, 100, 110, 124, 132, 139-140, 147, 166, 189, 195, 206, 230, 241, 247, 264, 303, 308, 317, 336, 344-345, 362
New England Blue Hubbard (squash), 365
New England Pie (pumpkin), 284
New Orchid (watermelon), 346
New Red Fire (lettuce), 204
New Star Mustard (mustard greens), 228
New York Early (onion), 245
New Zealand Journal of Crop Science, 20
New Zealand (spinach), 305
Nichols (catalog), 95, 305
nightshade, 143, 146, 148-149, 152, 161, 234-235, 266, 271, 275-276, 321, 326-327, 336, 364, 368,
nitrosamines, 193, 256
Nodak Pinto (bean), 47
nodal points, 4, 132, 148, 272
North and South Hybrids (okra), 234
North Carolina Potato Commission, 317-318
Northeaster (bean), 45
Northern Star (artichoke), 25
Novatov (cabbage), 84

Oaxacan Green (corn), 134
October Bean (shell bean), 46
Ohno Scarlet (turnip), 340
Okahijiki (agretti), 20
okra, 230-235
Old Brooks, (tomato), 326
Old Man Saltbush (orach), 351
Olympian (cucumber), 142
Olympus (carrot), 97
Omny Hybrid (radish), 290
Onaway (potato), 279
onion, 91, 109, 115, 122, 127, 155, 166, 170, 193-197, 236-247, 261, 272, 329
  as a tunicated bulb, 236
onion maggots, 242
O.P. Early Flat Dutch (cabbage), 84
O.P. Honshu (Chinese cabbage), 126
orach. *See* Wild Salad, orach
Orange Bells (peppers), 266
Orange Hokkaido (squash), 366
Orange Sunshine (watermelon), 347
oregano, 75
Oregon Giant (peas), 260
Orient Express (eggplant), 151

Osaka (mustard greens), 17
oxalic acid, 111-112, 349, 351, 354
Ozark (spinach), 304

pac choi. *See* Chinese cabbage
Pacemaker (beet), 53
Packman (broccoli), 67
Park's Whopper Hybrid (eggplant), 151
Parkinson's disease, 57
paprika peppers, 268
Parris Island Cos (lettuce), 205
parsley, 38, 160, 336-337
parsnips, 59, 76-77, 106, 199, 248-252, 288, 296-297, 299
parthenocarpic, 142-143
pasilla peppers, 268
Pastinaca, 248
patty pan squashes, 313-314
pe-tsai. *See* Chinese cabbage
pea, 38, 55-56, 59, 98, 127, 253-261, 277, 280, 295, 305, 340, 371-372
peanuts, 58, 255, 315, 320
Pediobius, 41
pellagra, 130
pelleted seed, 89, 108, 110, 156
peppers, 20, 145-146, 231, 247, 262-269, 301, 306, 323-325, 327, 336, 342, 364, 373
perception/perceptual, 2, 8-12, 281
Perfection (fennel), 158
Perfecto (radish), 289
Perpetual (chard), 114, 305
perennial sunflower (Sun Choke), 178-179
Pfeiffer, Ehrenfied, 8, 181
PH (of soil), 16, 23, 32, 40, 49, 56, 62, 73, 79-80, 99, 104, 109, 113, 120, 124, 131, 138, 147, 174, 189, 200, 208, 218, 227-228, 232, 239, 257, 264, 274, 292, 302, 309, 317, 321, 326, 329, 343, 356, 358
pharmacognosy, 163
Phaseolus, 42, 46, 254
phenomena, 10
phomopsis, 149
phylate, 248-249
Physalis, 321
phytophthora root rot, 148-149, 266, 312, 326, 362, 364
Picador (celery), 110
pigs, 58, 112, 200, 303, 315, 318, 349

pigweed, 137, 270, 349
Pike (melon), 221
pimento peppers, 267
Pink Beauty (tomato), 334
pink root, 245
Piricicaba (broccoli), 68
Pisum, 253
Planet (carrot), 87
plant hardening, 109
plantain. *See* Wild Salad, Plantain
plasticity, 15-16, 22, 78, 129-131, 225, 291-292
Plum Regal (tomato), 326
Primo (melon), 222
Ping Tung Long (eggplant), 151
Plantago, 352
Pliny, 22, 338
pod mottle virus, 41
polymorphism, 22, 23, 27
Poona Kheera (cucumber), 143
popcorn, 129, 137
Porrum, 194
Portulaca family, 352
potato, 47, 188, 248-250, 261, 267, 270-280, 295, 326-327, 336
potato beetle, 275, 280, 322, 328
potato onions, 246
powdery mildew, 41, 43, 95, 139, 141-142, 209, 221, 259, 284, 289, 312-313, 364, 366-367
Precoce de Argenteuil (asparagus), 36
pregnant onion, 246
Premium Crop (broccoli), 67
Progress (peas), 258-259
Prosperosa (eggplant), 151
prostaglandin, 164, 170, 238
Provider (bush bean), 39-40, 43
Pruden's Purple (tomato), 333
Puerto Rico (sweet potato), 319
pumpkin, 281-285, 359, 366
Purple (tomatillo), 322
Purple Beauty (pepper), 266
Purple Cape (cauliflower), 101
Purple Haze (carrot), 76
Purple Italian Globe (artichoke), 27
Purple Mustard (Brassica), 16
Purple Passion (asparagus), 33, 37
Purple Peacock (broccoli), 68
Purple Rain (carrot), 96

Purple Top Yellow (rutabaga), 295
Purple Top White (turnip), 295, 340
purslane. *See* Wild Salad, Purslane
pyrethrins, 210-211, 220, 233
pythium (fungus), 95, 148, 209
Quaker Pie (pumpkin), 282
Queen Anne's Lace. *See* wild carrot

raab. *See* broccoli, raab
rabe (rapini/rabine). *See* broccoli, raab
rabbits, 190, 200, 301
raccoons, 132-133
radichetta. *See* Italian dandelion
radicchio, 116, 119-121
radish, 47, 92, 144, 286, 290, 368, 372
Rainbow (carrots), 97
Rainbow (chard), 115
Rainbow Inca (corn), 134
Ralstonia (tomato), 326
Rampion/Bellflower (mache), 213
ramps, 194, 348
Ramshorn (pepper), 267
Rapunzel (mache), 213
Rattlesnake (pole bean), 45
Red Ace (beet), 53
Red Acre (cabbage), 84
Red Barn (onions), 246
red cabbage, 81, 84-85, 119
Red Calaloo (spinach), 305
Red Candy Apple (onions), 245
red chard, 111
Red Kuri (squash), 366-367
Red Drumhead (cabbage), 84
Red Dynasty (cabbage), 85
Red Giant (Brassica), 18
Red Giant (Mustard greens), 228
Red Gold (potato), 278
Red Hubbard (squash), 282, 365
Red Kuri (squash), 282
Red Meat (radish), 287
Red Mustard (Brassica), 18
Red Noodle (asparagus bean), 46
Red Norland (potato), 278
Red Oak Leaf (lettuce), 204
Red Orach, 351
Red Pearl (tomato), 335
Red Pontiac (potato), 278
Red Purslane (purslane), 353
Red Russian/Ragged Jack (kale), 185

Red Sails (lettuce), 204
Red Tinged Winter (lettuce), 203
Red Veined Sorrel (sorrel), 354
Red Velvet (radish), 289
Red Verona (radicchio), 119
Redbor (red-leaf kale), 185
Resistafly (carrot), 91, 95
rhizobial bacteria, 47, 208, 254, 255, 371-372
rhizobium, 255
rhizoctonia, 209, 228, 289
Rhubarb Chard (chard), 114
rhythm/rhythmically, 4-5, 11, 337
rice, 129
ricing, 65
Riverside Sweet Spanish (onion), 244
Rocambole (wild garlic), 165, 167-168
Roc d'Or (wax bean), 44
Rock Ford (melon), 222
rocket, 7, 28, 29, 58, 226, 355
rodents, 35, 52, 94, 274
Roma (tomato), 335
romaine, 281, 198, 201, 203, 205-206
Romanesco (broccoli), 66-67
Romanesco (cauliflower), 99, 101
Romanesco Minaret (broccoli), 67
Romano (bean), 44-45
Romano Gold (wax bean), 44
root aphids, 356
root cellaring, 292
root maggots, 124
root rot, 26, 266, 372
Rosa Bianca (eggplant), 151
rose, 254-255
rosemary, 75, 85, 91, 98, 127, 186, 368
Round-Up (weed killer), 293
Rouge d'Hiver (lettuce), 205
Rouge Vif d'Etampes (pumpkin), 285
Round of Hungary (pepper), 267
rotenone, 233, 293
Rubine (Brussels sprouts), 74
Ruby Red (chard), 114
Ruby Streaks (Brassica), 18
Ruby Streaks (mustard greens), 228
rucola (rugetti, rugola), 28-29
Rumex, 354
Running Vine (sweet potato), 319
Russian red kale, 68
rutabaga, 15, 78, 225, 230, 291-295, 338,
 as Swedish turnip, 291-292
rutin, 31
rye, 42, 88, 130, 151, 209, 273, 275, 276, 280, 311, 326, 336, 370-371

sage, 75, 85, 91, 98, 127, 186, 368
Safer's Mildew Cure, 220-221, 363
Safer's insecticidal soap, 242
Salad King (endives), 156
Saffron (squash), 313
Saint Valery (carrot), 97
Salad King (endives), 118
Salicornea, 20
salicornia (agretti), 21
salsa verde, 321
salsify, 296-297
Salsola, 20, 32
San Juan Hybrid (melon), 224
San Marzano (tomato), 335
sauerkraut, 84, 191, 338-339, 342
savory, 47, 59, 247
Savoy (cabbage), 74, 84
scallions (onions), 245-246
Scarlet Emperor (bean), 46
Scarlet Nantes (carrot), 94
Scarlet Runner (beans), 46, 105
sclerotinia (stem rot), 209, 228
scorzonera, 91, 98, 199, 296, 298-299
Scoville scale, 267
sea radish. *See* horseradish
seaweed tea, 33, 54, 64, 83, 91, 100, 110, 120, 124, 133, 139-140, 147, 189, 195, 202, 206, 230, 242, 264, 275, 292, 303, 310, 317, 326, 331, 336, 339, 344-345, 363
Seed Saver's Exchange, 222
Serrano del Sol (pepper), 267
Sessantina Grossa (raab), 70
Seven Hills (Brussels sprout), 74
Seven Top (turnip), 340
shallots, 105, 206, 246, 336
Shin Kuroda (carrot), 96
Shoepeg (corn), 135
short-day onions, 243
Short Vine (sweet potato), 319
Sicilian chicory. *See* Italian dandelion
Side Kick (watermelon), 346
Sierra (lettuce), 205
Sierra Blanco (onion), 244

silica, 4, 16, 27, 34, 41-42, 47, 51, 54, 59, 64, 68, 79, 81, 83, 85, 87, 91, 98, 105, 108, 110, 113, 115, 121, 124,-125, 127, 132-133, 137, 139-140, 143, 148, 152, 160, 166, 170, 184, 186, 189, 191, 195, 197, 202, 206, 219-221, 224, 230, 241, 247, 251-252, 258, 261, 263, 265, 269, 275, 279-280, 293, 295, 303-304, 306, 320, 328, 331, 335-336, 339-340, 344, 347, 350-352, 354-356, 358-359, 362-363, 367-368
Silver Moon (pumpkin), 284
Silver Queen (corn), 136
Sky Plus (lettuce), 204
Small Sugar (pumpkin), 283-284
smut, 246
snails/slugs, 202, 210, 220, 358, 362
snap beans. *See* beans, bush
snap peas, 258
snow peas, 254, 257-258, 260
Snow Ball, Self-blanching (cauliflower), 100
Snow Crown (cauliflower), 101
soft neck (garlic), 169
soft rot, 121, 126, 127, 149, 290, 294
solanine, 273
Sloanum, 270, 277
Sophie's Choice (tomato), 332
Sorbet Swirl (watermelon), 346
sorrel. *See* Wild Salad, sorrel
Southern Belle (onion), 244
Southern Exposure Seed Exchange, 33, 44, 89, 131, 134, 184, 233, 246-247, 311, 322, 346
Southern Giant (mustard greens), 228
Southern green stink bug, 210, 233
Southernwood, 85, 127, 186, 368
Southport Yellow Globe (onion), 245
Spanish onions, 242
Spanish oyster plants, 296-297
spargel /white gold (asparagus), 30
spider mites, 26, 210, 358
Spigaveillo Leaf (broccoli), 70
spinach, 21, 38, 44, 51, 54, 57, 76, 112-115, 154, 181, 215, 219, 224, 265, 269, 280, 295, 300-306, 330, 336, 340, 351, 353
Spinach Beet (chard), 305
Spinach Dock (sorrel), 354
spreen, 54, 351, 352
squash, 7, 32, 44-45, 137-139, 143, 178, 180, 200, 206, 217, 224, 233, 235, 280-282, 285, 301, 305-306, 309-314, 347, 368, 373
squash bugs, 311, 361, 368
Staddon's Select (peppers), 265
Stampede (Jerusalem artichoke), 177
Standard O.P. (corn), 135-136
Starship (squash), 314
Steiner, Rudolf, 5, 181, 193, 256, 275
  Agriculture Course, 256
Stella Natura Biodynamic Planting Calendar, 4, 12
stinging nettles, 112, 181, 307-308, 336, 348
Stokes (catalog), 90, 100, 120, 134, 185, 189, 267, 346, 368
Stonehead (cabbage), 84
Stout, Ruth, 216-217
Stowell's Evergreen (corn), 135
strawberry grand cherry. *See* ground cherry
strawberries, 7-8, 59, 206, 306
stem borer, 366
stem canker, 325
stem lettuce. *See* celtuse
Stuttgarter (onion), 242, 245
Styrian Naked (pumpkin), 284
sugar-enhanced corn, 136-137
Sugar Ann (peas), 261
Sugar Baby (watermelon), 346
Sugar Cube (melon), 222
Sugar Lump (tomato), 334
Sugar Snap (peas), 260
Sugar Sprint (peas), 261
Sullivan, General, John, 88, 248
sulphur compounds, 18, 31
Summer Crisp (Batavian lettuce), 205
summer squash, 281, 309-314
Sun Gold (tomato), 335
Sun Jewel (melon), 223
sunberry. *See* wonderberry
sunchoke. *See* Jerusalem artichokes
sunflower, American, 178
Sungold (wax bean), 44
Sunkyo Semi-long (daikon), 289
Sunny Delight (squash), 313
Sunshine Hybrid (squash), 366
Super Lakota (tomato), 333
Super Sioux (tomato), 333
Sugar Snax (carrots), 95, 97

Super Sweet (tomato), 100, 334
Sutton (fava), 59
Suyo Long (cucumber), 143
swallowtail butterfly, 92
Swedes (cole plant), 182
Sweet (cherry tomato), 324
Sweet Baby Jane (carrot), 95, 97
sweet corns, 129, 136-137
Sweet Banana (pepper), 267
Sweet Chocolate (pepper), 266
Sweet Dumpling (squash), 367
Sweet and Early Hybrid (melon), 222
Sweet Favorite (watermelon), 346
Sweet Gourmet Hybrid (squash), 314
Sweet Granite (melon), 221
Sweet Mama Hybrid (winter squash), 359, 366
Sweet Million (tomato), 334
sweet potato, 62, 182, 234-235, 249, 276, 315-320
Sweet Potato (squash), 367
Sweet Spanish (onions), 241, 245
Sweet Spot (peppers), 267
Sweet Treat (carrot), 96
Swiss chard, 283
Swiss Chard of Geneva (chard), 114

Table Queen (squash), 366
Takinogawa (burdock), 77
Tall Telephone (peas), 260
tampala (spinach), 305
Tango (celery), 110
tansy, 68, 85, 116, 127, 144, 186, 368
Taraxacum, 117, 350
Tasty Jade (cucumber), 143
Teosinte, 129
Tempo (artichokes), 27
Tendergreen (mustard greens), 228
Tennessee Red Cob (corn), 134
Tetragonia, 305
Thai Hot (pepper), 267-268
Thai Long Green (eggplant), 151
Thanksgiving (squash), 366
Theophrastus, 111
Thoreau, Henry David, 300
therapeutic, 3, 11
thistles, 22-23, 25
 bull thistles, 22
thrips, 167, 195, 170, 233, 239-240, 242, 245-247

thyme, 68, 75, 85, 186
Tiburon (pepper), 268
timothy, 151
tobacco mosaic virus (TMV), 149, 151, 265, 266, 268, 327, 332
Tokyo Cross Hybrid (turnip), 340
Tokyo Long White (onion), 246
Tom Fox (pumpkin), 284
Tom Watson (watermelon), 346
Toma Verde (tomatillo), 322
tomato, 32, 38, 45, 105, 110, 145-147, 160, 191, 261, 280, 302, 306, 312, 323-336, 342, 364, 372
tomatillo, 171, 321-322
 as husk tomato, 321
Tongues of Fire (beans), 47
Top Onion (Egyptian onion), 246
Topepo Rosso (pepper), 267
Touchon Deluxe (carrot), 94
Touchstone Gold (beet), 53
Tragopogan, 296, 298
Travista (endives), 118
tree cabbage, 72
tree kale, 72
Triple Treat (pumpkin), 284
triploid (seedless watermelon), 343, 344, 346
Tripsacum, 129
Triumphe de Farcy (bean), 44
Tromboncini (squash), 311, 314
True Honeydew (melon), 222
tumbleweed, 20
Turga (parsnip), 252
turnips, 15, 69, 188, 225, 291-292, 295, 327, 337-340, 371, 372
turnip mosaic virus, 175-176, 228
Turpin, P.J.F., 187
Turtle Tree Seeds, 84
Tuscan kale, 185

umbels, 10
Umbelliferae, 10, 48, 102, 106-107, 158, 191, 199, 206, 249-250, 252, 295, 320, 328
Umpquah (broccoli), 66
Underwoods Ornamental (corn), 134
upland or early winter cress. *See* Wild Salads, upland or early winter cress
Urtica, 307

Valencia (tomato), 333
Valenciano (pumpkin), 284
valerian (spray), 47, 91, 98, 105, 110, 137, 144, 160, 200, 206, 269, 318, 320, 336, 347, 368
Vardaman (sweet potato), 319
Vates (collards), 184-185
Vegetable Amaranth (spinach), 305
Venetian glass, 21
Veronica (cauliflower), 101
Ventura (celery), 110
Vert de Cambrai (mache), 215
Vert de Montmagney (dandelion), 351
verticillium wilt, 26, 149, 151, 227, 234, 235, 278, 327, 332
Vertus Savoy O.P. (cabbage), 84
vetch, 32, 56-57, 255, 329
Vicia faba, 55
vicine, 58
Vidalia onions, 244
vine borers, 311, 363, 368
Violet Queen Hybrid (cauliflower), 101
viral plant diseases, 149
Vit (mache), 215
Vitamin Green (Asian leaf mustard), 18
Viva Italiano (tomato), 335
voles, 52

Waldmann's Dark Green (lettuce), 204
wall/wild rocket, 28-29, 226
Walla Walla Sweet (onion), 244
Walking Onion (Egyptian onion), 246
Waltham (broccoli), 66
Waltham (squash), 367
Wando (peas), 260
Warted Hubbard (squash), 365
wasabi. *See* horseradish
wasps, 10, 41, 64, 158-159, 209, 328
water chestnut, 190
watercress. *See* Wild Salads, watercress
watermelon, 139, 341-347, 363-364
Watermelon or Red Meat (daikon), 289
"watery soft rot," 83
wax (bush) beans, 44, 47
Welsh onions, 192-194, 196
wheat, 129, 227, 231
White Bunch (sweet potato), 320
White Cobbler (potato), 279

White Half Runner (bean), 39
White Icicle (radish), 288
White Lady Hybrid (turnip), 340
White Lisbon (onion), 246
White Yam (sweet potato), 320
whiteflies, 328-329, 358
Witloof (chicory), 118-119, 121
Witloof Improved (chicory), 119
wild artichoke, 111
wild asparagus, 30
wild cabbage, 15, 22
wild carrot (Queen's Anne's Lace), 86, 88-89, 94, 102
wild garlic, 193
wild leek, 193
wild onions, 192-193, 239
wild morning glory, 87
wild mustard, 17
Wild Pigweed (amaranth), 349
Wild Salads, 348-373
  amaranth, 7, 137, 348-350
  dandelion, 7, 117-118, 198-199, 296, 350-351,
  lamb's quarters, 7, 48, 112, 115, 181, 270, 348, 351
  orach, 54, 113, 351-352
  plantain, 352
  purslane, 7, 137, 348, 352-354
  miner's lettuce, 354
  sorrel, 354-355, 351
  upland or early winter cress, 173, 355-357
  watercress, 356-358
wild sea beet, 111
wild seed fennel, 158
Windsor (broccoli), 67
Winter Bloomsdale (spinach), 305
Winter Density (romaine), 205
Winter Onion (Egyptian onion), 246
winter purslane (miner's lettuce), 354
winter squash, 45, 359-368
Winterbor (kale), 185
wireworms, 88, 221, 312
Wisconsin SMR (cucumber), 142
wonderberry, 161-162
Wong bok (Chinese cabbage), 126
Worcester Indian Red Pole (lima bean), 207, 211
wormwood, 68, 85, 127, 144, 160, 186, 368

Index

xanthophyll, 171

yams, 249, 319, 320
Yankee Bell (peppers), 267
yarrow, 144
yellow crookneck squash, 313-314, 359
yellow rocket, 355
Yin Yang (beans), 47
Young's Beauty (pumpkin), 284
Yukon Gold (potato), 278

Zavory (peppers) 268
Zefa Fino (fennel), 158
zucchini, 144, 220, 311, 314, 347, 361